COLONIAL AND COMPARATIVE STUDIES
EDITED BY MARGERY PERHAM

GEZIRA
A Story of
Development
in the
SUDAN

Colonial and Comparative Studies
edited by Margery Perham

*

Studies in Colonial Legislatures

THE GOLD COAST LEGISLATIVE COUNCIL 1606–1945
by Martin Wight

THE NORTHERN RHODESIAN LEGISLATIVE COUNCIL
by J. W. Davidson

THE NIGERIAN LEGISLATIVE COUNCIL
by Joan Wheare

THE LEGISLATURES OF CEYLON, 1928–1948
by S. Namasivayam

THE LEGISLATIVE COUNCIL OF TRINIDAD AND TOBAGO
by Hewan Craig

The Economics of a Tropical Dependency

MINING, COMMERCE AND FINANCE IN NIGERIA
by P. A. Bower, A. J. Brown, C. Leubuscher, J. Nars and Sir Alan Pim

*

THE METROPOLITAN ORGANIZATION OF BRITISH COLONIAL TRADE
by Kathleen Stalh

THE MAKING OF THE MODERN SUDAN: THE LIFE AND LETTERS OF
SIR DOUGLAS NEWBOLD
by K. D. D. Henderson

BRITAIN AND THE UNITED STATES IN THE CARIBBEAN
by Mary Proudfoot

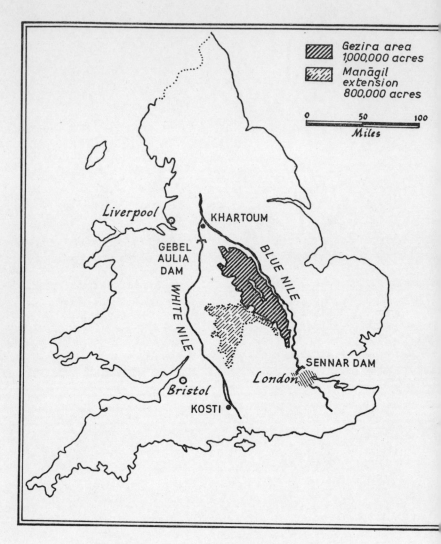

1. *The Gezira scheme superimposed on the map of England*

GEZIRA

A Story of
Development
in the

SUDAN

by

ARTHUR GAITSKELL

FABER AND FABER

24 Russell Square

London

First published in mcmlix
by Faber and Faber Limited
24 Russell Square, London, W.C.1
Printed in Great Britain by
Western Printing Services Limited, Bristol

c. 1

'Queen Victoria said: in their prosperity will be our strength, in their contentment our security, and in their gratitude our best reward.'

'Liberty will not descend to a people. A people must raise themselves to liberty. It is a blessing that must be earned before it can be enjoyed.'

INSCRIPTIONS ON THE ARCHES OF THE CENTRAL GOVERNMENT BUILDINGS, IN NEW DELHI.

CONTENTS

CONTENTS

Part 3. *The Cataract:* 1946–50

Epilogue

Part 4. *Full Flood: After* 1950

Appendices

LIST OF ILLUSTRATIONS

TABLES AND DIAGRAMS

MAPS

NOTE ON CURRENCY

Egyptian currency was used in the Sudan. The Egyptian pound was composed of 100 piastres or 1,000 milliemes, and was expressed by the symbol £E. Thus 1,000 milliemes = 100 piastres = £E1 = £1 0s. 6d. sterling. Conversely £1 sterling = 97½ piastres.

NOTE ON LOCAL ARABIC WORDS

Ardebb A measure of weight for dura, equivalent in the Blue Nile to 560 lb. and elsewhere in the Sudan to 336 lb.

Dura *Sorghum vulgare*, a millet, the staple food of the Central Sudan.

Feddan An area of land approximately equal to an acre. 1 feddan = 1·038 acres.

Kantar A unit of weight. For all practical purposes 1 kantar was taken as equivalent to 100 lb. of ginned cotton or 315 lb. of unginned cotton.

Lubia *Dolichos lablab*, a bean grown mainly for fodder (but also for human food).

Mudir The title given to the governor of a province in the Sudan.

Omda A local official in the administration responsible for a group of villages.

Samad A village representative responsible for the agricultural management of the tenancies.

Samadia A village agricultural unit supervised by a samad.

Sheikh A headman of a village.

ACKNOWLEDGEMENTS

The idea of writing up the story of the Gezira Scheme was often put forward by the late Dr. E. M. Crowther of Rothamsted at the meetings of the London Advisory Committee on Agricultural Research, and when I retired from the Gezira in 1952 I was asked by the Sudan Government to undertake the work. Fate took me into other fields and this book would not have seen the light of day except for the kindness of the Warden and fellows of Nuffield College, Oxford, and particularly for the warm persistence of an old friend, Miss Margery Perham, C.B.E., to whose lively interest so many who work in Africa already owe so much.

My particular thanks are due also to Sayed Mekki Abbas, Managing Director of the Sudan Gezira Board, to Sayed Ibrahim Ahmed, Minister of Finance in the Sudan, and to His Excellency Sayed Awad Satti, the Sudanese Ambassador in London, for their courteous permission to use the documents and records in their charge. Another old friend, Mr. G. R. F. Bredin, C.B.E., who was the Governor of the Blue Nile Province when I was Manager of the Gezira Scheme, very kindly read through the text and made me add to it the chapter entitled 'Down to Earth'.

I am indebted to Sir Ronald Wingate, Bart., C.M.G., C.I.E., O.B.E., for the interesting letters concerning Lord Kitchener, to Mr. R. Hewison, C.B.E., and Mr. W. A. Davie for first-hand descriptions of the early arguments about development, and to the British Cotton Growing Association for early reports connected with the Gezira.

Mr. Michael McWilliam, my young research assistant at Nuffield College, was a quite invaluable help. His personal interest in the theme of the story, and his capacity to synthesize the issues, made a stimulating contribution to the authorship. Mrs. Marshall, who succeeded him, and Mrs. Horton, lately of the B.B.C., made an equally valuable contribution in helping me to cut down the subject-matter and improve the syntax. For the photographs of Lord Kitchener, Sir Reginald Wingate, Sir Lee Stack, Sir Frederick Eckstein, Lord Lovat, General Asquith, Sir William Garstin, Sir Murdoch Macdonald, and Sir Alexander MacIntyre I am indebted to Messrs Elliott and Fry, and to the proprietors of *The African World* in whose Sudan Number in 1926 these photographs and Plate III were first reproduced. For the photograph of Sir William Himbury I am indebted to Mr Griffiths of the British Cotton Growing Association. Plates V and XV are reproduced by courtesy of the Central Office of Information, and the remaining Plates by courtesy of the Sudan Government.

I am also greatly indebted to Mrs Marshall for reading the final text and making the Index.

EDITOR'S PREFACE

When I first came to know the Sudan between the two world wars and visited that strange plain of the Gezira, made stranger by the gleaming geometrical pattern of the irrigation channels, I was deeply impressed by the need to spread knowledge of this unique achievement in economic partnership between a colonial government, a commercial company and what had been a very poor, semi-nomadic peasantry. I even went so far as to start collecting material in the hope that I might do something to spread this knowledge myself. Fortunately I soon realized that the task lay far outside my economic competence and was, indeed, the kind of book that must first be writte from the inside. After the war, with the development of the emotionaı recoil from 'colonialism' and 'economic imperialism' and of both the Communist attack and the Communist alternative, the need for such a study became more pressing. It was, therefore, most fortunate that Mr. Gaitskell was persuaded to accept a Research Fellowship at Nuffield College and so detach himself long enough from the claims that press upon a man of his experience in order to write this book.

Very few words are needed from the Editor of the Series about the importance of the subject. This is because Mr. Gaitskell has done more than write the much needed history of the Scheme, based on the records of the Sudan Plantations Syndicate and of his own personal experience. His record is illuminated by being related throughout to what is perhaps the greatest problem of our day—how the wealthy and economically experienced nations can help the poorer peoples of the world to develop their own resources without either economic or political subordination.

Mr. Gaitskell's experience has qualified him very fully to supply the growing demand for information about the Scheme. There was little that he did not know about it. From Winchester and New College he went out to the Sudan as a field executive in 1923 and worked his way up through the Finance Headquarters to Chief Field Executive, Assistant Manager and, from 1945 to 1950, General Manager. From 1950 to 1952 he had the experience of working as the first Chairman and Managing Director of the Sudan Gezira Board when the Sudan Plantations Syndicate retired from their large share in the undertaking and the independent Sudan took shape. No one, therefore, could be more fully qualified to write about the great revenue-producing and food-growing triangle between the two Niles. But as a member of the Sudan Executive Council 1945–50, and Chairman of the University College of Khartoum, he saw other sides of the Sudan. Moreover, since leaving that country he has held an interesting series of appointments as Chairman of a Mission to investigate Kalahari Ranching (1952), Member of the East African Royal Commission (1953–5), British member on the Committee of experts on the development of Africa, Council of Europe (1956–7), Member of the Board, Tanganyika Agricultural Corporation (1955–7), Member of the Board, Colonial Development Corporation (since 1955), and lecturer for the Foreign Office in the U.S.A. speaking on colonial policy (1956). These appointments have merited listing in this introduction because they will enable the reader to measure the weight which lies behind the generalizations Mr. Gaitskell makes in these pages about the problems and the possibilities which underlie the attempts of the Western nations to help the poorer peoples of this world.

MARGERY PERHAM

Nuffield College
October 1959

20

PREFACE

The practical in civilization has always been associated with dreams and ages of greatness with ideas. This is a story of the effect and the interplay of ideas upon a purely material development project.

It seemed worth telling for various reasons. There were the people in the story: the people of the land and those who came from outside. Their experiences reflect so many of the changes which we have seen who were born when the twentieth century opened. They reveal a little segment of our span for those who follow us. There was the land itself, huge, remote, and untamed, with nature dwarfing man for centuries. Together the people and the land made a case history in one of the most talked-of topics of our age: the search for a higher standard of living in underdeveloped countries. We still grope for the way to do this amicably and efficiently between us, and many of the problems we still face came into the story.

It was about agriculture not industry, but the big question marks are the same: the need but yet the fear of foreign capital; the paying and non-paying levels of investment; the discovery of an export product; the best way to sell amid erratic prices and demand. Some questions were specific to agriculture, especially yield and disease. But the most fascinating were the problems of society: the emergence from foreign paternalism to nationalism; the balance between state control, equity in economic advance, and individual freedom; the difficulty of participation between management and managed. These problems took the story into that borderland of so many of our difficulties, the discovery of an alternative to communism in the uncommitted world.

I have told the story chronologically.

This has drawbacks. It might have been easier to read everything about marketing in one chapter, social development in another, financial history in a third. But a vertical division would have meant a good deal of cross-reference and to some extent distorted an important truth. Development is not really like building a sectional bookcase. It is more like the

21

journey of a river. Tributaries join in and currents pass and repass, bringing to the surface different aspects at different times. So it is in this pattern that I have told the story.

There was another reason for using this simile. Development in the Gezira, to an unusual extent, was permeated by a cross-fertilization of ideas, like the intermingling of currents. This was one of the secrets of its success and of much of the human drama in this story. It may make the telling seem rather abstract in places for the reader but it brings out another truth about development: that all progress in the end depends on what is in men's minds.

This is the first book written about the Gezira. As such it has source material for the serious student of development. In places this is in rather concentrated detail because it may not easily be got together again. A reader interested only in the general narrative may be suddenly confronted by a close examination of financial negotiations suggestive of an auditor's report, or by the intricate history of Nile waters, or detail of crop rotations, too reminiscent of a textbook for his taste. I have tried to warn him in the text when these occasions arise so that he can skip them if he wishes. I had considered relegating them to appendices, but usually there was something in them significant to the general narrative which I did not want him altogether to miss.

In spite of this, there are aspects of the Gezira story which I have had to omit altogether. Prominent among them are the development of trade unions and the position of the permanent labour force in the workshops and factories of the Scheme. Conversely the central themes of the book will be gradually found to converge at the end to one point of paramount importance: what does the western world stand for?

It may seem strange that I have chosen the two inscriptions on the arches of the central government buildings in New Delhi as a text, for this book has nothing to do with India. But the reader will find that they form the heart of the matter.

Part 1
SPRINGS AND TRIBUTARIES
1900–25

Chapter 1

GEOGRAPHY AND HISTORY

This story takes place in the north-eastern quarter of Africa, in the country which used to be called the Anglo-Egyptian, but is now the independent, Sudan. This country lies to the south of Egypt, its capital, Khartoum, being about 1,750 miles up the Nile, or 1,000 miles by air from Cairo. The Sudan is large; nearly a million square miles, three-quarters of the size of the Union of India, but with, even today, only about twelve million inhabitants. Geography explains this. Its northern frontier starts in an almost rainless zone on the edge of the Sahara desert. Its southern frontier is in tropical forest adjoining the Congo. Between these limits the rainfall slowly increases from north to south, and this rainfall pattern has largely determined the way of human life there, making man a migratory animal.

A traveller flying level with the blue cranes, which come south to the Sudan every winter from Russia, could see the whole pattern below him. North of Khartoum there would be just a few camels grazing the thorn trees in the dry stream-beds. South of Khartoum would appear a little more general pasture for sheep and goats, and then the temporary landing-grounds of the cranes, the threshing-floors and the small earth banks put up to trap a first fitful rainfall and grow a crop of millet. Farther south, as the rain increased, would come the long grass and cattle country, and thorn acacia forest.

All this is the northern Sudan, a fringe of the Middle East and Mohammedan in civilization; the country, when this story started, of the nomad Arab following the rains with his flocks, and of his semi-nomad neighbour who grew his precarious subsistence crop. Through the lengths of this vast land of open horizons and great untracked distances flowed the two branches of the Nile, the sluggish White Nile from the great lakes in Uganda, and the Blue Nile, the flood-giver, from the mountains of Ethiopia. Where the rains faded as the rivers flowed north, the Nile added another way of human life to the overall nomad picture.

In narrow strips along its banks, where contours suited, with incessant work and small return, water-wheels could irrigate crops independent of the rains and so give rise to settled villages dotted at intervals along the river's course right down to Egypt. Where the rains increased far to the south huge stretches of swamp demarcated the southern Sudan, where the Middle East ended and Africa began; all part of this immense territory but outside the immediate scope of this story.

The blue crane is the crest of the Blue Nile Province in which lies the Gezira. It signifies the site of the sorghum belt where nature first makes agriculture, and so village settlement, possible away from the river. Gezira means 'island' or 'promontory' in Arabic and the name refers to the great plain, of about five million acres, which lies between the Blue and White Niles, north of the Sennar-Kosti line, before they meet at Khartoum, which means 'the trunk of the elephant'. Before development the Gezira in good rain years was the subsistence granary of the northern Sudan. In bad rain years there was nothing but the water-wheels and the river.

It would be difficult to imagine anything flatter than the great Gezira plain, two hundred miles long and eighty miles across. Some scientists say the brown, cracked soil was blown there, others that it was the bed of a huge marsh in primeval time. To this day graves of forgotten races can be found, not far beneath the surface, with, hard by, piles of big snail shells, suggesting dwellers in a sluggish swamp in wetter ages long ago. Dry when this story began, it had the boredom and the beauty of all great level landscapes. The eye searched in vain for some eminence or dell to break the monotony, and when on the far southern boundary it sighted the blue outline of the hills of Gebel Moya they had an allure beyond their true height.

Gezira was a land of mirage. At dawn in winter the horizon stood up like a pink cliff circling a giant hollow in which a curious refraction of light disclosed villages and fields beyond the range of normal sight. At midday great white sails, suggesting felukas on the river, became on closer view tiny flags on the grave of a holy man. Often on the path ahead the sheen of water disappeared as it was reached. It was a hard land. The few trees were thorny, and on hot, dry, windy days dust-devils turned to dust-storms, creating an inferno of flying particles like sandstorms in the desert. But when the rains came and the panorama revealed the thunderstorms in uninterrupted majesty the brown plain turned to green, chequered with carpets of white and pink convolvulus and other wild flowers, to be replaced in turn by orderly rows of millet.

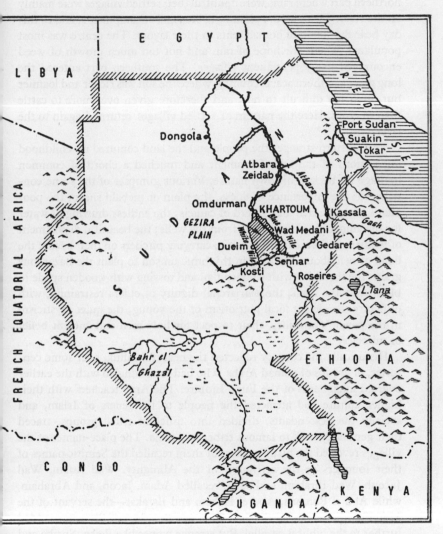

2. *General map of the Sudan*

The people in the Gezira followed the pattern of the weather. In the northern part where rains were doubtful their settled villages were mainly on the river. Those on the plain were seasonal encampments, and to this day bear the stamp of nomad tents in their layout. The centre was most populated, where fair hope of rain and not too much growth of weed encouraged many permanent villages. The southern part entered the long grass and thorn acacia country, where the soil was richer and loamier but often too difficult to hoe, and therefore given over more to cattle than to crops. Here the pattern of settled villages returned again to the river.

To a western stranger the people and the land conjured up childhood impressions of the Old Testament and touched a chord of common heritage far back in his own nature. Various glimpses of the scene contributed: the importance of flocks, the plain or piebald sheep, the poor man's goat, the rich man's herd of camels; the endless drawing of water for the animals in skin buckets from the wells; the beautiful deportment of women, in their dark blue robes, carrying pitchers on their heads; the band of neighbours working in rhythmic unison to plant the hazardous grain; the threshing with wooden flail and tossing with wooden spade to blow away the chaff; the patriarchal dignity of elders restraining with difficulty the violent local patriotism of the young; the quiet mysticism in the people's attitudes, their respect for holy men and current belief in miracles.

Historically the country reflected the peaceful influx, over some centuries, of groups of nomad Arabs, who had intermingled with the earlier negroid inhabitants of the Fung Empire. The Arab teachers with their higher culture had attracted the people to the tenets of Islam, and socially the descendants, divided into different tribal groups, traced their genealogy back to famous tribes in Arabia. The place-names of the villages revealed the history. Most of them recalled the Semitic names of their founders or the attributes of the Almighty. Wad Adam, Wad Jacoub, Wad Ibrahim, and such, recalled Adam, Jacob, and Abraham, while Abd el Rahman, Abd el Hakam and Barakat—the servant of the Merciful, the servant of the Just One, and the place of Blessing—added further to the biblical parallel. But strange names like Beika, Suriba and Meringan dated back to princesses of the Fung era. Abu Haraz, the tamarind, and Talha, the red gum, commemorated the pleasant shade of rare large trees, while for Hassa Heissa there could be only one explanation: the sound of the wind blowing on the great sandbanks at that bend of the river.

The pace of life was tied to nature and the people accustomed to extreme frugality. Time was of small importance, and men's delight was in stories and in the ceremony of social occasions, and at times in strife. A stranger would notice the white cotton robes and turbans of parties visiting nearby villages, the important personage riding his large white donkey, the others on lesser donkeys dangling their slippers from their toes. He might be invited to a village house, crowded with neighbours seated on the floor to hear big-turbaned, itinerant psalm-singers, cross-legged on the couch, praising in their verses the local religious leader. Outside he might meet other wayfarers, strangers to the region, armed with bows and arrows, clubs, or spears, or with flat-bladed swords fashioned with crusader's hilts. These were customary precautions, bred from years of uncertainty and violence, in a country where men were jealous of honour and indifferent to pain.

Down on the river, the curious creaking noise of the water-wheels slowly turning to the bullock's tread, the cry of a fish-eagle, and the lazy flapping of a goliath heron across the water added a peaceful sense of immemorial custom repeated and of fate accepted. It was upon this setting that a uniquely new system of agriculture was to descend.

This story begins in time at the very end of the nineteenth century. But events reaching out from deep in the past affected it, and the prologue must be put back to 1820. In that year Ismail Pasha,* grandson of the famous Mohammed Ali,† Viceroy of Egypt, invaded and annexed the Sudan. There followed sixty-five years of Egyptian rule which was terminated in 1885 by a national revolt headed by a religious reformer who proclaimed himself the Mahdi,‡ the chosen messenger of God. The Mahdi died in the year of his victory and from 1885 until 1898 the Sudan was ruled by his nominated successor, the Khalifa Abdullahi. In 1898 at the battle of Omdurman a joint Anglo-Egyptian army, under

---

* Ismail Pasha succeeded to the Egyptian throne in 1863. The Suez Canal was built during his reign. Egypt fell seriously into debt culminating in default in 1876, which led to the imposition of the Commission on Public Debt by the Powers. Ismail reacted against this, and the British and French secured his deposition in 1879.

† Mohammed Ali Pasha came to power in Egypt in 1805, and ruled the country from 1811 to 1841. During this time he regenerated Egypt and broke loose from Turkey. He annexed the Sudan in 1821 to secure his southern frontier.

‡ Mohammed Ahmed El Mahdi. Born Dongola: settled Abba Island, near Kosti, on White Nile: as religious reformer attracted great gathering in western Sudan: galvanized increasing resentment against Egyptian administration in 1881: defeated large Egyptian army under British General Hicks in Kordofan, 1883: headed patriotic and religious revolt culminating in fall of Khartoum and death of General Gordon, January 1885: died 1885.

British generalship and direction, defeated the Khalifa who was killed in a later engagement.

It is important to appreciate the fact that at this date the British were in *de facto* control of the policy of Egypt. A new form of dual sovereignty under both Britain and Egpyt, called a condominium, was set up after the battle of Omdurman to define the status of the country and to give it a separate name, the Anglo-Egyptian Sudan. The supreme military and civil command was vested in a Governor-General of the Sudan appointed by khedivial decree on the recommendation of the British Government. Proclamations by the Governor-General had the force of law.

A British Governor-General now began to rule the country with British officers in all the senior administrative posts and Egyptian assistants in the junior posts. The assumption was that Britain was the senior member of this partnership, Egypt the junior partner, and the Sudan the ward. This assumption and this condominium solution to the problem of sovereignty, which in later years was to bring in its train a very different situation, enabled the administration of the Sudan to be planned and executed in these early years to a quite remarkable extent by the administrative officers on the spot. Free of the 'capitulations'* which opened the door to foreign claims for consideration in Egypt, and equally free of responsibility to the Colonial Secretary in England, for the Sudan was neither colony nor protectorate, they fell only under the distant surveillance of the British Agent in Egypt. One effect of this independence of action was to make prominent in the administration of the Sudan a spirit of paternalism and a paramountcy of native interest, and this spirit is the first and perhaps the most potent stream persisting in the river which makes up this story of development.

An individual tributary to this stream flowed in from the earlier period of Egyptian rule. The last Governor-General of the Sudan for the Khedive of Egypt was the British Major-General Charles Gordon.† Gordon had a great reputation for courage, integrity and sympathy with

---

*Capitulations. These were privileges reserved to foreign residents in Egypt, such as Mixed Tribunals for civil and commercial suits connected with the ownership of land, Consular Courts for criminal cases involving Europeans, and no imposition of direct taxation without the consent of all the Powers, etc. For the hampering effect of these upon Government policy in Egypt see H.M. Agent's Report on Egypt, 1907, Cd. 3966, pp. 1 and 2.

† C. G. Gordon (1833–85), C.B. Originally famous as 'Chinese' Gordon and Commander for Emperor of China of 'ever victorious army' against rebels there, 1863–4: Governor of Equatoria in Sudan, 1874–6: Governor-General of Sudan for Khedive of Egypt, 1877–80 and again 1884.

the oppressed. He had been particularly active in attempting to put down the slave trade in his periods of service in the Sudan. The drama of his death—he was speared by the Mahdi's Dervish army overrunning Khartoum—had invested his name in Britain with a peculiar aura as a hero. It was as if a lone forlorn figure which represented the best intentions of our civilization had been deserted by us and overwhelmed by forces of maladministration which had provoked a flood of blind rebellion and swept the Sudan back into savagery. His epitaph in St. Paul's Cathedral recalls what his contemporaries thought of him.

> To Major General Charles Gordon, C.B.
> Who at all times and everywhere, gave
> his strength to the weak, his substance
> to the poor, his sympathy to the
> suffering, his heart to God.

Winston Churchill described him best.

He was the most disinterested of men. Wealth, rank, social distinction, the comforts and pleasures of life counted with him as little as obscurity, danger, or death from other quarters. 'Character', says Emerson, 'is always known' and in a queer way Gordon's personality had made its impression on the sub-conscious mind of England.

The first act of Lord Kitchener,* commanding the Anglo-Egyptian army, after the battle of Omdurman, was to hold a funeral service at Khartoum in memory of Gordon, and this was followed by a public appeal by Kitchener in England for funds to start a school in the Sudan in Gordon's name. The symbol was to endure, projecting on to policy ideas and ideals associated with Gordon's memory.

Early in 1899 Lord Kitchener issued a Memorandum to the provincial authorities defining in what spirit and for what purpose the Administration was to be operated.

The absolute uprootal by the Dervishes of the old system of Government has afforded an opportunity for initiating a new Administration more in harmony with the requirements of the Soudan.

2. The necessary Laws and Regulations will be carefully considered and issued as required, but it is not mainly to the framing and publishing of laws that we must look for the improvement and good government of the country.

* H. H. Kitchener (1850–1916), K.G., O.M., P.C., etc. Field-Marshal, Earl of Khartoum. Sirdar of Egyptian army, 1892: reorganized it and led reconquest of Sudan, 1896–9: Governor-General of Sudan, 1898–9: Commander-in-Chief South African War, 1900–2: Commander-in-Chief, India, 1902–9: Agent and Consul-General, Egypt, 1911–14: Secretary of State for War, 1914 until death by drowning in cruiser *Hampshire,* 1916.

3. The task before us all, is to acquire the confidence of the people, to develope their resources, and to raise them to a higher level. This can only be effected by the District Officers being thoroughly in touch with the better class of native, through whom we may hope gradually to influence the whole population. Mudirs* and Inspectors should learn to know personally all the principal men of their district, and show them, by friendly dealings and the interest taken in their individual concerns, that our object is to increase their prosperity. Once it is thoroughly realised that our officers have at heart, not only the progress of the country generally, but also the prosperity of each individual with whom they come into contact, their exhortations to industry and improvement will gain redoubled force. Such exhortations when carried in the shape of Proclamations or Circulars, effect little; it is to the individual action of British officers, working independently, but with a common purpose, on the individual natives whose confidence they have gained that we must look for the moral and industrial regeneration of the Soudan.[1]

The people whose resources were to be raised to a higher level by this policy were thought, by contemporary Europeans, to be in an extraordinarily backward condition as the result of the Mahdia.† In the southern Sudan, which the lack of communications in any case made extremely remote, there was still need to establish law and order by military expeditions. Only the central rainlands and the river-banks could make any contribution to revenue and here much of the land appeared to have been abandoned. Famine, service with the Khalifa's armies, and liability to arbitrary seizure of any surplus had discouraged any production beyond a family's minimum needs. The Sudan economy of 1898 was a subsistence economy with only a little gum, ivory, ostrich-feathers and hides and skins to be offered to external markets. The first year's revenue was only £E35,000.

'The Soudan', wrote Viscount Cromer,‡ British Agent in Egypt, submitting the first year's report to the British Foreign Secretary, 'is in a far more backward condition than was the case with Egypt when the work of reform was taken seriously in hand. The work of introducing civilization into the Soudan may not improbably present somewhat similar features. Time is above all things required. The main condition of ultimate success is, I venture to think, that whatever measures are

* Mudir was used in the Sudan as the title given to the governor of a province.
† The Mahdia is the term used for the historical period when the Sudan was ruled by the Mahdi and his successor the Khalifa.
‡ Evelyn Baring (1841–1917), P.C., G.C.B., O.M., G.C.M.G., etc. Earl of Cromer. Entered army, 1858: private secretary to Viceroy of India, 1872–6: British Commissioner of the Caisse de la Dette, Egypt, 1877–9: finance member, India, 1880–3: Consul-General, Egypt, 1883–1907.

taken should be deliberate, and that the work of reform should not be hurried.'[2] 'It is needless to touch on general economic conditions', wrote Mr. James Currie,* in submitting the first report on education, 'except to point out that one is dealing with a population steeped in poverty. As with the people so with the Soudan. Dependent as she is on the bounty of Egypt, with every problem of State complicated by chronic absence of money, the duty of proceeding slowly, of setting nothing on foot that has no real vital connection with the economic needs of the country, becomes plainer every day.'[3] 'The two most pressing needs in the Soudan', wrote Cromer, submitting the annual report for 1900, 'are, I think, first an increase in the number of British officials: and secondly, the expenditure of capital on railways and irrigation. . . . Little progress can be made in the Soudan without the expenditure of capital. I should add that I see little immediate prospect of unaided private capital, on any considerable scale, seeking for investment in the Soudan.'[4]

Modern eyebrows may be raised at the bland assumption of the superiority of western civilization disclosed by these quotations from the heyday of imperialism. What is interesting is that the confidence and faith behind this assumption led to a quite deliberate planning of development 'to introduce civilization', a planning, however, confronted by a financial dilemma of how to raise the capital. With different actors and changed slogans, the same drama is still being played over much of the world's stage today.

* Later Sir James Currie (1868–1937), K.C.M.G., K.B.E. Joined Egyptian Education Service, 1889: appointed first principal of Gordon College and Director of Education in Sudan, 1900: Director of Empire Cotton Growing Corporation, 1922–37; Chairman of Governing Body of Imperial College of Tropical Agriculture, 1927–37.

Chapter 2

FEELING THE WAY TO DEVELOPMENT

Governor-General Wingate,* reviewing the policy of the Government in a later report, continued the theme of planned purpose in development.

The task which the Sudan Government has set itself to perform is primarily to confer the benefits of civilization on the inhabitants by rendering secure, as far as is possible, their persons and their property; by improving communications across those wide stretches of desert or wilderness which intervene between the main centres of population and productivity; by adding to the fertility of the naturally rich soil by means of artificial irrigation suitable to the varying conditions prevailing over so large an extent of country; and finally by providing—in addition to the great Nile waterway and railway which bind the Sudan to Egypt—a good port and harbour on the Red Sea within easy access of the interior, whereby the inhabitants may be more economically furnished with their requirements from abroad, and may find outside markets for their natural products.[1]

These were the bare structures of public works and services without which a poor, scattered society could get no access to a higher standard of living. They form an interesting example of that basic sector of development indispensable for any move forward materially, yet very difficult to finance in a country starting from extreme poverty in assets of capital and skill.

How indeed was the Sudan to finance such a policy? High taxation of the local people was ruled out by Cromer. Past experience of the harm done by this method in the Sudan and Egypt had convinced him that low taxation should be the keystone of the political arch. It brought general tranquillity in its train, and was an essential preliminary to steady improvement.[2] Cromer himself had put the dilemma in his report for 1902.

* Sir Reginald Wingate, Bart. (1889–1953), G.C.B., G.C.V.O., G.B.E., etc. Saw service in India in early life: Director of Military Intelligence to Lord Kitchener before and during reconquest of Sudan: Governor-General of Sudan, 1900–16: High Commissioner in Egypt, 1917–18.

34

What the Soudan mainly requires is the outlay of capital on a large scale, notably to improve the very defective means of communication which at present exist. It is quite hopeless to expect that unaided private enterprise will supply this want. In view of the certainty that a considerable period will have to elapse before any outlay will be remunerative, it is impossible to arrive at any other conclusion than that recourse must be had to Government action. To obtain the necessary funds at the expense of the British taxpayer, even were such a course possible, would not, in my opinion, be either just or desirable. It is equally clear that the Government of the Soudan cannot, on its own unaided credit, raise money, for its expenditure is already largely in excess of its income. To impose additional taxation in Egypt, in order to meet Soudanese requirements, is a proposal which cannot for one moment be entertained. Under these circumstances, the problem might, at first sight, appear insoluble.[3]

A solution was found at first, not by imposing additional taxation in Egypt, but, as Currie wrote in his report, by 'depending on Egypt's bounty'.

The financial help was provided in three ways. The condominium Government was first presented with certain capital assets derived from funds voted for the military campaign, of which Britain had contributed some 40 per cent. The main item was the railway from the Egyptian frontier to Atbara. The extension of the railway from Atbara to Khartoum North at a cost of some £E400,000 was met by Egypt as part of the campaign costs. Secondly, Egypt made direct grants to strengthen the budget. Between 1899 and 1912 some £E2,800,000 was given for this purpose. In addition there was a military contribution which was the notional cost of the Egyptian army stationed in the Sudan as a defence and security force.

Thirdly, Egypt made a series of advances from 1900 to 1910 totalling some £E5,400,000 for capital development. These enabled the railway to be built from Atbara on the Nile to the Red Sea, and a new port (Port Sudan), with deep-water quays, to be developed there. Later, they enabled the Blue Nile to be bridged at Khartoum and the railway to be extended down the Gezira to Sennar and across to the White Nile at Kosti. Repayment terms and interest rates for these advances were not set at the time and not given much consideration until the middle 1920's, and it was not until 1938 that it was agreed that repayment of the £E5,400,000 should begin not later than 1949 by minimum annual instalments of £E150,000, without any accrued or other interest charge. The terms on which this financial help was provided, whatever the off-setting benefits to Egypt, must be considered most generous. Small as these sums seem compared to our inflated figures of today, they would have been a chronic burden on development, relative to the costs of those days, if they had had to be obtained on ordinary commercial terms.

Nevertheless the Sudan Government was clearly in a precarious financial position, and had at once a duty and a desire to develop production in the Sudan to make the country financially independent as soon as possible. But although there appeared to be places of potential production, any immediate action was confronted with a number of interconnecting difficulties. There were frustrations in the search to get access to water from the Nile without harming Egypt and uncertainties of how to get land for development without harming the indigenous Sudanese and these two themes form the main contents of the rest of this chapter. The history of the first ten years was of a very gradual build-up in confidence, in financial equilibrium, in experiment, and in experience, gained often at the expense of much disappointment. The motto *festina lente* dominated the period.

In the absence of known mineral wealth, the chief source of potential production was the land and the most certain way of increasing yields was by irrigation. As early as 1900 Wingate was musing about revenue and irrigation and wondering if their future lay together in the Gezira district.

I recently rode across the Gezireh from Wad Medani on the Blue Nile, to opposite Dueim on the White Nile, a distance of some 80 miles, across a perfectly flat plain, sown almost throughout its entire length with dura. As there is only one crop grown during the short rainy season, and as this cereal is planted and harvested within a period of sixty to eighty days, it follows that if a system of irrigation were feasible in the Gezireh, it would become a huge granary capable of supplying not only the whole Soudan but other countries as well.[4]

The first frustration was of course the lack of communications and he continued,

But without proper means of transport this rich district is of comparatively small value from a revenue point of view. Statistics show that in the Abud district of the Gezireh the tax collected amounted to 5,094 ardebbs,* but of this quantity 1,960 ardebbs were issued as payment to the native camelmen who conveyed it to Dueim. The existence of a light railway would of course obviate all this, but until improved irrigation increases the annual number of crops, it is doubtful if such a project would be a financial success.[4]

The lack of rail transport had the same deadening effect on the transport of gum from the interior of Kordofan where there was an inexhaustible

* An ardebb is a measure of weight for grain, equivalent in the Blue Nile to 560 lb. and elsewhere in the Sudan to 336 lb.

supply of this valuable product; and to the transport of grain from Gedaref where, for example, it could be had for 22 piastres* an ardebb but cost 160 piastres at Khartoum. In the eastern Sudan in the Gash delta, one of the few sources of irrigation not dependent on the Nile, excellent cotton would grow but hardly paid the camel freight to the Red Sea. On the Main Nile below Khartoum it was almost hopeless to expect that any staple article could be sold in the markets of Europe, if it had to be weighed down with the cost of freight from Khartoum to Alexandria. It is easy to understand how, as soon as money could be found, the priority claimant in the minds of the Government was a railway system. Thanks to the capital advances from Egypt, the Nile–Red Sea link was completed by 1906; the Blue Nile was bridged at Khartoum by 1909 and by 1910 the railway had been extended down the Gezira to Sennar and over the White Nile to Kosti.

Meantime between 1899 and 1903 the future irrigation possibilities of the whole Nile system were being explored by an eminent British irrigation engineer from the Egyptian service, Sir William Garstin.† Garstin had for many years directed important irrigation works in Egypt which, more than any other factor, had raised that country's condition from bankruptcy to prosperity. With these works approaching completion, the time had arrived when, for Egypt's own purposes, the question of dealing with the Nile in territories which lay outside Egypt could be advantageously considered.

The sources of the great river, which had mystified men since the days of Herodotus, had only been discovered in the last half-century by the great explorers, Speke and Burton, Baker and Stanley. In 1893 Sir William Willcocks,‡ the Director-General of Reservoirs in Egypt, proposed the idea of utilizing the equatorial lakes as reservoirs, but there was no reliable data on which to base a practical scheme for doing this. Garstin now made three expeditions up the White Nile to its source in the great equatorial lakes, and Dupuis, his assistant, up the Blue Nile to its source at Lake Tana in Ethiopia. They were the first occasions on

---

* Egyptian currency was used in the Sudan. 100 piastres = 1 pound Egyptian, £E = £1 0s. 6d.

† Sir William Garstin (1849–1925), G.C.M.G., G.B.E. Entered Indian Public Works Department, 1872: sent to Egypt, 1885: Inspector-General of Irrigation, Egypt, 1892: Under-Secretary of State for Public Works, 1892: adviser to Ministry of Public Works, Egypt, 1904–8. In Lord Cromer's words he 'raised himself to the rank of the greatest hydraulic engineer of this or any country'.

‡ Sir William Willcocks (1852–1932), K.C.M.G. Indian Public Works Department, 1872–83: Egyptian Public Works Department, Reservoirs, 1883–97: designed Aswan Dam, 1893, and irrigation works in Mesopotamia, 1911.

which these regions had been examined by competent hydraulic engineers.

Garstin's first report on the White Nile reads like an explorer's diary. [5] The name White Nile in those days was confined to the stretch of the river from Khartoum southwards to Lake No. Beyond that it was known as the Bahr el Gebel—the river that comes from the mountains—joined from the west by the Bahr el Ghazal—the gazelle river—and from the east by the Sobat. The mountain river itself had an alternative channel, 150 miles long, called the Bahr el Zeraf. Making a nexus near Lake No, these rivers drew their sources, apart from the main flow from the equatorial lakes, in innumerable watercourses and streams issuing from the great semicircle of mountains and high land which frames the southern border of the Sudan from Ethiopia to the Nile-Congo divide.

The distance from Khartoum to Lake Albert by river was over 1,300 miles, but in all this distance the fall in land level was only 300 metres. This negligible slope determined the character of the rivers, and so of what was known as the Sudd region. Few had ever seen this primeval phenomenon or had any suspicion of its extent. For two-thirds of the year and for 450 miles of its length, the main river meandered sluggishly through immense marshes, choked with tall papyrus grass and floating vegetation. For a further 250 miles northward there was a broad band of swamp on each side of it. Garstin described the Sudd thus:

> Throughout this whole region it is extremely rare to see any sign of human life. The Bahr el Gebel has an evil name for mosquitoes and one that is well deserved. With the disappearance of the sun they come forth in countless myriads and make life a burden. The whole region has an aspect of desolation beyond the power of words to describe. It must be seen to be understood. The dark green masses of papyrus, which hedge in the channel, although possessing a certain gloomy beauty, become monotonous to the eye when kilometre after kilometre is passed without any change in the aspect of the landscape. Even on the rare occasions when it is possible to see over this hedge no relief is experienced. In every direction the sea of vegetation extends without a break. . . .
>
> The air is hot and steamy and malarious to a degree. No one can remain long in this portion of the river without experiencing a feeling of depression. Through these dreary marshes the river winds in a continual succession of loops and curves. So numerous are these twists that the loss of slope caused by them must be very great, and it is evident that were it possible for the river to avoid these curves, and to follow a straight course between Bor and the White Nile, the surface slope would be very considerable. [6]

Depressed or not, Garstin hit on ideas which were going to influence thinking on the Nile for years ahead. He measured the discharge of the mountain river Bahr el Gebel, as it came in and as it emerged from the Sudd, and found that half its volume was lost in the swamps by evaporation. It was useless, he wrote, to create large reservoirs in the equatorial lakes, immense as might be the storage, if the greater part of the extra supply thus obtained was merely wasted in this vast marsh bottleneck. It would be difficult to imagine a river less fitted for bringing down water economically than the Bahr el Gebel, and no one who had seen it would think of large irrigation schemes for the benefit of the country through which it passed. But, if the great swamp region could be by-passed and the water conveyed to the north in a well-constructed and fully-controlled channel from Bor to the White Nile, then even the present water lost in the marshes could go a long way to supplying Egypt's needs, let alone the future storage of the great equatorial lakes which could thereby also be made available.

Dupuis, meantime, exploring up the Blue Nile, had found the complete antithesis.[7] The distance from Khartoum to Lake Tana was 850 river miles, but the fall in land level was over 1,000 metres. This steep slope had eliminated swamps and, in contrast with the wide shallow bed of the White Nile, the Blue Nile flowed rapidly with little loss in a deep rocky bed. The terrain offered a choice of potential dam sites, apart from Lake Tana, and the slope commanded a country of the richest alluvial soil in the eastern Sudan. On both sides of the river fertile plains extended for an immense distance, apparently only wanting irrigation to render them as productive as any land in the world. In particular the Gezira plain seemed predestined by nature for the purpose, for it sloped very gently from south-east to north-west, from the Blue Nile to the White Nile, and could be commanded from one of the dam sites on the former river.

The conclusion seemed clear. While the White Nile water could be little utilized in the Sudan but could immensely benefit Egypt if the Sudd could be by-passed, the Blue Nile water offered great potentialities for the Sudan.

Egypt, with her earlier civilization and utter dependence on the river, had naturally been the sole consideration hitherto in plans for Nile development. Returning from his explorations Garstin for the first time looked beyond the needs of Egypt alone. He wrote in 1901:

Were Egypt alone to be considered it would be scarcely necessary to go so far afield as the Upper Nile. A dam at Assouan could doubtless be built which would store sufficient water for the utmost requirements of Egypt. But such a work would leave untouched the countries bordering the river to the south. Their interests must be safeguarded by such a Scheme as will ensure them a proportional share in the prospective benefits.[8]

Even though the realization of these schemes appeared remote, especially considering the small population of the Sudan in those days, money spent in investigating them more fully would be well spent.

Garstin closed his report in 1904 with these words.

Those to whom the privilege shall be granted of assisting towards this consummation will have a chance given to them such as seldom falls to the lot of man. To rescue the Upper Nile from the marshes in which it has lost more than half its volume; to control and regulate the great equatorial lakes, making them add to the flow of the river at will; to cause the waters of the Blue Nile to rise and irrigate the fertile tracts through which they pass; to secure to Egypt a constant and sufficient supply for the entire area between the cataracts and the Mediterranean; to free that country from the ever present danger of a disastrous flood—these are tasks worthy of comparison with any previously recorded in the world's history, and, if successfully accomplished, will leave behind them a monument that will probably endure long after all evidence of those erected by an earlier civilisation shall have passed away.[9]

Garstin's examination of the steps necessary to increase the supply of water, on which the future development of Egypt depended, showed that the scene of action would have to be not in Egypt but in the remote provinces of the Sudan. It was always sufficiently obvious, Cromer had maintained, that the power which held the head-waters of the Nile commanded the Egyptian supply. Garstin's additional conclusion must surely convince doubters that there was real value to Egypt in making financial contributions to ensure stability in the Sudan. Egypt was relieved from the dread of Dervish invasion. All fear of interference with her water supply was removed. Indeed, in the country formerly dominated by the Dervishes, works might be executed which would eventually prove of the utmost service to all the inhabitants of the Nile Valley.[10]

Yet these considerations led to an additional frustration. For all potential irrigation in the Sudan had first to satisfy the authorities in Egypt that it would not interfere with her customary supplies or future needs of water. This was no idle formality. To avoid any risk of divided authority, Garstin himself had insisted that control over the flow of the river must always remain in the hands of one authority, which at that time could be none but the Ministry of Public Works in Egypt. The control of Nile water was accordingly concentrated in Cairo and permission had to be obtained from the Egyptian Government before any pumping machinery could be installed or low-level canals constructed anywhere on the Nile or its tributaries. The reason for this strict control was that Egypt had for some years required and used the whole of the discharge during the low-level period of the river, closing the mouths of the Nile into the Mediterranean with earth banks every year to do so. Any irrigation developments in the Sudan which used water in the low-level period would thus deprive Egypt of water to which she had a historic right of usage and on which she had come to depend.

This critical low-level period varied from year to year but for purposes of control was at that time defined as in the Sudan from 1st February until 15th July. Thus, whatever the size disclosed by survey of potential irrigation areas in the Sudan, the water was available for crops only from 16th July to 31st January, when the Nile flood was carrying to the sea a surplus above Egypt's usage. It was a matter for experiment, and open to doubt, whether in the climate of the Sudan this flood-water period was suitable and sufficient for bringing to maturity economic crops like cotton, wheat and sugar cane. It could provide additional dura, but this subsistence crop would not repay the capital costs. If experiment showed that these economic crops must have water in the low period then the only way of overcoming this water frustration would be to hold back flood water behind storage dams for use later. But these would be very expensive constructions, and their design dependent upon precise information on just how much extra water, outside the flood season, any particular crop required. Neither the money nor the information was available.

So the Government's attention was perforce transferred for the time being, away from the Gezira, partly to irrigation areas which did not involve the Nile, such as the Gash and Tokar deltas, and partly to the Main Nile north of Khartoum, to see if basin irrigation,* requiring only flood water and inexpensive guide works, could give more immediate scope for development. This led to other frustrating difficulties, how to deal with the ownership of land, and what to do about foreign concessions, a field of inquiry destined to have a profound impact on this story and, through the Gezira, upon the history of the Sudan.

* Basin irrigation was a system of ponding water on land by large earth banks, long enough for a thorough soaking. It was a method of utilizing the flood water to grow crops, in the absence of rain or of a continuous supply of water.

Chapter 3

THE PROBLEM OF LAND AND FOREIGN CONCESSIONS

The first objective of land policy after the reconquest of the Sudan was to get the local people back to work on the land. In the Nile strip fifteen years of instability during the Mahdia had driven many landowners and cultivators away. Disease and warfare had reduced their numbers. Many holdings were cultivated only in part and waterwheels had fallen into disuse. Although in the great nomad areas in the rainlands, where land was plentiful, it had been held in common by the tribe and distributed for individual usage by the chief, along the Nile, where cultivation was not a shifting uncertainty but involved fixed capital assets like water-wheels and bullocks, it had come to carry with it firm individual rights. It could be sold, transmitted to heirs, rented and mortgaged for money or a share of the crops.

The growing assurance, after the reoccupation, of a fair administration and reasonable taxation, and the Government's own desire to get cultivation going, brought out of hiding all manner of claimants and set off a wave of disputes as to rights. Without secure title cultivation and reinstatement of water-wheels would naturally be discouraged and settlement was urgent. For this purpose a Titles to Lands Ordinance was passed in 1899 and land settlement commissions were set up. A ruling was made that possession or rents for five years to the date of claim gave an absolute title in any event and, failing any superior claim, continuous possession since the condominium gave an apparent title to the land. These land commissions were started from the north in Dongola Province as the country became reoccupied, but it was difficult to find personnel to man the commissions and, particularly, reliable subordinate staff to demarcate the boundaries and record them precisely as evidence against further disputes.[1]

The delay caused by these staff difficulties was in some ways a blessing in disguise. The reconquest of the Sudan had created an opening for intensive land speculation both native and foreign. Much of this originated from Egypt where the increased rentals and high selling prices of land, due to the recent irrigation works, had engendered a land-hunger. So the second objective of land policy was to control the transfer of land in such a way that the native cultivator was not sacrificed for the speculator, while the genuine investor with capital was not discouraged from using surplus land which could be registered in the name of the Government. For this objective also a proper title was essential. These twin aims of protection and development were not always easy to reconcile and their interplay had a critical formative effect on the subsequent structure of the Gezira Scheme.

Protection, in the Government's view, was a vital consideration. The situation had provided a golden opportunity for far-sighted people with capital to speculate on buying up native lands and selling them at an appreciation. This gave rise to a fear that the only people who would later be able to afford to buy the land from the speculators would be wealthy landlords and companies, with the result that an independent peasantry might be converted into agricultural labourers or rack-rented tenants. The first necessity was to stop land being bought for a song from people who had no idea of its relative value with money. A Proclamation in 1900 makes vivid the happenings of the time.

Whereas it has been brought to the notice of His Excellency the Governor-General that certain persons taking advantage of the want of money in the Sudan are acquiring lands from the inhabitants at prices below the actual value, notice is hereby given that until such time as it may be found possible to establish a land register, as contemplated by the Titles to Land Ordinance 1899, all contracts for the purchase of lands should be submitted to the Mudir for approval and that power will be given to land Commissions which may be appointed to revise the terms of any sales . . . of which notice shall not have been given to the Mudir.[2]

Nevertheless speculation continued and was intensified in 1905 by the opening of the Red Sea railway and rumours about the irrigation plans for the Gezira. The Governor of Sennar Province reported in that year that 'in some matters the people still require to be fathered a lot, especially where land is concerned, several being only too willing to get rid of part or all of their patrimony at ridiculous prices for the sake of a few pounds in their hand'.

Most British officials in the Sudan, according to the Governor-General's report in 1904, were strongly in favour of creating a peasant proprietary class. The strongest protagonist of this philosophy was

Major Dickinson, the Mudir of the Blue Nile Province. He was convinced that the land would no more than suffice to keep the people in a reasonable state of prosperity, allowing for a natural increase in the population, and he thought that prosperous peasant proprietors were more likely to benefit the country in the long run than a class of large landowners who, being foreigners, would certainly be absentees.[3]

A further Proclamation in July 1905 brought the transfer of land under stiffer control. It decreed that no native might sell, mortgage, or otherwise dispose of any land without the consent of the governor of the province, that any disposition made without consent would be void, and that any monies paid for land when consent had not been given would not be recoverable. It further decreed that for the present no consent would be given to sales unless the land had been registered.

Wingate, in recording this Proclamation, reveals some apparent difficulty in the dual aim of protection and development.

The question still remains to be settled whether after the land has been registered, any restriction shall be maintained on the native owners' power to alienate, in order to protect them from their want of foresight and improvidence. There are obvious objections to placing all the land transactions of the country in the hands of the Government, not so much on account of the highly paternal character of such a measure—for I do not see how under present circumstances the Government of the Sudan can be other than paternal—but because of the very great difficulty of ensuring its effective execution. There can, however, be very little doubt that, unless some restrictions are imposed, almost the whole of the land will pass out of the hands of the natives into those of speculators.[4]

As far as the Gezira was concerned this Proclamation had a real effect in keeping land in the hands of local cultivators, for it was not until 1906 that survey and registration were begun there. By 1911 944,000 feddans* had been surveyed and registered in the Gezira and practically the whole of this land had been found to be in private native ownership. The amount registered as government land was small.

Wingate's dilemma in 1905 of whether to maintain any restrictions on transfer after registration was to remain a recurrent problem and soon after the Gezira survey was finished in 1912 a further Proclamation stated that permission would be refused for any sales or dispositions of lands in the Gezira 'except of such sales to other natives of the same locality as had hitherto been customary and were deemed by the Governor to be proper'.[5] In 1924, in the British Parliament, the Foreign

* A feddan may be taken throughout as approximately the same as an acre; actually = 1·038 acres.

Secretary, on behalf of the Sudan Government, was able to state that

The result of this policy has been that practically the whole of the land in the Gezira remains in native ownership divided into comparatively small holdings, so that it may be said that, not only has the foreign land speculator been kept out, but also the wealthy native absentee landlord, and the whole of the land remains in the ownership of the actual cultivators that work upon it.[6]

While this legislation was enacted to protect the Sudan peasant and had particular relevance in the Gezira, applications for land concessions were not everywhere looked upon with disfavour in these early years. According to Wingate in 1903 most governors agreed that, there being no Sudanese capital for investment, the best significant agricultural advance must be by foreign concessions, in places where these did not conflict with local interests. Such places were thought at the time to be available, especially along the Main Nile in the northern province. Here, while locals had their water-wheels along the river frontage, fairly large areas of land, lying a few hundred metres from the river, could be developed only by the installation of pumps and canals.

It is clear, however, that while some in the Government, and no doubt many outside it, welcomed such concessions, others experienced great difficulties over them. The Director of Agriculture wrote, in his report for 1904,

From the very outset this Department has had to tackle the question how to deal satisfactorily with the numerous applications for land which have been received, since, owing to the demand for cotton and the construction of the Nile–Red Sea railway, the eyes of capitalists and agriculturalists have been turned to the large areas available for cultivation in the Sudan. In most places where land was applied for, the rights of the natives had not been enquired into and settled, no cadastral survey had determined the areas, and no Irrigation Department had been formed to take levels and to devise schemes for irrigating the land, nor was it known how much water for summer irrigation Egypt would allow the Sudan to utilize for its own purposes.[7]

The difficulties were referred to an advisory committee of officials in Cairo, at which Lord Edward Cecil* made an interesting analysis of the issues at variance and a suggestion to reconcile them. The most important principle in this suggestion—that development by foreign capital should be looked upon as a problem of stages rather than of final and

---

* Lord Edward Cecil (1867–1918), K.C.M.G. Son of third Marquess of Salisbury. After taking part in reconquest of Sudan, served as military secretary to Wingate: Sudan Agent in Cairo, 1904–6: financial adviser to Egyptian Government, 1912–18.

permanent concessions—found a parallel later in the temporary nature of the foreign capital in the Gezira Scheme, and his views deserve quoting rather fully. He wrote,

I think it is as well to emphasize one general proposition, that an essential difference in our land policy should be maintained with regard to what may be termed the pioneer stage of land development as distinct from the permanent land settlement of the country. The Sudan is not, and never will be, a country suitable for permanent European habitation, and it is therefore the interest of the Government to encourage as far as possible native landowners. . . . But in order to bring under cultivation the vast tracts of land which only need water to make them fertile, it is necessary to provide a considerable amount of capital. Native landowners have not as a rule any considerable capital. . . . Under these circumstances I am strongly of opinion that land companies and syndicates will be of greater use to the country generally during its pioneer stage of development, than any attempt to develop the country through purely native agents. There is a certain danger, however, that people will regard the large purchases of land made by such syndicates or companies as being in opposition to the native landholder. Such is not the case, the business of the land companies and syndicates is merely to acquire land, place it under cultivation, and when its value is increased to a certain point, to dispose of the land which they have obtained. Provided sufficient encouragement is then given to the native landowners to buy land, the Government will succeed in settling a good class of native owners in the Sudan, and this I opine is their main object. The pioneer policy of Government should, therefore, be to encourage sound land companies by giving them fair terms under which they can make reasonable and fair profit, at the same time jealously guarding the native rights over any portion of such land, compensating adequately and fully any native owners whom it may be necessary to dispossess in order to carry out efficiently the larger schemes. The future land policy of the Government should be to facilitate the transfer of such land from the hands of the land company to smaller native owners. [8]

The Director of Agriculture doubted the ability to control the land companies. 'From my experience in other countries', he wrote, 'I do not think that we can calculate on the bulk of the land which is to be sold to European capitalists reverting to natives. Large estates have thus been kept in India and Ceylon in European hands and management, and there is no prospect of them going into native hands. . . . I myself believe that the small native landholder will have a tendency to disappear. The riverain lands will go into the hands of native capitalists (money lenders) and ultimately perhaps to Europeans.'[9]

For a while Lord Edward Cecil's view seems to have prevailed, and in July 1904 the Sudan Government offered government land for sale in freehold blocks of 10,000 feddans and upwards for basin irrigation.

Foreign applicants were not lacking in numbers but almost without exception they lacked capital. The files of 1904 and 1905 are heavy with correspondence of negotiations involving the Government in a great deal of wasted inquiry as to rights, for very little development materialized. Within a year, government policy veered more towards the viewpoint of the Director of Agriculture. The lack of effective response had suggested that most foreign applicants were merely speculators, although the uncertainty of profit must have been a deterrent also. Moreover the adjudication of native rights over these lands, even though they had been only occasionally exercised when flood or rare rain made the land usable, was proving troublesome and not easy to determine. The only province in which Government was ready to deal satisfactorily with applications was Dongola, and there, out of 53,000 feddans surveyed, 39,000 had been declared native land and only 14,000 government land. This did not leave much room for 10,000 feddan concessions. Other provinces would have to await settlement.

Early champions of the concession policy began to have second thoughts. The Governor of Dongola now drew attention to the fast-increasing population and urged that all land suitable for irrigation by water-wheel be reserved for the next generation. The Legal Department took the view that all existing native rights should be fully recognized, that Government should be able to grant concessions on areas where these rights were very partial, but that the people involved should be compensated with land in the resulting irrigation schemes. The Governor of the Blue Nile had all along been against alien concessions in his province. In the outcome only one concession of any size, of 10,000 feddans at Zeidab, about 180 miles north of Khartoum, was approved and taken up. The terms of this were recommended as a model for others. Henceforth concessions would only be granted on carefully surveyed localities, and the concessionaire would have to undertake to put through an approved plan of development on his holding.

Wingate summarized all this experience in his report of 1906, for the benefit of some critics of his policy.

There can be no doubt of the desirability of eventually bringing in foreign capital to assist in the land development of the Sudan, but in the first instance the conditions under which concessions of land should be made have to be carefully considered. I am aware that delay in this matter will not improbably be attributed to a narrow officialism which is reluctant to encourage private enterprise and is not sufficiently active in promoting the development of the country. It is scarcely an exaggeration to say that the whole future of the Sudan depends upon the treatment which this question receives. Not only do the facts speak for themselves but the experience of other countries shows the harm which can be done with undue haste. . . . Until the nature of the native rights has been clearly ascertained, and until the treatment which, in connection with those rights, shall be imposed when any land concessions are granted, be determined, I hold that it would be in the highest degree imprudent to deal with this question.[10]

The disappointing results of development by private enterprise on the Main Nile under these conditions led the Government to open up some flood irrigation projects to increase the returns from native lands. Initial success in a year of lucky flood encouraged investment of precious government capital in the hope of substantial returns from taxing the new food crops. In a few years, however, the irregularity of the flood had turned these projects into costly failures. Clearly, future development on the Nile could not be based on simple works and uncertain flood water: pumping machinery was essential. Only cash crops could pay for the machinery and they needed water outside the flood season. On any large scale Egypt could not spare this unless the river was dammed and the water stored from the flood. This argument, of course, led back to the big scheme in the Gezira, but there was still no finance for a project of this scale. Perhaps there would be in the future, but for the present policy must be concentrated on slow but regular financial improvement derived from a variety of products—more gum, more rain-grown dura, more hides and skins and—best contributor—more cotton from Tokar.

Tokar had three great advantages. It was near to the sea and had an easier transport problem. It was not connected with the Nile and had no water restriction from Egypt. And it cost nothing in capital works to get its water. Tokar was a silt plain, a small inland delta on to which poured an annual flood when the rains came to the Eritrean hills. Cotton, the new wealth of Egypt, had originally come from the Sudan, and Mumtaz Pasha, when Governor of Suakin fifty years earlier, had first introduced it to Tokar, and a small area had been cultivated there in the Mahdia. On the reoccupation, the area sown to cotton expanded sharply, rising from 2,000 to 40,000 feddans between 1900 and 1912, the yield rising from 15,000 to 115,000 kantars.*

Tokar was a forerunner in another direction. There was always a doubt about the volume and destination of the flood there and this precluded regular cultivation of particular areas. As a result no certain rights of ownership of the land had developed. The delta was therefore

* A kantar may be taken throughout as approximately equivalent to 100 lb. of ginned lint cotton, or 315 lb. of unginned seed cotton.

48

declared government land and allotments were made annually by Government to applicants who wished to cultivate. The government officer would refuse to allot to a bad cultivator and this measure of control was found to be a real benefit to the country itself when it became necessary to raise the quality of the product. It provided a way of eliminating degenerate local seed by permitting only government-supplied seed to be sown and so enhancing the value of the crop by grading.

Tokar thus gave the Government its first experience of the immense advantage, to the budget and to the individual peasants, of an agricultural policy which both controlled and helped them. Tokar also showed that economic advance could be made under such a policy by the natives of the country themselves. It showed, in fact, that foreign enterprise was not the only road to development.

Tokar, however, could never be anything more than a forerunner. The greatest flood there was negligible compared with the potentials of the Blue Nile. These in the meantime were being worked out with greater accuracy by the Sudan branch of the Egyptian Irrigation Department, started in 1905 and staffed by personnel experienced in irrigation in Egypt. By 1907 levels had been taken and contour maps prepared. From these, by 1908 Dupuis put forward the broad features of a project of a barrage, now chosen to be sited just south of Sennar on the Blue Nile, and of the alignment of a main canal for irrigating the Gezira by gravity flow from a point near Wad Medani.[11] A canal with this layout could command the irrigation of some three million feddans, an area vastly in excess of any possible requirement for many years to come, in view of the shortage of population and the difficulty of obtaining labour. For this reason, and because of the novelty of the scheme, it seemed highly desirable to introduce irrigation gradually, and to begin in the tract where rain cultivation was already most developed and villages most numerous.

The preliminary main canal could be made of small sections with provision for enlargement later. Half a million feddans was suggested as a suitable first-stage area, to be worked up to in the course of the next ten to fifteen years. But the problem of obtaining the water as economically as possible without detriment to Egypt was always dominant. Mainly for this reason Garstin had at first favoured the Gezira as a great wheat-producing area for the nearby Arabian market, with only a small emphasis on cotton, because wheat would not need water in the scarce months. The growing financial importance of cotton made it essential, however, to find out just how much 'scarce month' water cotton needed in the Gezira itself. In November 1910 a proposition was submitted by the Department of Agriculture to Government for a thorough experiment to answer this question,[12] and to determine whether cotton of a high grade could be produced in the area coming within the scope of the proposed Gezira irrigation scheme.

The policy of *festina lente* had served the country well. Communications were now established. Population was increasing. People were more settled. Land registration was well under way. The Sudan's revenue, although it did not overtake expenditure until 1913, had steadily improved from £E35,000 in 1898 to £E1½ million in 1913, but there seemed little prospect of going beyond a very primitive economy without a wholly new source of production. Thus influences were converging to the new point of development. The Trade section of the Governor-General's report for 1910 reads:

The Government has fallen in for some criticism as being dilatory and unsympathetic towards schemes of exploitation . . . but I wish to point out that the disappointments of the earlier days were almost entirely due to lack of recognition that the Sudan Government had no right to look beyond the first duty of providing Egypt with a firm buttress on her southern frontier at as little cost as possible. A new situation has now arisen. It may be summed up by saying that a policy of mere pacification has to be expanded into one which recognises as an end the creation of a community on an independent economic basis. . . . An encouraging agricultural feature is the large increase in rain-grown cotton from the Gezira. Much of this cotton is bad and carelessly grown and picked, but it is cotton none the less, and has been grown by the natives almost unaided and under very disheartening conditions. This is a base upon which it should be possible to build, and whenever the great Gezira canal comes to be made this preliminary acquaintance of the people with cotton cultivation should be invaluable.[13]

What sort of association with the local people, how best to use the land agriculturally, and from where the capital necessary for the project was going to be raised—for strong objection to providing any more from Egypt was being voiced there—were three major uncertainties. At this point in the river of development a new stream, a private enterprise stream, came in to join and merge with this first long tributary of government policy, effecting an important influence on just these three anxieties, and bringing new personalities on to the stage of this story.

Chapter 4

ENTER PRIVATE ENTERPRISE

In 1903, when the Sudan Government was welcoming the interest of private capital to develop lands along the Main Nile, a wealthy American, a Mr. Leigh Hunt,* after twenty years of strenuous efforts in many lands, was taking a long holiday in Egypt. Always attracted by the unsettled regions of the world, he ascended the Nile as far as the southern Sudan and on his return discussed with Wingate the possibilities of cotton-growing. Among his suggestions was a proposal to encourage the immigration of skilled negroes from the United States, such as blacksmiths, mechanics and dairy and other farmers, who had been trained in American agricultural schools, as technical demonstrators to the local Sudanese.[1] Leigh Hunt evidently impressed Wingate and Cromer as a capitalist with both the resources for and the genuine intention of development. It was to him that the only large concession on the Nile, that of 10,000 feddans at Zeidab, was granted.

To develop the Zeidab concession, Leigh Hunt set up in 1904 the Sudan Experimental Plantations Syndicate, enlisting the co-operation of certain merchants of the city of London, particularly Wernher Beit & Co., one of whose members, Mr. Frederick Eckstein,† had been one of the chief pioneers of the Rand goldfield in South Africa.

The first pump was installed at Zeidab in 1906 and 70 feddans of cotton planted. By 1907, 800 feddans of cotton and 800 of wheat were being irrigated. Initial costs turned out embarrassingly heavy and the early years were anything but remunerative. A population of only 600 local Sudanese lived there at that time on the narrow strip of river-bank which could be commanded by their water-wheels. Labour for levelling

---

* Leigh S. J. Hunt. President of State Agricultural College, Idaho: entered business in Seattle, 1886: developed Oriental Consolidated Mines, Korea: died 1935.

† Later Sir Frederick Eckstein, Bart. (1857–1930). Began life in indigo business in India: joined brother in Johannesburg: returned to England at beginning of century: Chairman of Central Mines Investment Corporation until 1915.

the land and digging the canals on the new concession, between this river fringe and the desert, had to be recruited expensively from Egypt. Only one batch of negro emigrants was tried. Leigh Hunt himself was frequently away on his many other interests in the world and in December 1906, in view of the financial position of the company, his salary of £E3,000 a year as Managing Director had to be discontinued.

In May 1907 the Company was reorganized and renamed the Sudan Plantations Syndicate Ltd. Eckstein became Chairman. Leigh Hunt, although remaining a director until 1909, gave place as Managing Director to a Scotsman of singular intelligence and force of character, Mr. D. P. MacGillivray, who had been one of the managers of a banking house in Cairo. Another Scotsman, Mr. Alexander MacIntyre,* the engineer who had erected the pumps, was made Manager. Yet another Scotsman, Lord Lovat,† joined the Board as Leigh Hunt's nominee, to continue and to develop, curiously enough, the same singular personal interest in the unsettled regions of the world. The appointment of such a man was an important indication of the standing of the company in the business world. Lastly, but most significantly in the outcome, British field inspectors were recruited from land companies in Egypt where they had already gained experience in irrigated crops and in supervising peasant tenants.

Good crops were obtained at Zeidab by careful management in 1908 and 1909 when 1,380 feddans of cotton and 1,200 of wheat were harvested, but deficient water supply, costly transport, shortage of labour, and lack of skill, enterprise and inclination to work on the part of the labourers made direct cultivation unremunerative. In March 1908 the Board had to limit future expenditure in the Sudan to £E1,000 per month. The attempt to produce crops by direct labour was abandoned and the Board concentrated on what appeared to be the only paying method of development—a tenancy system. An experiment had been made in 1906 with ten Egyptian fellaheen installed as tenants on the Syndicate's land, growing their own crops at their own expense under the Syndicate's supervision and according to the Syndicate's planned rotation, and paying a rental for the Syndicate's water. The Syndicate

---

* Later Sir Alexander MacIntyre (1879–1952). Civil engineer: Manager of Sudan Plantations Syndicate, 1907–19: Managing Director, 1919–46: Chairman, 1928–49: knighted in 1938.

† Lord Lovat (1871–1933), Major-General K. T., G.C.V.O., K.C.M.G., etc. A great Scottish landowner who was a director of the S.P.S. from its inception: Under-Secretary at Dominions Office, 1927–8: Chairman Overseas Settlement Committee, 1927–9. He played a notable part in raising the Highland Brigade in the 1914–18 war and was awarded the D.S.O. and C.B.

had erected a ginnery and undertook to buy the cotton and other cash crops for marketing in bulk. The Syndicate also advanced loans every fortnight calculated on the amount and quality of the work done by the tenant, as shown by the careful records made by the Syndicate's field inspectors. In 1907 there were twenty-five tenants and in 1908 102 tenants; by then local Sudanese were applying. An analysis of the 381 tenants in 1910 shows an interesting mixture of 100 Egyptians from Upper Egypt, sixteen Greeks, one Austrian, two Syrians and over 200 Sudanese, mainly from the locality.

The development of this tenanting association of capital, management and local cultivator was watched with considerable interest by the Sudan Government. Wingate reported in 1908 that it was clear from this experience that land reclamation rather than actual cultivation was the most promising field for land companies. This led him to wonder whether it was not best to confine enterprise to providing improved irrigation for riverain land owned by natives, and to invite private enterprise to assist in this form of development.[2] In 1908 the Syndicate, with surplus capacity from its pumps, offered to extend its water for a rental charge to natives owning 1,400 feddans nearby along the river-bank, in place of their water-wheels. The offer was warmly welcomed by both native owner and Government, for the water-wheel was inconvenient to run and the bulls that worked it consumed a large part of the crop. Everything possible was done to make the scheme a success. Government advanced loans repayable after harvest for clearing the land and digging the new water channels and the Syndicate provided cotton seed free of charge.

This rental association with local cultivators turned out later to be disappointing financially and had to be modified, but it had considerable significance in determining the subsequent history of the Gezira Scheme. For a Government preoccupied with reconciling the need for foreign capital, the protection and advancement of the local community and the enlargement of the country's revenue, the experiments at Zeidab offered an interesting combination. An unusual identity of interest seemed to be emerging. What the Government wanted from a social point of view the Syndicate was pioneering for its own financial reasons, and just on the eve of the first experimental station in the Gezira some of these thoughts and of the expectations then in the air were expressed in a remarkable address made in October 1910 by a man named Sir William Mather,* far away in Manchester.[3] Mather's address had a

---

* Sir William Mather (1838–1920), P.C. Chairman of engineering firm Mather and Platt; pioneered eight-hour day: Liberal M.P. 1885–6, 1889–95, 1900–4.

catalytic effect on the elements already present and brought into the river yet another stream of influence, this time from England, in the British Cotton Growing Association.

The B.C.G.A. was founded in 1902 to promote the growth of cotton in the British Empire. The necessity for its work was only slowly recognized but the failure of the American and Egyptian crops in 1909 brought home to Lancashire spinners the peril of relying on these two countries, especially for the longer and finer cotton then increasingly demanded for better-quality yarns. Such cotton could not be produced in India or West Africa, nor was the United States supply dependable, while in Egypt production had been static for ten years and practically the whole of the cultivable soil was already under cotton. That the Sudan could produce the quality needed was already known to the B.C.G.A., partly through Tokar cotton but especially from the increasing quantities of irrigated cotton produced at Zeidab.

Without the connecting link of Sir William Mather, however, it is open to doubt whether this particular stream would have joined up with the river at all, for the B.C.G.A. had approached Cromer some years earlier on the question and had been informed that there was nothing it could usefully do.[4] That Mather himself happened to be connected with the Sudan is an interesting illustration of how large a part the chance interests of individuals played in determining the final pattern of events, for Mather's connection with the Sudan was not economic at all; it was educational. James Currie, the Director of Education, whose reports show an astonishing interest in the economic needs of the country, decided, as soon as Garstin revealed the great potential of the Gezira, that his education department must begin to provide the basis for Sudanese technicians, for the civil and mechanical engineers which the future would demand. There was no money for such a purpose. The only thing was to appeal to philanthropists in Britain. The response came on the engineering side from Sir William Mather, who equipped the Gordon College with its first technical workshops and became a Governor of that Institution. This link with Currie put Mather, as a frequent visitor to the Sudan, in close touch with the problems and personalities in the Gezira itself, while in Lancashire, where he was a Vice-President of the B.C.G.A., he was at the centre of the cotton supply anxiety.

In his Manchester address in 1910 Mather gave an enthusiastic account of what was happening at Zeidab. He described the tenancy system, how the company had put up the pumping station and dug the canals, and how it provided regular loans to cover each phase of cultivation until a tenant could finance himself from his profits. And he made a specimen account of a tenant's receipts and costs which showed that this profit might be a very satisfactory figure.

Much too optimistically, as later years revealed, he estimated that a tenant's standard ten feddans of cotton should produce a crop of 4,500 lb. of lint cotton and 9,000 lb. of seed, based on a yield of 4·5 kantars per feddan, with the following result.

Costs		Receipts	
Ginning and Baling	£E7	Cotton (at 1s. per lb.)	£E225
Freight to Alexandria	17	Seed	30
Rent (at £E4 per feddan)	40		
Cultivation and Picking Loans	30		
	£E94		£E255
Tenant's Profit = £E161			

He spoke of Zeidab as a perfect object lesson for the development of the Sudan wherever cotton might be cultivated, either by pumps or by gravity irrigation.

The foundation of success has been found to be the principle of co-operation between native labour and the proprietors of the Estate. The effect on the natives has been to develop self-respect, and to inspire them with the ambition to become tenants of the 30 acre plots, each of which one man with his family is competent to cultivate to the best advantage. Instead of the former hopeless outlook for the natives as population increased, there is under the system at work at Zeidab a prospect of widespread comfort, the result of industry and perseverance, which must lead to the rapid increase of the population under improved social conditions, with the assured confidence in just and intelligent employers, whose goodwill and self-interest alike will lead them to make the well-being of the natives their constant care.

Turning to the bigger project of the Gezira Scheme, Mather urged that Britain should acknowledge a special responsibility to develop irrigation works in the Sudan. If this was accepted there were two alternatives for financing the Gezira Project. Either the capital might be raised, on the guarantee of the British Government, by the Sudan Government who would then construct the barrage and canalization. Or the British Government might authorize the Sudan Government to arrange for British capital to be found by a trustworthy syndicate in London. It would carry out the construction, provide subsidiary requirements to give the best cotton and prepare it for the market, and undertake the development of 500,000 feddans on such conditions as would confirm the natives in their properties and give them the full benefits of irrigation. The land owned by the Government in the Gezira might be leased to the Syndicate, and the whole area, both of native ownership and leased land, might, on using irrigation water, be assessed for taxation to yield revenue for the Government.

Mather concluded

I invite you to bring your influence to bear through the Cotton Growing Association, upon the British Government, to induce it to move without delay, and to do its part in the development of the Sudan on the lines I have ventured to suggest. If the Syndicate scheme should be adopted, you will have the opportunity of supporting it even from a personal interest. But, looking forward to the possibility of enormously increasing the growth of cotton in a territory under the part ownership and exclusive control of Great Britain, you may also feel pride and gratification in doing your part in removing the incubus that rests fitfully and disastrously on the industry of Lancashire. You may, moreover, experience a still wider satisfaction in knowing that you will help forward a great work of civilisation, in bringing to the native races of the Sudan, who have suffered for ages the greatest misery known to mankind, the benefits of freedom, justice, peaceful industry, ordered Government, and continuous prosperity.

A unanimous resolution was passed 'that the attention of His Majesty's Government should be drawn to the extreme importance of encouraging the further cultivation of cotton in the Anglo-Egyptian Sudan, and to the necessity of immediately adopting some scheme on the lines suggested by the Right Hon. Sir William Mather'.

Mather's speech drew the Sudan Plantations Syndicate and the British Cotton Growing Association together and in 1911, when the Syndicate first became connected with the Gezira under circumstances to be described in the next chapter, the B.C.G.A. took up 5,000 new £1 shares in the S.P.S., and their Chairman, Mr. J. A. Hutton, joined the board.

Valuable as this connection became in opening the first markets for Gezira cotton, the main effect of the interest of the B.C.G.A. was in the pressure which such a powerful trade group could bring to induce the British Government to guarantee Sudan capital loans for financing the project. The government attitude had been, as we have seen, that financing Sudan development was an Egyptian, not a British, responsibility. Although the provision of capital specifically to develop cotton growing in the Sudan, in competition with Egypt's own major national product, was hardly likely to find supporters among the ministers and legislators of that country, the alternative of applying to Whitehall for help had already had a very chilly reception. It is not easy to remember today, when colonial loans and grants and other forms of assistance are part of a recognized policy, just how different was the Government's attitude to overseas development in 1912. Wingate had continually urged that Britain should take an active financial part in the development of the Sudan, but to no avail. He had already proposed a Sudan loan, mostly for railway development, but nothing could move the Treasury.

The attitude of those days is vividly illustrated by a chance meeting in September 1912 between Wingate and Lloyd George, who was then Chancellor of the Exchequer. Wingate had been invited by H.M. King George V to Balmoral for a five-day visit when Lloyd George chanced to be there as minister in attendance. Wingate tried every day to get a word with him, without result. On the last day he tackled Lloyd George at breakfast and asked for ten minutes. It was refused, but Wingate followed him to his room and finally got his interview. Ten minutes became an hour as Wingate described the problems and possibilities of the great Nile river, and finally Lloyd George promised his support.[5]

Meantime following Mather's initiative, Hutton himself visited the Gezira in 1912 on behalf of the B.C.G.A., and also Mr. Arno Schmidt on behalf of the International Federation of Master Cotton Spinners Associations. The reports of these visits were widely circulated,[6] and culminated in a meeting between the B.C.G.A. and no less a person than the Prime Minister. *The Times* newspaper of 24th January 1913 gives an interesting picture of the meeting.

Mr. Asquith, replying to a deputation from the B.C.G.A. yesterday announced that the Government would at the earliest possible opportunity next session introduce a Bill, which has already been drafted, and which will authorize the Treasury to guarantee the payment of interest on a loan to be raised by Government of Sudan to the extent of three millions. . . . Mr. Asquith was accompanied by Mr. Lloyd George, Sir Edward Grey and Mr. Sydney Buxton. Lord Derby introduced the deputation, and the speakers on behalf of the Association were the Duke of Marlborough, Mr. J. A. Hutton, Sir Charles Macara and Mr. A. H. Hill, M.P. Mr. Hutton said that the development of cotton growing in the Anglo Egyptian Sudan was one of the most important propositions which had engaged the attention of the Association. The Gezira plain amounted to 5,000,000 acres of first class cotton soil, a country as large as the Egyptian Delta. The main difficulty that had to be solved was whether cotton could be grown as a winter crop, and the experiments which had been made in that direction had been eminently successful. He firmly believed that in the Gezira Plain they had the very finest cotton growing proposition in the whole world, and so they came to the Government to ask them to help in developing that wonderful country. Mr. Asquith in reply said

'We have long had under consideration the very important question upon which you speak with such special opportunities of knowledge and authority. When I was last year at Malta, I had the opportunity of several conversations with Lord Kitchener and he laid before me then many of the facts and considerations which you have presented today, because, as you are well aware, he has been from the first a most ardent, as well as a most powerful advocate and supporter of your scheme. It is a matter of interest, not only to Lancashire, but to the whole of Great Britain and the whole of the Empire, that we should both multiply our possible sources of supply of raw cotton and enlarge the area from which it is grown. Being as we are so largely interested, not only in the cotton industry here, but in the development of the Sudan, we approach the consideration of such a plan as that which you have laid before us with sympathy, and indeed, with the utmost possible prepossession in its favour.'

The poverty-stricken Sudan, searching to raise its standard of living, needed two allies before it could find the foreign capital. The first ally was a merchant-adventurer spirit, ready for risks and prepared to push into unknown fields of activity and profit. The second was an external demand for a product which the country seemed especially suited by nature to supply. Today the world is impatient for development but it is still difficult to succeed without these allies.

Chapter 5

PLANNING FOR PARTNERSHIP

Indispensable as were these external allies for obtaining foreign capital, they were looked upon by the British soldier-administrators of the Sudan with the same wariness with which they are looked on by emergent peoples today. Like them, these administrators feared that foreign capital, much as they needed it, would dominate the scene and take away their freedom to control the evolution of the country as they thought right. The interplay of this need and this fear, and the compromise arrived at to reconcile them, form the main theme in the next stage of the story.

In describing the influence of the B.C.G.A. in Britain we have overrun the story of events in the Gezira itself. There, following the Department of Agriculture's proposition for a thorough experiment, the first test pumping station had been opened by the Government in 1911 on 600 acres of land rented from local native landowners at Tayiba. The Sudan Plantations Syndicate had been invited to manage it on a fee basis and to apply to it the experience of its methods at Zeidab. In contrast to Mather's and Asquith's optimistic forecasts for their future the local inhabitants of the Gezira, who had no knowledge of what this would mean to them, were quite averse to change. Not one local peasant would take up a tenancy. Just as, at Zeidab, it had been necessary to get in Egyptians already skilled in irrigation as 'starters', so at Tayiba it was necessary to get in Zeidabis as the first tenants and to stimulate curiosity, envy, and finally imitation of their ways by locals in the Gezira.

Tayiba's first year was a great agricultural success. Yields of 5,300 lb. of cotton and heavy quantities of wheat, dura, and fodder were averaged by the first tenants on their thirty-acre holdings. It happened that outside this little irrigated area the rains had failed. When the Tayiba area was extended, for its second crop, to 2,000 feddans people came from all over the Gezira, offering to deposit money, gold bracelets and all kinds of jewellery in their anxiety to be accepted as tenants. A

59

contemporary report says that Lord Kitchener, who personally rode round Tayiba station and highly commended the company for the results there, suggested that those who had no experience at all in cotton growing should be sandwiched in between old tenants from the Zeidab estate. 'It is wonderful to see', the report goes on, 'how these novices at cotton growing have through the influence of their neighbours cultivated their own fields as well as if they had been used to cotton growing all their lives. There was no need to draw during the second year upon Zeidab farmers.'[1]

The second year at Tayiba gave even better results both in quality and yield of cotton than the first year. The Director of Agriculture in his report for 1912, after putting in a caution against too hasty conclusions before the effect of continued cropping on the Gezira soil was known, foreshadowed the next stage.

At the time of writing the prospects of this, the second year's experiment, are very good. One most gratifying feature is the ready way in which the native of the district, who, it must be remembered, has hitherto only cultivated in the most primitive methods, responds to the instructions afforded by the Syndicate's representatives and develops into a good cultivator. This disposes of the old idea that the Arab could never develop into a good husbandman.

This brings me to a very important point which bears directly on the success of any irrigation scheme on a large scale in the Gezira, namely, the education of the local native landowner and cultivator. The land is for the greater part all owned by natives who have been accustomed in years of good rainfall to sow their grain crops in a very primitive manner with no regard to preserving the fertility of the soil by rotations, etc. It is evident that under irrigation and intensive cultivation he will have to work his land on proper rotations and according to modern methods. In order to do this he must be taught. This certainly is being done to a limited extent in Tayiba, but it is all important that, when the time comes for water to be put on to the Gezira plain by means of a canal, and a large tract of country is ready, there must be sufficient native cultivators ready to avail themselves of the irrigation and work their land on the most economical system.

In order to bring this about everything points to the necessity of increasing the area at Tayiba, and, perhaps, establishing additional pumping stations at other points.

Furthermore, seed farms must be established so that an adequate supply of the best variety of cotton seed known to be suitable for cultivation in these regions may be available for issue to cultivators.

It is beyond the scope of this report to engage in discussing how this can best be brought about, but everything points to the application of a 'Tenant System' similar to the one at present in force at Tayiba.[2]

It is always tempting, when writing the history of some human undertaking, to attribute some specially interesting feature of it to the foresight of a particular individual. Without in the least minimizing the wisdom and determination of all those who appear at this stage in the story, it must be said that what was later to be regarded as the outstanding characteristic of the Scheme—the triple partnership between State, Private Enterprise and Tenants—came into being largely as the result of pressures from different directions and as the outcome of events already set in motion by many different people in the past. Nevertheless the ultimate voice was that of one man—Lord Kitchener. No arrangement of which he did not approve could have gone through at that date. He was the master and himself vitally interested in the human issues involved. Letters of the period reveal his dominant character and the mixture of awe and tact with which the great man was approached.

Lord Kitchener had a great personal interest in the people of the Sudan. For many years during the Khalifa's reign he had been training in Egypt the Anglo-Egyptian army destined to reoccupy the country and receiving intelligence reports on conditions in the Sudan. The reader may recall from Chapter 1 that he subsequently commanded this army and became the first Governor-General of the new condominium, that he founded the first school in Gordon's name, and laid down the principles of the new administration. Shortly after this he left for the South African war and was for more than ten years away from the scene. He returned to it in 1911 as the British Government's Agent and Consul-General in Egypt, the post which Lord Cromer had held earlier in this story, and which carried a tradition of surveillance over the affairs of the Sudan.

Just before his return, affairs in the Gezira had begun to operate around two major problems. First, who was going to manage the Gezira Scheme, and second, what was going to be the financial association between the peasant and the capital and the management.

As far as the first problem was concerned there were pressures from different directions. In favour of management by private enterprise was the Sudan Plantations Syndicate itself and particularly its forceful Managing Director, MacGillivray. The Syndicate was finding little scope for future investment on the Main Nile as the result of financial difficulties at Zeidab itself. The glowing picture which Mather had formed from the 1909 crop there had been rudely shattered when in the following year the cotton yield had been less than 1,000 lb. per tenant, and for the three subsequent years remained at less than 2,000 lb. per

61

tenant, instead of the 4,500 lb. Mather had forecast. Investment in the Gezira Scheme now appeared far more attractive. Moreover, the Syndicate felt that its methods, so successful at Tayiba, were particularly applicable in the Gezira.

Favouring the Syndicate also was the outspoken opinion of the B.C.G.A. to which the Sudan Government was so indebted for the government-guaranteed Sudan Loan, and which was exceedingly anxious to press on with more cotton growing. Its views were made plain in an illuminating letter written by its Chairman, Hutton, to Himbury* after visiting Tayiba in 1912.

The Zeidab experience has been more than valuable, and it is a mercy that the Government decided to hand over the management [of Tayiba] to MacGillivray. In this connection one cannot forget the invaluable services rendered by Sir William Mather. It was mainly due to his representations that the work was put into MacGillivray's hands. He pointed out rightly that commercial men of the right sort can work both more expeditiously and efficiently than any officials, however able . . .

Lancashire wants the cotton and I think the Sudan can supply it, though it will take some years to bring about any really large results. All the more reason not to lose a single minute and I think that hustle is needed here and we shall have to do more than a bit of clamouring at our end. Thank goodness Lord Kitchener is keen too, for, as we know from experience, official inertia is always one of the blocks to progress. Officials mean well but are so afraid of making a mistake or doing the wrong thing that they often do nothing at all. . . .

What is now needed is the provision of capital for railways, for irrigation works, and for commercial development, and also expert assistance and advice. As far as the latter point is concerned, the services of the Association are at the disposal of the Government. As regards the capital for commercial development, which will run into several millions, I think we can rely on the assistance of Mr. F. Eckstein, Lord Lovat, Mr. MacGillivray and their friends. The capital for railways and for irrigation works should, I think, be found by the Government, and when I say Government, I mean the British Government.[3]

A development committee had been set up in Khartoum but while some members favoured Hutton's views, others looked askance at entrusting all the commercial development to private enterprise. After all, the proposal to start an experimental test area in the Gezira had originated from the Sudan Government's Department of Agriculture. It had intended to run it itself as a prelude to running the Gezira Scheme

* Later Sir William Himbury, then General Manager and later Chairman of B.C.G.A.: member of Council of Empire Cotton Growing Corporation: Director B.C.G.A. (Punjab) Ltd.: member of Governing Body of Imperial College of Tropical Agriculture.

departmentally. It had some experience from Tokar. The land and the site of the pumping station were selected by Mr. Hewison of that department. The ploughing and canalization were undertaken by his official colleague Mr. Davie.* The soil was analysed by the government chemist. The pumps were erected by the Public Works Department.

But the whole Department of Agriculture consisted of Colonel Wilkinson as Director, a soldier who had been Governor of Kassala and according to tradition was reputed to be a very keen gardener, Hewison, Davie, and one other as trained British agricultural officials, and two Egyptian agricultural assistants. Inevitably there was scepticism as to whether such a tiny nucleus was appropriate for handling an undertaking expected to be so large and so highly specialized, particularly since the Syndicate was available. But the chief argument in favour of the Syndicate, and one of which the Government was very conscious, was that a successful experiment carried out by a commercial body would carry more weight in Britain when it came to raising a capital loan for the main scheme.

The decision made, in 1910, to use the Syndicate rather than the Department of Agriculture concerned only the management of the Tayiba experiment, and had been taken before Lord Kitchener returned to the scene. No decision had yet been made for the future management of the Gezira Scheme itself. The Tayiba agreement provided that the experiment, to prove conclusively that cotton could be grown on a commercial scale, should be carried out over a period of at least four years and should cease if the object had been attained before this period. Arrangements for the future had been left open.

There was, however, one feature of the Tayiba agreement which now caused the Sudan Government a great deal of trouble. MacGillivray had fully realized his value to the Government, both as a source of staff with technical knowledge and as a stalking-horse for attracting capital. When agreeing to manage the Tayiba experiment he had extracted from the Government an undertaking, if the trial at Tayiba was a success, to grant to the Syndicate an option to purchase 10,000 feddans of government-owned land within the area to be irrigated, or 30,000 feddans of rain-land in the Gezira. After the second season at Tayiba, all parties agreed that the trial had been a success and the undertaking was due to be implemented. But meanwhile the land settlement team had revealed that the only large area of government-owned land in the

* R. Hewison, C.B.E., and W. A. Davie. Each later became Director of Agriculture in the Sudan.

63

Gezira was of very poor soil at the northern tip far beyond the proposed canalization. Practically all the land likely to be irrigated had been declared to be the property of native owners. So the Sudan Government and Lord Kitchener had to face, in 1913, the questions both of who was to manage the Gezira and how to implement the promised undertaking to the Syndicate.

Objection to commercial management arose from something much stronger than the mere preference of officials for enlarging their departmental activities. There was the fear of being outwitted. Writing to Major L. O. F. Stack,* the Sudan Agent in Cairo, whom he used as a liaison officer to explain and supplement his letters and dispatches to Kitchener, Wingate speaks of the Sudan Government having to be on its guard against 'Gentlemen who are very well up in all company-mongering details, and would not fail to take advantage of the Sudan Government which has not much experience in such matters.'[4] He was not speaking of MacGillivray, but his remark typified an attitude. According to Stack Lord Kitchener also made some trenchant criticism of the Sudan Government's inefficiency in the matter of bargaining with MacGillivray.

Whenever I see Lord Kitchener on the subject of Tayiba he is rather more inclined to discourse on the bad bargain we made with the Syndicate than to confine himself to the point at issue. I have impressed on him again and again that the Agreement was submitted to the British Consul-General of that time who approved it . . . [He retorted] that of course owing to his knowledge of and interest he took in the country, he looked into things more than others in his position might.[5]

Kitchener had, a year previously, taken a considerably sterner view than had the Governor-General's Council as regards the Syndicate's claims for remission of taxation owing to bad crops at Zeidab. Writing to Wingate in April 1912 Stack says,

Lord K. thought MacGillivray's demands preposterous. . . . I hope to dissuade MacGillivray from going to him. Otherwise things may come to a deadlock and the Syndicate may in a huff go out of the Sudan altogether, which I take it is not in the interests of the Sudan. I have also represented to Lord K. that the fruits of the Company's experience have been an asset to Government, and that their withdrawal from the country after so many years would in financial circles in England have a bad effect.

Things are not altogether easy at present especially with regard to

* Later Major-General Sir Lee Stack (1868–1924), G.B.E., C.M.G. Joined Egyptian army, 1899: Sudan Agent, 1908–15: subsequently Civil Secretary: succeeded Wingate as Governor-General of Sudan, 1916–24: assassinated in Cairo, 1924.

council matters, for H.B.M.'s Agent and Consul-General is apt as you know to make up his mind pretty quickly and once he has decided he is difficult to turn from his decision. You see he only sees decisions and has not the arguments for and against before him, arguments which I have to supply for both sides when he asks me questions.[6]

The fear that the Syndicate, which was after all the only commercial company which had stayed the course in the Sudan, might pull out before the British Government had guaranteed a loan, and make it infinitely more difficult to find any capital for development, had in fact been the reason why MacGillivray had been granted his concession in the Tayiba agreement. Wingate now explained this in his reply to Kitchener's criticisms.

Personally, I was always strongly in favour of a Government loan, and, if we could have had any sort of promise that it would have been carried through, of course the conditions of the Agreement would have been quite different. Unfortunately, we had to be prepared to dance on either leg [Government Loan or Private Enterprise Capital] as the case might be, and although I quite agree we might have made a better bargain under different conditions, it must not be forgotten that the British public, especially Lancashire, have been to a considerable extent educated by action taken by outsiders, e.g. Sir W. Mather, the B.C.G.A., the Cotton Federation, and the S.P.S. Of course they took up the cause *con amore* because personal considerations largely entered into the matter and they saw that there was money in it.

I can appreciate Lord Kitchener's standpoint and I dare say that, au fond, he can appreciate ours, but he is not likely to say so.[7]

In reality Kitchener's standpoint, and Wingate's too, reflected their great anxiety as to the political and social effect on the country of giving too much power to commercial management. Their strongest principle was to make paramount the interests of the natives. Their greatest fear was lest they should lose their freedom to command this principle. In this respect the traditional reluctance of the British Government to put up any money for the Sudan was especially frustrating. With direct government finance and enterprise the situation could be kept under control, but as long as a government loan was uncertain, dependence on commercial capital posed always the problem of the repercussion of untrammelled private enterprise upon the Sudan Government's position and policy. Wingate reflected this view in a letter to Stack in April 1913.

It is quite true that had the Government refused to come to our aid, it would have been better to have resorted to the help of a Company rather than not develop the Gezira at all, but in that case the Sudan would have eventually become something like Rhodesia is today, namely the Company would have acquired such power as would probably have resulted in its eventually being given a Charter. [8]

The bad bargain over Tayiba had given the Syndicate a foot in this direction, so different from Kitchener's own views of the Sudan's needs. It had placed him under an obligation to the Syndicate, when he wanted its capital without losing his control over it. Moreover, in spite of the reassurances of Lloyd George and Asquith, the guarantee for a Sudan Government loan was not yet a certainty. It required an Act of Parliament. The money market early in 1913 was exceedingly tight and the figure of £3 million was for those days a relatively large one. Worse still this very figure now appeared to be insufficient. The £3 million had been originally estimated to cover other purposes besides the Gezira Scheme, which was supposed to need only £1 million. But a commission of irrigation experts, examining the dam site and canalization project in 1913, reported that £2 million would be needed for these works in the Gezira alone, and this merely for the dam and major canals. But capital was needed also for the Scheme's minor works, for levelling land and digging field-channels, for buildings, ginneries and offices; for current operations until sales were effected; for salaries to personnel and loans to tenants. If the Syndicate could fill these gaps it would be a very timely ally, but how could Kitchener avoid it becoming a master?

Kitchener's first action was to turn the tables a little on MacGillivray. He gave instructions that the Government should take over the Tayiba farm so that the Department of Agriculture should gain experience of management there, with the implication that the Syndicate would be shut out of the Gezira Scheme except for its problematic land grant. It was a shrewd move, for MacGillivray was far more interested in the big stake in the Gezira than a grudging implementation of his grant, only possible in poor soil, even if it cost the Government a lot to carry out its promise. Davie, who went back to Tayiba to take over from the Syndicate's manager, gives, in a private letter, a picture of a very disconcerted MacGillivray walking round the rest-house for the greater part of the night wondering whether there was justice in the world, until one morning a summons came to him to visit Kitchener in Cairo.

But Kitchener had in reality other plans up his sleeve, and Parliament's approval in 1913 of the Sudan loan placed him in a strong position to dictate his own ideas.

Kitchener's proposal was to take the Syndicate in as partner with the Sudan Government, utilizing its technical knowledge, its managerial ability and its money but for a limited time only. It was on the lines of

Lord Edward Cecil's earlier thinking, that development should be a matter of appropriate stages not of permanent concessions. On these lines the first tentative agreement between the Syndicate and the Sudan Government was for a period of ten years only, with an option for a further five years.

The period over which it would pay the Syndicate to accept an agreement with the Government was, of course, a matter of considerable bargaining and depended on what duties the Syndicate was expected to finance and what share it was to get in the profits, related to the capital it had to put up. The initial period agreed upon was in fact altered as these circumstances altered. But what did not change was the principle that the Syndicate should have a limited concession period and Government a right to terminate it at stated intervals if it considered the management unsatisfactory for political reasons. The financial provisions for early termination were a matter of free bargaining and precise definition and were part of the final agreement which will be discussed in more detail later. The point of importance here is that the result of forces operating both for and against commercial management was in the end a compromise: commercial management for a limited period.

While the actual partnership form of association between the Syndicate and Government was being arrived at a parallel problem was coming to a head over the future method of association with the tenants. Once again a play of different forces seems to have brought about the very critical decision to change from an association by rental to partnership in this field also.

The Syndicate had operated the Zeidab system of rental during the two trial seasons at Tayiba. The rental, which was to cover land, water rates and tax, had been fixed experimentally at £E2 per feddan for the first season and raised to £E2½ per feddan for the second season, a low figure when regard was had to the good crops, and the station had operated at a loss to the Government of £E6,000 over the two years. One purpose of the Tayiba experiment was, of course, to get some indication of the revenue which might be expected not only by the tenant but by the Government in return for its future capital investment. From this aspect the Tayiba results showed a clear need to raise the rents.

Apart from Tayiba, the rental system had in recent years at Zeidab been shown to have serious drawbacks. These had become particularly conspicuous when the company had supplied water to native landowners on their own land. It will be remembered that this system had been started in 1909 with the greatest enthusiasm by all parties, the Syndicate supplying water and cotton seed, and the Government advancing loans to the landowners for digging new water channels. After an initial success, a bad cotton crop caused the landowners to lose interest and there was difficulty in convincing them that they should pay the Syndicate for the water despite the failure of their crop. The Syndicate was forced to stop supplying water and to sue some landowners in the courts. Even on its own land at Zeidab the Syndicate was not making much profit. Its first dividend after eight years of pioneering was only declared in 1912.

The Syndicate had in 1911 requested from the Government certain changes in the terms of the Zeidab concession, particularly in regard to land tax, in order to afford a better prospect of profit there, and a government Zeidab Committee had been given facilities to examine the records. In this examination it appeared that income from rents alone would never bring enough profit to cover the capital investment and the Syndicate's revenue was supplemented by small profits on the charge for ginning and seed and on the differential between the price it paid to the tenant and the price at which it subsequently sold the cotton. To get tenants at all rents had to be low, for the idea of a fixed rent, regardless of the crop yields attained, was strange to the local cultivators, accustomed as they were to the considerable fluctuation in yield from natural hazards, locusts and variations in the river.

The rents charged in Zeidab were £E4 a feddan for cotton, £E2½ for wheat and £E1½ for the fodder crop. It was estimated that the rent roll, even if the full 10,000 feddans were let, would amount only to £E24,000 annually while the running costs and depreciation of the estate would be £E21,000. But in seasons of poor yield, such as had occurred from 1910, the company was not able to collect all its rents or recover its advances. The man with a good crop who could afford to pay more got away with a smaller contribution to the capital side of development than he might reasonably have made, while the man with a poor crop was apt to find the same rent a most discouraging burden and was liable to become a debtor. A solution by fixing differential rents according to quality of land had the drawback that often the cause of a poor yield was more due to climate or disease than to land.

There was therefore serious reason to doubt whether a rental system would ever be satisfactory from the point of view both of the capital investor and of the peasant himself. Experience of rental schemes in Egypt, with which Kitchener himself and some members of the Sudan

Government, in particular Hewison, were acquainted, also tended to corroborate fears that such a system might end prejudicially, above all to the peasant.

In these circumstances there was a general readiness to search for some alternative. The suggestion for the particular share partnership which came to be the basis of the Gezira Scheme originated from Davie, the Sudan government Inspector of Agriculture to whom the Syndicate handed over at Tayiba.[9] In 1912 a house had been built for him at Tayiba (jokingly known by the Syndicate as the watch-tower) and he was instructed to collect all the information available about the Tayiba experiment, especially to find out what the tenant could afford to pay.

Davie thought of ascertaining what the position was on the riverain lands in the neighbourhood, and in casual conversation with sheikhs, in particular at a place called Fedassi, with the help of diagrams drawn in the sand, they had illustrated to him the customary system of dividing the crops into shares, with so much for the landlord, for the owner of the water-wheel and for the labourer. When Lord Kitchener was visiting Tayiba in 1913 Davie, in conversation with his A.D.C., Captain Fitzgerald, mentioned these customary divisions. 'This would be of particular interest to Lord Kitchener', said Fitzgerald, and took him to explain the native system to Kitchener just when the latter was considering how to ensure financial success for the Scheme while giving the native cultivator a reasonable deal.

This native system was a partnership in which each factor of production had definite shares of the crops allotted to it according to the following custom:

The ownership of land entitled a claim to one-tenth of the crops.
Ownership and repair of the water-wheel entitled a claim to one-tenth of the crops.
Ownership of cattle entitled a claim to two-tenths of the crops.
Supply of cattle food entitled a claim to two-thirtieths of the crops.
Supply of seed and implements entitled a claim to four-thirtieths of the crops.

The total of these shares on behalf of the above capital assets came to six-tenths of the crops, leaving the working-tenant four-tenths of the crops.

Applied to the Tayiba pilot scheme it might be said that the modern substitutes of these capital assets were being supplied by the Government which was renting the land from the owners, while the tenant-cultivator was taking the traditional working-tenant's place. The suggestion had the merit of being already understood by the local people. It satisfied a feeling arising in the Government that it was 'desirable for the protection of the cultivators that the amounts payable by them for rent, water rate, taxes and other similar charges shall be dependent on and vary with the profits of their cultivation'.* It gave Government and peasant a mutual bond in adversity or in success, and it provided a practical method of doing the same between the Government and the Syndicate by passing on some of the Government's six-tenths share in return for technical management and for relief on some of the capital obligations.

In June 1913 when Kitchener summoned Wingate and MacGillivray to Cairo he presented the latter with the following basic proposals for the development of the Gezira. The offer was meant to cancel the existing Tayiba agreement and all rights under it.

1. The expense of leasing land from the native owners, of bringing water on to the land, and of constructing and maintaining the main works and canals, was to be borne by the Government.

2. The Syndicate were to act as Government agents in allocating their holdings to the tenants, to direct and supervise the cultivation, and to supply loans, as at Tayiba.

3. The gross profits of each individual holding were to be distributed in the following manner.

35 per cent to the Government.

To cover interest on the loan, amortization, maintenance of irrigation works and canals, and rent to the natives for the lease of their land.

25 per cent to the Syndicate

To cover the cost of roads, drainage, subsidiary canals, clearing and levelling, agricultural supervisory staff, accounting staff, and Syndicate's profits.

40 per cent to the Tenant

To cover the cost of labour, seed, agricultural implements, use of tillage animals, and tenant's profit.

4. Any arrangement made was to be limited to a term of ten years, with option for a further five years.[10]

Following a meeting on 21st July 1913 in London between Lord Kitchener, Wingate and government advisers on one side and the Syndicate directors on the other, at which the Cairo proposals were

---

* This sentence is taken from the first draft agreement drawn up by Sir Edgar Bonham-Carter, Legal Secretary to the Sudan Government, for consideration by the Syndicate. It is quoted as illustrating the intention in the minds of those who originated the Gezira partnership, although it was, with other such interesting detail, omitted in the final clipped draft.

tentatively agreed, subject to detailed examination in the Sudan in the following winter, the Syndicate again took over the running of Tayiba on August 1st but this time not on a fee for itself nor on a rental for the tenant but on the basis of the proposed commercial partnership.

The change from rental to partnership was far from beneficial in the eyes of the tenants at Tayiba who had done extremely well out of the low rents of the past two seasons and, being made after the start of the season, led to some feeling of bad faith. A petition from the tenants and some disturbance led Major Dickinson, the Governor of the Blue Nile Province, to look into the matter personally. His report gives an interesting contemporary picture of the difficulty of starting experimentally with too low a rental and then having to change the system and a glimpse at the periphery after the gathering of the great men in Cairo.[11] He wrote,

The demeanour of these tenants with the exception of one or two excited persons, was remarkably quiet and reasonable throughout, both yesterday and today. They represented to me that when entering upon the new agricultural year—March–April—they did so on the distinct understanding that the arrangement would be the same as in previous years, except for a proposal to raise the water rate from £2½/0. to £3 per feddan; and that later on they were clearly informed by Mr. Davie that the water rate would not be raised; in other words that the arrangement would remain in every respect the same as before. Now, after 4 or 5 months labour on the land they have suddenly been told that the entire system is altered and that their profits are to consist of two fifths of the gross receipts. They are sufficiently alive to their own interest to grasp clearly what an enormous reduction in profits this means, and it can scarcely be wondered at that there is a feeling among them that they have been 'let in' by the Government. As one man said to me today 'We don't know what may be done next. We may be handcuffed and marched off to prison for all we know.

Major Dickinson estimated that, compared with last year and assuming the same yields and prices, the tenants' profits would be reduced by 70 per cent under the new arrangements. He compared them as follows:

Receipts Last Year	£E
10 feddans of cotton yielding 5·5 kantars per feddan at £E3·25 per kantar	179
10 feddans of wheat yielding 5 ardebbs per feddan at £E1·60 per ardebb	80
10 feddans of dura yielding 4 ardebbs per feddan at £E1·88 per ardebb	43
Total Gross Receipts	£E302

Deduct Costs	£E	
Water rent at £E2·50 per feddan	75	
Cost of labour	80	155

Net Profit Last Year	£E147

Receipts This Year

Two fifths of gross receipts at £E302	£E121
Deduct Cost of Labour	80

Net Profit This Year	£E41

He went on,

It could hardly be expected that the tenants would accept such a reduction of profits without expostulation and the very large majority have expressed a wish to give up their holdings, and ask for compensation for their out of pocket expenses and for the profitless labour on which they have been engaged for the last four or five months, during which time they might have been working on their own sagias or preparing or sowing their rain land. . . . I do not presume to criticise a scheme planned by abler heads than mine, and under financial and other conditions of which I have a very imperfect knowledge, but I cannot help feeling that the introduction of it when a third of the agricultural year has gone by, and after the tenants had been clearly informed that they were working under the same system as before has somewhat seriously shaken the confidence of the native in our fair dealing.
A liberal compensation might make some amends.

The tenants concerned were given some compensation. The Government adhered to its decision that for the future a partnership and not a rental basis must be adopted, and those tenants who did not wish to continue under the new conditions were by then easily replaced by others. It was perhaps significant that after a succession of indifferent harvests and low rainfall material prosperity in the Gezira was, according to the Governor's report for 1913, at a low ebb.

The experimental nature of the percentage shares was, however, recognized by a clause in the agreement between the Syndicate and the Government providing for an increase in the tenant's share if circumstances warranted this. As a matter of fact no alteration was to be made in the share until 1950.

Matters now began to proceed apace. The area at Tayiba was increased by 1,000 feddans and the Syndicate built in 1914, at its own cost, another pilot pumping station to irrigate 2,000 feddans at Barakat, about twelve miles south of Tayiba. The original Gezira Scheme project for the development of 500,000 feddans was not adopted, as being too ambitious financially, and instead it was decided that an area of about 100,000 feddans only should be cultivated. The first loan bill passed by the British Parliament in 1913 was amended in 1914 to apply two of the three million pounds to the dam and major canalization, and the first sod of the Gezira main canal, originating at Sennar sixty miles south of Barakat, was turned on 1st January 1914.

It was now, at this period of quickening activity, that the 1914–18 war broke out, throwing all future development into suspense.

Chapter 6

THE SUDAN PLANTATIONS SYNDICATE AGREEMENT

The first world war had a significant effect on the Gezira project. It afforded a breathing space during which experience on the two pilot stations of Tayiba and Barakat accumulated. This enabled details to be much more effectively thought out and led to important changes in the irrigation and agricultural designs. It influenced decision on the critical question of how the Government was to acquire control of the land and who were to be the tenants. It gave time for attitudes to grow, particularly in two respects: the confidence between the Government and the Syndicate as partners and the confidence of the local people in the irrigation scheme. One adverse effect of the war was the phenomenal decrease in the value of money and corresponding increase in costs. Although for the same reason cotton prices rose, making the theoretical economic return also higher, the immediate practical effect on the Sudan Government was the need now for much more money to start the project. Immense drawback as this seemed at the time it had the effect of postponing until 1925 the completion of the dam and so of extending the period of preparation.

Something of the change in money values which makes the capital cost of basic development seem so remarkably low in the pre-1914 era is illustrated by the subsequent recurrent crises over Gezira loans. It will be remembered that the first estimate of requirement was £1 million, raised in 1913 to £2 million for the dam and canalization, out of a loan of £3 million to be guaranteed by the British Treasury. After the war a new estimate in 1919 put the cost of the Gezira works alone at £4,900,000. The British Treasury agreed to face the new situation and in 1919 guaranteed the interest on a Sudan Loan of £6 million (5½ per cent Guaranteed Bonds 1929–59)* to replace the £3 million loan promised in 1913 but never floated.

* £3,342,500 were issued in October 1919 at 95½; £2,649,600 were issued in February 1921 at 92.

A rise of more than double in the estimated capital costs would have been a much more serious risk if the Sudan had not been in the happy position of having ample additional land which could be irrigated from the same dam. In order to make the scheme a safer enterprise financially for the Sudan Government and at the same time not too large for the population and resources available, the area to be irrigated was raised in 1919 to 300,000 feddans instead of the 100,000 feddans contemplated before the war. This ability to bring in extra land, when the gap grew too large between capital cost and value of product, was to make a major contribution to survival of the Gezira in difficult times later on.

Nostalgia for the low capital costs of the pre-1914 era must be tempered by remembering the much smaller field for raising private capital in those days. In this respect the commercial history of the Syndicate up to 1919 is worth a digression, for it illustrates to what a degree enterprise in that period still originated in the audacity of a few friends and private firms willing to risk substantial sums from their own pockets on fairly hazardous hopes.

The Sudan Experimental Plantations Syndicate was registered in 1904 with a nominal capital of £80,000 in £1 shares. Members of Wernher Beit and Co. took up 41,000 shares, of whom Wernher and Beit took 10,500 each, Phillips 5,000 and Eckstein 4,000. Leigh Hunt took up 19,000 shares and other Americans a further 8,000. The shipowner, de Chastillon, took up 10,000 shares and two Irishmen took up 1,000 each. All shares were allotted for cash.

In 1907 the Sudan Plantations Syndicate replaced the earlier company, and the policy began to be changed from direct cultivation to a tenancy system. More working capital was needed but there was no profit yet to encourage subscribers. Leigh Hunt and MacGillivray came to the rescue. A block of building land in Khartoum, 100 acres bought earlier as a speculation, was sold by the Syndicate to Leigh Hunt for £40,000. It was actually paid for by MacGillivray when he replaced him as Managing Director, and the £40,000 put to reserve. Leigh Hunt also undertook to raise a further £80,000, for use as working capital, in the form of 3½ per cent debentures. MacGillivray personally paid off £22,000 of these debentures immediately and this amount also was added to reserve. This meant that MacGillivray had contributed £62,000 in all to the Syndicate's working capital. The remaining debentures, amounting to £58,000, were a first charge on the Syndicate's property and were repayable in 1916.

The first receipts from Zeidab came in 1906 and were worth £745.

In 1909, with 1,300 feddans of cotton, they rose to £12,700. These were merely gross receipts. It was not until 1910, six years after the start, that the first profit and loss account was presented. It showed a profit, covering the whole period to date, of £8,934, not enough yet for any thought of dividends. During 1910 the authorized capital was increased to £250,000 by creating 170,000 new £1 shares. But only 50,000 were issued, and they were to a single firm, Messrs. L. Hirsh and Co., at a premium of £2 per share.

The record of the company up to 1910 makes it surprising that they were able to induce a new subscriber to put up more money and at a premium! Clearly it was not the record but the prospects which were the attraction and these were a gamble on the Gezira. Zeidab had demonstrated that good quality cotton could be grown in the Sudan and it was beginning to get good prices. The Gezira Scheme was bound to come some time and the Syndicate was an experienced agricultural enterprise, fitted to the Government's concept. But 1911, the year after raising the new capital, witnessed the worst crop ever harvested at Zeidab. The directors had intended to declare a maiden dividend but decided not to do so. 1911 was also, however, the year in which the Syndicate was entrusted with the management of Tayiba, and the year when, on the strength of this, the B.C.G.A. took up 5,000 shares, also at a premium of £2, and their Chairman joined the Syndicate's board. The shareholders found this gesture of confidence reassuring. One of them said, 'When we first received the report of the directors it seemed rather unsatisfactory but it is very encouraging to know that such an important association as the B.C.G.A. consider the prospects so hopeful as to induce them not only to take a monetary but also an active interest in the Syndicate.'[1]

In 1912 the Syndicate began to receive income from its management fee at Tayiba as well as from Zeidab. Profits rose to over £16,000 and the event was celebrated by the first dividend in its history at 12½ per cent. This was repeated in 1913. In 1914, the new partnership arrangement began to operate in Tayiba but the yield was disappointing. From over 5 kantars per feddan in the first two seasons it dropped to 3·8 in the third. Other problems arose. With the outbreak of war, sales were difficult and half the cotton crop was still unsold in January 1915. The wheat crop at Zeidab had failed. Its inclusion in the rotation appeared to exhaust the soil both there and in the Gezira, and it was decided to stop growing it. The state of indebtedness of many of the tenants at Zeidab, still on a rental system, became disquieting. MacGillivray decided to give a rebate of £5,000 on rents and also to allocate £4,000 of the Syndicate's profit to the tenants. All this cut the net profit to under £5,000 and the dividend was reduced to 5 per cent.

The 1915 season saw the opening of the new station in the Gezira at Barakat. Yields were good, 5·3 at Barakat and 5·16 at Tayiba, but they struck the lowest price ever realized since the Syndicate started growing cotton. Profits fell below £2,000. A 5 per cent dividend was maintained but only at the cost of drawing on the carry forward. Prices revived smartly in 1916 but this time the yields dropped badly. The dividend was stopped altogether. This was not a happy moment for the repayment of the debentures to fall due but the Syndicate was able to arrange postponement until 1923, at the cost of increasing the rate of interest from 3½ per cent to 6 per cent. In 1917 yields did not improve but prices were extremely high. Profits rose to £14,000 and the dividend to 10 per cent. Yields were up again in 1918 and prices continued high. Profits soared up to over £50,000 and a 25 per cent dividend was declared. 1919 proved to be another good year, and the debentures were repaid completely, earlier than their due date, while the 25 per cent dividend was still maintained.

All these figures are given in table form near the end of chapter 7,* but they have been written descriptively in the text here so as to give the reader a mental picture of two features of development which are sometimes lost sight of. The first of these was the length of time—eight years—during which the merchant adventurers of the Syndicate were called upon to put up capital without getting any return on it, and without certainty that they ever would get a return. The second was the ding-dong result, when they did get on to a paying level, alternating elation and depression according to varying yields and prices. In the great desire to push forward with development today when those enterprises which have survived give an appearance of smooth success and iron out the hazards by the reserves they have accumulated, the impression sometimes arises that a higher standard of living can be attained merely by mathematical planning and the provision of capital on banker's terms. But the early history of the Syndicate reveals how potent is the element of risk in the process of development, how necessary is equity capital, and not merely bankers' loans, to meet this risk and how vital is the adventurous spirit in the human beings who handle the process. 'Break-even' principles and 'safety-first' slogans would never have started Sudan development.

* See page 94.

During the war the conclusion of the agreement between the Government and the Syndicate for the future running of the Gezira Scheme remained in abeyance. On the eve of resuming negotiations in the winter of 1918, MacGillivray died in the epidemic of Spanish flu. It fell to MacIntyre, who succeeded MacGillivray as Managing Director, to conduct the negotiations with the Sudan Government in 1919. The resulting agreement, defining the duties and shares of the partners, became the commercial textbook of the Gezira project, although new heads of agreement were signed in 1926 (not finally completed until 1929) and further modifications were made in later years.*

It is, however, interesting to mention here certain aspects of the 1919 agreement which throw light on the particular matters which the Government thought it important to safeguard, in the national interest, and the Syndicate, in its commercial interest. The partnership principle, and the provision of a term to the Syndicate's participation, arrived at in the 1913 agreement, provided a twin method of ensuring to the Government a powerful say in the present enterprise and freedom in the future. There were, however, still some official qualms about the intentions and possible conduct of the Syndicate as a major participant, and Kitchener, on seeing the first draft agreement drawn up by Bonham-Carter,† the Legal Secretary, was anxious to have an additional paragraph included, to the effect that the Syndicate should act in accordance with the views of the Government, provided that such views were not likely to hinder development.

There was also some suspicion that the Syndicate might make large profits in an ulterior manner at the expense of the tenant, particularly if it had a free hand in loans and rates of interest, sale of seed, and charges for ginning. At Zeidab the Syndicate had, in fact, made some portion of its profit from ginning and seed charges and from control of cotton sales and had had some difficulties over tenants' indebtedness, and Kitchener's previous experience of Egypt made him fear that the Syndicate might allow the tenants to get hopelessly indebted and in its power. Bonham-Carter inquired whether a 'fair profit' clause should be

* The full text of the Agreement can be seen in the Sudan Archives at Khartoum and Barakat and in the School of Oriental Studies, Durham University. As it is rather a long document it has not been printed in full here, but certain clauses in it which seemed of particular interest are given in Appendix II at the end of the book.

† Sir E. Bonham-Carter (1870–1956), K.C.M.G. Legal Secretary, Sudan, 1899–1917: judicial adviser, Mesopotamia, 1919–21: on retirement member of L.C.C. and Chairman of Letchworth Garden City Ltd. and of National Housing Council: Rugby football international for England in 1891.

inserted in connection with the Syndicate's agency duties of loans, seed, and ginning, to prevent it making undue profit from these services outside its share in the partnership. Wingate, writing of Kitchener's reaction, said,

He admits to being much puzzled as to how to prevent the Syndicate from making too much profit out of sale of seed, implements, ginning, etc., and goes as far as to say that he does not think that the Syndicate should be allowed to make more than about 5 per cent profit on these services and hinted that I should tell MacGillivray this straight. This is all very well, but I don't think we should interfere too closely in such questions, except to safeguard the tenants from undue extortion, and I hardly think it will be in the interests of the Syndicate to attempt anything of the sort.[2]

By 1919 the experience of working together seems to have tempered some of these fears. The 1919 agreement showed no jealousy of profit but contained special arrangements to eliminate these suspicions.

On the matter of ginning charges, in 1913 it had been anticipated that, as the Government had no available capital, the Syndicate would build and own the ginneries; this would have made it difficult for the Government to control the charges. By 1919, however, the Sudan Government set down a sum of £400,000 in the £6 million loan under Treasury guarantee as a provision for ginneries, etc., to be lent to the Syndicate. The loan was repayable to the Government with interest and the Syndicate was to provide, maintain and work the ginneries, and to charge only rates sufficient to cover the actual costs.

On the matter of loans to tenants, the 1919 agreement provided that the Syndicate should make loans for seeds, implements, labour and other agricultural operations to tenants who reasonably needed them, but would be free to refuse a loan in cases where it would not be businesslike to make one and would have absolute discretion as to the amount of any loan. But the interest charged and the terms of the loan had to comply with regulations agreed on with the Government. At the end of the concession period the Government was to pay the Syndicate the amount of the outstanding loans with accrued interest and to take them over. But to discourage extensive indebtedness this arrangement only covered loans contracted during the previous twelve months.

Finally, to allay Kitchener's earlier anxiety, there was a general clause in the 1919 agreement that the Syndicate was 'to consult the Government on all matters of importance affecting their joint undertaking with reference to the interests of the Government, the Syndicate and the Tenants respectively'.[3]

While these clauses were inserted to meet the Government's doubts about the Syndicate, the Syndicate had certain doubts about the Sudan Government. The most important concerned the area and period of the concession. Obviously, if it was to get its capital back and make a profit it would depend on how many feddans could be expected to be irrigated per annum over how many years, quite apart from subsequent uncertainties as to yield, price and marketability. Kitchener was at first extraordinarily dictatorial and cagy on both counts. He wished the period of the Syndicate's concession to begin from the time of the loan guaranteed by the British Government, irrespective of how long it might take the Sudan Government to build the dam and canalization and get the water on the land.[4] He was also reluctant to write into the agreement a guaranteed minimum irrigable acreage, and he wished to be free to act as he thought fit about renewing the Syndicate's concession after the first ten years.[5]

By the time of the 1919 agreement the Syndicate had obtained a clause which stipulated that the agreement would be in force for ten years from the date when the irrigation works could irrigate not less than fifty thousand feddans of cotton at the proper season for cotton cultivation. As for renewal, a compromise clause provided that if the Syndicate carried out the agreement fairly and to the satisfaction of the Governor-General, and if the agreement was not open to objection by the Imperial Government and H.B.M.'s High Commissioner for Egypt in the light of the good order of the district or political exigencies, the right to renewal should extend for a further four years on the same terms.

The Syndicate was also concerned to make sure that the Government would not take away with one hand what it was giving with the other. It feared that the Government might by taxation make nonsense of the partnership shares, and that it might prejudice the success of the Scheme by starting operations on its own, or making an agreement with another company within the irrigated area. Both these fears were covered by clauses in the agreement; one exempting the Syndicate from any profits tax, income tax or land or water rates in force in the Sudan, the other by guaranteeing its exclusive exercise of its function in the area.

The gross profits were to be divided as envisaged in 1913, namely 40 per cent to the tenants, 25 per cent to the Syndicate and 35 per cent to the Government, and they were deemed to be the sale price of all produce (from the cash crop, cotton) received by the Syndicate from the tenants, after deducting the cost of transport, ginning, insurance and other expenses incidental to marketing, including export tax.

(i) Lord Kitchener

(ii) Sir Reginald Wingate

PLATE I

(iii) Sir Lee Stack

(i) Sir Frederick Eckstein (ii) Lord Lovat (iii) General Asquith

PLATE II

There was yet a further uncertainty in the mind of the Syndicate: how much of its capital expenditure it would have to write off against its profits during the concession period. The Syndicate's first duty in the partnership was to provide an adequate and efficient staff to instruct and supervise the tenants, and conduct the general management. This was a running cost and could be estimated by the Syndicate from past experience. In addition, however, it was required, at its own cost, to clear and level the land, to carry out the subsidiary canalization, and to provide the houses, stores, offices and other buildings, and the heavy farm machinery, which it needed. These were capital requirements whose value would obviously continue beyond the Syndicate's concession period, and in the event an interesting bargain was struck.

The Syndicate was to get nothing back from the Government for clearing and levelling the land, or for the subsidiary canalization, and would therefore have to add the amortization of this capital expenditure to its annual running costs.*

With regard to the houses, stores, offices and other buildings, and the heavy farm machinery, the Government agreed to take them over at the end of the concession period at a valuation, provided that the former had been erected with the consent of the Government and the latter had been in regular use within a period of two years, and that both were in a good state of repair.

There remained the ginneries and they were the subject of a special arrangement. The Syndicate was to provide, maintain and work them and, during the concession period, a special reserve fund was to be set up, to which was to be credited a depreciation allowance of $1\frac{1}{2}$ per cent on the capital cost of the buildings and $7\frac{1}{2}$ per cent on that of the machinery. The rates were subject to a four-year review. These depreciation allowances were to be added to the annual ginning cost, which was a joint charge on all three partners. At the end of the concession the Government was to pay to the Syndicate the initial capital cost of the ginneries and to take them over and with them the reserve fund.

These details of the 1919 agreement illustrate the wide range of flexibility it was possible to bring into the capital structure to overcome the fears latent in the hearts of both foreign investor and government trustee for the local people. Before going on to the next stage, of how the tenants fitted into the picture, it is interesting for a moment to glance

---

* Provision was made for the cost of a certain part of the subsidiary canalization (the field channel abutting on his individual tenancy) to be recovered from each tenant.

ahead and notice the width of outlook with which the Syndicate's business leaders of those days regarded their enterprise, easily identifying their own commercial interests with wider objectives.

Speaking to the shareholders' meeting in December 1919, Eckstein, the Syndicate's Chairman, said,

It gives us particular pleasure to be able to tell you today all about the long delayed and much discussed agreement with the Sudan Government. It is a three-cornered partnership and I cannot emphasise the importance of this part of the arrangement too strongly. In fact I consider this the bull point of our agreement.

The sense of common purpose attained in the agreement was often touched on in Eckstein's speeches to the shareholders.

In 1920 he said,

We are doing a gigantic work. The undertaking is an immense one and a heavy responsibility is thrown on the directors. We have not only to look after the interests of our shareholders but also those of our partners, namely the Sudan Government and the native tenants who are not represented on the Board.

Lord Lovat took up his cue in 1925.

I should just like to remind you that you are not only owners of a great agricultural enterprise, but you are also associated with probably one of the greatest colonial development schemes going on at the present time. This is not only a scheme which will be materially advantageous to Great Britain and the cotton industry, but one also which is adding very largely to the welfare of the natives in the areas with which it deals.

Eckstein was Chairman for the last time in 1927. Announcing his intention to retire he said,

The longer I witness the work done by our Syndicate in the Sudan, the more I realise, and the more clearly I see demonstrated, the beneficial effects of the cooperative arrangement under which we are working, not only for the directly interested parties, but also for the country generally. This fact makes me venture to say that other tropical countries, if they more freely adopted this system and took a leaf from the book of the Sudan Government in this respect, would surely accelerate the development of their natural resources and likewise add greatly to the prosperity and contentment of their native population. . . . Were I asked to define the policy to be pursued by my successor in office I would reply:— cultivate to the utmost extent a loyal and harmonious working, in letter and spirit, with the Government in Khartoum, and show every consideration to the native population in the Sudan. If this policy is continued and adopted all will be well.[6]

Eckstein was created a baronet in 1929. He died in 1930.

Chapter 7

LANDOWNERS AND THE TENANCY
AGREEMENT

With the Syndicate Agreement signed in 1919 the Government turned its attention to the other partner. The pilot stations at Tayiba and Barakat, now in operation for more than five years, had provided a pattern for the main intention of the agreement: 'a joint undertaking in partnership with the Syndicate to develop the cultivation of the irrigated area and to direct and assist the cultivators'.[1] But the selection of a few volunteers to take up annual partnership tenancies laid out in thirty-feddan units on land which the Government had rented in two experimental areas was a small affair compared with applying irrigation to all the population living in 300,000 feddans.

But was it so different? If the direction and assistance, and the irrigation, were really going to be successful, it was desirable to lay out the land so that the water could be most effectively used, in units big enough substantially to raise the peasant's income yet not too large for him to manage, and under a rotation which was scientifically correct. None of this could be done by simply turning the tap on to the existing patchwork of privately owned land.

There was also the question of incremental value. The investment of government capital—an action on behalf of the whole community—was likely to raise the value of the land from five or ten shillings to ten or twenty pounds a feddan. Was this increase to go into the pockets of individual landowners who had made no contribution towards it? How, too, was sub-letting and rack-renting to be avoided, and the moneylender kept out? To help and protect the genuine cultivator the Government needed to get control over the use of the land. How could it do this and yet retain the co-operation of the people? What entitlement, if any, should landowners be given to participate in the irrigated area if the Government did acquire control of the land?

These questions had preoccupied the Government since 1912 and during 1919 arrangements were worked out to answer them. In March 1920 a notice was issued to all owners of land in the area, the gist of which was as follows:

1. Government intended to irrigate 300,000 feddans from a dam at Sennar. Plans of the intended area were available for view at local government offices.

2. The general scheme adopted at Tayiba and Barakat would be followed.

3. Owners of land would not be deprived of their ownership, and their present liberty to transfer or mortgage their rights of ownership to other natives of the same locality would continue.

4. The Government would hire all the land within the irrigation area and pay rent for it, but land required for permanent works such as canals and buildings would be bought outright by the Government.

5. The hiring would, in the first instance, be for a term of 40 years, the period laid down for repayment of the loan the Government had raised to carry out the irrigation. The Government's intention was that the hiring should cease at the end of the 40 years, but it reserved the right to extend the period if necessary in the public interest.

6. In assessing the rent to be paid for the hiring, both now and on any extension of the 40 year period, and also the purchase price of the land to be occupied by permanent works, the Government would not take into account any rise in value caused by the irrigation scheme. For the hiring, the Government would pay a fixed annual rent per feddan, which would be announced shortly.

7. The land in the irrigated area would be let annually to tenant cultivators on the system now in force at Tayiba and Barakat.

8. In the allotment of such tenancies owners of the land hired would be given the opportunity to take up such areas as they were able to cultivate, as far as possible in the vicinity of their land.

9. Tenants would be permitted to grow, in addition to the cotton crop, sufficient dura for their own food requirements, but not for sale.[2]

This was a preliminary notification. After full discussion of public reaction with the province authorities and others concerned, the proposals were embodied in a Gezira Land Ordinance in 1921. The preamble reminded the public of the reasons for the Government's decision: of the natural opportunity for irrigation in the district between the Blue and White Niles, hitherto cultivated only intermittently with rain-grown crops; of the costly works needed and the large loan raised to execute them; that the boundaries of existing holdings of land, if left unaltered, would make it impossible to carry on the irrigation and cultivation of the land in a businesslike and economical manner; that the landowners for the most part had no experience of irrigation and would not be competent to arrange for the cultivation of all their land; that the land at present was only cultivable in years of sufficient rainfall and so was of small value, whereas by the Government's irrigation works the value would be increased out of all proportion to its present figure. These were the reasons Government had deemed it expedient to acquire and hire the land as explained in the earlier notification.

The text of the Ordinance fixed the annual hiring rate at ten piastres (two shillings) per feddan, and the compensation for acquiring the full ownership of land by the Government at £E1 per feddan. These were the current rates applying to the highest quality of rain-land. The text also laid down that landowners would have the right to take up tenancies but only of such areas as they themselves were competent to cultivate, and subject to the same conditions as other tenants. The Government reserved the right to allot tenancies, on any land not assigned to owners, to such persons as they thought fit.

In 1923, to protect the tenants against moneylenders, an amendment was passed to the 1921 Gezira Land Ordinance, making any mortgage or recovery of money purporting to be secured by the crops or proceeds of a tenancy null and void, except with the consent of the Government in writing. Experience of certain difficulties in obtaining justifiable payments for alimony or for debts due to hired labour led the Government to repeal the ordinances of 1921 and 1923 and to re-enact them with certain changes in a new Land Ordinance in 1927.*

It would be difficult to exaggerate the effect which this land legislation was to have upon the economic and social life of the region and through it upon the whole Sudan. It will have been observed that the Government did not nationalize the land. It would probably have been impossible to do so and at the same time gain the confidence and co-operation of the people. By renting the land for forty years it postponed, of course, the problem of incremental value, and by permitting the owners of land to transfer or mortgage their rights of ownership, albeit only to other natives of the same locality, it left a loophole for acquisition and speculation on what might happen at the end of forty years, and this loophole was indeed to cause some anxiety later.

Nevertheless the Ordinance provided an ingenious way of establishing control over land without outraging the traditional right of proprietorship while preventing the landowner from using that right to extract

---

*Those clauses in the Ordinance which affected the tenants were incorporated as a schedule to the Standard Conditions of Tenancy and are reproduced in Appendix I (b).

anything from his future tenant. The right of ownership became only a right to a certain rental, a saleable security and quite a good financial investment in terms of interest, backed as it was by loans guaranteed by the British Treasury! But it was a right completely divorced from the real new element—the tenancy. The State took the place of the landlord and claimed its 60 per cent of the cash crop to repay its investment and augment its revenues. From this it passed a portion temporarily to the Syndicate for its services. But no private landlord had any power to increase rentals over the tenant's share in the new benefit.

Other unique features resulted from these arrangements. By establishing control over the land use and insisting on terms of tenancy related to an economic unit on a sound agricultural rotation the Government introduced to a peasant society advantages normally available only to large-scale estate management, for on to such a base could be grafted efficiently the instruments of modern agriculture, loans at low interest, machinery, selected seed, fertilizer, joint purchasing for crop needs, grading, processing, and marketing, all at cost and without middlemen.

By prohibiting mortgage of a tenancy and making all advances invalid except loans issued through the partnership, the individual peasant was made secure against the worst result of improvidence: the loss of his holding to the moneylender. By granting to landowners only such tenancies as they themselves, in the opinion of the Government,* were competent to cultivate, and by reserving to Government the right to let all other tenancies to such persons as it thought fit, the distribution of tenancies was made in such a way that very few persons had more than one unit. In this manner the wealth from the new enterprise was spread among a very large part of the resident population.

It is obvious that the new arrangements would affect the future shape of society, but meanwhile what was it likely to mean for the individual? The answer was—a mixture of control and help, a compromise between loss in freedom and gain in profit. By becoming a tenant a local peasant, landowner or not, joined an organization intended to provide him with marked advantages for raising his standard of living. Apart from the facilities, already mentioned, which organized for him planned assistance over his cash crop, the greatest attraction was the chance of water for his food crop, dura. The experimental rotation originally introduced at Tayiba, whereunder he shared all his crops with his partners, had by 1919 been modified and the profit-sharing now applied only to the

* The words 'in the opinion of the Government' were added in the 1927 edition of the Gezira Land Ordinance.

cotton crop. Wheat had been dropped from the rotation which was now a three-course one of cotton, grain and fodder (dura and lubia (*Dolichos lablab*, a bean), and fallow. The dura and lubia belonged to the tenant alone. On all crops he paid no rent for land or water and he was also exempted from all ordinary taxation on his private crops, the 60 per cent share of the cotton taken by the Government satisfying all such liabilities. This concession, incidentally, was destined in later years to be a great obstacle to obtaining local government revenue.

It would be difficult, of course, to foretell how the profit from the cash crop would turn out compared with pre-irrigation days. The Government did make out a rough economic balance sheet for the region, which worked out as follows.[3] The average annual production in the past of the whole area comprised in the Scheme was 20,000 tons of dura worth £E100,000. The future production of dura might equal 17,500 tons. In a year of bad rains, of course, the irrigated dura would total far more than the rain-land had given in the past. Moreover, in addition there would be the lubia crop to support the animals. As regards cotton, with a yield of three kantars a feddan the irrigated area would produce 300,000 kantars, equivalent in value, taking cotton at £E6 a kantar (i.e. about 14½ pence per lb.) to £E1,800,000. The tenant's share of this crop would be worth £E720,000. In addition to this the area would benefit generally from expenditure by Government and Syndicate out of their shares of the crop, and the total local circulation of money due to production in the area would be little short of £E1,000,000 a year as compared with £E100,000 under the old conditions. The profits of the tenants would depend on what would have to be paid as cultivation expenses and deducted from the tenants' share of £E720,000, but their total profit would probably not be less than £E350,000 against not more than £E20,000 under old conditions.

This was a regional estimate and it looked good, but against these advantages there were some uncertainties facing the individual. A tenant was responsible at his own cost for all operations on his tenancy until he had harvested his cotton and handed it in to the local collecting point. The Tayiba system of ascertaining his profit was as follows. A personal account was opened for each tenant at the local estate office and the weight and grade of all his deliveries of raw cotton were entered on the credit side. It was not paid for on delivery but, in order that he should not have to wait too long for his money, after sales from the whole crop had reached a safe proportion an estimated valuation was made of the ultimate proceeds less expenses of transport, ginning and marketing, and a preliminary figure of gross profit was arrived at for all three partners. Forty per cent of this figure belonged to the tenants as a whole and was then allocated over all the individual accounts *pro rata* to the weight and grade already entered there.

In an individual tenant's account this allocation represented a preliminary credit in money. Against it on the debit side had been entered already the cost of seed and ploughing and of any loans made to him. The deduction of these debits from the preliminary credit gave the individual preliminary profit payable to each tenant. As sales proceeded and proceeds exceeded the preliminary valuation, which was always a conservative estimate, further allocations were made from time to time bringing what were called 'appreciations' to the credit of each tenant and these were then paid out. When all the crop had been sold the exact amount still due to each tenant could be calculated and credited in a final appreciation. The total of the appreciations plus the preliminary credit then represented in each tenant's account his share of that crop. By deducting the original debits from this total the net profit of each individual for that season could be seen in the Syndicate's books and a tenant could check these figures with the sums which he had received.

The system, designed to help the tenant to get his money quickly and accurately, was nevertheless complicated and altogether remote. This was inevitable if the tenant was to get his proper 40 per cent share of the full net profit, for the partnership costs of ginning and marketing and the partnership credits from sales had to be kept in accounts at headquarters in Barakat. Moreover, as the progress of sales depended on market demand, the dates and amounts of profits and appreciations could not be foretold. This had the effect of making the system seem like a chance hand-out from headquarters, and the credit price per kantar and per grade had to be taken on trust. The purchase of cotton at a fixed price on delivery, as was done with many peasant commodities in other countries, would have been much simpler but less accurate, and would not have spread the payments so widely over the year.

There was one other feature of uncertainty about the tenant's profit level. Although the book profit of the individual tenant was a correct enough figure from the accountancy viewpoint and could be checked by auditors, it took no account of the tenant's own work or any expenses he might incur through hiring labour instead of working himself and which might not be covered by the Syndicate's loans. This was naturally the case since the whole theme of the Gezira project was that of an independent working peasant to whom help was being brought, not of an employee charging up his time.

Nevertheless these uncertainties as to how the tenant's share was arrived at, and to what extent a book profit really represented a true picture of the tenant's standard of living—and so of the equity of the 40 per cent figure—were in the course of time to become matters of very considerable argument, and it is reasonable to be surprised that the population of the Gezira accepted such a drastic change in their way of life and indeed welcomed it. Many of the province Governors' early reports speak of them as a thriftless, lazy, conservative and fanatical people. One of them had gone as far as to say 'The apathetic attitude of a large proportion of the people towards any change is remarkable, and has to be overcome by persuasion and argument. I have even heard of one sheikh who is said to have exhorted his people not to build water-wheels, saying that the rain which Allah sends on their crops is quite sufficient for all their needs.'[4] Moreover they were a people among whom for years all heavy work had been identified with slavery.

Their acceptance of the Gezira Scheme appears even more surprising when account is taken of the sticks as well as the carrots. The change was after all to be applied throughout the 300,000 feddans. No one was allowed to opt out and continue in the old way as far as his land rights went, and if he opted in as far as a tenancy was concerned, he came under a very marked constriction of freedom. The individual tenancy agreement in use at Tayiba, and Barakat and derived originally from Zeidab, was only in an annual renewable form and stipulated certain stringent conditions. A tenant must cultivate the land in an efficient manner according to the crop rotation laid down. He must not transfer or sublet his tenancy without consent in writing. He must obey the reasonable orders of the Syndicate's inspectors. If he neglected his cultivation the Syndicate might, without his consent, take steps to safeguard his crops and charge him with any expenses involved. Finally, breach of the tenancy conditions might involve the Government, through its agent the Syndicate, re-entering into possession of the land and terminating the tenancy. In short, on paper there were a good many obligations and not all that degree of security.*

Yet they were anything but a dumb, dragooned people. The whole of the British personnel in the Sudan consisted in 1914 of 110 persons, excluding technicians. In 1908 these very Gezira people had killed a

* A full text of a Tenancy Agreement, as modified in later years to cover provision for a reserve fund (1936), is given in Appendix I at the end of the book.

British administrative officer and an Egyptian mamur. Their acquiescence may have arisen from an attitude expressed in two Arabic sayings which were in common use in those days, for they were a people who delighted in expressing attitudes by sayings. 'The Master of the Sword is Master of the Land' and 'The Government is like a father'. They accepted the fact that the land had been conquered in war and was being administered with equity in peace.

In addition there was the evidence of the experimental areas. Hypothetical fears would be of less importance than the actual experience of those who had been tenants, and it is worth noting that in its notice of March 1920 the Government took care to say that the new proposals would follow the system already known at Tayiba and Barakat. The exceptionally high price of cotton in 1919 had brought quite extraordinary profits to these tenants.

As soon as the Agreement had been signed the Syndicate, with Government encouragement, began to put up further trial pumping stations, with a view to getting a nucleus of both staff and people used to the system by the time the dam could be completed and the full 300,000 feddans irrigated. 19,500 feddans were brought under irrigation in 1921-2 from new pumps at Hag Abdulla and a further 30,000 feddans in 1923-4 from a further pumping station at Wad el Nau. In this manner a fifth of the area was already finished and accustomed to the system before the dam water began to flow for the first time over the whole projected area in the 1925-6 season.

Individual officers also played a major part in overcoming the apathetic attitude to change and in spreading confidence in the Government's intentions. Mr. W. P. D. Clarke, an administrative officer, was detailed to superintend the allotment of tenancies and deal with all questions arising between the people, Irrigation Service and the Syndicate. He lived among the people and was for many the only government representative with whom they came in contact. His sympathetic personality and the opportunity such an appointment gave for easing individual adjustment to the situation provided an intimate example of government in action. It was also essential to get people to put their confidence in the Syndicate's supervision. As one of the directors, General Asquith,* said at the shareholders' meeting in 1926, 'All the technical achievements would have been of no avail if it had not been

* The Hon. Arthur Asquith (1883-1939), Brig.-General, D.S.O. (two bars). Third son of first Earl of Oxford (Prime Minister Asquith). Sudan Civil Service 1906-11: joined Syndicate Board, 1920: Chairman of Kassala Cotton Company from inception in 1922.

that the natives had absolute confidence in our young men: our inspectors. They had to sign tenancy agreements with 6,000 new tenants, individual natives, and these agreements would not have been signed if, from past experience of the Syndicate, the people of those parts had not had confidence in being fairly dealt with by our people.'[5]

There was one other factor, a factor so important in the mind of the Government that in 1925, when the dam was completed and the project finally launched, the Governor-General, Sir Geoffrey Archer, made it a predominant feature of his summary of the Scheme's advantages. The Government, as this story has frequently shown, was convinced of its duty to keep control of development for the protection of the people. It believed that economic progress should come, not as an imposition from outsiders, indifferent to the effect on local society which must be fitted in to suit it, but as a process of evolution from the inside, suited to the existing social system of the people. The unique feature of the Gezira partnership to the Government was that it fulfilled these aims. The Governor-General wrote:

It is, I think, an entirely new conception that the applications of western science to native economic conditions, in a project of such moment to the country, should take the form of a partnership in which the native, the Government, and the Company managing the concern on behalf of the Government, each take an agreed percentage of profits. . . . But another aspect of the scheme should be emphasised. Unless particular care is taken, economic considerations may run counter to accepted administrative principles and endanger the development of existing social systems. Administrative policy in the Sudan is concerned with fostering all that is good in native institutions, and the method adopted in the inauguration of this economic project conforms entirely with our administrative policy. The native cultivates land which is his own property. The social system to which he is accustomed remains undisturbed. In fact, just as we endeavour to improve existing native institutions by the addition of consistent elements from more civilised countries, so have we endeavoured in the Gezira project to improve native cultivation with the aid of scientific methods without alteration of the normal social development of the community.[6]

There seems little doubt that this suiting of the development to the people's society played a big part in securing their acquiescence and enthusiasm for it.

In this description of how the tenant and his land were fitted into the picture, the story has jumped yet another financial hurdle which threatened to put an end to the whole project. It is necessary to turn back to 1921.

The Syndicate agreement had been signed, and the decision taken upon the treatment of the landowners. The cotton crops at Tayiba and Barakat in 1920 had been the best on record. Prices were phenomenal. For the Syndicate, profits had rocketed to £220,000 and a dividend of 25 per cent and a bonus of 10 per cent was distributed. With the big project at last in view the Syndicate's authorized capital had been increased in 1920 by £500,000, of which 150,000 shares were issued at £3: the first time that its capital was raised in the open market. It looked early in 1921 as if everything would be plain sailing.

But this set-fair prospect was to be rudely shattered by another financial crisis. Sir Murdoch Macdonald,* Irrigation Adviser to the Egyptian Ministry of Public Works, which still controlled construction in the Sudan, reported to the Sudan Government in 1920 that the cost of materials and labour had increased to such an extent that the previous estimates for the Gezira Scheme were quite inadequate.[7] The irrigation works could not be completed without raising yet more funds. A Sudan Government delegation was compelled once more to go cap in hand to the Treasury in Great Britain. With cotton prices high their importunity might have seemed reasonable, but by ill chance their arrival in 1921 coincided with a tremendous fall in price from 45 pence per lb. in 1920 to 8·5 pence in 1921. The post-war slump had arrived and the Geddes'† axe was beginning to strike in Britain. It was no time to ask for more capital.

After considerable discussion it was decided that the work should be carried on with existing funds for another season, that an expert examination should be made of the cost of completing the work, and a report rendered early in 1922. As a result of this report, the contract with the Sudan Construction Company, which until then had been responsible for the dam and the major canalization, was cancelled, and the Sudan Government was faced with either closing down the project altogether or finding additional funds. It was a critical moment, and the British Government was understandably hesitant.

The Syndicate's profits after its £220,000 in 1920 slumped to less

---

* Sir Murdoch Macdonald (1866–1956), K.C.M.G. Adviser, Egyptian Public Works, 1911–21: Liberal National M.P. for Inverness, 1922–50: President, Institute of Civil Engineers, 1932–3: constructed second heightening Aswan dam, 1929–33, and Great Ouse protection works in England and hydro-electric schemes in Scotland.

† Rt. Hon. Sir Eric Geddes, P.C. Chairman of the committee, appointed by the Chancellor of the Exchequer, to advise on all questions of national expenditure, 1921–2. In other words a credit squeeze.

than £10,000 in 1921, but it determined to show its faith in the project by paying a 15 per cent dividend. General Asquith, previously an administrative officer in the Sudan Government for five years, marshalled the arguments for continued support at the Company's meeting in 1921. He argued that since the British Government had already guaranteed the interest on the £6 million loan it would have to act up to its guarantee at the expense of the taxpayer if no project resulted. Lancashire would lose potential trade and unemployment would increase. Moreover the confidence of the Sudanese, who were relying on the dam to bring them prosperity and insurance against starvation, must not be abused.

After careful investigation, the British Government, to enable the work to proceed, agreed to guarantee the principal and interest on a further loan of £3½ million. Opportunity was taken to transfer supervision of the work from the irrigation service in Egypt to the Sudan. In October 1922 tenders were called for and Messrs S. Pearson and Sons secured the contract, under the terms of which the dam and canalization were to be completed by July 1925. In 1924, under the Trade Facilities Act of that year, the Treasury was authorized to increase the amount guaranteed in 1922 from £3½ million to £7 million. This approval, together with the £6 million loan of 1919, made a total authorization of £13 million. £700,000 of this was for railway extension and £400,000 was a loan to the Syndicate to erect the ginneries, and it was estimated that the full cost of the dam and canalization of the 300,000 feddans would now be approximately £11½ million.

And so, at last, near the sleepy little village of Sennar, where a few crumbled ruins still reminded the traveller that this had been the capital of the Fung kingdom in the seventeenth and eighteenth centuries,* the great Blue Nile river was harnessed. For a brief spell an immense burst of activity startled the quiet countryside, for 20,000 men were at one time employed scraping and carrying to make a firm foundation for the dam. In the midst of the work, yet another sudden anxiety confronted, this time, the contractors and their agent in charge, Mr. J. W. Gibson.†

---

*Sennar means 'tooth of fire' and a reader interested in the Fung kingdom will find a history of it in H. C. Jackson, *Tooth of Fire* (1923).

† Later Sir John Gibson (1885–1947). Left Messrs Pearsons after Sennar dam built and undertook contracts for canalization during extensions of Gezira Scheme: built Gebel Aulia dam on White Nile, 1933–7: during second world war Controller of Building Construction, Ministry of Supply: knighted 1945. He was responsible for the famous 'Mulberry Harbour' breakwaters used in the allied re-entry to northern Europe.

At the point of greatest depth an unexpected overlay of weak rock was struck. It was a race against time to remove it, reach the firm quality and lay the foundations before the seasonal flood of the river should sweep away the coffer dams. The race was won. The foundations were laid and upon them, when the river flood had receded, the superstructure was erected. It was completed on time by July 1925.

The Early Financial History of the Syndicate

Year	Authorized Capital	Issued Capital in Ordinary £1 shares	Debenture Capital	Profits	Dividends
	£	£	£	£	%
From 1904 to 1909	80,000	80,000	58,000 (3½%)	Nil	Nil
1910	250,000	130,000	,,	8,934	,,
1911	,,	135,000	,,	6,169	,,
1912	,,	,,	,,	16,384	12½
1913	,,	,,	,,	16,608	12½
1914	,,	,,	57,000	4,761	5
1915	,,	,,	,,	1,392	5
1916	,,	,,	,,	2,678	Nil
1917	,,	,,	,, (6%)	14,238	10
1918	,,	,,	,, ,,	58,492	25
1919	,,	,,		57,146	25
1920	750,000	297,790		223,259	35
1921	,,	300,000		8,968	15
1922	,,	,,		126,520	35
1923	,,	450,000		45,082	17½
1924	,,	531,119		112,934	20
1925	,,	600,000		162,885	25

The visitor to the Sudan today will find the countryside around Sennar once more quiet and sleepy, for the irrigated area does not begin until thirty miles north of it. Turning to the river he will come down suddenly on the great dam and may be surprised that such a thin bar stretching across for nearly two miles, and creating a great lake for fifty miles back, can hold the river. The dam's million tons of masonry, and its height of 128 feet from deepest foundation to top of parapet, are concealed. If he is a fisherman he will choose the downstream side and, casting his line for Nile perch and tiger-fish, with the roar in his ears of the water passing through its eighty sluice gates, he may wonder about its origin. He will find on the dam the conventional plaque recording the names of the designing and constructing engineers, and of Lord Kitchener, Sir Reginald Wingate, Sir Lee Stack and Sir Geoffrey Archer, the Governors-General during whose terms of office the Gezira irrigation project was planned. But nowhere will he see the names of Sir William Garstin, of Hewison and Davie, of Leigh Hunt, MacGillivray and MacIntyre, of Eckstein and Lord Lovat, of Sir William Mather and Hutton. Nor will he see anywhere the words 'Built for the people of the Sudan by the paternal pride of their British administrators and the adventurous enterprise of their British commercial partners'.

'With the roar in his ears of the water passing through its eighty sluice gates.' The Sennar Dam, 1925

PLATE III

(ii) Sir Murdoch Macdonald

(i) Sir William Garstin

PLATE IV

Part 2
THROUGH THE DESERT
1925–46

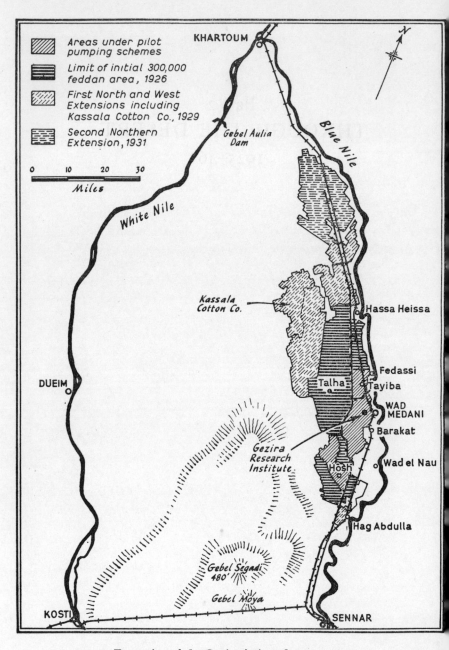

Legend:
- Areas under pilot pumping schemes
- Limit of initial 300,000 feddan area, 1926
- First North and West Extensions including Kassala Cotton Co., 1929
- Second Northern Extension, 1931

0 10 20 30
Miles

KHARTOUM

Gebel Aulia Dam

White Nile

Blue Nile

Kassala Cotton Co.

Hassa Heissa

DUEIM

Talha

Fedassi

Tayiba

WAD MEDANI

Gezira Research Institute

Barakat

Wad el Nau

Hosh

Hag Abdulla

Gebel Segadi 480'

Gebel Moya

KOSTI

SENNAR

4. *Expansion of the Gezira irrigated area 1910–31*

Chapter 8

ORGANIZATION AND A HOPEFUL START

The great dam was finished. The maximum area of cotton irrigated from the pilot pumping stations had been 21,600 feddans. In the first season of gravity flow from the dam the cotton acreage rose to 80,000, and in the second season to 100,000 feddans. This meant that the main canal from the dam, the major and minor canals, and the countless smaller field-channels were now spread like a great network over a gross area of 300,000 feddans, bringing water to every metre of the ground. The scheme had been brought to the people. But how did the Syndicate's organization actually work and affect them?

Administratively the irrigated areas had been divided by the Syndicate into blocks. These were simply estates which varied in size as their boundaries conformed conveniently to the canals. An average block would be 15,000 feddans and would have a block inspector in charge with two junior field-officers under him. They had been learning their job on the pilot stations. A group inspector supervised from six to ten blocks and was responsible for these to the headquarters at Barakat. There were, of course, civil and mechanical engineers for construction of buildings, machinery and so on, but it was the Syndicate's field personnel who were responsible for the agricultural efficiency of the project, and who were superimposed like the canal system itself on the life of the Gezira.

Picture a typical village in the chosen region and see the process beginning! Talha, 'the red gum tree' village, was situated about ten miles west of the province capital at Wad Medani, and fifteen miles from Barakat. It had a pleasant site at the edge of a depression where water collected in the rains, encouraging the gum trees and making a good duck-shoot. It was distinguished by the white conical tomb of Sheikh Ahmed El Tereifi, a local ancestor of the Arakiyin tribe. The same tribe inhabited the Tayiba experimental area, so that some of the people already knew from their cousins what the irrigation might mean.

Talha was a large village and, on the basis of 30 feddans gross per tenancy, the people were entitled by right of ownership of some 3,000 feddans to 100 tenancies. They had seen their lands gradually covered by the irrigation grid, the canals laid out and dug by the Irrigation Department, the field-channels under the supervision of the Syndicate's block inspector. They already knew him. They had sought his intervention to get a canal diverted round the graveyard at Heleiwa village and his help to get compensation for Mohammed Dafalla when the excavators ran through his dura before he had a chance to harvest it. They had seen his new house and offices being built and they knew that most of their village lands were to be included in his Abd el Hakam block, No. 10 in the Gezira Scheme. Some would fall, however, across the drainage line in the neighbouring block, Medina, which was No. 11.

The Syndicate's block inspectors had already been giving work to local contractors, putting in the road pipes, levelling the rain-banks and clearing the fields of bushes and grass, but now was the day when tenancies were to be allotted. Years ago, when the land survey team had registered everyone's land rights, their individual holdings had been plotted on maps and numbered. The numbers were registered in the Government's land office, each with its area and name of owner, who had himself a duplicate card of these particulars. The Syndicate's inspectors had copies of these maps, overprinted with the canals and field-channels, so that each owner's number and plot could be viewed in relation to the new layout, and his tenancies allotted as near as possible to his own land.

Allotment takes place at the village. Putting partnership into practice, the Government's Gezira Commissioner, W. P. Clarke, is present to check with omda and sheikh (the local authorities) the bona fides of each claimant in addition to his registration card. The Syndicate's assistant manager, W. P. Archdale, is present to make sure that the new block inspector does this original allotment properly, and to resolve with the Gezira Commissioner the treatment of any dubious cases. Some owners may be too infirm, or they may be women too shy to undertake the work, and a male relative must be registered as the responsible tenant. For here is the first change that the scheme is bringing: the tenancy has to be managed competently. The rights also of young people must be noted, when an uncle agrees to work the tenancy until they are old enough to do so. 'Wicked uncles' are not unknown. The owners, of course, have their rent, but this is of small account compared to the advantages of a tenancy.

Gradually the privately owned land is allotted. The biggest landowners in Talha are the heirs of Sheikh Ahmed El Tereifi, a local aristocracy owning some 780 feddans. 180 feddans is the next largest unit, but large units are rare and less than 30 feddans admits a preferential claim to a tenancy. A few large owners may get two tenancies in their own name, but never more, for the rule is that an owner's personal allotment is confined to what he can manage and it is strictly adhered to. The Government's aim was that each tenant should work his own holding. An owner can fill up his entitlement by nominating his sons, relations, servants, or villagers who used to cultivate his lands, and this he does, but each now becomes a tenant, beholden not to the owner but to the Syndicate's resident inspector. Some owners may not fill all their entitlement and to these vacancies, as well as to all government-owned land, any local villager may present himself for selection.

In this first allotment most of the adult male population get tenancies. Later, as children grow up, absentees return and economic changes bring new employments, the non-tenant population will increase and within twenty years tenants will form but half the population. But in these early years local casual labour is hard to find. This would not have mattered in the past. Traditionally everyone is used to planting, weeding and harvesting the rain-grown dura. But irrigation means more than this. It means regular attendance, much more rapid planting and weeding, and harvesting in months which were previously idle. In the past neighbours could call on each other for help. It is not easy now when all are busy at once. So the Scheme introduces two new problems to life— one practical—the need to find casual labour when weeds threaten and harvests are heavy: one mental—calculation as to whether the extra work is worth while. The practical need for labour and the mental attitude to it were to form a psychologically important part in the tenant's relationship with authority.

To help out with the cotton harvests the Arakiyin in Talha welcome their kinsmen of the Hassania tribe, whose lands lie just outside the irrigated area. Complete families come for a spell like hop-pickers to Kent in England, glad to get the money and the grazing not available at home. As the fame of the scheme grows, others drift in from further afield. Nigerians, making a slow pilgrimage to Mecca, set up a little settlement on the edge of the village. Bands of bachelors drift in from the western Sudan and French Equatorial Africa. All these help the labour load but their arrival is uncertain and their services competitive. The responsibility of finding and employing them is a new one for the individual tenant. The alternative is for the family to do more work.

There is the choice between the visible benefit on one side, the visible additional work on the other.

Authority is coming much closer to the tenant. The water is being brought to his land to give him a chance of a higher standard of living. He has to do the work on the land, but his partners, the Government and the Syndicate, have an interest, and the latter a management responsibility, for teaching him to do it well. The principle of control and help has come into being in Talha.

With the allotment finished at Talha, each new tenant must be shown where his thirty-feddan tenancy is located. It will be near his own land, but this has now had its old rain-bank boundaries levelled, and been laid out in units of ten feddans. An average of nine such units forms the scope of one field-channel. In future his holding will be known by the name of the canal and the number of the field-channel. He will be given a folio number, too, for his personal account in the Syndicate's block office. He will be going to the office to draw tools to make up the irrigation furrows within his own tenancy, and to draw a loan when this work has been done. All these are the symbols of a new direction, the start of a new routine, for his agricultural life. The Syndicate inspector will come round his tenancy regularly, expecting him to be there, showing him how to water his land; giving him an issue chit to draw pure-bred seed, grown on a seed-farm, from the store; telling him the sowing programme; when to thin the plants and when to expect the next watering; warning him to get on with weeding before the rain catches him out; giving him a quick loan, and in general chasing him along to keep up to date with his work.

There was a time when it was hoped that peasant proprietors would actually live on their tenancies. It never happened. The wives refused to leave the pleasant gregarious society of their villages. Later this turned out a great advantage, for the village became the basis of local community development. There were economic disadvantages, however, for our tenants from Talha had to go backwards and forwards once, and often twice, a day from the village to their tenancies, on foot or on donkeys, a few yards or a few miles according to location. Time taken in these journeys would have been of little moment in the leisurely days of rain-grown crops. It was more important with the greater demands of irrigation.

It put a certain strain on the relationship between the Syndicate inspector and his tenants. Making his agricultural round, enthusiastic to see all work on time to get the best results, he had often to search out his tenants from their villages instead of meeting them on their tenancies. Keen as they all were on making money, the level of energy and competence was not outstanding. According to the tenancy agreement, an inefficient tenant could have work done for him by the Syndicate and charged to his account. Theoretically, too, he could be evicted. But these sanctions, although a threat to the idle, were of limited value when alternative tenants were no better. Moreover, they had to be used sparingly to avoid the worse evil of too great a sense of insecurity. Thus, an element of 'drive' became at times difficult to avoid. This could have virtue in the result as long as it did not become a vice in the relationship.

From this small picture of how the Scheme first came to Talha village, something of the organizational pattern can be seen. It was not like a plantation. It was not a Port Sunlight* in the Sudan, with the Syndicate employing the people and responsible for their welfare. The people continued their normal social lives in their villages. The district commissioner and local native authorities continued to administer them as before. But in their future agricultural life, in the economic opportunities it offered, their most intimate adviser and director was the local Syndicate inspector. Although he was not a direct employer he was the manager of the block in which their tenancies were situated. He organized the distribution of their water, their seed, their fertilizer, their ploughing, their loans and their profits. He was their supervisor, resident among them, and his influence was far more concentrated than the intermittent uplift of a government agricultural officer. His job was to make them succeed.

Above all, in a country where government officials were rare and sparsely scattered, an organization outside Government, with many British inspectors so closely linked to their livelihood and permanently resident among the people, was something quite unusual. This personal continuity was of immense importance in the success of the project but it raised new administrative problems. Inevitably the people discussed with their inspectors many of their affairs and the distinction between the purely economic and the other aspects of their newly evolving life was blurred.

A description of a working year will be given later in Chapter 18 when the reader has formed a more comprehensive view of all aspects of the Scheme but here it is relevant to say something about these Syndicate inspectors. What sort of men were they? They had been recruited

* A model settlement, founded by Lord Leverhulme in Britain for the workers in Unilever Ltd.

from various backgrounds, some from public schools and universities, some from highland crofts. Few had agricultural degrees. Most had come abroad to get an open-air life in a developing creative concern. The job demanded no great intellectual attainments, but rather energy, honesty, executive ability, a sense of humour and tolerance, a capacity for getting people to work and working with them. In very rare moments the job gave satisfying flashes of the picture as Garstin had seen it. Often it seemed exasperatingly dull. The life could be lonely, but not with the splendid loneliness of really remote places. Put out early on his own to pick up the language, Arabic, from the peasants around him, a Syndicate inspector had little hope of staying if, in the press for efficiency, he did not find friendship among his tenants and they find it in him. Yet he had to be wary, for they were a people who sought the Achilles' heel in any weakness of character. Conversely, among his own kind, all concentrated on the same job, he would often experience a staleness of outlook which could only be dissipated by the excitement of playing in a good polo match or riding in the races. Many left, and the turnover in field personnel at one time rose to a hundred per cent in twelve years. But among those who stayed an *esprit de corps* arose, blended with many a friendship among the tenants whose interests they served as readily as those of the shareholders who employed them.[1]

At the apex the Syndicate was managed by a triumvirate, each of whom, by some trick of fate, contributed some dominant personal characteristic which the others lacked. The Managing Director, MacIntyre, has already been mentioned. Mostly engaged in negotiations with the Government and with sales policy, he used to spend some five months annually in the Sudan. He came from Inverness and all his earlier experience at Zeidab, combined with a childhood knowledge of the struggles of highland crofters, gave him a hard-headed but intensely human interest in the real welfare of the individual tenant. Obstinate as a mule, he often refused to accept only the logic of figures, holding that some reserve capacity or awkwardness in human nature was bound to defeat them. His personal tenacity was destined to be more important than any other factor to the survival of the Scheme through days of disaster.

The Manager, H. Poyntz-Wright, had experienced disaster before he joined the Syndicate. He was the son of an English doctor who had died suddenly and left his family unexpectedly badly off. He found himself removed from public school at sixteen and put to work at erecting the Big Wheel at the White City exhibition in London. A disastrously wet winter brought on tuberculosis and to cure it he joined his brother ranching in western America. It was a hard life, often eighteen hours a day in the saddle, and at the end of five years, seeing no future in that job, he accepted an offer from a friend to work with him in Egypt. From there he joined the Syndicate at Zeidab and came to the Gezira to open the Tayiba experimental farm. From his pay he had to support his mother and sister. These personal misfortunes made him an excellent Manager. Quiet and shrewd, he brought to the task two unusually important qualities: extreme carefulness over expenditure and an excellent memory. To a youngster coming into his office to take orders he would say, 'Leave your notebook behind and train your memory.' It was good advice and he practised what he preached.

The Assistant Manager, Archdale, was a son of Sir Edward Archdale, Bart., for many years Minister of Agriculture in Northern Ireland. He had learned farming the hard way working as a young man with cowmen and shepherds. Later he too worked in a land company in Egypt and transferred to Zeidab. He brought to the Gezira some of the quality of his homeland which has bred so many great soldiers. Archdale was restlessly energetic and contemptuous of all obstacles. He spoke Arabic like a native, was a born leader on the outside job and carried staff and tenants with him in impulsive enthusiasm. He too had pertinent advice to give. Confronted with a complexity of courses men would turn to him. 'Do the difficult thing,' he would say. 'It is almost sure to be right.'

It is easy to forget how much depends on the tradition set by the first leaders of any project. Later-comers tend to follow like sheep and to do in Rome what the Romans do. Sympathy without softness, tenacity, shrewdness, economy and energetic enthusiasm made up the blend of tradition which the triumvirate started in the Gezira. It gave the Scheme a liveliness and resilience of its own.

One of the objects of the Government in developing the Gezira was to obtain a greater stability of revenue, and the first two seasons which followed the opening of the Sennar Dam, those of 1925-6 and 1926-7, gave striking confirmation of its value in this respect. The yield, which in the last year of the pilot schemes, 1924-5, had caused some anxiety by falling as low as 2·2, rose in the first two seasons of irrigation from the dam to 4·8 and 4·7 kantars per feddan. These splendid cotton crops from a vastly increased area were sold at an average price of 16 pence and 18 pence per lb., and brought a net return, divisible among the three partners, of £E2,300,000 and £E3,300,000 respectively. These figures represented returns of £E29 and £E33 per feddan. As the budget estimate was for £E20 per feddan, the revenue from the Scheme was unexpectedly large for the Government. The Syndicate's net profit for these years was £482,394 and £588,382 and its dividends 25 per cent and 30 per cent respectively, on a capital now increased to £1,500,000. The tenants' 40 per cent share amounted to an average credit per individual tenancy of £E117 in 1926, and £E134 in 1927, bringing more than two million pounds of unaccustomed wealth into the hands of the tenants. Apart from these direct financial benefits, the value of the irrigated food and fodder crops made a great impression on the people. This was contrary to their expectations. They had been afraid that the Gezira Scheme, which earmarked so much of their land for cotton, would mean less and not more dura.

By contrast these two years were critically bad over most of the Sudan, owing to inadequate rains. Inhabitants of the surrounding country were in serious straits for food for themselves and their animals, and many thousands of men and animals were saved from actual famine by the demand for labour and the abundance of food and grazing in the irrigated area. With the failure of the grain and, in addition, of the Gash and Tokar cotton crops, the country was able to turn to the Gezira project for protection against a financial condition which otherwise would have resulted in very heavy deficits. In all these circumstances the vast new enterprise of cotton growing was a tower of strength and its popularity with the people of the Gezira continued unabated.

Nevertheless the Sudan Government was conscious that the step from comfort to poverty was a short one. 'The essence of the matter', wrote the Financial Secretary, Sir George Schuster,* to Sir Otto Neimeyer at the Treasury in Whitehall, 'is that the Gezira Irrigation Scheme is an absolutely dominating factor in the whole Sudan position, and until that Scheme has been working on a large scale for several years, it is impossible to say whether the Sudan is rich or poor.'[2] The important words were 'on a large scale'. The Sudan Government aimed to attain a position where the Gezira could be relied upon to provide enough direct revenue to balance the current costs of irrigation and land rent and the service of the Gezira loans. The country would then have the benefit of the indirect revenue which the Scheme provided in additional rail freights, customs dues, and in a variety of ancillary activities, while any accumulated reserves could be invested in extensions.

* Sir George Schuster, K.C.S.I., K.C.M.G., etc., chief assistant on credits to League of Nations, 1921: member of advisory committee to the Treasury, 1922: Financial Secretary, Sudan, 1922-7: financial adviser to Colonial Office: member of East African Commission, 1928: finance member, India, 1928-34: Liberal National M.P., 1938-45.

Unfortunately, ever since the 1921 crisis over costs, the Sudan Government had been aware that only exceptional yields or exceptional prices could provide enough revenue to balance the current costs of the Scheme, unless the cotton acreage was again increased. But to do this meant raising the problem of the equitable distribution of water between Egypt and the Sudan. At this point therefore the story of the Gezira becomes merged again in the turbulent history of the Nile, and some technical digression is now necessary to explain its significance.

Chapter 9

NILE WATERS: THE CONTROVERSY

Every year the Nile has a regular season of flood, followed by one of low water. On an average the flow of the main river (north of Atbara) at the peak of its flood is sixteen times greater than the flow at its lowest stage. Half of the total discharge occurs in two and a half months of high flood from mid-July to the end of September, while no less than four-fifths passes down in five and a half months from mid-July to the end of December. The exact dates vary from year to year, but in general this is the period of surplus. The rest of the year is a period of shortage.

Until the early nineteenth century irrigation in Egypt was practised only during the flood, either by water-wheel or by making cuts in the banks into basins. As the nineteenth century progressed, perennial irrigation, or watering throughout the year, was increasingly used for growing cotton and other cash crops and gradually Egypt's needs used up the whole of the natural flow of the river in the period of shortage and established a prior claim to it. Countries upstream of Egypt had, at this date, no established irrigation, and were regarded as quite uncivilized.

No more could be done with the natural flow alone, and there then began the process of storing water from the time of surplus for use in the time of shortage. The first step was the building of the Aswan Dam in 1902 which provided one milliard* of stored water. In 1904 Garstin published his review of the possibilities of the whole Nile basin, already described in Chapter 2. Investigation into his suggestions continued and, at the same time, the Aswan water being found insufficient the dam there was raised in 1912 to provide a storage of 2·4 milliard. By this date the area under perennial irrigation in Egypt had increased to

* The unit used on the Nile is a cubic metre of water. A milliard is a thousand million, known in the U.S.A. as a billion. The average total annual flow of the Nile is 84 milliards at Aswan.

4 million, while that under basin irrigation had fallen to 1·3 million feddans.

It will be remembered that because of Egypt's vital interest in Nile waters, the British advisers in Cairo retained strict control of irrigation development in the Sudan. At first licences for perennial irrigation there were only approved on 2,500 feddans for experimental stations. On completion of the Aswan Dam an increase of 10,000 feddans was permitted and a further 10,000 feddans when the Aswan Dam was raised in 1912. In addition open permission was given in 1905 for pump irrigation between 15th July and the end of February—the permits were known as flood licences. The first proposal for the Gezira had been for a mere diversion barrage to irrigate 100,000 feddans from the flood but, before anything was undertaken, there occurred in 1913 the lowest Nile discharge for 180 years.* Following this experience, and when increased costs demanded the increase of the irrigated area to 300,000 feddans, the Gezira proposal was altered to provide a storage dam at Sennar. With this change came new uncertainties.

Sir Murdoch Macdonald was at the time Irrigation Adviser to the Ministry of Public Works in Egypt. The problem facing him was two-fold. Firstly, what area in the Gezira could be watered at all from the Blue Nile in the low period of river, if another year like 1913 occurred? Macdonald calculated that the proposed Sennar reservoir, allowing for evaporation losses, could store 487 million cubic metres from surplus flood waters and that this volume, plus the natural flow of the Blue Nile in this period, could irrigate 660,000 feddans in the worst known year and more than a million feddans in the next lowest year (1907–8).

But the second part of the problem was how much area could be watered in the Gezira without detriment to Egypt. For this purpose he calculated that in the lowest recorded year Egypt's shortage would have lasted from 18th February to 25th July at Aswan, equivalent, allowing for the travel time of water, to 18th January to 25th June at Sennar. After 15th April the Gezira would require only a small quantity for domestic supplies as cotton watering could cease at that date, but between 18th January and 15th April the crop would require water and, if the criterion of the worst year was to be used, this could not be drawn from the natural flow at all between these dates without detriment to Egypt. The only water available to the Gezira in this period would be

* Records of Nile levels existed at Cairo for over 900 years and it was computed that such a low discharge had only occurred four times in all this period. See the S.P.S. Agreement, 1929, schedule II.

the 487 million cubic metres stored in the Sennar Dam. According to data from the pilot schemes a gross area of 300,000 feddans* would need between these dates 500 million cubic metres, so that at first sight it looked as if this area would have to be the ultimate limit of the Scheme.

But Macdonald had a wider plan. While the Sudan had been pre-occupied with the Gezira, Egypt had been about to undertake another of Garstin's proposals, a dam on the White Nile at Gebel Aulia, near to Khartoum, to impound 4 milliard of new storage for Egypt. Macdonald proposed that, as this quantity was far in excess of Egypt's present needs, a portion might be reserved to make up for a gradually increased use of the Blue Nile water by the Sudan.

Macdonald's views amounted to the following conclusions:

(a) Since the Blue Nile with the Sennar Dam could guarantee 660,000 feddans against the lowest recorded Nile, in the next lowest 1 million feddans, and in years of average flow much more, ordinary engineering practice would warrant one million feddans forthwith.

(b) The only area intended for cultivation now was 300,000 feddans. Before it could be completed Egypt should have finished the Gebel Aulia Dam. When it was thought expedient to extend the Gezira to, say, 660,000 feddans, this could be done by earmarking 20 per cent of the Gebel Aulia storage which would cover even the lowest year. In all other years a million feddans could be cultivated without detriment to Egypt once the Gebel Aulia Dam was constructed.

(c) These stages of development could overlap, producing ample and continuous security of supply. Before the Sudan could deprive Egypt of any Blue Nile water the White Nile storage could be ready, with the bulk of its supply for Egypt and with a percentage, in excess of Egypt's requirements for many years, temporarily available as compensation for any abstraction from the Blue Nile. So also, before Egypt was ready to use this compensation water herself, either upper Blue Nile or upper White Nile works† could provide more storage, and leave Egypt 'indifferent to even the most brilliant future of the Gezira Scheme'.[1]

---

* The requirements were calculated on the assumption that the rotation, water intervals, crops, and amount used per feddan per watering, would be as per data supplied from the pilot schemes. Later experience of economizing water, together with a changed rotation, and greater storage capacity at Sennar, was to show that the reservoir could suffice for a much larger gross area.

† Mainly the works already suggested by Garstin and noted in Chapter 2. On the Blue Nile, storage dams were envisaged at Roseires in the Sudan about 165 miles above Sennar, and at Lake Tana in Ethiopia. On the White Nile the only good storage sites were the great lakes of Uganda, but their immense capacity

Macdonald suggested that the Sudan should undertake that, until the Gebel Aulia Dam was completed, 300,000 feddans would be the maximum area of the Gezira Scheme; Egypt should agree that, after completion of the Gebel Aulia Dam, 20 per cent of its storage would be ear-marked as compensation water to allow the Blue Nile to be drawn on to an equivalent amount by the Gezira for, say, twenty years. After this, this compensation water would be released to Egypt by the provision of other storage on the upper Blue Nile or some further arrangement on the upper White Nile.

These proposals were suggested to get over difficulties in the period of shortage. But there was also a difficulty in the period of surplus. Any serious abstraction of water for the Gezira during the flood might affect the levels of the main Nile in Egypt and operate to the detriment of the remaining basin irrigation there. It was clearly unfair to hold up all irrigation in the Sudan for such a reason, and yet undesirable for such detriment to assume large proportions. The risk could be greatly reduced by the construction of a barrage at Nag Hamadi in Egypt. There was thus an additional reason why any programme of work on the river should be executed simultaneously and as part of a common plan.

Macdonald's conclusions, which were published in detail in 1919 in a volume entitled *Nile Control*, gave rise to immense controversy. Certain British engineers cast doubt on the accuracy of some of his data, suggesting particularly that he had overestimated the discharge of the Blue Nile at the lowest period of the worst years, had underestimated the needs of the Gezira crops in the period of shortage, and was not necessarily right about the periods of river surplus and shortage in Egypt. The controversy reached the press in Egypt and public opinion became alarmed. Apart from the uncertainty about the data, there were some cultivators in Egypt who feared that the loss of the silt-carrying Blue Nile water might harm their land.

To resolve the situation the Egyptian Government appointed in 1920 a Nile Projects Commission of three independent experts to report on the physical data on which all the projects advocated in *Nile Control* were based, on the manner in which the increased supply of available water provided by them should be allocated at each stage of development

could not be used effectively until measures had been taken to deal with the excessive losses (exceeding 12 milliard in an average year) in the Sudd region of the southern Sudan. To do this it was proposed to excavate a by-pass channel some 200 miles long, which has come to be known as the Jonglei canal project.

between Egypt and the Sudan, and to advise as to the apportionment of the costs. Meanwhile it pressed for the stoppage of all work, and the Minister of Public Works, Ismail Sirry Pasha, threatened to resign unless this was done.

The Sudan Government, it will be remembered, had in 1919 just negotiated the agreement with the Sudan Plantations Syndicate, and obtained Treasury consent to raise the loan of £6 million. It was therefore most anxious to continue with the Gezira Scheme, and afraid that a postponement would operate to its discredit both in Lancashire and in the money market. Macdonald himself suggested a compromise which was accepted, and in February 1920 the British Government gave an undertaking that the initial area of 300,000 feddans in the Gezira would not be exceeded without reference to the Egyptian Government. The work was thereupon carried out within this limitation. The report of the Nile Projects Commission found that the projects were based on reliable data and advocated their execution, although the majority felt unable to advise on the allocation of future water supplies, and the only proposals made in this connection, those of Mr. Cory, the American member, were not adopted.*

Almost immediately after this occurred the second financial crisis about capital funds for the Gezira, to resolve which the total loans authorized were raised to £13 million. But when these loans were negotiated, a new estimate was made of the paying level of the Gezira Scheme which indicated that the direct revenue from the Government share on 300,000 feddans would only show a credit if the average yield was as high as 3 kantars per feddan, and the price as high as 18 pence per lb. If the area were extended to 450,000 feddans, however, the Scheme would show a credit even at 15 pence per lb., while on an area of 600,000 feddans the financial position should be altogether more certain.

Outside these Gezira calculations Schuster, the Financial Secretary, now had to anticipate additional burdens on the Sudan budget.[2] Some of these related to political changes in Egypt, including the possibility of having to finance a Sudan Defence Force in place of the Egyptian army in the Sudan, and the possibility of claims for interest, and perhaps

---

* Cory's proposal was that established water rights should be recognized, and that thereafter the unappropriated water made available by conservation should be divided between the two countries according to their potential irrigable land. He assessed this potential as practically the same in Egypt and the Sudan, and consequently recommended an equal division of the unappropriated waters between the two countries.

for repayment of principal, on the Sudan's development debt to Egypt. Within the Sudan there would probably be a falling off of some £E100,000 a year in revenue derived during the construction years of the Gezira Scheme, and of £E150,000 a year in customs and railway receipts on withdrawal of the Egyptian army. On top of this there was now a probable £E100,000 a year increased liability for pensions and rates of pay as well as an increased establishment.

Schuster's conclusion was that the Gezira Scheme must be extended. But any extension of the Scheme had now to be referred to Egypt and, unfortunately, while the Sudan had gone ahead with the Gezira, the Egyptian Government, in view of the heavy estimated cost of the Gebel Aulia Dam and complementary works, had in May 1921 decided to suspend all operations connected with that project.

Political relations between Britain and Egypt had been steadily deteriorating since the close of the 1914–18 war, and among the points of difference had been the future status and control of the Sudan. In November 1924 these differences were brought to crisis point by the murder in Cairo of Sir Lee Stack, the Governor-General of the Sudan.[*] When this occurred Lord Allenby, the British High Commissioner in Egypt, presented an ultimatum to the Prime Minister of Egypt which required the Egyptian Government, among other matters, to 'notify the competent department that the Sudan Government will increase the area to be irrigated in the Gezira from 300,000 feddans to an unlimited figure as need may arise'.[3]

In January 1925 Notes were exchanged between the President of the Egyptian Council of Ministers and the High Commissioner, in which the President emphasized the anxiety aroused in Egypt at the prospect of unlimited irrigation in the Gezira, and contended that the Egyptian Government had always held that this development ought not to be harmful to the irrigation of Egypt, nor to prejudice projects required there to support the growing population. The High Commissioner then agreed to rescind this clause and to have a commission appointed to propose the basis on which irrigation could be carried out, in view of Egypt's interests and rights.[4]

The Nile Commissioners of 1925 confined their objective to 'devising a practical working arrangement which would respect the needs of established irrigation while permitting such extensions as might be possible under present conditions, and those of the near future, without at the same time compromising in any way the possibilities of the more

* See page 64 n.

distant future'. Their report recognized that an important feature of the projects recommended in *Nile Control* was that they should come into operation simultaneously, and their task was made easier by the knowledge that the Egyptian Government had now definitely sanctioned the Gebel Aulia Dam, the Nag Hamadi barrage and the initial investigation of the Sudd channel.

The chief novelty of their report was the recommendation that control over abstraction of water from the river would be better maintained by proposals in volumes and seasons than by area limitation, and that as far as the Sudan was concerned this control should, for the time being, be exercised by concentrating everything on an agreed procedure for regulating the Sennar reservoir. The suggested procedure was based on a 'standard' rather than on a 'worst' year, with cover for the unusual by providing that certain minimum criteria of flow on the river should have been reached at certain dates and should be used to control the rate of abstraction. These principles gave a wider opportunity to the Sudan without detriment to Egypt, for they enabled the Sudan to increase its irrigated area to any extent it liked by economies in water usage within a certain total available quantity, both for the period of surplus and the period of shortage.

For the period of surplus, Sir Murdoch Macdonald had suggested in *Nile Control* that a maximum discharge of 84 cubic metres a second in the Gezira canal would be sufficient for the first stage of the Scheme. The 1925 Commission confirmed this figure, and then went on to consider what water, additional to this, could be taken in the Sudan in the period of surplus, consistent with the interests of Egypt. They recommended that, although there was a large volume of unused water in the flood, the Sudan should accept a limited rate of progress so as to allow Egypt to catch up with the work which formed her part of the programme. They therefore laid down a scale providing for specific increases in the Gezira canal discharge from 84 cubic metres per second in 1926, to 96 in 1930, and to a final total of 168 cubic metres per second, or double Macdonald's figure, in 1936.

For the period of shortage, the 1925 Nile Commission confirmed Macdonald's conclusion that the whole natural flow of the river, from 19th January to 15th July at Sennar, ought to be reserved for Egypt. They went further than Macdonald and insisted that even after 31st December the natural flow should not be drawn upon in excess of 117 million cubic metres, which Macdonald had estimated the Gezira could draw without detriment to Egypt and would need from 1st to 18th January, in its initial phase. It will be remembered that, apart from the Gezira, pumping permits had been granted some years before for small areas of perennial irrigation, and an unlimited licence for flood irrigation up to the end of February, a date which had at that time been thought of no detriment to Egypt. As the Commissioners had now determined that the natural flow ought not to be drawn upon by the Sudan after 31st December, it followed that if these permits were exercised and extended, on top of the provision for the Gezira, Egypt might be adversely affected. Yet, if pumping was to be prohibited in the Sudan after 31st December, valuable crops like cotton would be restricted to the Gezira alone.

To get over this difficulty the Commissioners suggested a compromise which confirmed existing licences and allowed for some extension. No restrictions were to be placed on pumping up to 31st December. After that date the whole natural flow, except for pumping permits already granted, was to go to Egypt, but by a special way of operating the Sennar Dam water which would otherwise have been held there, although unavailable for irrigation, was to be utilized instead for extending the pumping areas. Macdonald's original plan of operation had envisaged holding the level in the reservoir throughout the period of shortage at the height necessary to command the Gezira canal, so as to supply the Scheme with domestic water. The Commission now suggested that the pumps of the pilot schemes might fulfil this task and eliminate the need to hold up the reservoir level. Some 150 million cubic metres of water, hitherto held uselessly in the reservoir, could thus be released and used by pumping areas in the period of shortage.

These recommendations meant, in effect, that until further storage works on the river reopened the problem all water used by the Sudan from 1st January to 15th July inclusive should be recorded in a credit-and-debit account.

The credits were to be as follows:

		million
1.	Computed capacity of the Sennar reservoir	781
2.	Allowance for evaporation loss from the reservoir	24
	Allowance for Gezira from 1st to 18th January	117
	Allowance for pumps previously approved	143
	Total credit	1,065

The allowance for pumps was to cover the 22,500 feddans of perennial irrigation and 38,500 feddans for flood irrigation to the end of February, for which permits had already been given.

The debits were to be:

1. Quantities actually drawn off in the Gezira.
2. Quantities estimated to have been drawn off by irrigation pumps anywhere in the Sudan on the Nile or any of its tributaries.
3. Actual evaporation loss of the Sennar reservoir.

The Sudan could then dispose of her water as she thought fit as long as she did not let the debits exceed the credits.

Although the report of the 1925 Nile Commission was not immediately adopted, the working of the Sennar Dam, and the allocation of water to the Gezira Scheme and to pumps, was carried on in accordance with its recommendations from 1926 to 1929. In May 1929 Notes were exchanged between the British Government and the Egyptian Government, which have gone down to history as the Nile Waters Agreement of 1929.[5] These Notes accepted the findings of the 1925 Nile Commission as an integral part of this Agreement.*

The most important effect which resulted from this water settlement concerned the potential irrigable areas which for the moment it made available for the Sudan. It was found to be sufficient, under the rotation and water intervals and quantities which came to be standard in the Gezira, to irrigate a gross area of a million feddans there, and in addition more than 500,000 feddans by pumps elsewhere in the Sudan. If an earlier cessation of cotton watering was practicable in the period of shortage, the area could be extended further. The Agreement therefore enabled the Sudan to increase irrigation and in particular removed the problem of supplies of water for the Gezira during the period of this story.

The water problem of the future is another matter. The Nile Waters Agreement of 1929 was concerned with reassuring Egypt about her water needs at a time when the future water needs not only of the Sudan but of Uganda, Kenya and Tanganyika had hardly become apparent. A clause in the 1929 Agreement contained this wording:

Save with the previous agreement of the Egyptian Government, no irrigation or power works or measures are to be constructed on the Nile and its branches, or on the lakes from which it flows, so far as all these are in the Sudan or in countries under British Administration, which would,

---

* With one exception. The date and volume schedule in the flood season was modified so that the Gezira should not draw more than 126 cubic metres per second before 1936, in view of further delay in the construction of the Gebel Aulia Dam, which was finally completed in 1937. By agreement with Egypt in 1936 the Gezira was to reach its total entitlement of 168 cubic metres per second in 1940. In the event, the final widening of the main canal to take this discharge was only completed in 1956.

in such a manner as to entail any prejudice to the interests of Egypt, either reduce the quantity of water arriving in Egypt, or modify the date of its arrival, or lower its level.[6]

While this wording clearly acknowledged the historical rights of Egypt, in the last generation the rights and needs of other countries bordering on the Nile have come to the forefront and have equally to be considered.

In the Sudan the ultimate success of the Gezira Scheme created an immense interest and demand for further irrigation. Huge areas of land have been found suitable, but their development awaits the construction of those additional storage works envisaged so long ago by Garstin, and also some international agreement on how to share the remaining water equitably. 'Precedents in this matter of water allocation', wrote the Nile Commissioners of 1925, 'are rare. The Commission is aware of no generally adopted code or standard practice upon which the settlement of a question of inter-communal water allocation might be based. Moreover, there are in the present case special factors, historical, political, and technical, which might render inappropriate too strict an application of principles adopted elsewhere.'[7] The neutral Dutch Chairman of the 1925 Nile Commission, Mr. Canter Cremers, died in the course of the inquiry, and the report was really written by the two technical members, Mr. R. M. MacGregor, the British Delegate, and Abdel Hamid Soliman Pasha, the Egyptian Delegate. Their readiness to agree on a practical working arrangement played a great part in making possible the first phase of the Sudan's emergence from a mere subsistence economy. They left to others the choice of emulating them over the next stage of storage works or of seeking for the elusive fundamental principle for dividing up a river's water for ever.*

* When the Sennar reservoir was filled to its original top level of 420·7 metres above the sea the total water credit for the Sudan was 1,065 million cubic metres, as already explained on page 115. It remained unchanged until 1951, but during the next three years the top level of the reservoir was gradually raised by one metre. This raised the computed capacity of the reservoir from 781 to 929 million, an addition of 148 million cubic metres. At the beginning of 1954 the total Sudan water credit was increased by a further 200 million as the result of an agreement with Egypt, the top level of the Gebel Aulia reservoir being raised 10 cm. by way of compensation. For the year 1955 a further increase of 200 million was granted on the same terms. These various changes raised the total credit for the Sudan to 1,613 million cubic metres.

If the capacity of the reservoir had not been increased, there would have been a deficit in the water account for 1952. Even so, there would again have been a deficit in 1955 but for the first advance of 200 million. With the construction of the Manāgil Extension to the Gezira Scheme and the present rapid expansion of pump irrigation in the Sudan, a deficit is almost certain to occur by 1960 at the latest unless something is done to prevent it.

EXPLANATORY NOTE: NILE COMMISSION 1925

The reader will, I am afraid, be confused by the different ways in which measurements of water are expressed in this chapter.

The volume of water made available to the Sudan in the period of shortage (1st January to 15th July) had to be expressed as a total of 1,065 million cubic metres, and was determined primarily by the storage capacity of the dam. Any water taken in excess of this total in the period of shortage was held to be liable to deprive Egypt.

In the period of surplus (16th July to 31st December) it was not a question of depriving Egypt but of going fair shares in using the surplus. The Sudan's fair share was calculated by the quantity of water she was likely to need per day as the Gezira Scheme extended, and this was expressed by the scale 84 cubic metres per second in 1926 to 168 cubic metres per second in 1936.

In making these suggestions the Nile Commissioners pointed out that they were devising practical arrangements for the present and near future, without compromising the distant future.

The basis of the calculation of 84 cubic metres per second in 1926 was as follows:

In 1916 the volume of water needed to irrigate the Gezira crops had not yet been determined. It was essential to Macdonald to have some figure upon which to base his works. Two factors required to be known.

(1) The water interval between waterings.

(2) The volume of water required per feddan per watering.

In Egypt the water interval for cotton was 18 days, and the volume per feddan per watering 450 m.^{3} This amounted to a need of 25 m.^{3} per feddan per day. The Sudan climate was much hotter and, according to the Syndicate at Tayiba, the water interval required was 10 days and the volume 600 m.^{3} per feddan per watering, or 60 m.^{3} per feddan per day.

This was at variance with all known data, and Macdonald compromised with an estimated need of 50 m.^{3} per feddan per day for cotton. For other crops he assumed that the same volume was needed per feddan per watering but that the water interval might be 20 instead of 10 days, making an estimated need of 25 m.^{3} per feddan per day.

Out of the 300,000 feddans the intended areas were 100,000 cotton, 100,000 other crops, and 100,000 fallow. On this basis the formula of need worked out as follows:

Cotton—
100,000 feddans @ 50 m.³ = 5,000,000 m.³ per day, or 58 m.³ per second

Other crops—
100,000 feddans @ 25 m.³ = 2,500,000 m.³ per day, or 29 m.³ per second
Total = 7,500,000 m.³ per day, or 87 m.³ per second

For various reasons Macdonald, in *Nile Control*, reduced this total to 84 cubic metres per second.

In the event, over the years, it was found that the average water interval for cotton need not be as close as every 10 days, nor the volume as high as 500 cubic metres per feddan per watering. Similar economies applied to the other crops. It was these economies, compared with the original estimate, which enabled the area to be so greatly extended, and the Nile Commission's settlement by volume of water rather than by land area to be so beneficial.

Chapter 10

NILE WATERS: THE FARMING PATTERN

A second important effect of the water settlement concerned the form of agriculture which resulted. In the early years of the century, when speculators hastened to get hold of land in the Sudan, they anticipated entering into a second Egypt, with all the wealth of two crops a year on similar marvellous land. No one had any knowledge of the climate, the soil or the availability of water. It was at Zeidab, Tayiba, Barakat and a few government research stations that the farming year for crops appropriate to the Sudan's needs was discovered, and then trimmed and fitted to the water restrictions from Egypt. In the Gezira, with the exception of scattered storms, the rains begin in July and end in September. The rest of the year is dry, relatively cool in the winter months from November to February and blazing hot in April, May and June. In the rains everything grows green. In the rest of the year it turns brown and dies.

It might be thought that irrigation water could make its own climate and that these natural seasons could be ignored. For most annual crops the contrary was found to be true. The rains were nature's period of beneficial development. Of course, if water could have been available to get crops planted just before the rains such development might be enhanced, but the water needs of Egypt, preventing any offtake in the Sudan before 15th July, excluded this advantage. On the other hand, postponement of planting until towards the end of the rains stunted the crops by shortening their enjoyment of the beneficial season and by throwing their growing period into a drier climatic environment.

The farming year for cotton had therefore to begin as soon as water was available for planting in July and go on for maturity and harvesting from January to April. Dura and lubia also required planting in the rains. The consequent concentration of planting and weeding all three crops at the same time had to be modified in practice for labour purposes so that one crop came after the other, but all had to be sown and

120

weeded within six weeks. Any extensive staggering might involve watering dura and lubia in the period of shortage, which meant using precious stored water for a much less valuable crop than cotton.

So the farming pattern began with a great rush to get cotton and dura, and then lubia, planted and weeded within a very short period, imposing a considerable demand on the energy of the tenants and availability of labour. Dura watering ceased in November to enable harvesting to be finished before cotton picking began in January. Lubia watering ceased in December and that crop came to maturity in fodder and beans during the cotton picking. Wheat, which might have been a suitable winter crop, could be planted with the onset of the cold weather in November but would need, of course, water after 1st January, an encroachment on cotton in the period of shortage and so economically ineligible. Any extensive use of vegetables, fruit trees or perennial fodder crops like alfalfa, all of which were found to grow satisfactorily, was excluded because no water at all was available from 15th April to 15th July, the command level having been released in this period at the Sennar Dam.

The form of agriculture which developed in the Gezira was thus not in the least like that of Egypt. Only one crop could be grown on the same land in one year, which meant a much more extensive rotation, dominated inevitably by the most paying crop, cotton, to enhance the yield of which a preceding year of fallow was found desirable. Dura was the essential food and lubia the essential fodder for the people. No other crops could really qualify. Gezira agriculture thus began, concentrated but simple, with a three-course rotation: cotton, followed in the next season by dura and lubia each taking half of the field, followed in the next season by fallow. The dura and the lubia exchanged sides at regular intervals so that the nitrogenous crop should offset the draw on the land from the cereal crop.

In any one season each individual tenant had three ten-acre plots parallel and alongside each other, watering independently in their appropriate numbers from the canal. The first was in cotton, the second half in dura and half in lubia, and the third was fallow. The standard watering number was divided into nine such ten-acre plots, one for each tenant. Looking down from the air the scene would be something like this (see following page), for two adjacent units of nine tenants each.

This little diagram has been made deliberately bald and impersonal to draw attention to a fundamental change which the introduction of irrigation made to the lives of the people of the Gezira. Mohammed Ahmed

TALHA MINOR CANAL

CANAL ROAD

BASATNA MAJOR CANAL | CANAL ROAD

Field No. 1	No. 2		No. 3	Field No. 4	No. 5		No. 6
Tenancy 1 COTTON	1 DURA	1 LUBIA	1 FALLOW	Tenancy 10 COTTON	10 DURA	10 LUBIA	10 FALLOW
Tenancy 2 COTTON	2 DURA	2 LUBIA	2 FALLOW	Tenancy 11 COTTON	11 DURA	11 LUBIA	11 FALLOW
Tenancy 3 COTTON	3 DURA	3 LUBIA	3 FALLOW	Tenancy 12 COTTON	12 DURA	12 LUBIA	12 FALLOW
Tenancy 4 COTTON	4 DURA	4 LUBIA	4 FALLOW	Tenancy 13 COTTON	13 DURA	13 LUBIA	13 FALLOW
Tenancy 5 COTTON	5 DURA	5 LUBIA	5 FALLOW	Tenancy 14 COTTON	14 DURA	14 LUBIA	14 FALLOW
Tenancy 6 COTTON	6 DURA	6 LUBIA	6 FALLOW	Tenancy 15 COTTON	15 DURA	15 LUBIA	15 FALLOW
Tenancy 7 COTTON	7 DURA	7 LUBIA	7 FALLOW	Tenancy 16 COTTON	16 DURA	16 LUBIA	16 FALLOW
Tenancy 8 COTTON	8 DURA	8 LUBIA	8 FALLOW	Tenancy 17 COTTON	17 DURA	17 LUBIA	17 FALLOW
Tenancy 9 COTTON	9 DURA	9 LUBIA	9 FALLOW	Tenancy 18 COTTON	18 DURA	18 LUBIA	18 FALLOW

Crop Rotation and Watering System

Abdulla, of Abu Seneina village, who had previously been the independent owner of an irregular plot of land somewhere on the Gezira plain, became instead tenant number 1 on field number 1 on the Talha minor canal. His agricultural life was now less a matter of his own whim and judgement, for he and his companions in tenancies 2, 3 and 4 had to be present on an appointed day to take water on their cotton. They had to complete this watering in four days so that the water could pass on down to tenants 5 to 9 in their turn. Moreover, all the tenants in field number 1 had to finish their cotton watering in eight days so that their field outlet-pipe in the Talha minor canal could be closed in time for field number 4 to be opened in alternating fashion on its correct watering day. Here Mubarak Osman Dafalla, of Mahla village, had become tenant number 10 and had to be waiting with his companions in tenancies 11, 12 and 13 to receive their water on the right date and in turn close their water correctly so that tenants 14 to 18 could get their turn. What was necessary for cotton was necessary too for dura and lubia, although the intervals between waterings would be longer in the case of these crops.

This system of balancing one field outlet-pipe against another was essential to maintain, as far as possible, a stability of discharge in Talha minor canal, relayed correspondingly to the Basatna major canal and so to a main regulator on the main canal, and finally to the control outlet from the Sennar Dam. Without this intricate balancing time-table the immense volume of water discharged into the main canal head, reaching at its peak ten million tons a day, could not be evenly distributed over the whole network of canals as the crops needed it without chaos.

The watering time-table determined all the other farming operations. Related to the due watering date the crops had to be sown, weeded, thinned, ridged up and even harvested. In particular, to allow water on to weeds or unpicked cotton was to increase labour costs and to risk a serious fall in yield, for in a soil deficient in nitrogen weed competition was vitally damaging, while unpicked cotton when watered simply fell in the mud. Mohammed Ahmed Abdulla and Mubarak Osman Dafalla and their companions were not Egyptian fellaheen with two thousand years of dependence on Nile water in their ancestry. They were subsistence farmers who had hitherto led unregulated lives sowing their rain crops and sending out their animals to graze. From this leisurely existence they suddenly became part of a pattern of farming which demanded regular attention and foresight for most of the year. From now on each individual's action or inaction was liable to affect his neighbours and he had to operate constantly as a unit in a community plan.

Irrigation engineers in India and Egypt had customarily maintained stability of discharge in their canal systems by passing the water on to the fields day and night, and the cultivators, immensely aware of the preciousness of water, were expected to handle their ration efficiently whenever it came. The first plan for irrigation in the Gezira was designed accordingly. The Syndicate in its pilot schemes had watered by day only by the simple process of stopping the pumps. Clearly it would be impossible to use this process on the main canal or over a large area of canalization, yet the Gezira tenants, who had already accepted immense changes in daylight farming, could hardly be expected to turn out by night. But if water flowed on the land uncontrolled at night how could the farming operations be conducted without confusion and loss and in time with the water?

To meet this human difficulty an ingenious solution was invented by A. D. Butcher, an outstanding engineer in the Egyptian Irrigation Service. Stability of discharge was maintained in the main and major canals and at the minor canal heads. But in each reach of the minor canals a simple weir was built in front of each regulator.* During the day the field outlet-pipes were opened and water taken on the land, leaving the minor canal empty by sunset. During the night the field outlet-pipes were closed but the constant discharge from the head of the canal continued, quietly filling the first reach and then spilling over the weir into the second reach and so on, until at dawn the canal was at full supply level, ready for the opening of the field outlet-pipes again.

This ingenious system of night storage, designed to help a people unused to the intricacies of irrigation, was not, however, without its penalty. Apart from extra capital cost it encouraged excessive silt deposit and made the maintenance of minor canals abnormally expensive. Later on, when the routine of Gezira farming had become second-nature to many people, the night storage system was dispensed with and in extensions today the people are expected to manage with more orthodox ways of irrigation.

In irrigation in the Gezira different crops needed different quantities of water at different times of the year. A bare fallow, cracked by the heat of summer, took a great deal more water to saturate it for planting than the cool earth which had already had plenty of rain, and the same crop which was small in size in humid days in September would need more water when it was tall and leafy in drier October. In the cool of winter it would again need less. Although theoretically these changes might have been satisfied by some optimum scientific ration of water, in practice a much more rough and ready method had to be adopted. The arrangement was for the Syndicate's field officer to make a forecast once a week, on a fixed 'indent' day, of the water likely to be required for the next seven days on each of his minor canals. With a little experience he would get to know that under certain weather conditions, and with due regard to the tenants' capacity to be on time with their agricultural

* A regulator was simply an earth bridge over a canal with a pipe through it. A door on this pipe controlled the discharge through it. The purpose of a regulator was to hold the water level high enough in each reach to command all the field outlet-pipes. The number of regulators, and so of reaches, on any canal would depend on the downward gradient of the canal from contour to contour.

operations, he should estimate a discharge of so many cubic metres per twenty-four hours for each of the field outlet-pipes which were due to open. Under certain conditions it might be 3,000 cubic metres, under others 5,000 cubic metres per pipe. This figure, multiplied by the number of pipes watering in that week, would give the discharge required at the head of each minor canal per twenty-four hours, and this discharge could then be held constant until the next 'indent' day. The sum total of these indents for the respective minor canals would then determine the discharge to be fixed at the head of the major canal which supplied them, while the sum total of the majors in their turn gave the discharge required from the main canal head at the dam.

This system whereby the agriculturalist indented on the Irrigation Service for what water he wanted served admirably the needs of a people completely unused to irrigation. There is, however, one long-term danger lurking in the process. The Gezira tenant has never come to regard water as precious. The nature of the partnership, admirable in so many other respects, implied a duty on the Government to supply the water without any charge, and the method of indenting adjusted the quantities supplied very much as the farmer thought he needed them. With a sense of claim on the water, and with everything organized to make it easy for them to get it, Gezira farmers have not yet acquired that attitude of mind to water which automatically endeavours to make the most of it. They are not yet actively interested, as are most farmers in irrigation, in the minimum quantity in amount and depth really needed to mature a crop. It is an interest to which they may soon be compelled for water in the Sudan of the future is likely to be more precious than land.

Chapter 11

EXTENSIONS AND A NEW AGREEMENT

The prospect of a settlement of the Nile waters dispute enabled the Sudan Government to consider extending the Gezira Scheme, and Schuster lost no time in beginning negotiations with the Syndicate for a new agreement. The Government had two main problems: how to raise further capital, and for what area and for what percentage of the profits the Government should aim, to enable it to meet its direct outgoings on the Gezira.

To raise capital was as difficult as ever. Only a small balance remained unused of the £13 million raised by loans in the United Kingdom (£11½ million having been spent in the Gezira), and the British Treasury now made clear that it would oppose any further attempts to raise guaranteed loans and would not permit the Sudan to borrow on the London market without Treasury guarantee. The Sudan Government revenues had reached a figure, by 1925, of just under £E5 million compared with £E1½ million in 1913, but there had been wide fluctuations. The British Treasury's attitude was therefore understandable, for considerable risk had already been taken in relation to the resources of the Sudan, when the amount borrowed represented between two and three years' government revenue from the country as a whole.

Sudan budgets had traditionally covered little more than the maintenance of the government departments but, by stringent economy, had yielded small surpluses. These were credited to a general reserve fund, and all capital expenditure, derived from internal saving, was made from this fund. In this manner, from 1919 to 1925, the Sudan had been able to put aside an average of £E430,000 annually, or £E3 million in total, as an internal contribution to capital development, but at the beginning of 1925 the unallocated balance of this general reserve fund stood at no more than £E750,000.

Thus, while it was essential for the Government to extend the Gezira Scheme in order to increase revenue and bring down the overhead costs, it was still extremely difficult to find capital merely for the irrigation works. Reliance on the Syndicate to find the rest of the capital needs was a close corollary.

The second main problem for the Government concerned the probable earning capacity of the extended scheme. When the net cotton area was 100,000 feddans, the Government's annual charges came to £E8 per feddan of cotton area. On a 35 per cent share of the crop, this meant that there must be a net divisible return for the partnership of £E23 per feddan per annum to enable Government to cover its costs. Such a situation was altogether too risky. A yield of 3 kantars per feddan at a price of 15 pence per lb. gave a net divisible return of only £E18·8 per feddan.

But on 150,000 feddans of cotton, the Government's annual costs would fall to £E6·5 per feddan. This meant that the Government would cover its costs at a net return of £E18·5 per feddan if its share remained at 35 per cent. But if this share could be raised to 40 per cent it would cover costs at a net return of £E16 per feddan.[1]

These considerations determined the objective of the Government in negotiating a new agreement with the Syndicate. It was not thought reasonable to estimate for more than an average yield of 3 kantars per feddan and for more than an average price of 15 pence per lb. At such a yield and price Government could not hope to break even unless the area was increased to at least 150,000 feddans of cotton. Even on this area a 35 per cent share would allow no margin of direct profit and an increase to 40 per cent was indispensable for safety.

The bait held out to the Syndicate to fall in with these plans was the prospect of a longer period over a bigger area for its concession. Negotiations with Eckstein and MacIntyre opened in May 1926. They were extremely reluctant to allow the Syndicate's share to be reduced from 25 per cent to 20 per cent even for these advantages. Eckstein gave in only when Schuster intimated that the Government would carry out the extension on its own if the Syndicate refused to come to terms, and then called in Lord Lloyd—the British High Commissioner in Egypt—to say that he would not give his approval to a longer concession period unless the Syndicate's share was reduced to 20 per cent.[2] As a compromise a sliding scale was introduced as the area was extended, until by July 1930, when the addition of the full 150,000 feddans was due to be completed, the shares would finally change to 40 per cent for the Government and 20 per cent for the Syndicate. The Heads of Agreement were signed on 9th November 1926. The period of the concession was extended to

1950, making twenty-five years from the completion of the dam in place of the fourteen years of the 1919 agreement.

The Government was still preoccupied with the possibility that the Syndicate's activities might run counter to its social and political objectives, and insisted on a clause providing for the possible early termination of the concession by the Government, either in 1939 or in 1944, after one year's previous notice in writing. The Syndicate naturally found it difficult to accept this sword of Damocles. It was finally agreed that in the years and subject to the notice mentioned, the Government might take over from the Syndicate the management of the whole undertaking and the assets of the Syndicate in the concession, as a going concern, including an agreed sum for working capital. To this end a schedule to the agreement laid down in detail an exact method of valuing these assets, and the value so arrived at was to be paid to the Syndicate in 1950. A corollary to this clause, however, provided that if the Government did exercise this option it would compensate the Syndicate for the loss of prospective profits. This was to be done by paying it an annuity each year until 1950, based on the average annual value of its share in the net divisible returns, less its working expenses, for the five years preceding early termination. In this case also a schedule laid down in detail how this average profit was to be calculated. In both cases interest at 6 per cent was allowed to the Syndicate on the working capital and assets on which it was already entitled to charge interest under the agreement. A final point provided that fair and reasonable arrangements would be made to take on such staff and employees of the Syndicate as the Sudan Government might require.

The Syndicate was not entirely comforted by these arrangements and it pressed the Government to agree that, if its management was satisfactory in other respects, it would not exercise this option purely for financial gain. Schuster's reply of 9th November 1926, to Eckstein, is worth quoting in full, for it illustrates how difficult he found it to give an undertaking on behalf of the Government which might hamper its freedom of decision on a point of sovereignty.

With reference to Clause 8 of the Heads of Agreement which we have just signed, you have asked me to put it on record that the intention of the Government in insisting on the right to premature termination is not that this right should be exercised merely for its own financial gain provided that your management is working satisfactorily in every way.

I am quite ready to confirm that this is so; but I must make it quite clear that this statement of the Government's intention is not to be taken as in any way modifying the legal effect of the provision in Clause 8 of the Heads of Agreement as it stands. The possibility of limiting the provision to one giving the Government the right to terminate for certain reasons only (e.g. political reasons) was indeed considered by the Governor-General's Council, and was deliberately rejected by it owing to the impossibility of finding a definition which would not give rise to disputes, and possibly hamper the Government's freedom of action. We have, therefore, insisted on an absolute right to terminate, and endeavoured to protect you by fixing very generous terms for compensation. If in the future the question of terminating the agreement should arise, the Government itself must be the sole judge of its own motive, and this letter must not be taken as altering that position. But it might be of some value to your Company in inducing those who at that time are responsible for the administration of the Sudan, to analyse carefully their motives for doing so, and in representing to them that, if the agreement is working satisfactorily in every other way, and if their only reason for making a change is the expectation that they will have to pay you less under the compensation clause than you would receive if you continued your management, they will be acting in a manner contrary to the intention of those of us who have concluded the present agreement on behalf of the Sudan. But it is not intended that you should have any legal remedy if these representations are disregarded.[3]

As it turned out, this option of termination was never exercised but the story is worth telling because these same arguments obstruct the path of negotiations between foreign capital and new but poor states today. This story shows how flexibility and method can help to bridge the difficulties when both sides really desire to do so in spite of their apprehensions. Credit for the flexibility in this case must largely go to the respective auditors of the Syndicate and Government, Cooper Brothers and Deloitte Plender Griffiths and Co., for, once given the principles of the settlement, they were able in the schedules to lay down the details so clearly that disputes about the financial meaning of early termination could be negligible. Thanks to these schedules, in 1950, when the concession did end, the transfer of the going concern from management by the Syndicate to management by a new National Board was effected with the minimum of friction.

Later, in November 1926, the Syndicate reopened negotiations by asking for protection should it be necessary to increase the tenants' share. In the new agreement this had been left, as before, at 40 per cent. But in the 1919 agreement there had been a clause providing that, if it should be found necessary to increase the tenants' share, such increase should be taken equally from the Government and the Syndicate. The Syndicate now felt that the situation had been completely altered by the reduction of its share to 20 per cent.

Unlike the Government and the tenants the Syndicate had no indirect revenues to look to, and it could not afford to work for an uncertain percentage of the crop. It particularly feared two possibilities: the effect of rising labour costs, and the effect of Government starting other schemes on better terms for their tenants which would force the Syndicate to follow suit, or other Government action over which the Syndicate would have no control. The Government felt that this demand was justified and it was agreed that the first 2½ per cent of any increase in the tenants' share should fall on the Government, and that any increase thereafter should be carried by Government and Syndicate in proportion to their shares in the crop.

Another item changed in the new agreement was the method of recovering tenants' debts. In the 1919 agreement the Syndicate had been entitled to charge tenants a rate of interest on their loans sufficient to provide a sinking fund to cover bad debts. In the new agreement the Syndicate was given the right to charge interest at 6 per cent, or 1 per cent above bank rate, whichever should be the higher, on those items of working and fixed capital on which it had been entitled to charge interest in the 1919 agreement, and it was required to allow the same rate of interest on any funds belonging to the Government and tenants temporarily in its hands from sales of the crop. At the same time there was substituted for the previous arrangement a new provision for the recovery of tenants' debts. In future the Syndicate might deduct, from any money payable to the tenants as a whole, debts owed by tenants written off as bad, less sums recovered.

When all had been settled Eckstein wrote to Schuster:

I desire to acknowledge the generous spirit in which you have conducted a settlement of the difficulties which have arisen and to assure you that everything possible will be done by my colleagues and myself to reciprocate this spirit.[4]

Schuster left the Sudan at the end of 1927 to go on to service in East Africa and India. But the new concession agreement was not finally signed until 17th October 1929.

Little did anyone imagine, in these early years of abundance, how these clauses about the tenants' share and tenants' debts were destined in harder times and with other personalities to disturb the relationship of Government and Syndicate with a storm of controversy.

Meanwhile development in action outpaced the paper plans. These had envisaged that if the Syndicate managed to economize in its water usage the Government would consider favourably the possibility of allowing it to extend the concession area still further.[5] It was found that the Syndicate area could be increased to 465,000 feddans, and in 1927 an additional 45,000 feddans was allocated in the west to the Kassala Cotton Company, a sister company in which the Syndicate held a majority of the shares.* By July 1929, that is to say a year ahead of schedule, these basic areas had been made ready for cultivation and, with slight additions, the grand total of the irrigable area at that date had reached 527,000 feddans.

Notwithstanding this rate of progress, it was then decided to undertake a further extension in a northerly direction with a view to bringing in a further 100,000 feddans. This region, which was called the second northern extension, by contrast with the earlier north and west extension, was the subject of a special supplementary agreement whereunder,

* Mention has already been made of the Gash delta as a potential cotton-growing area hampered by the lack of communications with the coast. Kassala, on the border of Eritrea, was the main town in the delta. In 1924 the Government negotiated with the Syndicate for the development of cotton growing in this region, and a separate company, the Kassala Cotton Company, was formed for this purpose. The principles followed those of the Gezira Scheme, that is to say of a partnership between Government, Company, and local tenants. The Company undertook also to finance the building of a railway link to the Khartoum-Port Sudan line. Difficulties arose on two counts. The area selected for irrigation had been a traditional grazing preserve of the Hadendowa tribe. They proved very indifferent cultivators and preferred to drive their cattle into the cotton-fields to the Company's considerable vexation and loss. Government administrators in the province, remote from their financial secretary's preoccupation with developing the country's economy, were inclined to sympathize with the Hadendowa and gave little assistance to the Company in a situation unmanageable without their help. A second difficulty arose when the Italian Government in Eritrea threatened to interfere with the discharge of the Gash by starting a cotton scheme of its own higher up the river. These twin problems completely invalidated the basis of the agreement. To avoid further friction both parties agreed to accept instead a new concession of 45,000 feddans for the Kassala Cotton Company in the western Gezira. Although a separate company, with its own shareholders, for administrative purposes it was treated on lines parallel to those of the Sudan Plantations Syndicate. There were special terms in this concession to enable the Company to try to recover some of the capital spent on the railway link and in the Gash delta. Government took over the Gash irrigation scheme and put the management under a special board. The change was, in the long run, satisfactory for all parties.

This story of the Kassala Cotton Company in the Gash delta is a classic example of the difficulty of reconciling development and tradition. The government administrator's view of it is given in pages 37–40 of *The Making of the Modern Sudan* by K. D. D. Henderson (Faber, 1953). This book, published in this series, which concerns the life and letters of Sir Douglas Newbold, subsequently Civil Secretary to the Sudan Government, has many references to the Gezira Scheme, upon which Newbold's views were later to have great effect. Newbold at this time was himself the administrative officer of the Hadendowa tribe in the Gash.

for the specified area in question, because of the poorer quality of the soil there, the Syndicate's normal share was increased to 22½ per cent, with provision, however, for reversion to 20 per cent or increase to 25 per cent, if the proceeds per feddan were much above or below the basic expectation.

The completion of the second northern extension brought up the total area comprised in the Scheme from 300,000 feddans in 1926 to 682,000 feddans by July 1931. On this gross area, assuming a three-course rotation, and allowing for some decrease in the Government's percentage share on the second northern extension, Government's fixed annual costs, if one excluded interest on capital derived from internal funds, could be covered by a net divisible return as low as £E10 per feddan.

The transfer of the Kassala Cotton Company's concession had meant an additional £E200,000 capital cost in the Gezira to the Government. The capital cost of the second northern extension was estimated in 1929 to involve another £E810,000. To this expenditure was allocated the whole remaining capital balance of the country, estimated at £E555,000. The rest had to be found by drawing on the Gezira Reserve and Equalization Funds.[6] It was taking a big risk to draw out the last source of capital to this extent and to call up reserves. It meant commitment up to the hilt, but it looked worth it for the capital cost of the whole under-taking would then have been brought low enough to make it reasonably certain (so it was thought) that, even on a conservative estimate of yields and prices, the Scheme would pay its way over an average of years.

The Results to the Government of the First Four Seasons[7]

	1925–6	1926–7	1927–8	1928–9
Area of cotton in feddans	80,031	100,058	100,768	131,292
Government share	35%	37½%	37½%	38½%
Yield per feddan in kantars	4·8	4·7	3·3	3·6
Average sale price in pence per lb.	16	18	20	19
Net divisible return per feddan (budget estimate)	£E20	£E20	£E20	£E20
Net divisible return per feddan (actual)	£E29	£E33·5	£E24·5	£E25
Amount of Government Share—				
Allocated to cover costs	£E703,212	£E721,412	£E814,009	£E1,008,038
Retained in Gezira Equalization Fund	£E21,227	£E477,941	£E142,904	£E243,134

Moreover, in comparison with these figures the actual results of the first four years were considerably better, so much better that the budger estimates could be based on a net divisible return as high as £E20 per feddan and then in practice be exceeded, as the following table reveals. The Government had been able not only to cover the direct costs out of the direct revenue but at the same time to put by some £E900,000 to the Gezira Equalization Fund. It had been wisely decided that the Government's receipts from the Gezira Scheme should not be credited directly to the country's revenue in the first instance, but should be paid into this equalization fund. Transfers were then made from this fund to the budget, but only to cover the annual expenses of the Gezira, the balance in the fund being retained as a cover to meet a bad crop or low prices.

Apart from these direct returns, the indirect benefits of the Scheme were not inconsiderable. There were the increased revenues for the government-owned railways and from the customs, export duty and profits tax. As early as 1927 Schuster estimated them to be worth about £E200,000 per annum. A later calculation made for the 1929–30 season increased this estimate to £E380,000. The contemporary view of the Governor-General's report for the year 1928, written from the standpoint of the first four years' results, gives a yet wider impression of these benefits. 'If a close analysis of the distribution of money earned in the Gezira could be made,' reads one passage, 'it would probably be found that most of the central area of the country has derived benefit from it in greater or lesser degree, and that it is the Gezira Scheme which has kept native trade solvent during the last few years of drought and misfortune by providing employment and putting money into the home market.'[8]

Taking the value of external trade as a whole as a criterion of prosperity, the last seven years had shown a continuous upward growth, and the value in 1928 was nearly double that of 1922. Cotton now overshadowed all other exports, its value in 1928 amounting to £E4 million, or some 70 per cent of that of all exports. The spending capacity of the country was increasing. Increased imports of cotton goods, tea, tobacco, motor vehicles, petrol and machinery were all signs of expanding wealth. Considerably more money was spent on sugar consumption and this was always a gauge of native prosperity, particularly in the cotton-producing areas. The eating of meat was becoming much more common and there was considerable evidence that the diminution in the export of sheep was due to increased consumption in the Sudan. All in all, although few satisfactory statistics were available to demonstrate it, there could be no doubt that the native standard of living was rising in many parts of the country.

For the tenants, crop areas in the Gezira Scheme had been mounting steadily to the following totals in feddans:

Season	Cotton	Dura	Lubia	Fallow	Total
1925-6	80,031	32,286	8,990	114,693	240,000
1926-7	100,058	50,091	49,017	103,092	302,258
1927-8	100,768	50,404	53,005	100,845	305,022
1928-9	131,292	65,334	57,478	143,526	397,640

the curve striking even more sharply upward with the planting of the 1929-30 crop.

| 1929-30 | 174,164 | 98,838 | 76,164 | 178,018 | 527,184 |

A poorish dura crop in the Scheme in 1927-8 had totalled 150,000 ardebbs. That of 1928-9 jumped to 250,000. The steady grain and forage from the irrigated area, in years when others were experiencing poor rains, continued to make the Scheme immensely attractive locally. There were large numbers of applications for tenancies on each extension, and labour was drawn to it as to a magnet, from districts alongside it, of the White Nile and Blue Nile, from Berber and Dongola (particularly for positions requiring skill and ability to read and write), from the western Sudan, from French Equatorial Africa, and from Nigerian pilgrims on their way to Mecca. In the Gezira villages tenancy credits in 1927-8 and 1928-9, even on lower yields than those of the exceptional opening years, were, thanks to better prices and quality, still averaging around the £100 mark per annum.

It was an immense contrast to former days! It may be worth while shifting for a moment to the human scene, as this writer recalls it. In the village of Medani Kawahla, where the sheikh had been the only man living in anything but a grass hut, his grandson Tayib Ahmed Medani was having a square house of mud bricks built for himself and his young bride, after the fashion, but not yet quite the size, of a town man's house. Nearby in Alim el Hoda village, Belal Mohammed was marrying young also, far younger than custom had permitted in the past, for both were typical of a new generation growing up with independent incomes of their own. Belal's bride was changing the fashion in clothes, for his father was the village shopkeeper and they had relatives in town. Her wedding dress had a beautiful embroidered waistcoat and crimson silk trousers caught at the ankles with silver anklets and she had a string of gold coins across her hair. Old Ahmed Abu Seneina looked at the wardrobe with six changes of clothing and recalled the days when a man had but one new garment in a year. Abdel Rahim Abdel Rahman, the sheikh of Wad Asha village, was spending some of his income on the pilgrimage and bringing back carpets from Arabia to refurnish his house. His friend, Mohammed Mustafa, had gone with him on the pilgrimage and taken his aged mother too, fulfilling the dearest wish of her life, and had paid four stalwart Tekruri slaves to carry her on her bed round the holy Kaaba in Mecca. The thoughts of many with new-found wealth turned first to their spiritual adviser and every appreciation pay-day witnessed tenants taking the train to Khartoum to pay their respects and contributions to the Shereef Yousif El Hindi, the particular patriarch of the central Gezira.

More mundane forms of investment were not hard to come by. Nur El Imam, of Heleiwa village, represented many who, starting with nothing, were now contractors for bull-ploughing and ran herds of sheep and goats on their own lubia and on any keep they could hire from their neighbours. Trading in dura had always been a popular line of business for anyone with capital. The principles were simple. One bought on an abundant harvest and held until a lean year. Irrigation might make the gain less sure, but there was an immense new field of trade in all kinds of consumer goods and the rising purchasing power was the smart man's opportunity. For the long-term investor with a shrewd eye on the distant future there was land. It was true that it was divorced from a tenancy, but if one could buy it for a £E1 a feddan, the Government's rent gave one a 10 per cent return, not much compared with other immediate opportunities, but no one could be sure what irrigated land would not be worth to the owner in the end. Some were cautious and held for a rainy day. Everyone had laughed at Mohammed el Kheir, bitterly bemoaning the three hundred pound notes which had gone up in smoke when his thatch caught fire. Anyway he was a foreigner from the west and notoriously close-fisted. Still, how was a man to keep this money concealed from his wife? Abder Rahman Teleiha had buried his in the ground, but even there the white ants had got at it.

Not all were successful. Beshir Sheikh Ahmed El Tereifi, of Talha village, had twenty-six tenancies in his own and brothers', sons', and servants' names, for he had been a big landowner, but it was not his line of country. The commercial management, the conception that the master's foot was the best manure for the crops, was too exacting for the aristocrat whose values inclined to the open hospitality and gracious living of a leisured class. Like many a contemporary in Britain his prestige waned, and in a competitive world he paid the penalty of losing most of his tenancies. Surprisingly enough not many shared his fate, for there was a virility in the people expressed in their own proverb, often spoken at the time: 'The seeker finds, but he who chooses leisure is lost.' No one, of course, could deal with bad luck. Dafalla El Araki had the tenancy at the end of the number just by the estate office. It was a beautiful crop of cotton and he had done all possible, by erecting bulls' horns along his field-channel, to avert the evil and envious eyes of all and sundry who came by on their donkeys and camels and compared it covetously with their own crops. Alas, it was of no avail. Gradually the leaves fell off until his cotton looked like rows of raspberry canes with little bunches of foliage at the top. It gave a miserable yield. They called it 'Hurug', from the same word root as 'fire' in Arabic, because it looked as if someone had put a flame through the field. But no one seemed to know how to stop it, or why other people's plants so affected seemed sometimes to recover. Still, there was always a chance that next year would be better.

Away in Britain the Syndicate's shareholders were reaping their sector of the prosperity. The capital had been increased in 1927 to £2,250,000 by the issue of 750,000 £1 shares, to pay for their side of the extension programme and to finance the vast cotton crops which were now being produced. Dividends were maintained at 25 per cent in 1928 and 1929 on the past season's results. At one of the Syndicate's annual meetings Hutton, the chairman of the British Cotton Growing Association, put in a word in season about its contribution to the partnership's prosperity. He began by explaining the arrangements for marketing the crop by consigning it to Liverpool for sale under the superintendence of the B.C.G.A.

As you all know, the B.C.G.A. is a philanthropic body run on sound commercial lines. They have only one object in view, namely the extension of cotton growing throughout the British Empire, and they are well aware that the best means of obtaining this object is to make it a profitable occupation for the grower. Consequently, thanks to their experience and also to their close touch with the Lancashire spinning trade, we are able to obtain the very best prices for our cotton. I am also glad to say, thanks largely to the B.C.G.A., Sudan cotton has now obtained a well-deserved reputation in the world market. . . . The whole of the work is done for a commission of 1 %, and the usual army of middle men, each of whom wants his profit, is entirely eliminated. I should also mention that the B.C.G.A. guarantee the payment for the cotton, a very important point with the present deplorable conditions in the cotton trade.[9]

'Looking down from the air the scene would be something like this.'

Aerial view of the Sennar Dam showing in right foreground the main canal, in the left foreground the Blue Nile river and in the background the reservoir

PLATE V

Aerial view of the layout of fields and canals on the Gezira Plain

PLATE VI

(i) Sir Alexander MacIntyre

(ii) Sir William Himbury

PLATE VII

'A Celebration in the Gezira'

PLATE VIII

In 1884 General Gordon had written in a dispatch, 'The Sudan is a useless possession, ever was so and ever will be so.' His chief-of-staff, Colonel Stewart, had endorsed the opinion.[10] Were they going to be right or was the Gezira partnership, with its unorthodox and imaginative new methods of development, to prove them wrong?

Chapter 12

DISEASE, DEBT AND DISASTER

The blow, when it came, was devastating. It hit the young economy of the country when it was outstretched like a runner getting into his stride and sent it reeling. And it hit at the two most vital spots: the yield and price of cotton.

The first enemy was *Xanthomonas malvacearum*, the scientific name not of some rare flower but of an insidious bacterial disease. Blackarm, as it was more commonly known, was the cause of the 'thing' which had ruined Dafalla El Araki's tenancy and reduced it to a row of raspberry canes. The bacterium, infecting the leaves and stems, caused the defoliation and, in severe cases, the death of the cotton plants. If there was no recovery the effect on yield was extremely serious. The phenomenon had been observed in the early days in Tayiba but only sporadically. It was attributed then to the vagaries of climate.

In 1918 a Gezira Research Farm had been started near Wad Medani, the capital of the Blue Nile Province, to study soil and water management, crop varieties, rotations, cultivation practices, fertilizer response and, of course, diseases and pests. With the setting up of this scientific station in the heart of the Gezira there began a close association between the back-room boys of the Research Farm and the field staff of the Syndicate, not at all times easy but always stimulating and destined to play a vital part in the survival of the Scheme.

It would not be possible, without greatly extending the scope of this story, to pay adequate tribute to much of the work or many of the scientists of the Gezira Research Farm. It was financed and staffed (with a small annual contribution from the Syndicate) by the Sudan Government, and later became the Agricultural Research Institute for the whole Sudan. In innumerable ways it played a continuously valuable part, and although here only the more dramatic moments can find mention it would be difficult to exaggerate the benefit brought by it. Its situation in the middle of the Scheme stimulated a two-way traffic.

Experimental discoveries on the Research Farm could be quickly applied in the field. Pests and problems of the field could be quickly given priority at the Research Institute.

Nor was it just a local research station, for it had connections with the Empire Cotton Growing Corporation and with the Rothamsted Experimental Station in Britain. These connections not only attracted staff of high calibre to the local research station but brought out scientific agriculturists of the highest class to visit and advise.

In 1924 Sir John Russell, F.R.S.* and Dr. Martin Leake† were invited to the Research Farm to suggest a basis of work, which Sir John Farmer, F.R.S.,‡ further elaborated in 1930. In 1925 Dr. E. M. Crowther, of the Rothamsted Experimental Station in Britain, stayed for several months at the Gezira Research Farm, advising on field experimentation. Thanks to his initiative the method of experimental layout evolved at Rothamsted by Professor R. A. Fisher§ was introduced in the Gezira in 1926, the year of its general adoption at Rothamsted. In 1928, Professor F. G. Gregory, F.R.S., of the Imperial College of Science and Technology, also worked for some months in the Gezira, advising on plant physiology experiments. These contacts with some of the foremost agricultural scientists in Britain were given a more permanent link by the setting up of a London Advisory Committee‖ on Agricultural Research, to review the work regularly and to criticize constructively year by year the programme of experiments.

But, while many outstanding men came in this way to be connected with the problems of Gezira agriculture, it was R. E. Massey, appointed in 1911 as the first government botanist, who more than any other scientist found himself called upon to discover the elusive causes of blackarm and to advise on their control.

In describing a fight against disease it is not easy, from the standpoint of later knowledge, to convey the baffling puzzle which it once

* Sir (Edward) John Russell, O.B.E., F.R.S., D.Sc. Director of Rothamsted Experimental Station, 1912–43.

† Dr. Martin Leake, D.Sc. Principal, Imperial College of Tropical Agriculture, 1924–7.

‡ Sir John Farmer (1865–1944), F.R.S., D.Sc. Director of Imperial College of Science and Technology: member Advisory Council Scientific Research and of Agricultural Research Council.

§ Sir R. A. Fisher, F.R.S., D.Sc. Expert on mathematical statistics. Professor of Genetics, Cambridge University, since 1943.

‖ Sir Edwin Butler, C.M.G., C.I.E., F.R.S., Sir Frank Engledow, C.M.G., and Dr. E. M. Crowther himself were for many years the chief technical members of the Committee.

presented. Blackarm was recorded by Massey in 1922 and was first mentioned in the Governor-General's reports as harming the yield of the 1923–4 cotton crop, which gave the lowest yield yet experienced at 2·8 kantars per feddan. In the following, 1924–5, season the yield fell to only 2·2 kantars. It had been hoped that treatment of the sowing seed by sulphuric acid as a fungicide would kill the blackarm but its recurrence, in spite of this treatment, suggested the presence of seed-borne internal infection. For the 1925–6 season, the first from the Sennar Dam, when the cotton area jumped to 80,000 feddans, entirely fresh seed was therefore imported from Egypt and from Tokar. The superb yield of 4·8, followed by 4·7 kantars in 1926–7, appeared to indicate that this measure had been effective.

A fall in yield of 33 per cent to 3·3 for the 1927–8 season was known to be affected by blackarm. It was difficult to see what had caused its recurrence, but once again unfavourable climatic conditions were thought to be responsible although the Research Farm now recorded it as an exceedingly dangerous cotton pest. In 1928–9 the yield improved to 3·6 which, although the crop was again affected by blackarm, was thought to be very satisfactory considering the large area now under cotton. But in 1929–30 the storm burst, both physically and metaphorically, and a very heavy rainy season revealed what had been hidden by light rain years and the continually expanding area. Surreptitiously but continuously blackarm bacteria had been penetrating from old land to new until, with climatic conditions in 1929 most favourable to its spread and continuance, it flared up everywhere and the average yield of the 1929–30 crop fell to 2·3 kantars.

There was another enemy to good yields besides blackarm. It was a virus disease called leaf curl. Instead of branching out and bearing flowers and bolls, the plants were sterile and spiralled upwards with incurling, crinkled leaves. A few such plants were noticed as isolated curiosities in the 1925–6 crop. There were patches of them in the two subsequent years, and in 1928–9 at the very end of the season it was noticed that leaf curl, although too late to be of much harm, was general everywhere. But once again it was the 1929–30 season which alerted all to the real danger. Like the bacteria, the virus seemed to have been spreading insidiously all the time and it seized on the new growth that year as soon as the plants were recovering from blackarm.

Massey ascertained that blackarm bacteria were at their most virulent stage under the temperature conditions prevailing in a heavy rain season and that the disease was rapidly transferred from plant to plant and field to field by the power of the wind during rainstorms. He also traced the carry-over of the bacteria in the infected volunteer seedlings which grew up in the previous season's cotton numbers. T. W. Kirkpatrick, the entomologist appointed to grapple with leaf curl, found that the virus was transferred by white fly, which bred in myriads, particularly in lubia. He also discovered that a major source of the carry-over of the virus lay in infected ratoon plants which sprouted in the lubia crop from the previous season's cotton planting.

These discoveries prompted the next attempts to control the danger. The 1929 rains had been exceptional, double the normal incidence. It seemed reasonable to hope that if the 1930 rains were not above average and if the tenants put in a special effort to cut out in the rains any seedlings and ratoon plants, a break might be made in the carry-over circuit and the power of the two diseases crippled.

A stop to the rot was certainly needed. The poor yield had been a shock, but this was now aggravated by a heavy fall in cotton prices due to falling world demand. At the end of 1929 MacIntyre wrote to Sir Arthur Huddleston,* who had succeeded Sir George Schuster as Financial Secretary.

I think we shall have a difficult year in the Gezira, and I think it right that you should know this before you complete your budget. Owing to the exceptionally heavy rains the crop is very late and backward, and Blackarm is unduly spread all over and has done a lot of damage everywhere. There is a very large proportion of very late sown cotton and this cold weather will retard its growth and it will probably be too late to obtain anything but a poor yield.

Financially, the world seems to be in a very criticial condition and new money will be very difficult to obtain for undertakings. It looks as if more taxation will have to be imposed at home, which will be a further burden on industry which is in a bad enough state as it is, and this will not help cotton or seed prices.

With all these things on the horizon, I consider that economies in every direction ought to be the order of the day.[1]

The prospect was depressing. Instead of the usual surplus the 1929–30 Gezira crop was estimated to result for the Government in a deficiency of £E350,000, and this at a time when it was faced with all the ancillary commitments of the recent economic development, and with its loan funds and part of its reserves fully pledged for the extensions. In addition the poor yield was bound to cause a contraction in the indirect

* Sir Arthur Huddleston (1880–1948), C.M.G., O.B.E. Governor of Blue Nile Province, 1922–7: Financial Secretary, Sudan, 1928–31: Director of Royal Technical College, Glasgow, 1933–45.

revenue from customs and rail traffic, and a falling-off in receipts from trade in a more than local manner.

In the middle of 1929 the average selling price of the good 1928–9 crop was around 21 pence per lb. By the end of that year this average had fallen to 18 pence, but by then most of that crop had been disposed of. By the time the 1929–30 crop had been harvested the price had fallen to 15 pence and showed no signs of halting there.

An even more disturbing feature began to appear: it became more and more difficult to sell cotton at all. By July 1930 the customary date had been reached for paying the tenants the first profits on the 1929–30 crop, but next to nothing had been sold, and it became a matter of extreme difficulty to make the usual conservative forecast of the final selling price, or *pro forma* valuation as it was called, upon which the tenant's profits distribution must be based. Huddleston, in a note to MacIntyre, thought that 14½ pence per lb. might be taken as a reasonable probability.[2] Even this figure, on the wretched yield of 2·3 kantars per feddan, only equalled a net divisible return of £E5 per feddan, compared with that target of £E10 per feddan still needed to cover Government's outgoings, even when the extensions had been completed, and which, only a year ago, had seemed such a safe figure to aim for. MacIntyre suggested a lower *pro forma*, 10½ pence per lb., equal to a net divisible return of £E3·7 per feddan. But with terrifying rapidity the deterioration in the world's economic life made a mockery of all these figures. By January 1931, when the crop of the 1930–1 season was beginning to be harvested, the price of cotton had fallen to 7½ pence per lb.If yet another disastrous yield occurred, it would give rise to very grave anxiety.

It did occur. The measures taken to combat blackarm and leaf curl proved totally inadequate and the yield of the 1930–1 crop dropped to all-time low at 1·4 kantars per feddan. The long-desired expansion to the 200,000 feddans of cotton had been attained. This, at a yield of 3 kantars and a price of 10½ pence, would have paid its way. The difficulties of water and finance had been overcome. To double the acreage since 1925 only a fifth of the original capital cost had been required. 196,000 feddans had been planted. But the yield that transpired had fallen to about a quarter, and the price to about a third, of the 1925–6 season. The extent of the contrast is revealed by the following figures:

Season	1925–6	1926–7	1929–30	1930–1
Yield per feddan	4·79	4·74	2·3	1·4
Estimated price in pence per lb.	16	18	8	6
Net divisible return per feddan	£E28·5	£E33	£E5	£E1·7

A terrible gap had thus to be bridged.

'The course of events', wrote Sir John Maffey* in his Governor-General's report for 1930, 'has temporarily shaken the confidence in the financial soundness of the Gezira Scheme, with the success of which the prosperity of the Government is so closely bound up. We may conceivably be forced into the position that for many years to come we shall have to regard the Gezira as on the whole a liability to be liquidated by annual subsidies, not only from the direct receipts attributable to the Scheme, but also from the normal administrative revenues of the Government.'[3] But these in turn were in trouble. The external trade of the Sudan, which in 1929 amounted to £E13,665,000, fell in 1931 to £E5,646,000. It had totalled £E3,400,000 in 1913. This gives a measure of how far the clock was being set back. The revenue in 1931 fell short of the estimate by over a million pounds. The deficit was met by drafts of £E541,000 on the Gezira Equalization Account, of £E238,000 on the Railway Renewals Account, of £E167,000 on the General Reserve Account. The balance was scraped up from sundry small accounts.

It was clear that further and more drastic measures of economy were called for if rapid depletion of the liquid assets of the Government was to be prevented. In August 1931 a Treasury official from Britain, H. E. Fass,† took over the Financial Secretaryship from Huddleston, and a sub-committee of the Governor-General's Council recommended measures of retrenchment expected to result in savings of £E720,000 a year. Higher customs duties were imposed and the price of sugar increased. New well-boring and water-storage schemes, new hospitals and medical expansion were postponed. Rail and postal services were curtailed. A thousand classified posts, 20 per cent of the government staff including 207 British, were retrenched. In addition the strength of British officers in the Sudan Defence Force was reduced from 152 to 91. All these retrenchments threw heavier burdens on those who were left. Nevertheless their salaries were reduced by from 5 to 10 per cent. Allowances hitherto regarded as recognized emoluments were abolished and the charge for amenities provided by Government was increased. The retrenchments, salary cuts, and reduction of amenities on the part

---

* Sir John Maffey, first Baron Rugby, G.C.M.G., K.C.B., etc. Indian Civil Service, 1899–1905: Governor-General, Sudan, 1926–33: permanent Under-Secretary of State for Colonies, 1933–7: U.K. Representative to Eire, 1939–49.

† Later Sir H. E. Fass, K.C.M.G., C.B. Board of Education, 1909: Treasury, 1915: seconded to Sudan as Financial Secretary, 1931–4, to lead retrenchment drive (in Arabic his name means axe!): Public Trustee, 1934–44: Custodian of Enemy Property for England and Wales, 1939–44.

of the Government were matched by similar measures among the Syndicate's staff while the dividend to shareholders, reduced to 10 per cent in 1930, was omitted altogether in the following two years.

But even then the end was not in sight. At the close of 1931, 30 per cent of the 1929-30 crop and 60 per cent of the 1930-1 crop were still unsold and, what was worse, no one could be quite certain how to overcome blackarm and leaf curl, or even whether the trouble was more radical and that measures to control disease were furnishing no remedy because the soil was in progressive deterioration.

Certain soil scientists had all along distrusted the effect of irrigation on the heavy Gezira land with its 60 per cent clay content, high alkalinity, and marked deficiency in organic matter and nitrogen. They had feared that waterlogging and accumulation of salts in the upper layers might lead to a rapid deterioration in fertility, and they recalled instances in other countries where land had gone out of cultivation after a few years of irrigation. The miserable appearance of the Gezira at this nadir in its fortunes certainly lent colour to these fears. Within the incredibly short space of six years the virgin land which had started with such splendid crops appeared to be worthless, filthy with weed and foul with disease. The raspberry-cane effect of blackarm, removing the lateral branches of the cotton plants and leaving only a small bunchy top of foliage, exposed the soil to continuous sunlight which at each irrigation stimulated the competitive growth of a forest of weeds. Normally weeding had ceased after three intensive operations during the planting period. Now it became a continuous duty, and with the certainty of lower profits and on reduced loans the tenants inevitably shirked it: indeed, of what avail was such work when the diseased cotton itself seemed to lack the vitality to take advantage of it?

Moreover there was a certain weed which had increased with irrigation like a cancer on the land, *Cyperus rotundus*, a nut-grass locally known as seid, which no surface weeding could eradicate. Its underground structure was made up of roots and tubers interconnected by rhizomes to a depth of fifteen inches. Crops planted in seid remained hopelessly stunted. Its spread was causing land to pass out of cultivation, and the only effective form of control was expensive mechanical ploughing in depth.

A certain hold over the standard of agricultural work was always possible on the cotton crop as long as the tenants could look to individual loans appropriate to each cultural operation. Their dura and lubia crops, however, were their own property and no specific loans were advanced for their cultivation. Consequently standards of work in these crops had always been lower than in cotton. Less cash from profits and from loans now made tenants more reluctant than ever to dip into their own pockets to finance a clean standard of work in these crops, and this, along with the weed growth, led to a falling off in these crop yields also. The lubia crop, in particular, which had jumped to 98,000 feddans in 1929–30 and 111,000 feddans in 1930–1, passed beyond the capacity and interest of the tenants to treat as a farm crop any longer. Weeds grown on free irrigation water could, after all, keep their animals alive at no expense at all. But the dura and lubia crops were being grown on the previous season's cotton land, and it was in such cultivation conditions, over some 200,000 feddans, that the tenants had to be induced to hunt out and eradicate infected seedlings and ratoons in addition to their other work in the rains.

The country could not possibly afford yet a third crop failure, and there now arose a certain divergence of opinion between the scientists and the field executives on the question of rotation. All scientists had been agreed that, in the peculiar circumstances of Gezira soil, the inclusion of a leguminous crop like lubia was indispensable in the rotation. On the Research Farm, operated without costings by direct labour, it was possible to ensure eradication of seedling and ratoon and establishment of good lubia and dura crops, and there was no scientific reason for supposing that a change in rotation would help matters. MacIntyre felt that something must be done to break the choking combination of weeds, disease and costs. A wider rotation, from which for the moment the farcical lubia crop might be omitted and in which the dura might be grown in some other place than on last year's cotton land, might kill two birds with one stone. By not irrigating last season's land the amount of seedling and ratoon might be enormously reduced, and the task of seeing and eradicating it made more feasible. By leaving two year's fallow before the cotton crop more time might be given for weeds to die out (reducing the need of mechanical ploughing), and for land to dry out from excessive irrigation.

The Syndicate's view was accepted with some reserve and the rotation was changed. At Zeidab, long ago, the Syndicate had changed its original close rotation in a similar manner, and had thereby lowered its costs and increased its yields. But Zeidab had been its own estate, in which it could do what it liked. In the Gezira the abolition of lubia, and the concentration of dura in blocks no longer adjacent to each man's cotton tenancy, might well raise opposition from the tenants as well as the scientists, for the immediate disadvantages to their own personal crops were clear, while the advantage to the cotton was in the partnership crop and anyway problematic. The Governor-General's report of 1929, when the first onset of the depression halted the economic progress, deplored the set-back as 'discouraging the somewhat scanty initiative of a simple and fatalistic people at a time when roads and motorcars in the new areas into which they were penetrating were just beginning to widen the horizon, creating fresh wants and giving new stimulus to life'.[4] By 1931 it was the fatalism rather than the initiative which was the virtue. While the British staff sought desperately for solutions the patience and calm of the indigenous people, facing often with remarkable cheerfulness the complete reversal of their fortunes, weighed in with a solid contribution to survival.

The banishment of lubia and the blocking of dura were not the only devices planned with the planting of the 1931-2 crop. Once again a complete sweep was made of all old seed and a new supply was imported from Egypt. It was treated with 'Ababit B', a new mercuric disinfectant sought out and tested on the Research Farm. Furthermore, Massey had noticed that the intensity of blackarm was related to the actual number of storms which a plant experienced. So a delayed sowing date had the advantage of exposing the cotton to fewer storms. The Syndicate kept records of the annual yield of every cotton tenancy and the incidence of rain on some 150 rain-gauges covering the Scheme. Observation in the field and examination of these records confirmed Massey's view and led to the adoption of a planned sowing programme. Everything had to be concentrated, because sowing after the end of August meant poorer yield, poorer grade and late development, when leaf-curl risk would be wider spread. And so, in the 1931-2 season, nothing was sown until 1st August, only 23 per cent by the 15th, but 88 per cent by the 31st. Each tenancy had its particular planned date, those adjacent to areas of last year's heavy blackarm infection being placed last. In addition an intensive drive was maintained against all seedling and ratoon which might sprout from rain on the last season's cotton numbers.

To the intense relief of the whole country these measures were successful. The soil pessimists were proved wrong and an excellent average yield of 4·1 kantars per feddan was obtained over 194,000 feddans. Blackarm was, in spite of everything, extensive but the penetration was slight and recovery good. One of the most heartening features was the comparative absence of leaf curl. On such a crop even a price of $7\frac{1}{2}$ pence per lb. would enable the 1932 budget to be balanced, while every additional penny per lb. would put £E120,000 to government reserves. Price and rate of sales were beyond the control of the Sudan, but at least the sneaking fear of progressive deterioration in the soil had been belied.

There was, by now, another and even more pressing reason to be thankful for the recovery in the field. The tenants were getting hopelessly into debt, but unless the Syndicate continued to finance them with loans they could not be expected to carry on, while without them the Scheme would collapse. This problem led to a bitter difference of opinion between the Syndicate and the Government, and to explain this it is necessary to describe the relevant accountancy.

It will be recalled that the Syndicate made small loans to the tenant at each stage of cultivation. These, with the cost of ploughing and seed, were debited to his account. Very large sums of money from the Syndicate's working capital were needed for these loans but normally, except for a small proportion of bad debts, they would be repaid when the cotton crop was sold. The bad debts left outstanding were, in accordance with the 1929 Agreement, debited to the General Tenants' Cotton Share Account and this corporate form of security was held to be justified because the amount of residual bad debts was expected to be so small that the disadvantage to the tenants was likely to be far less than any alternative system of carrying the risk. In fact up till 1929 the bad debts were of negligible importance, as the following figures show.[5]

Bad debts left outstanding against the General Tenants' Cotton Share Account at the end of the season (these were still liable to collection from the individuals concerned from future years' profits).	1925–6	1926–7	1927–8	1928–9
	£E	£E	£E	£E
	132	20	86	277

But when the preliminary valuation was fixed for payment of profits for the 1929–30 crop it appeared that, with the low yield, bad debts would be abnormal, and with the falling market the estimated price might prove too high, so that the General Tenants' Cotton Share Account might itself be in debt.

However, it looked a temporary difficulty at that early stage, and Huddleston, in agreeing to MacIntyre's suggested preliminary valuation, had written: 'We consider that in the interests of the Scheme as a whole it would be wrong to fix lower prices which would discourage the tenants to an undesirable extent in a year of very low yields.'[6] There was at the time an outstanding credit of £E158,000 due to tenants on account of the final appreciation on the 1928-9 crop. Instead of being paid out in cash this sum was credited to the individual tenants' 1929-30 accounts as well as the preliminary valuation, so as to reduce the bad debts. The bulk of the tenants thus had a profit which would see them through to the next harvest and, to minimize debt risks, new cash loans prior to harvest were cut to £E5 per tenant. It was hoped in this way to fight the economic blizzard.

In fact, what happened was that an arrangement made to deal with the possibility of a debit balance, due to one low crop and to over-estimating the preliminary credit by a penny a pound or so, had to meet a situation where the price fell from the 14½ pence per lb. thought by Huddleston to be a 'reasonable probability' in June 1930,[7] to 7½ pence by January 1931, and where a second, even more disastrous, crop failure was encountered.

The full seriousness of the debt position became apparent by January 1931 and its financial magnitude continued to grow as prospective prices for the unsold 1929-30 crop and new 1930-1 crop dropped even further. By contrast with the small debts of previous years, the figures now became staggering. The individual tenants' debts, after the passing of the preliminary valuation for the 1929-30 crop, amounted to £E56,000, but on top of this the General Tenants' Cotton Share Account for that year was overdrawn by £E197,000 because the actual sale price was so much less than the preliminary valuation. In addition to this estimated total of £E244,000 of debt on the 1929-30 crop, a further £E326,000 of debt was incurred on account of the loans of the 1930-1 crop.

Therefore the Syndicate had to face the prospect, at a time when its own income was badly affected, of continuing to support the tenants with loans which for the moment there was no prospect of their repaying. The Syndicate was especially bitter over this as it had previously urged that part of the appreciations paid out to the tenants should be set aside to form a Tenants' Equalization Fund, to meet the problem of debt, but the Government had argued that it was unfair to ask individual tenants to contribute to a fund to cover debts which they themselves had not incurred.

MacIntyre now raised the matter again in January 1931. He urged that unless some equitable scheme could be evolved, it would appear practically impossible to finance tenants already heavily in debt, carry two crops which were practically unsold and go on incurring heavy expenditure with the preparation of a third crop. The Government and Syndicate had each its own reserve funds, but the only provision in the agreement for the tenants was that in clause 28 relating to a rise in their share, of which the Government was to bear the first $2\frac{1}{2}$ per cent and thereafter two-thirds and the Syndicate one-third. Rather than raise the tenants' share in order to meet the temporary crisis of a world slump and two bad crops he suggested that the Government and Syndicate should pay into the tenants' cotton account the sum needed to meet their debts up to a maximum of £E450,000, which then seemed sufficient.[5] Each party would make their contribution to this loan as they would have had to do under clause 28. The loan was to be recovered by suitable machinery when cotton prices had improved, proper provision to this effect being introduced into the Tenancy Agreement.

After some argument the Government accepted this suggestion, but on condition that contributions to the fund were made equally by the Syndicate and Government.[9] The Board of the Syndicate accepted this condition and for the time being the question of raising the tenants' share was dropped.[10]

Alas, this compromise could not solve the problem. The slowness of sales and the continuing fall in price pushed the inevitable debt right over the agreed maximum. By October 1931 it had been exceeded by £E100,000 and the Government agreed to raise it to £E550,000.[11] By June 1932 a current valuation of sold and unsold stocks of the 1929–30 and 1930–1 crops left the bad debts of those years at over £E600,000. The Scheme was now getting even deeper into difficulty. The 1931–2 crop had given a good yield and the tenants would expect a profit from it. It was the time for fixing the preliminary valuation but the price at Liverpool had dropped to 6 pence a lb. When marketing costs of 2·3 pence were deducted from this, the tenants' 40 per cent share of the balance would only amount to $1\frac{1}{2}$ pence per lb. or 60 piastres per kantar. A tenant with the average of 4 kantars per feddan could thus only get a credit of £E24, which would not cover his cultivation and picking loans. Additional debts must be expected therefore on this crop also and only the exceptional tenants could expect a profit.

MacIntyre approached the Government once again. Would they agree to continue with the fifty-fifty arrangement?[12] Not merely to cover the exceeded maximum of the two bad years, but also the potential bad debts of 1931–2 and even for 1932–3, for a loans policy must be decided for the new crop. If the tenants got no profit after the good 1931–2 crop

Changes in Gezira Rotations

Year	Gezira rotation	Average Price	Average Yield	CANAL 8	7	6	5	4	3	2	No. 1
1925–26	1st Gezira rotation	18d	4·8					C	F¹⁰	D⁵	C¹⁰ / D
1926–27		18	4·7			F / D	D / L	D / L	C / D	L⁵	L / D
1927–28		19·7	3·3			C	F	F	C	F	F
1928–29		18·4	3·6			D / L	C	C / D	D / L	C / D	C / D
1929–30		7·9	2·3			F	D / L	F	F	D / L	F / L
1930–31		6·4	1·4			C	F	C	C	F	C
1931–32	2nd Gezira rotation	8·5	4·1	F / D	C¹⁰	F	F	F	F	C¹⁰	F
1932–33		8·1	1·9		F	C	F	C	C	F	C / D
1933–34	3rd Gezira rotation	8·6	2·3	L	F	L	F	⁵D / D⁵	F	F / D	F
1934–35		8·2	4·5	F	F	F	C	L	C	D / L	C
1935–36		7·9	3·7	C	C	C	F	F	F	F	F
1936–37		8·6	4·5	F	F	F	L	C	C	L	C
1937–38		5·9	4·6	F	C / D	C	F	F	F	F	F
1938–39		6·2	4·5		F / D	C	D / L	C	L	C	C
1939–40		9·6	3·8	F	L / D	F / D	F	F	F	F	D / D
1940–41		8·9	4·0	C	F	D / D	F	F	C	F	L

1. This diagram illustrates the annual cropping through the years of two adjacent tenancies.

2. In the first Gezira rotation one tenant's holding was in Nos. 1–3 of the canal, the other tenant in Nos. 4–6. This rotation was self-contained and compact but broke down for reasons explained in the text.

3. In the second Gezira rotation the tenants continued in their same canal numbers, but they were allowed no lubia, and their dura was concentrated away from their tenancies in large blocks of land taken out of the rotation for dura. No fallow land was allotted for dura, the continuous cropping of which, coupled with no provision for lubia, meant that this rotation was suited only to a short emergency.

4. In the third Gezira rotation, which continued, dura and lubia were returned to the rotation. Dura now followed a fallow period, while cotton followed two fallows or a lubia and a fallow. This enhanced the yields, particularly of dura. The system was lavish with land but sparing with water.

Its greatest drawback was its lack of compactness. The tenant from Nos. 1–3 now rotated his cotton in Nos. 1–4, and the tenant from Nos. 4–6 in Nos. 5–8. The gross area of each unit increased from 30 to 40 feddans. But although the cotton was confined to the four fields of a tenancy, the dura and lubia ranged over the eight fields of two tenancies, and every other year a tenant had to plant his dura and lubia in his neighbour's numbers.

plants on each tenancy. They had had no profit now for three crops, and could obviously expect nothing from this fourth one with its additional fatigue of root-pulling. Fatalism was indeed a virtue and perhaps it was just as well that the best known of their many proverbs was 'It is a dog that barks. A camel keeps on going.'

During 1932 discussions had been going on between the Government and the Syndicate to devise a new permanent rotation, for it was clear that the emergency step taken in 1931 of blocking the dura and banishing the lubia was only temporizing with the problem. Although it provided two years of fallow preceding cotton, it allowed no fallow at all for dura and no lubia at all for the tenants. Both crops had somehow to be reincorporated in as compact a holding as possible and yet avoiding those features which might encourage disease. This difficult problem led once again to divergence of opinion between the research scientists and the field officers of the Syndicate. If the dura and lubia were brought back into a three-year rotation they had to be grown either immediately before the cotton, to its known detriment, or immediately after, when the water supplied to them would encourage ratoon and seedling. Inadequate fallowing by watering for two seasons out of three might also be detrimental to the soil and increase the need for ploughing weeds.

A complex eight-year rotation was devised by the Syndicate to meet the difficulties.* It involved two tenants operating together over eight numbers, instead of each tenant having his own three numbers, and to this extent was a sacrifice in personal proprietorship and compactness. It also involved the individual tenancy unit going up from thirty to forty feddans gross, but the areas of its crops remaining as before, with cotton at ten and dura and lubia at five feddans each per tenant. The cotton acreage thus fell from one-third to one-quarter of the gross area, with a consequent diminution in the number of tenants by some two thousand five hundred in the Scheme as a whole. With the hard times, although the bulk of the tenants held on, some locals had deserted in discouragement, and some from other parts of the Sudan had returned home. Many of these had been replaced by 'westerners', mainly Borgu from French Equatorial Africa, who were often temporary immigrants. Their retrenchment and the elimination of waverers in general was felt to be no hardship.

But a financial problem arose in the implied reduction in the cotton

* A diagram of the rotation is given on pages 152-3 with an explanation of how it worked between two adjacent sets of tenants compared with the previous rotations.

area from 194,000 to 167,000 feddans. If it could be assumed that the land would give the same yield of cotton on a three-year rotation, which included dura, as on the proposed new eight-year rotation, then the Government would clearly lose by the latter. But if, as the Syndicate maintained, a three-year rotation which included dura would involve a falling off in yield of at least half a kantar a feddan then, with cotton at 8 pence a lb. and a yield of three kantars, Government would just gain by the eight-year rotation. The calculation revealed a notable diminution in the probability of tenants' indebtedness under the wider rotation. At 8 pence a lb. a yield of 3·25 on 167,000 feddans would cause £E3,000 of debt, while a yield of 2·75 on 194,000 feddans would cause £E31,000 of debt. At 7 pence a lb., the figures would be £E37,500 and £E109,000 respectively. This reasoning clinched the matter. It was felt that the effect of the change on the individual tenant must be good. He would have a better chance of profit. He would get more grain and get it more conveniently, and he would get back the lubia which he had lost in 1931.*

By now the 1933–4 crop was due for planting. Once again entirely new seed was brought from Egypt and treated with ababit. And for this 1933–4 crop two new advantages applied. It was grown, for the first time in the history of the Gezira, after two preceding fallows. And it followed a crop that had been pulled out. From the point of view of blackarm, fertility and leaf curl it looked a good bet. A very critical change was, however, made in the technique of sowing. As a result of the depressing experience of late sowing in the past season the policy of a delayed and planned sowing programme was abandoned, and a return was made to sowing from 1st August. The year was dry and sowing went quickly. Fifteen per cent was in by 5th August, 32 per cent by the 10th. This early sowing undoubtedly gave rise to considerable blackarm, and

---

* At the same time, as a check on the decision, one estate was continued on a modified form of three-year rotation suggested by M. A. Bailey, Controller of the Research Institute. The Gezira has continued ever since on the wide rotation although time was to prove that there was hardly 10 per cent difference in the cotton yields. The dura yield, however, appreciated by 50 per cent under the wider rotation owing to the preceding fallow provided for it. It became possible also gradually to get the land much cleaner.

As population pressure has increased in the Gezira, the tendency has been to split the forty-feddan unit into two tenancies and to use more fertiliser, rather than to revert to a three-course rotation, which today would involve remodelling the canal system to carry the extra water. In the Manāgil extension, however, due to be first opened in 1958, it is intended to adopt a three-course rotation and a smaller gross area per tenant so as to reduce dependence on outside labour and cater for more tenants.

heavy late rains in September and October spread the disease from which in many places the crop never recovered. It was a bad year again, with a yield of only 2·3. But there was one bull point. Leaf curl was negligible. Pulling out had largely eliminated ratoon, and the result was striking. Although by careful search infected plants were found in the crop, highly correlated with ratoon survivals, it was not until very late in the season that the disease became noticeable.

It was, though none yet knew it, the turning of the road. The years of endurance were over and the patient search for the techniques which could control the two dread diseases and bring back fertility was at last going to pay its dividend. Other pests were destined to bring anxiety in the future but in no comparable manner. The 1934-5 crop, for which a planned sowing programme was again introduced, gave a yield of 4·5 kantars. It marked the beginning of a recovery from the run of bad crops to a long run of good crops. Looking back later, it was astonishing how often particular changes in technique, which had seemed the hoped-for panacea, had turned out a disappointment. It was the planned combination of all these techniques which gradually overcame the legacy which the quick degeneration had bequeathed.

1934-5 added two more pieces to the pattern. In that year yet another task was put on the tenant. After pulling out, all debris was swept up by hand—a laborious process on ten feddans—and included in the burning, as a further control against blackarm. And, most significant of all, a new variety of cotton, resistant to both blackarm and leaf curl, was tried out on 12,800 feddans scattered all over the Scheme. It gave a yield of 5·3 compared with the 4·3 of all the rest, indicating its astonishing recuperative and high-yielding power in the deep rich soil of the southern Gezira. The botanist at the Research Farm, A. R. Lambert, searching in 1930 among the sakel plants, selected a few which appeared to develop late and would expose less foliage to early blackarm. They were found to be resistant also to leaf curl. Passed on to Bailey for breeding up, the new variety took its name from its number in the progeny lines—X1530 and X1730—but the symbol 'L' on Gezira bales, well known today in most long-staple cotton mills in the world, and the variety 'Lambert' in the Sudan cotton quotations, perpetuate the name of its discoverer.

The measures necessary to combat disease entailed the most rigid supervision by the field officers and the people themselves epitomized this in one of their sayings:

The man on the East Bank is free like a nomad. The man on the West Bank is like a soldier in a camp.

156

But curiously enough they did not necessarily dislike it. The Blue Nile Province report for 1934, at the end of the long run of bad years, has this record:

The financial position of some tenants, particularly in the Northern area, has improved. The demand for tenancies there exceeds the supply, and people living outside the Scheme clamour for their land to be included in the rented area. The inhabitants of the province have awakened to the fact that tenancies which they surrender are eagerly taken up by Westerners, and ex-tenants are anxious to have a second chance. Total profits issued to the tenants during the year were over £E85,000. Advances for work done total over £E383,000, and include an average of nearly £E16 cash per tenant. Over £E73,000 was paid in rent. This makes a grand total of over half a million pounds put into direct circulation by the cotton scheme. The actual profit made by the average tenant is admittedly small, but seems sufficient to encourage the hope of better times to come.[16]

It was all a matter of relativity, and in the general economic stagnation it was still better to be in the Scheme and put up with the discipline than to be out of it. £E85,000 profit might be small compared with the million pounds a year of the early years. But one got the guaranteed food crop, now enhanced in yield by the new rotation, and one got the Syndicate's loans.

But how was this vital loan service being continued and what had happened about the debt problem?

The stalemate between Syndicate and Government continued but a ray of external light now softened the gloom. The price of cotton moved slightly upward. In April 1933 it was possible to fix a preliminary valuation for the good 1931-2 crop at 7 pence a lb. The resulting bad debts of £E33,000 were almost extinguished when the crop actually averaged a sale price of 8½ pence. Even the debts of the bad 1932-3 crop, which at one time looked like totalling £E144,000, ended up at £E50,000 when the crop sold at an average of 8 pence. Negotiations continued and a draft ancillary agreement was made out in October 1933, 'to substitute a more workable plan, when returns to tenants were inadequate, and to legalise the establishment of an Equalisation Fund and the treatment of tenants as a corporate body'. By January 1934, when yet again a poor yield was apparent from the 1933-4 crop, even MacIntyre was nearly in despair. He had all along really preferred the Equalization Fund solution as being more practicable for the debt problem than a rise in the tenant's share. But now his own board of directors began to have doubts. He wrote to Fass in May 1934,

One of my main difficulties over the Ancillary Agreement is that the Syndicate Board regard it as an attempt to make the tenants provide, out of their share of the crop, sufficient funds for an Equalisation Fund, whereas on yields and prices since 1930, the tenants' share has not been sufficient to pay for growing the crops.[17]

Indeed in February 1934 Asquith, on behalf of the Board, had drawn up a masterly résumé, pressing again the case for a rise in the tenant's share, and had had it forwarded to the Governor-General.[18] The Syndicate Board, he said, had a feeling that the Sudan Government was not trying to work the existing agreement but was trying to improve on the bargain it made in 1926. The past four years' difficulties had arisen owing to the fall in prices and in some of those years to low yields. The problem was twofold: firstly to provide the tenants with enough to repay advances and to leave a reasonable profit as an incentive to continue efficiently, and secondly to build up an Equalization Fund to protect tenants against bad seasons in future and to make good to the Syndicate and Government the £E600,000 advanced for 1929–30 and 1930–1. The second problem would not have arisen if a reserve fund had been created as suggested by the Syndicate. It had been turned down on the grounds that the tenants could not be treated collectively, but it was now clear that this difficulty could have been overcome by provision in the tenancy agreement. Indeed, in their original 1919 agreement the Syndicate had been entitled to charge the tenants a rate of interest sufficient to establish a sinking-fund to cover bad debts, and in this sense the principle of treating the tenants collectively and of assuring to the Syndicate protection against loss on bad debts had been established. In the 1926 agreement the same principle was upheld when, in place of the previous arrangement, the Syndicate was empowered to deduct from any money payable to the tenants 'debts owed by tenants written off as bad less sums recovered'.

Without some increase in the tenant's share and with prices at present level it was impossible for the tenants to repay advances, get a fair profit and contribute to an Equalization Fund. The memorandum concluded by suggesting that, from the 1932–3 season onwards, the Syndicate and Government should agree to such an increase as provided in the main agreement. Once this had been agreed it should not be difficult to agree the scale of a levy on future tenants' profits in varying circumstances, and the allocation of such a levy towards future protection and past indebtedness.

The memorandum was never answered. The tenant's share was not raised. The clauses concerning it in the agreement were not cancelled. The Equalization Fund was eventually legalized by a supplementary agreement signed in 1937. By then good yields were beginning to restore confidence. And the story of what happened about the £E600,000 of debt and then, on top of it, the £E50,000 from 1932–3, followed by another £E50,000 of debt from 1933–4, belongs to the history of the years of recovery. But the unresolved argument left for a long time a certain coolness between the Syndicate and the Government, each side feeling that the other had been less than punctilious in its obligations. What the tenants thought was not made vocal until much later. They were still in the nursery.

Chapter 13

THE SLOW RECOVERY

In the preface I have claimed that the development of the Gezira was more like the natural history of a river than the growth of a mechanical structure. The reader has seen from the beginning how intermixed were social, political and economic motives in the setting up of the Gezira Scheme. Harmony had been sought by the partnership pattern adopted, but naturally at different periods in its history different aspects predominated. In the first period (Part 1) were described the various tributaries of influence which converged to determine the peculiar pattern of the project. In the second period (Part 2), which carries the story on to 1946, the river of development started off as one confident stream but ran into the desert of depression just described. Henceforth this period was dominated by the need for economic recovery, the story of which is told in this chapter. Closely connected with it were the problems of research and marketing which came to light in this period, and chapters on them follow next. But the most fascinating phenomenon, and in the end the most powerful, was in this decade still underneath the surface. This was the history of the people, of the different views of what their society ought to be like, and of their own emergence from the nursery. Chapters 16 and 17 are concerned with this phenomenon. Underneath the surface of a very gradual financial recovery the currents of these subjects pass and repass, interacting on each other until, at the end of the decade, and in the next part of the book, the river sweeps into a cataract of new ebullience.

The economic future of the Gezira was not rated very high by outsiders in the depth of the depression. The *Egyptian Cotton Year Book* in 1932–3, in an article 'Sakellarides Cotton Growing in the Anglo-Egyptian Sudan', forecast that Sudan sakels would never compete with Egyptian because of the high cost of production and because of the Sudan's uncertain future as a cotton-producing country of importance. Local opinion in the Gezira was not much different. A report of the

160

Governor of the Blue Nile Province noted that during the recent years of low cotton prices and erratic yields the cultivation of cotton seemed to the tenants a hopeless labour, and many of them were only kept on their land by the prospect of an assured, irrigated grain crop. The condition of the country outside the Gezira was described as a plethora of grain, meat and milk but a complete lack of cash.[1]

There was, however, one advantage in this state of affairs. It brought down local costs to a minimum and made even small profits valuable. As long as loans continued and some profit was paid a tenancy, with its irrigated grain crop thrown in, tended to give a better standard of living than could be obtained outside it. It was on these terms that a gradual haul out of the slough of despond was accomplished. But they depended all the time on getting a consistent yield and no more debts. Price made little contribution at this stage to prosperity. Indeed, in that respect the situation cast an ironical doubt on the virtue of estimates. For the Scheme, which had been planned on an estimated minimum of 15 pence per lb. as the average sale price, had not only to withstand the sudden fall to 7·9 pence on the 1929–30 crop, but it never saw 15 pence again for fifteen years. It had to manage with a maximum of 10·6 pence until after 1946, and in the years immediately preceding the second world war the price fell to an even lower level than in the depression, with an average of only 5·9 pence for the 1937–8 and 6·2 pence for the 1938–9 crop.

It is interesting to make a pause at 1946, which marks the end of the recovery period, and see how the partners had fared up to that date. After 1946 the story enters the post-war era and changes in prices and policies make it convenient to treat that as a separate period. The tables at the end of Chapter 20, which show the final results of the partnership when the Companies' concession ended in 1950, also give the position year by year, with a subtotal in 1946 to demonstrate this distinction.

The table on page 271 shows the Companies' (S.P.S. and K.C.C.) share in this period, and the table on page 273 shows what this meant in terms of dividends to an S.P.S. shareholder. (The K.C.C. had an analogous history.) The S.P.S. capital had been increased in 1926 and again in 1928 and 1935. It will be seen that the average dividend over the twenty-one years came to 13 per cent, but if the premiums that shareholders were required to pay when taking up the shares are added in the dividend averaged 8 per cent. Out of this they had to pay income tax. Considering the depression years this was not an unsatisfactory return but, bearing in mind the limited period of their concession, it could not be called excessive.

To judge the Government's average return requires consideration of the indirect as well as of the direct results. The former are not easy to assess with confidence but the table below does give an idea of the slow but steady recovery of the country's economy by 1946 in some of its main indices.

The Gezira, of course, was not the only contributor but it was still the major element for good or for bad in the general economic activity. Cotton and seed furnished 70 per cent of all exports in value, and 80 per cent of this was produced in the Gezira. The higher yields were an important contribution in themselves for they meant more money in circulation in tenants' loans, in rail traffic, and all ancillary activities. Their value was reflected in those standard tokens of economic well-being: imports of cotton goods, tea, coffee and sugar, the number of ships coming into Port Sudan, the extent of building activity, savings and travel, all of which had reached new records by the end of the period.

Sudan Finances from 1934 *to* 1946
(in million £E)

	Revenue	Expendi-ture	Imports	Exports	Liquid Assets	Gezira Yield (Kantars per Feddan)
1934	3·8	3·7	3·9	3·8	3·4	2·3
1935	4·1	4·0	5·4	4·6	4·6	4·5
1936	4·5	4·2	5·4	5·6	6·3	3·7
1937	4·7	4·5	6·3	8·1	8·5	4·5
1938	5·1	4·9	6·3	5·5	9·2	4·6
1939	5·1	4·9	5·9	5·4	5·9	4·5
1940	4·6	4·5	5·6	5·0	6·7	3·8
1941	5·4	5·0	8·1	8·5	8·4	4·0
1942	5·8	5·3	8·1	7·2	8·7	4·0
1943	5·9	5·6	9·2	6·4	9·5	4·8
1944	6·6	6·5	10·0	8·7	10·7	3·1
1945	7·8	7·5	10·0	10·6	12·1	4·9
1946	8·3	8·2	11·5	9·3	12·3	3·4

The indirect revenues of the Gezira Scheme were the main contributing factors to the steady improvement.

A notable advantage of the economic recovery was taken in 1939 when £5 million 5½ per cent Guaranteed Bonds 1929–59, borrowed in 1919 and 1921, were repaid. A new loan of £2 million was raised at 3¼ per cent, resulting in a net saving of £202,000 per annum, together with a reduction of £3 million, or 24 per cent, of the total market debt of the Sudan. This transaction had been made possible because the liquid assets of 1938 had risen to over £E9 million. The repayment reduced them to £E6 million but by 1941 they were up again to £E8¼ million.

Another notable feature of the period was the quicker rate of cotton sales. The year 1939 touched a record for sales in one year of 295,000 bales. In 1941 307,000 bales were sold, and for the first time in fourteen years there was no stock unsold at the end of the year. From 1942 onwards all cotton was sold and paid for during the year, making a marked contrast with the depression years. These quick returns were due to the contract negotiated during the war with the United Kingdom, the story of which must come in the marketing chapter. The benefit of them was made very evident in 1944 when the Gezira gave a shock by a fall in yield to 3·1, just when the country's expenditure figure reached a record of £E6½ million. It was the worst crop for ten years. Providentially the position was reversed in 1945 when the Gezira produced the largest crop yet, restoring the net divisible return to over £E20 per feddan for the first time since 1929. It was thanks to this bumper crop that the indices shown in the table reached their zenith. Yet all this time the price of cotton had not gone over 10·6 pence per lb. since 1930.

Nothing spectacular emerges from this analysis. Gezira results in this period continually added to the security of the country's economy, but not always, and not sufficiently to lessen the Financial Secretary's anxiety about the yield efficiency of the Gezira. That this must still be his paramount preoccupation is clear from a glance at the table on page 268 where the Government's direct revenue from the Scheme is compared with its direct expenditure. This table shows how, separated from the indirect revenue, the Gezira, on its own bald costings, was not a very showy investment, even by 1946.

An analysis of how the tenants fared in this period is given in the table on page 270.* This shows the tenants' collective share from each particular crop and the amount of credit that this gave per standard tenancy. The distribution of this credit over what was absorbed by the average loans, by levies to the Reserve Fund, and by payment of profits (including appreciations) is shown in the last three columns. The table brings out how low was the credit per tenancy (column 6) in the

* In the report of the Select Committee of the Legislative Assembly on the Future Administration of the Gezira Scheme, 1950, slightly different figures are given for the average tenancy profits. The reason for the difference is that the figures in this table are per annual crop whereas those in the report are per twelve months.

depression years 1930, 1931, 1933 and 1934, and how inevitable were the bad debts unless the service of loans had been suspended. Even in the good year, 1932, part of the profits had to be appropriated to keep down the debts of 1933. Clearly the margin of profit after repayment of loans was negligible in the depression period.

The profits of the first four seasons were relatively very high for a people almost unused to a cash economy at all, and the tenants had acquired new habits of living which had now become necessities. When the depression came many began to sell their capital assets to buy at least tea, sugar and clothes. Sales of land from the poor to the less poor began to pass in the Gezira for as low a price as six shillings a feddan. The Government intervened in 1933 to buy 42,000 feddans at twelve shillings a feddan, and a further 33,500 feddans in 1934. Without government buying it was thought that much land would have found its way into the hands of moneylenders at much below fair market prices, and incidentally government purchase of land reduced the annual rental payments and helped the taxpayers. As material conditions improved, the rush to sell subsided and government purchase of land fell to 17,859 feddans in 1935, 15,885 in 1936, 11,607 in 1937 and 6,493 in 1938.

Because the Gezira provided practically the only source of cash, costs were low, and the purchasing power of money was enhanced. Therefore the figures up to 1946 were more satisfactory than their face value suggests. Conversely, the close connection between the amount of money in circulation in the Gezira and the cost of labour to the tenant held equally true in the reverse direction. When loans and profits were high, labour costs went up. Later in this story, when figures for tenancy profits went very much higher, their real value has equally to be discounted owing to inflation of costs.

A true impression from this table, therefore, would be not one of extravagant profits but a small but steady build up, dependent on good yields, to a fair competence at the end of the decade. By 1945 the tenants were beginning to become prosperous. As long as the cost of living was reasonable, and the tenant's loans covered the cost of hiring extra labour when necessary, his lot was enviable and there was plenty of competition for any vacancy. And by this time there was the additional security of about a year and a half's profit put by for each tenant in the Tenants' Reserve Fund against a rainy day. The rest of the story of the creation of this fund must now be told.

The stalemate between the Syndicate and the Government over the bad debts and the rise in the tenant's share was finally overcome by the setting up of a Tenants' Reserve Fund, confirmed by a supplementary agreement in 1937. It had three objects: to repay the bad debts of the depression years, to afford security for future loans, and to provide an equalization fund to subsidize profits in future bad years. The better yields reduced to some extent the Syndicate's anxiety to increase the tenants' share and certain alternative methods were adopted to put the tenants in a better position to meet levies for the fund, and to start the fund off. The Government at last agreed to grant a rebate of £E1 per ton on the rail freight on lint cotton to Port Sudan as from the 1935 season, provided that the Syndicate made over its share of the rebate to the tenants. The Syndicate on its side agreed from the same season to reduce the rate of interest on tenants' loans from 6 to 5 per cent. These benefits increased the tenants' share of the proceeds.

An opportunity to start the fund off with a credit was taken also in 1935 on review of the Gezira Sinking Funds. As the depreciation rate for machinery, charged since 1926 to the tenant in the cost of ploughing and to the partnership in the cost of ginning, had proved higher than was needed, the tenants' share of the surplus was transferred to the Tenants' Reserve Fund. The Syndicate also agreed to transfer its share to the Tenants' Fund, and the Government matched the Syndicate's contribution. The surplus from the ginneries fund amounted to £E88,808, of which £E46,632 was the Syndicate and Government contribution. The surplus from the ploughing fund amounted to £E54,650, and the total from both funds, of £E143,458, made quite a substantial start to the Tenants' Reserve Fund.

It had been agreed that the first objective of the fund, the repayment of the bad debts, should not apply until a sufficient sum had accrued to meet the second objective, security for future loans. The level required for this purpose was initially fixed at £E10 per standard tenancy. It was also agreed, after considerable argument, that the best method of taking a levy from the tenants' current profits would be simply at a flat rate per kantar. This of course meant that those who had done best would put most into the fund. Contributions, however, were not to be individually recorded. It was a collective, not a personal savings, fund.

The next problem was when to take a levy and for how much. A government board had been set up in 1934, called the Gezira Advisory Board, to co-ordinate the views of different government departments so that there could be a uniform government policy on the Gezira. The Syndicate was not a member and continued to deal direct with the

You not only charged no interest* but you postponed any repayment until a particularly prosperous year rendered the contribution no hardship.

In Nigeria I created a reserve fund in the native treasuries as an insurance against famine, and both the living and posterity had the satisfaction of knowing that they were insured against famine. If no famine occurred during the lifetime of those whose taxes had built up the reserves, the living were paying for what they would never receive. Surely this principle is constantly admitted? It is perhaps (as Himbury observed) more cogent in a commercial company than in the case of a Government, but both are trustees of other people's money—taxpayers or shareholders.[4]

Lugard's argument was accepted, and these principles had in fact been accepted when the negotiators of the original main agreement approved the collective principle for treating bad debts, even though they could hardly have anticipated their magnitude.

Mayall had long suggested that a statement on present and future policy towards the Reserve Fund should be issued to personnel working in the Gezira to help them to answer questions on the subject. A document giving the history of the Scheme to date, with details of the debts and levies, was made out by the Government and Syndicate jointly at the end of 1938. It contained the following summary of the collective argument:

The Gezira Scheme is designed to allow as much reward as possible to individual enterprise subject to certain cooperative features which are regarded as being essential to its success. One of these features is the collective treatment of tenants' debts. The individual Gezira tenant has no adequate security to offer for the repayment of his debts to the Syndicate, and the Syndicate under its agreement with the Government is entitled to charge the debts owed to it by individual tenants against the Tenants' Collective Account, while the tenants concerned have to reimburse the Collective Account as and when they can afford to do so out of their future profits. Without such a safeguard neither the Syndicate nor the Government could, of course, contemplate the financing of the tenants unless this liability was reduced by an increase in its share of the profits. This procedure means in effect that the tenants collectively have to pay temporarily, and, if the debtor dies or departs, permanently, the individual tenant's debts. It is important to understand that the principle of collective recovery of debt means that the profits not only of the tenants who incurred these debts but also of existing tenants who may not have been in the Scheme in the bad period are being drawn upon to meet these debts which in some cases are those of tenants who have died or left the Scheme. Under the special circumstances of 1930 and 1931, and since 16th March 1937, individual debtors of those seasons are no longer called upon to repay their individual debts.

* No interest had been charged on the £600,000 advanced since October 1932.

Present and future tenants will benefit from the existence of those monies in the reserve fund derived from the sinking fund surpluses which were contributed in part by tenants who are now dead or departed. Although new tenants are contributing towards the repayment of benefits received by the tenants of 1930 and 1931, it should be borne in mind that the new tenant in, say, 1945, or in any bad period which may lie ahead, may receive benefits from the Tenants' Reserve Fund which has been built up by the contributions of tenants of past years who may then be dead and may never have received any benefit from the fund themselves. An inevitable element in any scheme of mutual insurance is that existing members pay for the benefits received by those dead and gone while the dead and gone have paid for benefits to be received by existing and future members.[5]

But whatever the principle, there was something to be said in practice for the Government and Syndicate reducing the burden gratuitously. There were really two debt points to be dealt with. There was the £E600,000 due to the Government and Syndicate for the loan they had put up to pay off the debts of the 1929–30 and 1930–1 crops and the £E100,000 of bad debts on the 1932–3 and 1933–4 crops. As far as the Syndicate was concerned this latter money had been recovered from the collective accounts, to which however the individual tenants who had incurred these debts had still to repay them. MacIntyre had suggested in 1937 that this liability should be cancelled. It seemed to him undesirable to pay out the meagre profits with one hand and then to take back for the collective account such a large share with the other.[6] But the legal advice had been that the Government and Syndicate lacked the power to waive any of these debts owing to the tenants as a body. On the other hand there was nothing to stop the Government and Syndicate paying them off, and this they now did by relinquishing £E100,000 of their £E600,000 claim and using this credit to cancel these individual debts to the collective account. This meant that the debts owed by individual tenants were now back in small figures.

There remained the balance of the £E600,000 claim against the Reserve Fund. By 1940 the levies taken into the fund, and the interest on their investment, had not only brought the fund up to the £E10 per tenancy level but had enabled the repayment of £E260,000 towards liquidating this debt. There had been three successive years of excellent yields and prospects looked better. There remained £E240,000 of the debt and both Government and Syndicate were anxious to be quit of it. The Government decided to waive the remainder of its claim, but the Syndicate felt unable to justify similar action to its shareholders. A compromise was found. A levy was made for the Government half of the remainder, and the £E120,000 placed by it as the capital of a new Tenants' Welfare Fund. To be quit of the Syndicate half there was a different possibility. By a curious oversight the Syndicate had until now never charged any interest on the capital cost of the ploughing machinery, the operation of which at cost fell within the tenants' normal liabilities. In return for the right to make this charge for the remaining ten years of their concession, to the extent of £E12,000 per annum, the Syndicate agreed to waive any further claim on account of the £E600,000. If such interest calculation exceeded the £E12,000 the excess was to be credited to the Tenants' Reserve Fund.

The first objective of the Tenants' Reserve Fund, the recovery of past debt, was thus concluded and it was felt desirable to build up the fund to a considerably higher level to permit it to function, on its third objective, as an Equalization Fund. Shortage of consumer goods following the outbreak of war added an anti-inflationary motive, and levies were continued and rather intensified, as the following table shows:

Totals in the Tenants' Reserve Fund

in 1938	£E310,088
in 1939	£E313,540
in 1940	£E348,532
in 1941	£E501,564
in 1942	£E969,187
in 1943	£E1,192,150
in 1944	£E1,120,925
in 1945	£E1,317,432

This total, at 1946 prices, was equivalent to about a year and a half's profit. Bearing in mind the long history of debts and the adjustments made to help the tenants, it seemed at last a satisfactory outcome.*

The Gezira Scheme was a curious blend of collective and individualist principles. While the individual tenant derived an individual advantage from any better yields he obtained, and there was in no sense a general pooling of results, still less an issue of reward according to hours worked, there were other collective features in the accountancy, in addition to the collective security for loans and the reserve fund, whereby the lucky and successful contributed to help the more heavily burdened. The methods of charging the cost of ploughing and of fertilizer were illustrations of the truth that a bundle of sticks is harder to break than a single twig.

* The position of the Tenants' Reserve Fund at 30th June 1950, which gives a picture in totals of these transactions into and out of the fund, can be seen on page 274 at the end of Chapter 20.

Mechanical ploughing, to clean the land ready for planting, was carried out by the Syndicate, but it was held to be the tenants' liability, and its cost was debited to a collective Tenants' Working Account and allocated at a flat rate per feddan to each tenant according to his cotton area. Different treatment was needed according to the condition of the soil. The poorest land was often the hardest and required cultivating and ridging separately. Land heavily impregnated with seid grass needed ploughing in depth, while good clean land needed only one ridging operation. Had the cost of the work been debited according to the individual cost of these operations it would have borne heaviest on the lowest-yielding land, throwing it still further into debt. By pooling the cost the burden was spread over the tenants as a whole. This system of accountancy, unfair as it might seem to the individual, enabled large areas of land which had deteriorated during the depression years to be brought back into good condition economically.

The same considerations applied to fertilizer. At low prices of cotton extensive use of fertilizer, if charged out individually, was an overhead of some risk, but by charging the cost against all three partners like a marketing expense fertilizer could be applied to raise the yield of the worst land without debiting the tenants thereof with the full cost. These collective methods played a useful part in helping to raise the lowest level of yields near to the average and thereby to keep down the annual total of debt to comparatively modest figures. By 1946, apart from the four bad years whose debts were liquidated by the processes described previously, the whole outstanding debt to the Tenants' Collective Account, from all individuals for all years since the start, amounted to less than £E5,000. As the price of cotton rose after that date the once nightmare problem of debt faded like a bad dream.

Chapter 14

A VISTA FROM RESEARCH

The Research Institute, with its resident director and team of scientific workers, plant pathologists, botanists, soil chemists, plant breeders and experimental farm managers, played a continuously valuable part in various aspects of the Gezira Scheme. Some of this work—the discovery of control measures against blackarm and leaf curl, and of resistant strains of cotton—has already been woven into this story. Much of it—the search for cash crops alternative to cotton, water economy experiments, the breeding of a dual-purpose herd of indigenous cattle, to mention only a few items—must be passed over without adequate tribute. But some of the more important problems the Scheme put before the Research Institute and some dramatic issues raised by research should be described.

None of the collective techniques of internal self-help mentioned in the last chapter—the communal reserve fund and the methods of allocating ploughing and fertilizer costs—would have been effective if the overall yield had fallen again to the level of the worst years. The major preoccupation of the Syndicate's field administration and of the Research Institute, working in close co-operation, was to prevent this happening.

The high yields of the X1530 and X1730 strains and their resistance to leaf curl suggested that plant selection and breeding was a good line of attack, and these 'L' varieties were rapidly extended until they filled half the planted acreage. At this point marketing considerations came in. The 'L' variety, although originally selected from a sakel plant,* emerged with a rather coarser fibre and was not accepted by the market as a substitute for fine sakel cotton except in its highest grades, so it sold

* Sakel was the shortened name of the best variety of cotton grown in Egypt when the Gezira Scheme started. It was discovered by a Greek landowner named Sakellarides. Sakel seed, imported for the Gezira from Egypt, came from the pure strains produced on the state domain seed farms.

172

at a lower price. Its high yield and high ginning out-turn would have offset this disadvantage, but there was another consideration. Sakel cotton had almost a monopoly for materials requiring strength and fineness. Few parts of the world were climatically suited to produce it. Egyptian sakel had deteriorated and it seemed unwise not to plant in the Gezira a sufficient acreage to keep a foot in this high-quality market. The decision to do so was vindicated very shortly by the outbreak of war, when Gezira sakel cotton came into particular demand for airmen's clothing, parachute cords, rubber dinghies, and a whole range of high-tenacity uses.

The Gezira Scheme possessed unusual organizational advantages which also helped to maintain high yields. The control of seed supply, already mentioned, was one of them. The risk of seed-borne infection was further prevented by sending the pure product of the Gezira seed farm to be sown for a season in the Gash delta where blackarm was negligible, and then using the product of the Gash delta for sowing the following year in the Gezira.

Another organizational advantage was the standardization of grading made possible by the central ginnery system. All cotton was brought in from the fields to two main centres (each with four large ginneries) situated for convenience of delivery about thirty-five miles apart. At these centres a team of classifiers examined every bag and graded it in a uniform manner, according to length and strength of staple, wastiness,* lustre and dirt. Each variety, whether 'S' (sakel) or 'L' (lambert), was divided into eleven different grades and ginned separately. This procedure enabled full opportunity to be taken, on sale, of the substantial premiums available for quality.

These advantages enabled a planting policy to be adopted which had twin objectives. The first was to supply spinners, as far as possible, with a regular, reliable product for their yarn mixtures year after year. The second was to breed into this product resistance to blackarm and leaf curl, which could enhance the yield without impairing quality. This latter objective not only required very competent scientists with adequate time to fix such new strains but also a slow and steady testing of the field and market response to them. For these reasons, and with the retention of the susceptible sakel variety, it was necessary to maintain for a long time strict supervision over the clean-up and eradication of plants and debris liable to be a focus for the carry-over of disease, and

* Wastiness: an assessment of the proportion of short, weak fibres which were likely to come out as waste in the process of spinning.

the fall in yield in 1940, 1944 and 1946, although it had other causes as well, was a continuing reminder of these persistent dangers.

Other experiences began to add to the factory-like appearance of Gezira farming, and to accentuate the value of constant watchfulness and ability to apply scientific discoveries quickly to the field. After three consecutive good years the crop in the northern Gezira in 1940 began to develop the appearance of brown paper. The leaves withered and curled up at the edges. For a while this was attributed to water strain and the poorer soil was suspected until, by caging a few plants, the real culprit was revealed in the jassid fly. The incidence seemed to vary from year to year but, as in the history of blackarm and leaf curl, the jassid danger spread sporadically until under suitable conditions in 1944 and 1946 they covered the Gezira as a major menace and seriously reduced the yield. Wisely the scientists at the Research Institute had already experimented successfully with Bordeaux mixture and in 1946 Pest Control Ltd. had been contracted to spray 1,000 feddans experimentally with D.D.T. The result was a 40 per cent increase in yield, and from this date contract spraying was stepped up both by air and land machines until, with the exception of control areas, it came to be a routine operation debited to the joint account as a marketing expense.

As disease was reduced by control measures it gradually became apparent that the wide fluctuations in yield between one season and another, and between one area and another in the same season on the same sort of land, must have some other cause. The Syndicate had observed a correlation between heavy rains preceding sowing and high subsequent yields, and between a severe shortage of rain before sowing and subsequent bad yields. The Research Institute, meanwhile, had observed a negative correlation between the yield of one year and the total quantity of rain in the preceding year.

Dr. Frank Crowther* at the Research Institute put this data into an equation, giving a certain weight as a factor decreasing yield to every fifty millimetres of the preceding year's rain, and a certain weight as a factor increasing yield to every fifty millimetres of pre-sowing rains. These rainfall statistics were of course known at the time of planting, and the equation was used to foretell the probable yield before a seed went into the ground. Amazingly enough this forecast turned out to be

---

* A brother of Dr. E. M. Crowther of Rothamsted. One of the outstanding scientists of the Research Institute who had the rare quality of looking beyond his particular subject to try and trace the interaction of different factors in phenomena affecting yield and grade. His untimely death in 1948 was a great loss.

remarkably accurate, and at the end of the decade excellent agreement was found between the actual yields from 1936 to 1946 and yields estimated by the rainfall equation. This curious phenomenon suggested that irrigation in the Gezira was not just a straightforward substitute for rainfall, and that a large part of the aberrations in yield was connected more with the effect of rain on the land before sowing than with all other factors affecting the crop afterwards.

The fascinating and exceedingly complex task now facing the team of research workers was to find the cause of this in order to increase the factors favourable to yield. Did the rain dominate the yield by altering the physical structure and permeability of the soil? A soil-firing experiment had shown some remarkable yield increases and suggested that physical condition might be a potent factor in yield. On the other hand, did the rain simply provide additional moisture reserves or did it activate nitrogen-forming bacteria in the soil? Alternatively was it changes not in the soil but in the climate which affected the plants' ability to take up nutrients? Or was the result related to the physical effect of rain on the survival of pests and disease or on the growth of weeds, and the possibility of eliminating weed-competition before the growing period? Such questions revealed the extraordinary ignorance of the basic causes of good and bad crops. The pursuit of the answers underlined the value of trained research workers, and of an intimate contact between them and the field officers. An annual post-mortem survey of the past crop and joint planning of future experiments became a most valuable feature of the Scheme's administration.

On top of this puzzle about yield came the problem of grade. The qualities assessed in the grading process, the length and strength of the cotton staple, the fineness, lustre and percentage of waste, varied enormously from season to season. If research could have discovered methods of encouraging the phenomena which stimulated better grade as well as higher yield, the results could have been of vast financial value to the country.

Nature was not prepared to release its secrets easily and these two branches of research continue to challenge the scientists of the Gezira. Experiments in pre-watering the crops to simulate the effect of pre-sowing rains were conducted but they did not respond in the same way. However, certain discoveries about the effects of the previous year's rain did suggest possible action. As is so often the case in research these discoveries originated in a different purpose. In a chequer-board experiment at the Research Station to test the effect of different dates of precultivation of land, all those fallow plots which, contrary to the usual practice, had been cultivated during the preceding rains gave marked increases in yield. From this experiment it was only a step to discover that the chief cause of the depressing effect of the previous year's rains in the rainfall equation was the habit of allowing weeds to grow on the fallows in the rains. Whether this was due to a draw-off of nitrogen or of moisture, continuing experiments revealed that if weeds were prevented from growing on both years of fallow preceding cotton a substantially bad year, such as 1945-6, could be turned into an average one, and in a substantially good year, where pre-sowing rains were heavy, such as in 1944-5, this process increased the yield phenomenally.

The experiments were taken further. If the increase in yield was a matter of increased moisture content why not irrigate fallow out of season but keep the resultant weeds from growing? This treatment indicated a further yield increase. Here was indeed a full turn of the circle of knowledge. The fallow, and the cracking out of the soil which accompanied it, used to be deemed the main asset to soil fertility and part of the basis of the wide rotation. Irrigation out of season seemed now to make nonsense of this belief. At this point more conventional measures were fitted into the experiments. With closer control of disease and a rising price greater use of nitrogenous fertilizer became economic and desirable, and response to it was found to be greater in a good season. Using all these results combined—irrigation out of season, spraying, nitrogenous fertilizer and X1730 seed—in one of the out-station plots run by the Research Institute in excellent land in the southern Gezira, Crowther touched an all-time record yield in the Gezira of seventeen kantars per feddan. Commercial yields in that district had already topped ten kantars, but Crowther's experiment raised the sights to revolutionary ranges.

But the experiments were now reaching a wall of practical difficulties. Irrigation out of season enormously encouraged seid grass. Expensive ploughing in depth was the only known control and to kill the seid the land had to be dry. Moreover, from where was the water to come, on top of that needed by the crop? Altogether this discovery about the harmful effects of fallow weeds presented practical and social difficulties. Weeds naturally grew on the fallows most in years of heavy rain, when all labour was already occupied with them on the cropped land so they could not be eliminated by hand labour. Moreover, the weeds grew extraordinarily quickly and each day's survival decreased the benefit of removing them. It seemed essential to use machinery continuously during the rains over small areas per unit machine. The discovery of the right machine with the right tractor power for the purpose (and the suitability of such tractors for other uses during the year to make it an economic proposition) was to take some years.

Meanwhile the social effects acted as a brake on agricultural progress. Harmful as the weeds were for the crops, they were invaluable for the tenants' animals and these were needed for milk and meat supplies in the villages. Of course, if the tenants could suddenly have become modern farmers and had conserved their irrigated fodder as silage in the summer and rains, the weeds might have been dispensed with. But they could not do that without much more hard work than traditional nomadic grazing required, and to eliminate this work demanded another technical discovery: how to cut and carry the irrigated lubia crop by machinery.

It was becoming clear that with anti-jassid spraying, seid grass control, fallow weeding and mechanical fodder conservation, the Gezira Scheme was opening up prospects of a machine age very different from the conception of peasant farmers working by hand labour with their families, and the social effect of these new techniques had to be taken into consideration as much as the effect on profits. They were by now touching off disquieting speculations about the objectives of the Gezira. Supposing fallow weeds could be controlled by aerial spraying, and picking and pulling-out and sweeping done by machinery, where did the peasant farmer fit in the picture? Supposing the country's most important objective was high financial returns from the Scheme, could this be best met by a central organization controlling the machinery and utilizing the peasants as fringe labour? Or was the development of the tenant's society more important to the country than finance?

Such questions were taking the Gezira into the problems then facing the peasantry in Russia or India, the section-farming society in western Canada and the small family holding in the United States. Was the machine and economic efficiency to determine the society on the land as it had in industry, and if so, what did one do about the human beings? Such thoughts, although they were still premature for the state of technical advance in the Gezira, illustrate how inevitably social, and thus political, considerations were impinging on what had at first seemed a purely economic project. As a matter of fact, the question of how far the social should influence the economic aim had already arisen in connection with the political policy of indirect rule and had been the subject of a great deal of argument and negotiation between Syndicate and

M 177

Government. The moral and managerial problems raised by mechanization fell to be considered in that context, and the origin of this theme has to be traced back from an earlier stage. But before embarking on that story one indispensable section of the economic history of the Scheme must be described—the marketing of the cotton.

Chapter 15

MARKETING

As the problem of marketing the products of underdeveloped areas often comes up for public consideration, the varied history of marketing the Gezira cotton crop through some thirty years may provide a case study of some interest. Unfortunately some aspects of the subject are rather technical but cannot easily be avoided, for cotton is one of the great primary commodities of the world and there has developed round it in the main centres—Liverpool, New York and Alexandria—a most complex marketing system.

The problems of debt and of yield which occupied so much attention in Gezira history from 1929 to 1946 were intimately linked with price. The lower the price the greater the risk of tenants' debt, and the greater the need for efficiency to produce a good yield.

The price, of course, depended upon outside trade demand, but this demand might be affected by the method of offering the product to the trade, in other words by the efficiency of the marketing. Although marketing was naturally a continuous process from the start of the Gezira, differences of opinion about how best to sell the cotton became more acute when price margins were low, and for this reason a chapter is devoted here to the marketing theme from the start until 1946. The theme will be taken up again in Chapters 20 and 21.

The first marketing problem which new producers face is how to get their products accepted at all in the trade. They have somehow to cut in on the existing organization of supply. In this respect the Gezira was lucky. It will be remembered that Lancashire had taken a powerful interest in the development of Gezira cotton right from the beginning and that the British Cotton Growing Association had bought shares in the Syndicate and been given a seat on the Board. The Association was following a similar policy of encouraging cotton growing in other parts of the Empire—Nigeria, Uganda, India, Tanganyika, Nyasaland, and to a small extent in the British West Indies. Apart from supplying expert advice and machinery the Association also undertook to act as marketing agent on a small commission. This was a very valuable function, for it meant that cotton from the Sudan and other out-of-the-way places was handled by an organization of the highest standing and introduced to the Liverpool market under its auspices. It helped to overcome the natural reluctance of spinners to change from established connections and to alter their machinery and try new growths. The alternative for the struggling new projects would have been to depend on local merchants who might lack interest and experience of the crop, would require a middleman's remuneration, and might have mutual understandings detrimental to the producer.

Part of the technique of the B.C.G.A. in persuading spinners to take up Sudan cotton lay in having, ready at store in Liverpool, sufficient stocks to enable spinners to choose lots which suited their particular yarns at times when they wanted them. As a corollary to this, the first system of marketing adopted by the Syndicate was to consign all the cotton to Liverpool to the B.C.G.A. for sale on commission.

Once the main scheme was launched the desirability of developing, in addition, sales by local auction came up for consideration. The Syndicate was the partner responsible for sales management, although it had to consult the Government. MacIntyre, in whose hands, with those of Sir William Himbury of the B.C.G.A., selling policy was largely concentrated, agreed to an experiment and auctions were held at Barakat in the Sudan in 1926. But it was an unhappy venture. Four auctions were held but every lot but two was withdrawn for failing to meet the reserve, and the experiment was suspended.

A flood of protests then descended from the Alexandria export houses who had been invited to send representatives. The Syndicate was criticized for giving too little time for sampling, for selling in too big lots and for refusing to disclose reserve prices. Buyers complained that they were being asked to buy a pig in a poke. The leading firm, Carver Brothers, put their view of it in a telegram to Schuster, the Sudan Government's Financial Secretary:

There are as yet no cotton exporters established in the Sudan of any substance or with any connections in spinning countries, and these are the only sort of firms who can get your cotton known and ensure a steady demand. After the way we were all treated this year it will be a long time before most firms will send up buyers to the Sudan again.[1]

There was some truth in the criticisms and there is little doubt that the Syndicate exhibited a common characteristic of producers everywhere:

suspicion of the middlemen who operated the marketing. But on the straightforward issue of price the auctions were plainly disappointing. In a public statement the Syndicate made clear that this was the reason for discontinuing them.[2] The reserve prices had been fixed by the Syndicate in agreement with the Government. They had been fully justified by sales effected later in England at prices considerably above the reserves. The advantage anticipated from local sales—better prices and quicker settlement of the cotton accounts—had just not transpired.

Hewison, now Director of Agriculture, supported the Syndicate's view in a comment to Schuster and thought that local buyers expected much too large margins for the service of coming to the Sudan. 'A point for consideration', he wrote, 'is that if the firms have not sufficient enterprise to chance their arms to a slight extent in order to get into the business, what is our position going to be when they have become established at our expense and we are more or less dependent on them?'[3] He was touching on the real point at issue in the minds of MacIntyre and Himbury. Were they likely to spoil what appeared to be an excellent market at good prices via the B.C.G.A. by operating through other channels at lower prices? This particular problem, of whether continuity of supply to a known market should or should not take precedence over the unknown risks or advantages of attempting to widen the market, was to dominate the theme of Gezira sales for a long time.

For the moment the position was summed up by Schuster in a circular letter to the protesting firms. He was evidently in two minds about it. 'It may of course be argued that it is in the interests of the Sudan generally that outside merchants should be attracted even at the cost of some sacrifice in price', but however strongly such a view might appeal to the Government it was the Syndicate's duty to get the best possible price for the cultivator and as long as it was doing so the Government could not complain or seek to influence its judgement. He concluded, 'Nevertheless I assure you that the matter has been fully discussed with the Syndicate and that I still hope the time may come when we find a basis of working which will satisfy everyone.'[4] And there the matter rested for the time being.

But marketing in England was not without its difficulties as conditions moved from a seller's to a buyer's market, and before long the problem of alternatives had to be faced more seriously. The system of consigning the crop to Liverpool for sale by the B.C.G.A. on commission involved the partnership in heavy storage charges in England. Was it best to use this system of marketing direct to spinners and pay carrying charges

while awaiting their choice, or to sell quickly to local merchants, even at
lower prices, and let them take the risks and profits of carrying stocks?
Would their prices be so much lower that marketing direct would have
been better? Local sales might widen the market but at too high a cost.
Could one be sure of selling quickly to local merchants anyway? Or
could one get the best of both systems without being completely dependent on either?

The question became increasingly urgent. To provide a wide selection
in England the amount there was always far in excess of immediate
demand and could hang rather threateningly over the market. This
tended to have an adverse effect on the prices and quantities that could
be unloaded from time to time and enhanced the attraction of a wider
market. Sir William Himbury managed the sales in England and tried
to counteract the sensitivity of the market by always selling on a slight
rise, but this was often a slow business. The whole position became
aggravated by the world slump after 1929. The sakel market became
increasingly narrow. The Liverpool stock was frequently the only sakel
cotton involved and operators knew all about its sales position. In this
restricted sphere the selling of a small number of 'futures' was apt to
be followed by an immediate fall in prices, sometimes by as much as
$\frac{3}{4}$ pence per lb., a dangerous drop with cotton at only 8 pence per lb.

It is necessary here to make a technical digression into the meaning of
the word 'futures'. The futures contract originated historically as a
forward sale, and was an undertaking to deliver so many bales at a certain
price and date in the future. But in practice it was very seldom intended
as a real sale or purchase of actual cotton. Much the most important use
of futures in the trade was for 'hedging'. Hedging was simply a self-
balancing system of insurance whereby a holder of cotton could cover
himself against a fall in price between the time he bought the cotton and
the time he sold it. This was done by setting up for each contractual
obligation a parallel contract which would work the other way so that,
if the original contract resulted in a loss, the parallel contract would
produce a profit to set off against the loss.

For example, without a hedge a merchant who bought cotton stood
to lose if the market went down before he found a buyer, although to
gain if the market went up—an uncertain and risky position. If, however, at the time of his original purchase contract he hedged himself by
selling futures under a parallel contract (i.e. contracting to deliver the
cotton at a known price and date in the future), he stood covered while
he sought a buyer. When later he sold his actual cotton he would buy

back his futures contract at the price quoted at that time. If, since his original purchase, prices had fallen, he would not get as much as he had hoped for the sale of the actual cotton, but he would be able to buy in his futures contract at a lower price than he had sold it for and this gain would offset his loss on the actual cotton. If, on the other hand, the price had gone up in the period, he would lose the difference on the futures contract, but this would be offset by the higher price at which he would sell the actual cotton. The sale of actual cotton was called a spot sale contract to distinguish it from the parallel futures contract.

It may be surprising to the general reader to find that cotton traders were so concerned to have a system of security which, while protecting them against a fall, also obviated any gain from a rise in price, and were content as long as they covered the cost of moving the cotton from producer to consumer and made a marginal profit. In point of fact the creation and use of the futures system reveals how much more important to the trade was stability than speculation. Also, the value of the futures contract was that a much greater degree of trade was made possible by the system for, in a futures contract, the price of cotton was quoted for a choice of months ahead, and by using it merchants could carry larger stocks without speculation.

Without such facilities they must either buy only for immediate usage or buy and hold in expectation of orders without any cover over the price they had paid. The futures contract, in fact, was actually first used to enable Liverpool merchants, buying cotton in the United States for import to Lancashire, to avoid the risk of a decline in market value during shipment and while awaiting purchase in the United Kingdom. From this stage the facilities of hedging and the Liverpool Futures Market, provided by the Liverpool Cotton Association, became available to anyone who wished to use them.

On the consuming side also all sections of the trade used the system, manufacturers to hedge their cloths and increase their forward-buying of yarn, and spinners to hedge their yarn and buy their raw cotton ahead. They represented the other half of the futures contract. If, for example, a spinner had been asked to quote for a big weight of yarn to be delivered over some months ahead, if he should do so without knowing what his cotton was going to cost him he would be speculating in a most dangerous way. He might of course buy the actual cotton first, but there were several difficulties in the way of doing this, such as lack of storage, of capital, or of cotton of the right kind and quantity at that moment. He would therefore usually base his quotation on the prices of futures for the various months ahead required by the contract and when he booked the yarn order would buy futures accordingly. A manufacturer booking a big sale of cloth ahead would cover himself in the same way by buying his yarn ahead. Or again, a spinner might be offered cotton he thought he would want in the coming months, although he had not yet got orders which would call for it. If he bought the cotton and afterwards the market went down his customers would expect to get the yarn at the lower price, which would mean a loss to the spinner. If, however, at the same time as he bought the actual cotton he sold futures as a hedge, then if the market went down he would be covered for the loss on the actual sale by his profit on the futures.

Finally, producers also might use the system to cover unsold portions of their crop. If they thought the price of futures relatively high they too might sell futures, and, if their view was correct, they could buy them back when their crop was sold, and would gain whatever difference the drop in the market gave to offset the loss on actual sales. If on the other hand the price had gone up they would have to buy back the futures at the higher price, but to offset this they should have sold their cotton at the higher price.

The fair working of the system, however, depended on there being enough activity in the trade to make such sales, and on there being enough transactions going on in the futures market to obviate the risk of being squeezed by speculators. The Syndicate was trying to sell futures to cover the unsold portion of the Gezira crop. But when spot sales were going very badly there was a danger that the futures contract would mature without it being able to make equivalent spot sales. In these circumstances it was then left with the alternative of either delivering the cotton against the futures contract (which was called tendering), or buying in its futures and selling futures again for a more distant date, still hoping in the meantime to dispose of its cotton by spot sales. In a narrow market, where such a position could be easily detected, there was a serious risk of heavy loss outside ordinary business. For if this embarrassment was detected by speculative operators they would squeeze their victim by making him pay high for the futures that were being bought back while depressing the distant position on which he was trying to sell. The Syndicate was caught in this manner during the winter of 1933–4.

Matters reached such a pitch that in October 1935 MacIntyre decided—on Himbury's advice—to obtain coverage outside the narrow Egyptian futures market, and switched to the large American market.

This policy rather worried the Government, which inclined to the view that it would be preferable not to sell futures at all in the circumstances. The Director of Agriculture wrote:

I presume that MacIntyre considered that any change in American Government policy resulting in lower prices would reflect to a corresponding extent on Sakel and that by using the American contract he could protect his cotton from any serious fall in price.

My own view is that, as America is not tied to Sakel, the companies in dealing in the American contract are taking a risk. They have no American cotton to tender if called upon, and, so far as I can see, they are relying on taking in at a profit. The operation is at the moment a financial success. They have a profit on the futures placed in the American market which, if placed at the time on Sakel, would have been a loss.

I look upon it as a transaction justifiable in the case of a merchant who was prepared to take his own view of the market, but I feel it should not form part of the selling policy for Gezira cotton when the interests of others are involved.[5]

In July 1936 the Syndicate switched back at a loss of nearly £45,000; and at the beginning of the next year stopped selling futures altogether. This decision was largely forced upon it by an action by the Liverpool Cotton Association, which prejudiced its ability to use the alternative, if buying back its futures meant a heavy loss, of tendering its cotton.

Although it was perfectly legitimate to tender cotton under a futures contract the use of this method of selling cotton on any extensive scale, in lieu of spot sales, would have upset the whole mechanism of hedging. The futures contract was by nature a contract by description; the cotton involved was not there. It might not even have been harvested, let alone examined as in a spot sale, so that the contract had to permit a wide possibility of quality. Whatever the conditions of earlier days when the contract originated, the growing specialization in manufacture was making the requirements of spinners as to grade and staple increasingly exact. Spinners could not fulfil these requirements if they took delivery under a futures contract, on which several different qualities might be tendered. What they did therefore was to buy the actual cotton they required, when the time came, on a spot contract, paying the current price for the particular grade and staple they wanted, simultaneously selling out their futures which were in the main merely negotiable instruments. For the same reason merchants who had sold futures when they bought their cotton would not normally tender against the futures contract because they would get better premiums for quality by spot sales.

The Syndicate, however, was in a rather different position. Its main objective was bound to be to get rid of its crop. It was not merely able to tender—for, unlike the ordinary holder of a futures contract who would have no intention to tender, it was in a particularly monopolistic position to do so because it controlled the marketing of the whole Gezira crop. It might choose to sell futures for large quantities of cotton which nobody wanted and then tender them, leaving the ultimate holder of the contract, who could not use the cotton, with the problem of selling it at a certain loss. Although it might be deterred from doing this by the probable slump in price, its dominant position could enable it to operate to the detriment of other merchants who had bought Gezira cotton. However unlikely it might be that the Syndicate would use its position for these purposes, such a powerful organization, with a very large crop at its disposal (and incidentally these considerations apply equally to many a lint marketing board), could wreck a delicate instrument like a futures market, and the Liverpool Cotton Association felt it essential to take precautions against this possibility.

Its fears were aggravated by the refusal of the Syndicate to base its selling prices entirely on the fluctuations in the futures market. In such narrow and risky conditions the Syndicate sought to fix its asking prices on a basis that was not constantly fluctuating, though in line with Egyptian prices, rather than allow the fair value of its cotton to be depreciated by every market pressure. But the fact that it was the sole seller of Gezira cotton made it difficult for those who had bought futures to be sure of buying this cotton at a known relation to them, and the operation of this separate sales system over an increasingly large part of the long-staple cotton crop was naturally resented by the Liverpool Cotton Association as upsetting to its futures market.

By the summer of 1936 the long-staple market was so obviously unsatisfactory that the Association revised the Egyptian futures contract. In the revision a new variety, Giza 7, which was rapidly replacing sakel in the Delta, became the basis. Giza 7 was shorter and coarser than sakel and was valued then at $1\frac{3}{4}$ pence per lb. less. An allowance extending to 400 'points on' (hundredths of a penny) was allowed in the new contract for premium in quality, but a special clause was inserted which laid down that for Gezira sakel no premium would be allowed above good standard Giza 7. This meant that Gezira sakel could only get a premium of about $\frac{1}{2}$ pence per lb. at a time when Egyptian-grown sakel of the same quality could draw the full 4 pence per lb. premium. Thus the effect of the new contract was to penalize high-grade Gezira cotton, if it was tendered against the contract, by as much as 3½ pence a lb. The clear intention was to discourage the Syndicate from unloading its cotton in this way, by refusing to allow it a premium for it if it did. The effect was to make the purchase of Sudan cotton by merchants more hazardous than the purchase of Egyptian cotton of equivalent quality.

While the fears of the Liverpool Cotton Association were understandable and real, its method of protecting itself put the marketing of Gezira cotton under a great and deliberate disadvantage, and MacIntyre was exceedingly sore at this discriminating treatment. The proper solution, in his view, would have been to establish one really wide futures market. The new Giza 7 contract was nothing of the kind. It was not only objectionable for its discrimination. It repeated the former narrowness. He said at the 1937 shareholders' meeting,

The whole of the Egyptian and Sudan crop is relatively a small amount on which to establish a futures market. When broken up into several contracts the market is subject to the manipulation of speculators. This means that genuine growers and buyers who want to cover their sales or purchases ahead, find they are liable to be squeezed to such an extent that it is impossible to risk covering in futures. Consequently, the Liverpool futures market is rapidly diminishing, and the limited business now transacted makes the market more subject than ever to manipulation. We cannot use this contract in its present form.

Although the Liverpool Cotton Association improved the Giza 7 contract, it did not go far to meet his views. 'At present', MacIntyre concluded at the 1938 shareholders' meeting, 'those who wish to provide cover for any substantial quantity are compelled to effect this in American covers, where there is a free market. But this is not satisfactory as the prices of Egyptian and American cotton do not always keep in step',[6] a conclusion which revealed a situation as unsatisfactory as in 1935.

The discrimination against Gezira cotton in the futures contract would have been less important if direct spot sales to spinners via the B.C.G.A. could have been counted upon to take up all the crop, for in such cases individual prices were arranged with the mills concerned and the futures market could be more or less by-passed. If, however, it was desirable to widen the selling circle and call upon cotton merchants to explore new openings, they would need to cover their purchases of Gezira cotton during this process, and in their case the discriminatory clause in the futures contract increased their risk and so reduced both their interest and their price offer. The terms of the futures contract thus represented an additional hazard when the alternative systems of marketing came up for consideration. Nevertheless during the thirties the custom of consigning the whole crop to Liverpool was becoming increasingly a case of putting all the eggs in one basket. Bigger crops were being produced in the Gezira while Lancashire sales were declining. Alternative outlets had to be found.

Action became increasingly urgent, particularly, in the opinion of the Sudan Government, owing to the slowness of sales. The Syndicate itself needed proceeds quickly because of the large sums of money which had to be paid out to tenants for the preliminary valuation, but the Syndicate's need was tempered by the fact that it was all the time earning interest on its loans. It was more urgent for the Government because its share was always a major revenue item. But another aspect which worried the Government was that it took such a long time to settle the tenants' accounts. It was common for them to be receiving appreciations on a crop more than a year after it was harvested. This divorce in time between the profit and the crop which produced it encouraged in the tenants an impression that the proceeds were some external mystery managed by others for whom they did the work. It was a manifestation which ran counter to certain social objectives about which the Government was feeling increasingly concerned, and which are discussed in the following chapter.

The upshot of this reasoning was to reopen the question of local auctions. The Government had been holding auctions at Tokar for many years, but in 1935 they started auctions in Port Sudan for all government-controlled cotton. Much of this was American-type cotton suited to the world's widest market, but the Government now took away their Gash delta crop, an Egyptian variety hitherto entrusted to the Syndicate for marketing, and added it to their Port Sudan auctions. At the same time they put pressure on the Syndicate to change the marketing methods of Gezira cotton. 'I put it bluntly to the Chairman', wrote Rugman* in a later minute to the Governor-General, 'that the Syndicate were failing in their obligation to market the crop, and that their position was one which demanded energetic action and early rectification.'[7] This prodding had its effect, and in February 1936 MacIntyre agreed to try out some sales at Port Sudan at least of the 'L'

---

* Sir Francis Rugman (1894–1946), K.C.M.G. Chartered accountant: entered finance department, Sudan Civil Service, 1920: Financial Secretary, Sudan, 1934–44.

variety, the coarser quality of which was not attracting much sale among the fine spinners in England.

Over the next few years marketing policy reflected a serious difference between the Government and the Syndicate: Rugman and the Government in a great hurry to get rid of the old system and conduct all sales by local auction, and behind them the Alexandria merchants, MacIntyre and the Syndicate much more cautious lest the established trade with the United Kingdom spinners be prejudiced, and behind them Sir William Himbury and the B.C.G.A. It is an interesting example of the genuine difficulties which arose in operating the partnership and put quite a test on the patience of the parties.

The 1936 auctions were hastily organized and, in the opinion of the Government, were conducted by the Syndicate with little sign of its having learnt anything from its experience of ten years ago. In 1937 auctions were started in better time, trading conditions were good, and over £E1¼ million worth of cotton was sold. The result elicited an approving comment from the Governor-General for its quick effect upon the country's revenue returns.

The Syndicate's representative, A. M. Telford, conducted the auctions but all important decisions were taken in London. The reserve prices were fixed there in consultation with Himbury and were related to sales actually made in the United Kingdom, or to valuations made by Wolstenholme and Holland, the well-regarded brokers who had valued Gezira lots in Lancashire for years. Reserve prices were not disclosed. Only the 'L' variety was put up for auction. Any inquiry for the finer 'S' variety had to be referred to London. If auction bids failed to reach reserve prices the cotton was withdrawn and could only be sold thereafter by private treaty. Clearly the whole procedure was a cautious attempt to explore possibilities, with a care not to prejudice the established take-off in the United Kingdom, rather than an enthusiastic acceptance of auctions as an alternative system. As such it once again came under a flood of criticism from local merchants, which was reported by Telford with some sympathy.

The first complaint was over sampling. The proportions were too low, but more important was the refusal of the Syndicate to give time for samples to be sent abroad. Telford reported.

If time is not given to the buyer to have his local valuations confirmed by Liverpool or his clients, he has to rely entirely on his own valuation made under difficult conditions of light and climate; with the result that his price is naturally on the low side. In fact he will only give his maximum bid after confirmation from home. [8]

Especially in the lower grades spinners would not commit themselves without seeing samples. This led on to a second complaint: the Syndicate's refusal to reauction withdrawn cotton. 'Until the lower grade samples got to India this year,' wrote Telford, 'not a sale was made for us in that market. Immediately the samples did arrive, buyers here received cabled advices to buy, but found that the cotton had already been auctioned and withdrawn.'[9] But the biggest complaint was that the Syndicate would fix its reserve prices according to its own valuations and would not follow the daily fluctuations in the futures market.

The government sales manager at Port Sudan, A. P. Thompson, was, like Telford, a daily target for the views of the local buyers and his report on the auction of 1937 was even more critical.

After much pressure the Syndicate agreed not to auction until samples had been available for three weeks. Later this concession was summarily withdrawn. The change suited those firms with experts on the spot with full discretionary powers but had the effect of shutting others out of the market to a large extent.

The effect is being felt now. Firms still represented here, anxious to do business, and receiving constant enquiries (especially from India), assure me that they would have made considerable purchases of cotton which has been withdrawn, if only their correspondents overseas had had samples in their hands when the cotton was offered. But the Syndicate only offers lots once for auctions, nor is the cotton available for negotiation till the auction is closed.

But the greatest obstacle to successful selling is at the moment, in my opinion, the Syndicate's refusal to adjust reserve prices in conformity with the market.[10]

Thompson's report was passed to the Financial Secretary and Rugman was moved to write this minute on it for the Governor-General.

In my view, the report reveals an astonishing lack of appreciation of the most elementary principles of salesmanship.

In the early days of the Scheme, Lancashire absorbed without difficulty the total products. The bulk of the crop was disposed of in the year of harvesting and the balance in the following year. From 1930 onwards the area under cotton was progressively increased; Lancashire trade and off-take progressively declined, and unsold Gezira stock showed a corresponding increase. The function of selling the crop had from the beginning been farmed out, on a one per cent commission, to the B.C.G.A., a body which had little experience of cotton selling and which in turn employed outside professional brokers whose advice, I have been informed, was frequently ignored.

The holding of enormous stocks of cotton involved the Government and tenants in heavy charges for interest, storage and insurance. . . . The

Government took the selling of the Gash crop out of the hands of the Syndicate and started the Port Sudan auctions for Government cotton.

In 1936 the Syndicate followed our example, but with a very small grace. They were late off the mark and gave totally inadequate facilities to buyers. In 1937 they started their auction early, but, as the present report shows, their methods of marketing remain the last word in amateur incompetence. In spite of this they have surprisingly enough sold over £1¼ million worth of cotton in some three months, a result which indicates that buyers, unless and until they become disgusted with the facilities offered to them, are prepared to come and pay fair prices for locally sold Gezira cotton.[11]

The picture of MacIntyre which emerges from these criticisms is of an obstinate Scot who refused to heed his clients' obvious needs and had no idea how to do business properly. But was it incompetence or shrewdness? In reality these strictures were projections of a real difference in policy. MacIntyre, whose mind was apt to operate more by shrewd intuition than by elaborate reasoning, made no public reply to them, and his relationship with merchant buyers continued to be one of some mutual distrust.

He had a conviction that the later in the season that auctions were extended the lower the price was likely to be. They could not be started earlier than the cotton could be harvested, ginned and dispatched to Port Sudan, but if they started late the influence of the new season's Egyptian crop coming to maturity might dominate them. Buyers knew that Government was anxious to get proceeds quickly and, in any period of slow sales, MacIntyre felt that he might be vulnerable to pressure if they got together to hold off purchasing and force prices lower. There were not enough buyers to be certain there would not be a ring. However reasonable it might sound to allow ample time for sampling and ample opportunity to buy later at a reauctioning, such facilities might operate to discourage bids earlier in the season, permit buyers to pick out all the plums at reauctions and leave him having to sell large stocks of withdrawn cotton later at much lower prices. With the restricted market in futures, there might be a tendency for a few sales to cause a substantial fall in price, and if he regularized his reserves to follow the market quotations, there might be a continual lowering of prices during the period of auctions.

All these considerations might have a permanent adverse affect upon the established trade connections in Lancashire and the prices being obtained there. It would be preferable therefore to offer at first only 'L' variety cotton rather than the 'S' variety for which, in top grades especially, Lancashire fine spinners had a consistent demand at high prices. Clearly there was reason for proceeding over auctions as experience revealed desirable, rather than for adopting any precipitate policy: especially one recommended by merchant buyers.

By contrast with this sceptical attitude to new merchant clients the Government became increasingly anxious to get all sales transferred to an auctions system in the Sudan. It made light of the risks of losing its direct contact with spinners in Lancashire and believed that local auctions would promote its main objective which was the maximum sale of bales in a year and the quickest return of money both to itself and to the tenants, even if this meant lower prices.*

Thompson wrote another report at the end of 1937 which reflected the belief that all would go well if the Syndicate were not so cagy.[12] He picked out three factors which seemed to run in a vicious circle: the difficulty of hedging under the futures contract, the lack of adequate competition, and the Syndicate's failure to regularize its reserves. As a result of the first factor purchases of Gezira cotton, except against a definite order from a spinner, were attended by considerable risk to the buyer. This in turn led to the second factor, the lack of competition, for, without a safe system of hedging and in face of the Syndicate's arbitrary methods of fixing reserve prices, many firms anxious to do business were, he reported, nervous of doing so. The second factor in turn led to the third, for the Syndicate was unwilling to adjust its reserves in accordance with market fluctuations if there was any risk of a lack of competition. The Liverpool Cotton Association would not alter its discriminatory futures contract until the Syndicate altered its selling policy, and Thompson suggested that the only way of breaking the vicious circle was a courageous gesture in this direction. If the Syndicate would fix its reserves to follow the market the confidence of firms hitherto nervous would be restored, the present small circle of buyers increased, and fair competition assured. With the attainment of a free market in place of the Syndicate's separate price system there would appear little doubt that the difficulty of arranging a suitable futures contract, not discriminatory against Sudan sakels, could be overcome.

---

* The reader who perseveres with the marketing theme will be interested to know that twenty years later, after an auction system had been adopted, there still remained the problem of what reserve price was appropriate. The auction system proved no panacea for automatic selling, and serious consideration was proposed for re-establishing a sales office (like the B.C.G.A.) and holding stocks in Lancashire so as to enhance direct contact with spinners. See the *Manchester Guardian*, Trade Notes, 'Selling Sudan Cotton', 19th July 1957.

As an approach to such a policy Thompson recommended for the 1938 season that reserves should be reduced, published, and tied to the fluctuations of the Liverpool futures market.

MacIntyre was unwilling to take such a sanguine view of obtaining fair open competition but he made a cautious move forward and agreed to relate reserves to the closing price of Giza 7 futures on the day before an auction. According to Telford, buyers appreciated this change which enabled them to buy and hedge on the same basis. The 1938 auctions were, however, carried out under poor selling conditions, owing to falling prices, a big American crop, and poor spinner demand. They were the direct opposite of conditions ruling at the auctions of the previous year. 68,000 bales were sold and 56,000 withdrawn. MacIntyre still refused to give a twenty-one-day sampling period and still allowed no reauctions. Telford passed on clients' comments on these restrictions and also pleaded to be allowed to auction 'S' variety cotton to make the market more attractive, but this MacIntyre refused and his comment on Telford's report is illuminating.

Telford seems to think that all that is important is the number of bales that are sold at the auctions irrespective of whether these prices pay the Syndicate and the tenant. We have already told him that the time has not yet come when we are prepared to sell our S cotton through the auctions. It is quite likely that if we sold our S cotton at low enough reserve prices, the amount of L cotton sold would be even less than the small amount which we did sell through the auctions this season at miserable prices. The buyers can quite well buy now from us S cotton ex-store Port Sudan, if they want to, on the basis of Liverpool prices, but they won't, as there is not enough in it for them at our prices.[13]

But although prices were low, the Government was convinced that the auctions had accelerated sales and resulted in quicker payments to tenants and increased activity in all markets in the Blue Nile Province. These direct and indirect results suited it, and the Director of Agriculture, Dr. Tothill,* pressed its point of view in a report in March 1939 strongly critical of the cautiousness of the Syndicate and sanguine of the results of a purely local sales policy.

Reserve prices are still being withheld from buyers. . . . The policy of not re-offering withdrawn lots is apparently being reconsidered, and if this

* Dr. J. D. Tothill, C.M.G. After service with United States and Canadian Governments, joined Colonial Civil Service: Director of Agriculture, Fiji and Uganda: Director of Agriculture, Sudan, 1939–44: Principal of Gordon University College, 1944–7. His book, *Agriculture in the Sudan* (1947), is a mine of agricultural information about the country.

should result in cotton once offered being made available through the auction on request, I am convinced it will result in more sales.

The practice of shipping all the S cotton without exposing it for public sale means a continuance of the old monopoly which has been so strongly criticised, and which undoubtedly affects trading in this type.

To make these sales a success buyers must have some assurance that in selling they will not be competing with stocks held by the Syndicate. This will entail the selling of all cotton at Port Sudan, there must be no question of stocks being carried for old customers; they will have the same opportunities as others in obtaining their requirements.[14]

Once again MacIntyre made a step towards the Government's viewpoint but refused to abandon the policy of gradual experiment. At the 1939 auctions at last some 'S' cotton was auctioned, though only in the lowest grades, and it was all sold. But to avoid undercutting sales made through the B.C.G.A. a ban was placed on buyers against shipment of the 'S' crop to the United Kingdom or to India, where the B.C.G.A. had developed a useful outlet through one firm, Gill and Co., of Bombay. Then further steps were taken. After the sixth auction, reauctioning of all the 'L' cotton withdrawn was permitted, and at Government instigation reserve prices were reduced and for the first time disclosed. There was no dramatic result. Merchants still said the cotton was too dear and that action had been taken so late that many of their clients had filled up with other growths. 20,000 bales were sold at the 1939 auctions, 6,000 more at reauctions, but 42,000 were withdrawn unsold.

Nevertheless 1939 culminated in the record number of 295,000 bales being sold in one year, and although world demand had increased this result reflected in some degree justification of the Government's pressure. MacIntyre, however, maintained his usual caution when telling the results to the shareholders at the 1939 meeting.

Sales have not been too easy to effect and prices have been low. Nevertheless we have been able to dispose of larger quantities than in the previous year at approximately equal prices. We are continuing to develop sales by auction at Port Sudan. The Giza futures contract in Liverpool still remains in the same unsatisfactory form, resulting in a restricted market in forward sales. When such are made to any large extent, there is a tendency for a continual and substantial lowering of our cotton prices during the period of these auctions.[15]

Looking back at this story of Gezira marketing before the war it is not easy to deduce what was significant. The record closes in rather a confusion of counsel. But that in itself may be significant, for it discloses how complicated the problem of selling a major world product can be. The operation touches established interests which everywhere limit independence. There was first the question of how to get in the trade at all. There is little doubt that if Lancashire had not been actively interested this problem might have been much more difficult. Thanks to the B.C.G.A. direct contact with spinners was established in the United Kingdom. Then later the protégé grew too big for its promoter. The market narrowed for its particular fine-quality product. The producers found the existing trade system—the Liverpool market—liable to manipulation against them and sought to run a price system outside it. But this in turn frightened the Liverpool Cotton Association. In the effort to seek a wider outlet in the world the producers' problem then was how far to trust merchants, in whose hands the channels of trade lay, to promote new openings at good enough prices without prejudicing the prices and off-take of those spinners who already knew and valued the cotton. On this problem the partners split, the Government eager to trust the new and discard the old, the Syndicate sceptical of merchants' talk and of dependence on them.

Curiously enough in the end the most important feature was that neither partner pressed its view to the limit. The market was undoubtedly increased, particularly in India, by the Government's pressure to get local auctions going. But MacIntyre's caution also came into its own. With the outbreak of war, the predilection for old customers, which had seemed an obstinate vice, became a contact of considerable virtue, and the system of a separate selling price, sustained at a higher level than the open auction had provided, became the basis of an invaluable war-time contract.

For a while in 1940 auctions continued. 53,000 bales were sold and 90,000 withdrawn. Sales at the earlier auctions were good but, after the invasion of Holland and Belgium in early May, they fell away to nil. Shipping facilities, after a first shock of dislocation, had been improving and it was decided in March, at Himbury's suggestion, to ship all high-grade 'S' cotton to Liverpool, in order to take advantage of supplying spinners who might get government contracts. With the entry of Italy into the war in June shipping again became difficult, and thenceforward the outstanding problem for the Gezira, and the Sudan, was to get the cotton accepted as a war necessity.

The Syndicate tried to hold auctions again in 1941 but buyers preferred to buy privately after the auctions. In March 1941 the Liverpool market, in common with other commodity markets in the United Kingdom, was closed, the Sudan being notified that all cotton in Britain would be controlled by the British Government who would merely order forward what it required. Conditions of sale for other customers continued to be published by the Syndicate even in 1942, but the buyer bore his own war risk and found his own shipping. There were no takers for auctions and few private treaty sales. These were the last flickers of life in the pre-war system. On 23rd August 1942 the Syndicate closed its Port Sudan office.

When the commodity markets were closed in the United Kingdom all raw material imports were controlled by special boards. For the cotton industry it was a body called the Cotton Control. With the Gezira and government cotton crops of 1941 on its hands with no buyers, the Sudan Government approached the British Government for help, for the marketing in such circumstances was beyond the Syndicate's scope and became a Government to Government problem. In April 1941 the Cotton Control inquired from the Sudan Government the minimum number of bales needed to be purchased to cover the overheads of the Gezira Scheme. In July the Control offered to buy 17,500 bales after shipment of all cotton already licensed for import to the United Kingdom.

In August 1941 a contract was negotiated with the Cotton Control by Sir William Himbury, acting for the Sudan, for the sale of a further 48,550 bales of 'L' and 11,350 bales of 'S' cotton. Prices were negotiated for each grade produced in the Gezira and the prices and differentials between the grades in this contract were destined to be the basis of sales to the Cotton Control throughout the war.

In the following year the Cotton Control agreed to buy any unsold cotton from the 1942 crop, and in March 1943 a new contract was signed, under which the Control undertook to buy all the Gezira cotton crops during the war and for one full crop after the war. Prices were fixed at sixty points above those of the 1941 contract and provision was made for a further rise if costs of production justified it. A rise of forty points was agreed for the 1944 crop and of a further twenty points for the 1945 and 1946 crops, with which season the contract ended.

This war-time contract was criticized in some quarters in the Sudan in later years as having been unduly low-priced as a deliberate help to Britain at the expense of the Sudan. This was not true. The original price basis in 1941 was related to prices for Gezira cotton current at that time for United Kingdom spinners which, as has been seen, were usually above the auction prices, and when it was first negotiated the purpose of the contract was as much to help the Sudan as the United Kingdom, when, with the seas dangerous and impossible for transport outside governmental control, there ceased to be a market for Gezira cotton at all.

It might be claimed that the 'points on' for increases in expenses, which were related mainly to joint account items ascertainable from the accounts, did not very generously cover rises in the tenants' costs outside these accounts. But the main feeling of criticism arose from the year after the war when the contract was still in force but external prices were once again being quoted and were by then at a higher level than those in the contract.

But against these drawbacks the contract brought immense advantages. The anxiety of marketing, so long the major problem, simply ceased to exist. Delivery and payment were made in monthly units of 30,000 bales irrespective of shipping delays, the Cotton Control paying for storage at Port Sudan after delivery and accepting all risk of loss at sea. With the entire crop guaranteed sold and paid for during the year, at known and, as appeared then, fair prices, the Government's objective of quick returns had been reached, albeit fortuitously, and a marketing system attained, of stability through bulk purchase, which is still often put forward as an ideal for raw material producers. Why this system did not work out ideally in the end is another interesting feature of Gezira marketing experience, but it belongs to a later chapter (Chapter 20) dealing with the history after 1946.

Chapter 16

FIRST VENTURES IN SOCIAL
DEVELOPMENT

The reader may be thinking that the original purpose of the Sudan
Government, 'to introduce civilization', has got a little lost in
the maze of technical detail in the last few chapters. The partnership was designed for social as well as economic progress but soon after
the Scheme was launched economic problems began to assume priority
and unless they were settled there was a risk that the Scheme which
could bring such social benefits would collapse. The technical chapters
have shown just how varied and how vital were the economic problems
which had to be solved before the Scheme could be regarded as safe or
stable.

But the reader's bewilderment at being led down paths of technical
details and left wondering what is the main theme of the story was a
feeling strongly shared by many government officials in these very years.
What, they increasingly demanded, was the Scheme for? Should not
policy be directed more to the needs of society in the Gezira and less to
the dictates of economic efficiency? They were questions typical of the
age, and the search for an answer became the predominant theme as the
Gezira gradually emerged from the economic doldrums. It may be
wondered if there was any need for such philosophizing. Why not get on
with the job of growing cotton? Surely the Scheme was to produce
money? But this was precisely the bone of contention. Was the purpose
of the Scheme for the tenant, or its effects on his social life, being given
enough attention compared with responsibility to shareholders or claims
to revenue for the central government?

These questions were grounded in the old fear that the Syndicate
might administer the Scheme in a way different from the Government's
objectives, and we have already seen that Sudan administrators were as
touchy on this point as any batch of nationalist politicians. One might
argue that the Syndicate had no concern with the social or political

development of the people. But even in developed countries today the pursuit of a just society causes social and political considerations to impinge on economic life. In the less-developed Sudan a paternal Government, with the same aim, had greater power and, they believed, duty to interfere. It is important to appreciate this attitude because the emphasis on government control in many emergent territories is less an ideology than a legacy of paternalism based on the same outlook, conditioned by the same circumstances.

The government administrator's attitude was not just one of jealousy, but was definitely coloured by the expectation that all aspects of life ought to conform to his interpretation of desirable policy. Now although the agricultural was only one of such aspects it permeated 90 per cent of the people's lives in the Gezira and the decisions concerning it were made, not by the sparse cadre of district commissioners with their occasional visits, but by a large staff of resident Syndicate field officers, whose policies were dictated by the Syndicate's headquarters at Barakat.

Government policies were notably inspired by ideals of trusteeship but the concept of what was best for the ward varied with different generations of officials. The early administrators followed Kitchener's injunction of direct personal interest in the lives of individuals, and their anxiety to make sure that the fruits of economic development were equitably spread was evident in the Gezira land laws and in the regulations controlling the distribution of tenancies to landlords and others. The Syndicate's administration of the Scheme followed these ideals, which were also suited to efficiency. It was a direct administration consciously emancipating, by the opportunity of economic independence, the individual tenants from the control of masters and fathers to whom otherwise they would still have been subservient. In the process it was incidentally enveloping them in a new dependence upon the Scheme and its field officers.

The result was not very palatable to the generation of government administrators which took over in the twenties and thirties and established the golden age of 'indirect rule'. This doctrine of administering a country through the 'natural leaders of the people', of which the great protagonist had been Lord Lugard, was generally accepted as desirable in the British Colonial Service at that time. Although the Sudan came under the Foreign Office, conditions were in many respects similar to a dependent colonial territory, and the prevalence in most of the country of a tribal and patriarchal form of society made this prevailing doctrine particularly applicable. Two factors in the Sudan itself in any case greatly influenced a change from direct to indirect administration: the financial stringency of the time which made cheapness in government a necessity, and the expulsion from the Sudan, after the murder of the Governor-General, Sir Lee Stack, in Cairo in 1924, of all Egyptian personnel. These had hitherto held most of the subordinate posts in the service, and although in the long run their expulsion played a crucial part in encouraging the training of educated Sudanese for civil and military posts in their own country, the immediate result was to transfer much greater responsibility to the indigenous tribal authorities.

The Syndicate's administration of the Gezira Scheme formed a rude contrast to this policy, and the political officials of the Sudan Government felt that efforts to introduce devolution of powers to the natural leaders of the people in the judicial and administrative spheres would prove of little value if agriculture and irrigation continued to be administered directly and intensively by the Syndicate. As early as 1926 many government officials thought that the Syndicate should be compelled to conform to government policy as the price of getting extensions. As important a man as MacGregor,* the Irrigation Adviser, who negotiated the Nile Waters Agreement, wrote:

There is the question of the communal organisation of the people, and of making provision for the building up of a system which can eventually dispense with intensive Syndicate management. I feel that the Syndicate should be definitely made to acknowledge some obligation in this respect if their concession is to run for 25 years. Arising out of this is the question whether government should retain the right to insist on a certain number of larger holdings to be held by men of substance and standing.[1]

The more commercially minded men in the Government were more cautious. Huddleston, then Governor of the Blue Nile Province, and later Financial Secretary, had seen devolution in action in Dongola, where use had been made of omdas and sheikhs (posts in the local native administration) for water control and agricultural supervision. The experience had been disappointing and, in view of the importance of sanitary control (because of malaria) and of the financial risks, he considered it essential that the Government should carry out independent experiments in devolution before trying to influence the Syndicate. Schuster, the Financial Secretary, had shared Huddleston's opinion and

* R. M. MacGregor (1882–1946), C.M.G. After service in Public Works Department, India, was Irrigation Adviser to the Sudan Government, 1923–37: Sudan member of Nile Commission, 1925 (see Chapter 9).

refused to risk blindly the fate of the Gezira Scheme. Nevertheless his view was that before long the pioneer stage would be passed and with it the necessity for close direct administration by the Syndicate. In a note in 1927 which was passed on to Eckstein he concluded:

I think it is most important that this principle should be recognised now on both sides. Otherwise there is likely to be friction and loss of efficiency owing to each side pulling in different directions. A proper understanding in this point ought generally to help in promoting good relations between the Government and the Syndicate. On the Government side suspicion that the Syndicate wants to extend its grip on the country would be removed, while on the Syndicate side it is hoped that they would view plans for extensions by the Government on its own account without jealousy.[2]

The Governor-General, Sir John Maffey, penned a short minute on this statement which was often quoted in later years.

There is no future for the Syndicate as a power established between the Government and the people. Similarly there is no future for the Government as a cotton magnate. This ought not to mean divorce but a new relationship, and the present discussions may be productive of good results if they enable the Government and Syndicate to coordinate their final objectives.[3]

Huddleston expressed a like sentiment and added pertinently that it would be difficult enough anyway for the Government to decide between its own financial and administrative interests.

The Syndicate, however, had considerable doubts about the efficacy of a policy of devolution of agricultural control in the Gezira and Mac-Intyre set these down when, a year later, the Government asked him to participate in an experiment in looser control on an extension in the south. Highest among these he placed justice to the individual tenant and a measure of financial success whereby he could live better than he used to do. Without honest treatment and straightforward financing of loans and distribution of profits both tenants and workers attracted to the Scheme might disappear. Then there were the various technical aspects which required constant supervision of a high standard, efficient distribution of water to synchronize with the daily discharges supplied by the Irrigation Department, proper agricultural methods for the growing of all crops, adequate ploughing, clean picking which affected subsequent grading, and finally baling out of water after irrigation, a breakdown in which would increase risks of malaria. He wrote,

The maintenance of all these factors is dependent on the individual cooperation of our inspectors with the individual tenants, and I cannot see how a third party can be introduced without jeopardising these services so essential to the success of the Scheme.

On 15,000 feddans we employ three British inspectors. Taking leave into consideration this means that for half the time there are only two inspectors who have each to supervise 7,500 feddans of which 5,000 may be under crop and 2,500 fallow or being ploughed and prepared for next season's crop.

I cannot imagine that at any time in this generation you will be able to do with less British supervision without endangering the revenues of the Scheme. The introduction of a third party between inspector and tenant would mean not a decrease but an increase in control, to supervise how the third party was dealing with the cultivator, and adjust innumerable grievances which might be legitimate or otherwise.[4]

W. P. Clarke, the same man who had been the first government commissioner to make contacts with the local people for the introduction of the Scheme, drawing on his recollections of those days, gave a typical picture of the administrator's attitude in 1929.

The kind of arguments against it [the Gezira Scheme], which were advanced, especially by the older and more patriarchal type of native, were 'The Sheikhs will be nobodies, the Syndicate inspectors will be kings of the country.' 'I now own and control large areas of rain land, under the new scheme I shall have only 30 feddans just the same as my slave.' 'We hate these straight lines, we would rather be hungry once every few years, with freedom to range with our cattle unconfined, than have full bellies and be fined if we stray outside these horrid little squares.' 'Our children and our slaves will become swollen headed and no longer regard our authority.' One entirely sympathised with this point of view but the only thing to be done was to stress the arguments on the other side. These arguments consisted in appeals to the grosser and more materialistic side; the probability of wealth beyond their dreams, water laid on without the trouble of drawing it, security against famine, were, one was compelled to argue, of far more value to them than freedom and administrative powers and responsibility.

Although by now the desire for material gain has overcome all the objections, the latter remain just as valid as they were in 1920. They are only buried under a layer of gold. The levelling effect of the present system has been decried by all who have had anything to do with the Gezira, and we have heard a lot of promises about devolving agricultural control to the bigger natives in the future, but nothing definite has yet been done. If the Syndicate insist on methods of direct control, let us keep the area as small as possible. If we must have an extension, let us not give it to the Syndicate except in return for official recognition of devolutionary methods.[5]

The Government, however, did not press the case and the matter was dropped for the time being. Soon the great depression (1930 to 1934) ruled out any question of social experiments in the fight to keep the Scheme alive.

But the depression itself accentuated the difference in outlook. With the fall in prices, yields and profits, the picture of a tenant as a newly emancipated individual with a rising standard of living began to fade. In the first years of prosperity protagonists of the Gezira Scheme, by contrast with the disciples of indirect rule, saw it as an island of new ideas in a stagnant sea of almost biblical society. But in the years of adversity, with their stricter discipline and added work, the tenants seemed to have precious little liberty or economic advantage. They seemed little more than labourers on their own land, cogs in a cotton-production machine. The wisdom of having attached them to a world economy at all was doubted, and measures for raising their standard of living thereby, if not disparaged altogether, were felt by government officials to be much less important than the encouragement of self-management under their natural leaders.

These conflicting attitudes put a strain upon the relations between the political service and the Syndicate throughout the depression and, as is so often the case, they tended to be enlarged into caricatures. Broadly, the Syndicate feared that the Government was about to sacrifice the economic well-being of the Scheme and the economic emancipation of the small man, in the interests of an out-of-date system of tribal aristocracy. Genuinely, MacIntyre, with the emancipation of Scottish crofters from their lairds in his mind, regarded this as a be-trayal of the tenant's interests, and the Syndicate staff had little belief in the integrity of those natural leaders of the people whom the Govern-ment had set up in judicial and administrative responsibility in the Gezira. Meanwhile on the White Nile the Government had gone farther and had established certain individuals, by grant of pumping stations, in positions of material power and advantage which in the Gezira had been deliberately reserved for the state. Pursued to its logical conclusion this policy had an affinity with the oil and land sheikhdoms of the Middle East and it carried the great danger of corrupting traditional authority rather than revitalizing it, producing pashas in Packards rather than a progressive peasantry. On its side the Government tended to suspect that the Syndicate was completely out of sympathy with any attempts to get away from plantation management.

There was enough truth in these caricatures to confuse the problem for some years. Too many administrative officers interpreted their func-tions as game wardens in a Garden of Eden. There was need to abandon attempts to preserve a static patriarchal society and to recognize that economic changes required new instruments of responsibility in which all citizens could share. On the Syndicate side it was necessary to accept that in a scheme of such national importance financial considerations alone were not enough. It was a most serious reflection on the development of the Gezira inhabitants that they were completely excluded from the administration of an enterprise which had really enveloped the whole of their lives. Indirect rule might be out of date, but this did not remove the crucial point that under the Syndicate no start had been made in associating the local people with the management.

The gradual improvement in the economics of the Scheme in the late thirties brought the attitudes of the two partners closer together, and MacIntyre took the opportunity of the appointment of R. C. Mayall as Province Governor in 1936 to try and get a common objective worked out. He wrote,

> While I am sure of your wishes for the heartiest cooperation, it would be so much easier for everyone if the ultimate objective and outline of the running of the Scheme after the Syndicate's tenure were known now, so that all could work towards a common objective irrespective of whether the Syndicate could be usefully brought into the picture or not after 1950. [6]

The right to revise the concession agreement in 1939 gave Government the opportunity it needed for a major review of Gezira policy. The financial position at that time made it probable that the Syndicate's services would still be welcome even after 1950, provided that agreement could be reached on social policies. The prospect of being able to pay off the Gezira debt and the take-over value of the permanent assets of the Syndicate was a distant one. Even the annual interest burden was heavy enough, in relation to the country's resources, to rule out any hazardous experimentation. Moreover the probability of being able to double the size of the Scheme during the next twenty years made the wisdom of parting with the Syndicate open to doubt. There was therefore considerable reason for taking up MacIntyre's opening and laying down a common objective.

Rugman, the Financial Secretary,* invited senior members of the administration to submit papers on the future of the Scheme, which produced a valuable survey. The vision of an Arab squirearchy had by now been dropped and Mayall, the focal agent of new-deal planning for the Gezira, summarized the administration's new view of the future.

---

* Rugman described his own views in a memorandum of such interest that I have included a large extract from it at the end of this chapter.

The ideal object of government, if she is to be faithful to her principles of trusteeship should be, before the concession period is ended, administratively and agriculturally to have trained up a class of small peasant proprietors, who can, when the control period is ended, make the best use of the irrigation system.[7]

There were three main prongs in his policy to attain this objective. First, progressive devolution on to village communities (as represented by village councils), of self-control over their own civic and agricultural life. This involved a combined operation between Government administrators and Syndicate staff, so his second prong was a local board of field management with Syndicate and Government (and later tenants') representation. A corollary to this was that the previous practice of referring everything to the Managing Director must be replaced by a generous devolution of authority to this local board. The third prong was that as much attention ought to be paid to the training of the tenant as a general farmer, to his food and fodder crops and animal husbandry, as to the cash crop, cotton.

Rugman embodied many of Mayall's ideas in a letter to the Syndicate in April 1939.

Generally speaking our review has up to date, shown that an extension of the concession period would necessitate not so much a drastic recasting of the financial basis of the Scheme as a reorientation of the Companies' attitude to it. I think you would wish me to speak frankly. I do not think that any responsible critic could deny that as a purely cotton producing proposition the Gezira Scheme has been highly successful or that the duties of the Companies in raising and handling the crop have been carried out with admirable efficiency. But mere technical efficiency is not the sole quality which a government must expect from a chosen implement in an undertaking which represents a substantial portion of the public debt and the welfare of 150,000 inhabitants. There must also be free recognition of the fact that the Government is not only a principal partner in the Scheme but also a trustee for the local population. And that recognition must be translated into practical and sympathetic cooperation with Government in the development of its native policy.

This sounds rather abstract but in concrete terms it implies, I think, closer liaison to be achieved by a local joint standing committee representing the Government and the Companies (with facilities for the inclusion of tenants' representation when necessary), further decentralisation to the Companies' representatives in the Gezira, the gradual devolution of agricultural control of the individual tenants to native agencies, the substitution of non-British staff by native staff, the provision of agricultural education facilities, and a recognition of the equal importance of the non-cotton activities of the tenants. These are matters of machinery rather than money but they are of great importance from the government point of view.[8]

MacIntyre had had the misfortune to be attacked by tuberculosis of the lung in 1938 and Rugman's approach fell to be dealt with by Mr. Harold Wooding,* who succeeded him as Managing Director, although MacIntyre still remained Chairman. Wooding had visited the Sudan occasionally as a director but his professional background was that of a city banker. MacIntyre, with all his intimate experience of the Gezira project since the days of Zeidab, had, like many a Scotsman, built up very much a one-man empire around him. His stubborn and decisive personality, of immense value in days of trouble, made it difficult for the views of any other person to penetrate the Companies' policy. Changes were, to a very high degree, dependent upon his personal inclinations. It was this dependence upon one dominant personality that the Government was anxious to alter in its new proposals. Wooding's appointment afforded the opportunity.

The writer was by now Manager-Designate and began to play a personal part in the future policy. Both I myself and my colleagues among the senior local staff of the Syndicate had an awareness of a dual loyalty in our position. We had a duty to obtain the best commercial returns for our shareholders and for the country. We had equally a duty to advance the general interests of the tenants. The Government's social policy of indirect rule had seemed to us to threaten rather than advance these interests. But the new proposals were a different matter. They provided for all tenants gradually to share in running their own local management. We knew that the Sudan was slowly moving to an independent political destiny. It was important that the countryman should not be left behind the townsman in the process. He had had some years of direction in his agricultural job from us and ought to know it. That we should now turn to be tutors of a local democratic community, fading out ourselves and teaching them gradually to make all their own decisions, was an understandable ideal to us. Spoon-feeding had been wise in the early years, and drive and direct control essential through the depression, but if the tenants were ever going to stand on their own feet the habit of waiting to have everything organized for them had to be changed.

We were, however, more apprehensive than the Financial Secretary of the effect of the new policy upon the monetary returns. We could envisage a gradual transfer of responsibility from our field staff to the village councils. To begin with, these bodies could take over arbitration duties, which often took up a great deal of our time and arose out of

* Later Sir Harold Wooding. Director, Sudan Plantations Syndicate, 1929–46: Managing Director, 1946–9: Chairman, 1950: knighted in 1950: died 1953.

disputes between tenants over water or labour or assessment of animal damage. Gradually their horizon could be raised to include the allotment and termination of tenancies, supervision of the work of absentees, planning of ploughing, fertilizer and sowing programmes, distribution of loans, indenting and local control of water. The mere enumeration of these items reveals the intensity of supervision which lay behind Gezira efficiency. Clearly the efficiency was still essential to the three partners. Our problem was how far it was likely to be diminished by the transfer of responsibility.

On this score we were particularly worried by the disappearance of the two most powerful factors in efficiency: the immediate contact between the tenants and our field officer and the connection between loans and work done. They did not amount to compulsion but they were strong stimulants to timely action in a land where lethargy was climatically natural and leisure a man's first purchase.

The problem of integrity also worried us. In a poor country the risk of corruption was great and the effect might be disastrous. To reduce it, it might be necessary to standardize loan payments and make them independent of performance. In short, efficiency must depend ultimately on the tenants themselves, on their desire to change to a new way of life with its greater independence and social opportunities. A crucial part of the devolution programme would therefore have to lie in a great expansion of education in its widest sense. There were thus two economic differences which the partnership would have to face in the new policy compared with the simple principle of maximum cotton profit which underlay the original agreement with the Companies. The first was the extra risk to efficiency, the second was the on-cost in time and staff, at any rate at first, of training the local people to do things themselves instead of doing them for them.

Our local view was to a certain extent shared by Sir Douglas Newbold,* the new Civil Secretary, in an opinion given to Mayall. He wrote,

I consider it essential that both parties understand that under the new policy some loss of efficiency, and therefore of revenue, is inevitable. This loss of revenue can be wholly or partly made up by the Syndicate in a dilution of British staff. The last half kantar may not now be picked. This loss of revenue is the price which the Syndicate must pay for an extension

* Sir Douglas Newbold (1894–1945), K.B.E. Joined Sudan Political Service, 1920: Civil Secretary, Sudan, 1938–45. See K. D. D. Henderson, *The Making of the Modern Sudan, The Life and Letters of Sir Douglas Newbold* (London, Faber and Faber, 1953), for his biography and, incidentally, the political history of this period.

of the agreement, and which the Government and tenants must pay for the advance in social development which is overdue. I do not feel that either side will gain anything by burking this issue. Comparative loss of efficiency does not mean bankruptcy or slovenliness, and is compensated by the gain in contentment, agricultural education and local government.[9]

It will have become apparent by now how very close our ideas and those of the Government had become. At a formal meeting at Barakat, in February 1940, the accord was cemented when Wooding, on behalf of the Syndicate, accepted a declaration of policy drafted by Mayall which was later to become known as Schedule X. It read as follows:

The Government's general policy is to train up a class of small farmers, who, when the concession period is ended, can make the best use of the permanent irrigation system established in the Gezira.

The Government's administrative policy is:—

(a) The development of an orderly organisation of village communities controlled by headmen selected by themselves.

(b) The devolution of civic and agricultural control of the farmers to agents of this organisation (e.g. agricultural sheikhs) and the use of village and other councils and of native courts to support and enforce the authority of these agents.

(c) The gradual substitution of Sudanese for all non-British employees and eventually the use of Sudanese agriculturalists in the field in an advisory capacity.

The Government's agricultural policy is:—

(a) The production of a class of mixed farmers with a permanent stake in the land which they farm. To this end:—

(b) The cultivation of food and fodder crops should be given as much importance as the money crop.

(c) Provision should be made for the agricultural education of native agents and selected farmers.[10]

Schedule X was a very sketchy document and it remained to work out how the new policy was to be implemented. As in the early days pilot pump schemes had been used to work out the best agricultural pattern for the Gezira so, for the new social policy, a pilot experiment was set up. On both occasions there was too much at stake to think of rushing in headlong. For agricultural administration the Syndicate had divided the Gezira into forty blocks (estates). One of the older blocks, by the name of Hōsh, was selected for the social pilot scheme.

It was not, as a matter of fact, the first experiment of its kind. During the years leading up to the determination of this policy tentative experiments had been going on, both within and without the Syndicate's sphere of operations. When the Gebel Aulia Dam had at last been built by Egypt on the White Nile certain tribal lands had been inundated. To provide an alternative livelihood for those affected, the Government had tacked on an extra block to the north-western end of the Gezira main canal at a place called Abd El Majid. This Abd El Majid block, which had its first season in 1938, was managed by the Government through a special board, and in it were applied many of the principles of devolution now approved for the Gezira. There were, however, significant differences which made a more tentative approach in the Gezira desirable. The tenants in Abd El Majid had been brought from the White Nile under their tribal chiefs. The land had been registered as government-owned and there were no settled villages. Thus it afforded an appropriate opportunity for tribal administration in a way no longer applicable in the more sophisticated Gezira. But more significantly Abd El Majid was essentially an alternative livelihood project. Unlike the Gezira its efficiency was not a criterion, for it was not, like the Gezira, indispensable to the revenues of the country. Thus deductions from Abd El Majid experience had limitations in applicability to the Gezira.

Apart from Abd El Majid, within the Gezira there had also been some tentative experiments. Two lessons in particular had been demonstrated by these. In the one case, in a block named Fawar, devolution of powers merely to the headman (sheikh) in each village had been practised. These headmen were appointed traditionally by a tribal leader in whose territory the block lands lay. The tenants, however, were mostly of another tribe. The substitution of these headmen for the Syndicate's field officer, whose only contact with the tenants was through the headmen, was felt by the tenants to be detrimental. The headmen favoured the interests of their own tribesmen. The tenants requested leave to elect their own headmen. This placed the district commissioner in a difficult position. By the tenets of indirect rule he had to support his tribal leader. By contrast the tenants sought the support of the Syndicate's field officer. Co-operation in a joint policy became difficult.

In the other example the Syndicate had been invited in a number of blocks to select outstanding tenants of their own choice and devolve powers on to them. It was hoped that this method of devolution would result in each cultivator understanding more clearly the necessity for various operations since the reasons could be explained to him at leisure by one of his own people. It was hoped also that the gradual relaxation of direct control would encourage a greater sense of personal responsibility. In this case the results were more satisfactory than in Fawar, but it became clear that unless the selected tenant genuinely regarded himself as a representative of his people the devolution of powers gave him the opportunity of developing into a petty official of the worst type.

All these experiences were taken into consideration when the Hōsh pilot block was planned, and measures were laid to try to avoid repeating the mistakes. In each village headmen were elected, and with them a number of village councillors. The headmen were made presidents of their village councils. In each village, an individual tenant was selected, jointly by the Syndicate's field officer and the villagers, to be the village representative responsible for the agricultural management of the tenancies. For this purpose he was under the tuition of the Syndicate's field officer. These men were called samads. The council was equally under his tuition and was intended, on the one hand, to support the samads in maintaining satisfactory standards of work on the tenancies, and on the other to prevent them becoming petty autocrats. The development of devolution on these lines was entrusted to the Syndicate's block inspector who had in addition a block council, consisting of one representative from each village council, for discussion and execution of matters of general interest. Just what these matters were was left undefined. Clearly they were mainly agricultural, but with the new social purpose they soon began to embrace everything that was not obviously the known province of some existing department of government or local government.

The Hōsh experiment was intended to initiate a new phase in Gezira history, marking the beginnings of community control of agriculture through village councils and their agricultural samads. It was the experimental prelude to afford evidence on which a new agreement might be hammered out between the Government and the Syndicate, to carry the Gezira Scheme a stage further on its journey. But almost as soon as it was started, World War II enveloped us and was destined to have quite an influence on these plans.

EXTRACTS FROM A NOTE BY RUGMAN SUMMARIZING THE
EXPERIENCE OF THE GEZIRA SCHEME UP TO 1938
30.5.1938. S.G. (763-11-1)

The motives behind MacIntyre's inquiry are understandable. The two companies represent the investment of some £5,250,000 of capital and they need good time to know what to do with it if the S.G. terminate their concession and so repay most of it.

Unless the Sudan is to attempt to adopt a purely totalitarian or purely socialistic economic policy it must continue to rely, to an increasing extent, on outside capital and enterprise. The S.G. cannot indefinitely continue as the principal commercial organization in the country. This view may not be consistent with that Father Christmas concept of administration which labels all outside commercial enterprise as 'exploitation', but it is difficult to see how the native can eventually learn to run the country's commerce unless outside interests are allowed to come in and provide the example for teaching him.

Three fundamental factors have to be kept in mind:

1. The Gezira must remain primarily a financial problem so long as the debt service remains. 1959 is the earliest date for repayment.

2. The Gezira land laws. We are pledged to pay 10 piastres per feddan per annum for forty years from the time the land is brought into the Scheme.

3. Liability to the companies for taking over capital assets on termination of the concession. Even if the Sudan struck another favourable period comparable with 1934–7, the S.G. would probably wish to apply any free reserves up to £5 million in repayment of the Egyptian debt.

What has been the value of the co-operation of the companies? The Gezira Scheme is a—I believe unique—partnership. Up to date the companies have not made excessive profits. Taking into account premia on share issues the Syndicate shareholder has secured an average return of about 6 per cent on his money. The K.C.C. paid no dividend during the first twelve years of its existence.

The Government's return cannot be accurately assessed owing to the large indirect benefits and liabilities accruing from it. Taking only its direct receipts, the Government, i.e. the general taxpayer, has lost £2 million since 1924.

I think it is fair to say that anyone who was familiar with the Gezira before the Scheme would agree that the tenant is far better off now than he was then.

What has been the working record of the companies? So far as mechanical operations are concerned their duties have been carried out economically and with great efficiency. On the other hand a number of features call for criticism. Their marketing policy was shortsighted. Their general administration has lacked flexibility. There is insufficient devolution of authority. Everything is referred to H.Q. and, if the Government is involved, the matter is usually passed to the Managing

Director who is normally outside the Sudan. The attitude of the companies has lacked the broad and statesmanlike qualities which a partner of the Government and a chosen implement might be expected to possess. Certain of the Cadman criticisms of Imperial Airways could be applied to the companies.

On the other hand, the Government itself is not blameless. Its attitude has been lamentably inconsistent. The central government and the local province authorities left everything to the Syndicate. Then came the bad times and a lot of wrangling over tenants' debts. One Governor told the companies 'Hands off my Sheikhs'. His successor blamed the companies for impeding the progress of native administration by failing to use the sheikhs. Relations between the Central Government and the companies are now normal and it is to be hoped that Syndicate inspectors and local government staff will appreciate each others' points of view and difficulties.

The answer to MacIntyre's inquiry should, I think, be that the Government would be prepared to extend the concession provided that the Agreements are suitably revised. To my mind the most important question is the agricultural control of the Scheme. I am convinced that the proper way to run the production side of the partnership is through a local board representative of all three partners.

Chapter 17

SOCIAL DEVELOPMENT AND
THE WAR

The second world war quickened the programme of social development immensely. The objective of self-management, novel at first to tenants and staff, became a much more conscious ideal from its connection with the war aims of the allies. Pressures, awakened by the war, from educated Sudanese and tenants alike for a greater say in affairs were in this sense evoked rather than resisted. In particular the Atlantic Charter had a profound effect. However much a later generation may have come to look back on it as a statement of pleasing platitudes, the affirmation at that time of the right of all peoples to choose their own government was in the northern Sudan unequivocally taken to heart as a declaration of policy, which gave immediate urgency to the local build-up of responsibility.

Practical stimulus was given to this policy by the acute staff shortage, occasioned by the departure of many British field officers to the forces. It had been intended that the system of devolution at Hōsh should be very gradually spread as the experiment proved itself. Now it became necessary to supplement the field staff with more samads immediately. There were 250 of them by 1941. This hasty arrangement at first forced the Syndicate into an expedient contrary to the devolution principle. Unlike the samads at Hōsh, these wartime samads were not connected with village councils, and they were paid by the Syndicate as *sous-officiers* of their staff, as opposed to the Hōsh samads who (as the experiment in devolution was not financially a company liability) were paid from government funds. There was thus some danger that they might form just that cadre of petty bureaucrats which their association with village councils had been designed to avoid.

The training of village councils and samads in a new mutual responsibility meant a patient weaning from years of accepted direct authority and was a very different matter from the creation of *sous-officiers*. It

213

of their own contribution were meant to lie. Schedule X had laid down the aim but had never been carried to the point of a new agreement between the Syndicate and the Government.

Uncertainty on these issues was making it difficult for us as local managers of the Scheme to know how far to go and, by way of extracting a more definite plan, we set down in a memorandum in 1943[3] an imaginary programme and forwarded it to our board for their consideration as a basis of discussion with the Government. The memorandum reflected the ideas we exchanged locally and the organizational problems which permeated that period.

Our basic assumption in this programme was a future picture of a co-operative community of farmers capable of managing their local affairs through their village units, assisted meantime by our organization whose duty was to make this community one of healthy, intelligent and progressive men and women. For development at the centre, we envisaged the village councils appointing representatives to the block councils and from these, later, a small representative board of tenants for the whole Gezira. The idea was that through such a board consultation at first, and much later on control, might pass from the present system to an appointed or elected body of tenants representing and managing the Tenants' Co-operative Society. We looked on this social development programme as something additional to, not competing with, economic efficiency.

In pursuing this ideal we felt that the Gezira Scheme offered in a remarkable degree an opportunity of carrying into practical effect the aims of the Atlantic Charter. The existence, in a previously backward country, of a large peasant community organized to trade as a unit, controlling its own reserve funds and mutual-help machinery, highly socialized and yet offering wide scope for individual initiative and advancement, might, as the Scheme changed to a more democratic administration, have an interest outside the Sudan, and advertise one sort of solution to a political and economic problem now facing many parts of the world. Such a view of the Scheme's future went a long way beyond mere cotton production, but was the logical outcome of the Schedule X conception. It would require, however, the co-ordination in one programme of the needs of agriculture, social services and local government.

In agriculture we saw a need for widening the farming outlook of the tenants. In the existing Gezira agreement the management's job was concentrated on cotton. The tenants' food and fodder crops were simply permissive adjuncts. Neither money nor staff time was allocated to improving these and to encouraging the tenants to develop mixed farming interests as a subsidiary to the main cash crop. Seed quality of dura was often poor and far too much of the crop sold forward to merchants at low prices. Nothing like full productive value was made of lubia. The indiscriminate grazing of nomadic days was the custom. Cutting, storage and silage were never practised. As a result there was little feed for stock for several months in the year and milk and meat supplies, which from an irrigation scheme might have been expected to be available for the better nutrition of a rapidly growing population, were unnecessarily short. Water of course was limited under the existing Nile Waters Agreement but new dams on the river might alter this in future. An American visitor during the war observed how well alfalfa grew in the Gezira, and struck a spark by forecasting that within another generation the Scheme would be sending beef to southern Europe. But if fat-stock production was to be a new sideline there was need for a complete change in the traditional outlook on stock. Organized stockbreeding would have to be arranged and the value of quality rather than quantity taught. Another sideline in cash income could be obtained within the rotation by vegetables, groundnuts, and pigeon peas, while fruit gardens could be established in village compounds. But these also were outside routine and needed a special horticultural section.

Direct British control had been a useful first teacher, and wisely concentrated on the cash crop, but its effect, like a drug, was wearing out. To get across an active interest in mixed farming among the tenants it was essential to do more about practical agricultural education as a supplement to the mere giving of orders. We did not want anything bookish. The desirable curriculum we had in mind was quite simple and specific to the Gezira. A special school for samads seemed a sensible suggestion. But many of the samads owed their selection to their authority and personality, not to their aptitude to learn new ideas. It seemed wiser therefore to choose young intelligent tenants for this special education, who later on could take over the samad's job in their villages.

In addition to the simple syllabus we thought that opportunity should be taken at the school to explain the financial organization of the Scheme, the intention behind the devolution to village councils, and, finally, the need for better village living conditions and for a social services plan. What we were after was a demonstration, by doing, of how a progressive village could get the most out of the Gezira Scheme.

'What a man hears he may not believe, what he sees he may forget, but what he does with his own hands he will always remember' was the motto of our educational aim. It was obvious that schooling of this type, highly specialized to the demands of the Gezira, was not obtainable in ordinary government schools. New institutions and new finance were required for it.

The need for special social services impressed itself on us in the disappointing conditions in the villages, considering the money which had passed through the Scheme. Our organization had provided the cash from the cotton crop but had kept clear of responsibility for social conditions. But routine government departments did not cater for these needs either.

Gezira villages were dirty and hygiene primitive. Dysentery, malaria and bilharzia were endemic. The attitude to sanitation and health was passive. There was a dispensary in each block in the Scheme and public-health inspectors had erected corrugated-iron latrines, but this had small effect. A clinic, recently opened in the province town, Wad Medani, away from the hospital and where women could see a British woman doctor privately near their homes, had attracted large numbers. What was needed, we felt, was a welfare service, like the Wad Medani clinic, extended to the women in the villages, where the provision of advice to them and their children, and of better midwifery facilities, would impart a new attitude to health at the base.

The material environment in the villages was disappointing. Grass huts had been replaced by mud huts but many houses were decrepit. It was a region devoid of stone and, because of excessive lime in the soil of the plain, the brick kilns were all situated on the river-bank where river silt made good bricks. Resulting transport costs made a brick house too expensive for most villagers. Experiments were needed to discover better methods of protecting ordinary mud houses from the weather. With the house went a need for better-made doors, windows and furniture. This in turn revealed the lack of any simple technical education where local boys could learn carpentering, house-building, shoemaking and other crafts which they could later practise in their villages. There was an analogous need to teach girls how to cook better and thereto to invent a better stove and better fuel than cow-dung and cotton stalks. Irrigated timber plots to supply wood for such fuel and for house-building—for it had become very scarce and expensive—and new wells to give cleaner drinking-water than the canals were other typical practical needs in villages.

Most of the people were illiterate and elementary schools were few and far between. As a result they tended to turn out boys who wanted to better themselves by getting away from the land. This had advantages, for it added country boys to the educational stream of the nation, hitherto confined to towns and to the sons of merchants and officials. But there was by now an enormous demand for education, and the chief educational problem of the future was bound to be that of making the vast majority of boys and girls, whose living was going to be derived from the land, into more competent and intelligent users of it. Close co-operation with the education staff was a natural need, for our aim to build a democratic co-operative community provided a real follow-up in adult life for a great deal of the new teaching in the schools. But till now we had practically no contact or interest in each other's activities.

The absence of any recreation facilities was a gap in village life. The main occasions for breaking monotony were births, circumcisions, marriages and deaths, but the leisurely periods which custom used to allot to such matters had tended to be foreshortened as the irrigation made more claims on time, and increasingly the dispeller of boredom was the beer-shop. In the more egalitarian atmosphere, and with the much greater spread of transport and news, story-telling and gossip in the courtyards of the chief men's houses had lost its attraction, and the chief men themselves had lost their position as the focus for community life. There was, especially, nothing attractive for the younger generation. There seemed a need to organize football and athletics, scouts and clubs, and an occasional cinema to brighten their lives. Village halls were needed if village councils were to become a new focus for the dignity and self-respect of the people.

Affecting us more directly as managers of the Scheme was the problem of debt in the villages. Extortionate conditions for loans were known to exist. How far these were due to extravagance, or to the driving needs of urgent work on crops for which no loans were provided, was not easy to assess, but if in future the village moneylender got into a dominant position the concept of economic democracy would have little validity. While everything to do with the cotton crop, as administered by direct British control, had been planned to obviate the moneylender, and was in one sense a giant co-operative, no co-operative societies as such existed. There seemed a need to encourage them for a variety of purposes outside the routine running of the Scheme.

One of our difficulties was to know the true facts. No one living outside the villages could really tell the extent of all these, or other, needs and their comparative importance. There seemed a real need for an intelligent social investigation.

It might be argued that these social needs could be best met by voluntary organizations. In fact, in the setting of a paternal colonial government, voluntary action by the people themselves on such matters was rare and any initiative in this respect would have been expected of the Government. We were experiencing phenomena shortly to become general to the age, to deal with which, after the war, a great many territories have set up community-development departments and district teams.

Although we were partners, hitherto Government and Syndicate had been content not to interfere in each other's department, but this had brought disadvantages. The general hierarchy of native administration had, to a lamentable degree, been uninterested in the agricultural efficiency of their districts, because they were fundamentally the district commissioner's men, and their job had been exclusively political administration. Yet the influence of these important men was vital. If now the district commissioner was to work out in isolation the new plans for local government it might result in village councils which took no interest in agriculture and in the appointment of sheikhs unfitted to play their important part in agricultural devolution. The position was inescapable because at the bottom it was one body of people, one unit, the village, with which both parties had got to deal and unless they worked in harmony the result was likely to end in failure.

On their side the British field officers of the Syndicate, with their close contact with the people, could help social progress enormously. Our conclusion was therefore that the Syndicate and Government must work together to some common plan which needed its own co-ordinating board and special finance and staff.

Proposals of this kind would also, we felt, provide an opportunity for educated Sudanese to play a part in planning and in action, which would give them a much greater sense of association in the development of the community than our use of them, mainly in clerical posts, had so far offered. But we were anxious that they should be working for the new objective of devolution, not in a perpetuation of the old régime with new personnel.

No director from the board of the Syndicate had been out to the Sudan for three years and it was difficult for those in England, very much in the front line of the war (the Syndicate's offices in London had been destroyed by a direct hit), to appreciate in 1943 the anxiety of some of us in the Sudan to press forward changes of the type suggested in this plan. In their infinitely worse situation they saw no need for difficult and extensive changes in the administration of the Gezira, whose main war-time job to them was to keep up production. As far as any immediate action was concerned the memorandum came to nothing.

One reason for our sense of urgency locally to get a more definite objective in the Gezira was the pace of political development in the Sudan as a whole. It is necessary for a moment to assess its significance.

The Sudan was still ruled in 1943 by the Governor-General in a Council of senior civil servants. There were no formal provisions for local consultation. But the small educated class had begun to take note of the world around them and an increasing interest in the future of their country. The first event to affect them deeply was the Anglo-Egyptian treaty of 1936, wherein important decisions about the future of the Sudan were taken by the two condomini. For the first time there was a feeling that local opinion should have been consulted. In 1938 a Graduates' Congress* was formed to give expression to educated opinion. But since there were no avenues for political expression this body was a cultural organization and was warned off politics by the Civil Secretary, Sir Douglas Newbold. They soon developed an interest in the Gezira Scheme, with its potential for the employment of educated Sudanese, and its capacity for generating emotions on the great issue of foreign development and control. A prescient comment by Newbold in 1940 is illustrative.

I do not know if the Gezira Advisory Board is aware of the increasing interest taken by educated Sudanese in the Gezira Scheme. Apart from one or two actual petitions, there have been several articles in the Vernacular press, mostly critical. . . . I do not want to raise a bogey of either local strikes or Congress agitation, but unless the Sudanese can soon have some more intelligent participation in the Scheme than that of a labourer, we are bound to have trouble. Moreover, we now have a post-secondary school of agriculture. Are its products to be denied participation in the largest agricultural operation in the Sudan?[4]

It is appropriate here to draw attention to the damaging effect of a phenomenon all too common in the history of the British Empire in dependent colonial territories. As the British staff of the Syndicate we were preoccupied with our agricultural tasks, and spent our leisure

* It should be pointed out that these were graduates of the Gordon College, which was not at that time even a university college. But they represented the majority of the educated class among the Sudanese and many of them already held important posts in the government services.

hours in our own community. We had no personal contact with the educated Sudanese and little conception of their ideals and capacities or they of our work in the Scheme. We should have been allies. Instead, mutual misconceptions derived from ignorance of each other swelled suspicions which human friendship in a task made common might never have allowed to arise.

While the challenge of the war and the declaration of the Atlantic Charter made the British more receptive to change it made educated Sudanese more aggressive in demanding it. In April 1942 the Graduates' Congress presented a memorandum to the Government with a list of demands of which the first was the right to self-determination after the war. Another was the termination of the Syndicate's concession in the Gezira and a third a demand for increased 'Sudanization'. The memorandum was rejected rather brusquely. It so happened that a few days later Sir Stafford Cripps* passed through the Sudan on the way back from his mission to India. To Newbold he advised the immediate setting up of an Advisory Council, and to the local press he said,

> We are all looking to the future. The Sudan is playing its part in the war effort very well, and this will gain it a place in the new era which we hope to see in the world when we have finished with the evil forces. There are a lot of things to be done: and we must perhaps do them more quickly than we have in the past.

In September of that year Newbold presented a note to Council in which he surveyed the development of political thinking in the Sudan, the new trend in colonial thought in Britain from trusteeship to partnership, and offered the conclusion that the Sudan should hasten to get into step with these forces. He proposed that local government devolution should be extended, Sudanization accelerated, and the expediency of forming an Advisory Council for the northern Sudan examined. An ordinance promulgating the new council was signed in September 1943. The first meeting was held in May 1944.

While the Syndicate board in London was somewhat remote from the trend of events in the Sudan, the Government was increasingly concerned that the administration of the Gezira should be identified as closely as possible with the future of the country. In order to minimize public doubt on the question, and to provide the maximum freedom of action, the Government decided in 1944 (the second termination date

* Sir Stafford Cripps (1889-1952), P.C., C.H., F.R.S., etc. British ambassador to Russia, 1940-2: Lord Privy Seal and Leader of House of Commons, 1942: Chancellor of the Exchequer, 1947-50.

provided by the 1929 agreement) to notify the Companies that they did not, after all, wish to renew their concessions after 1950.

There is no doubt that this step was welcomed politically in the Sudan. The board of the Syndicate expressed regret at the passing of the partnership which had seemed to many a model for the development of a country, but appreciated that social and political considerations had determined the Government's decision. They expressed their readiness to co-operate with the Government, in so far a s their duty to their shareholders permitted, in furthering its policy during the remaining period of the concession.

Paradoxically, the fact that the Syndicate was now terminating in 1950 slowed up the prospects of a rapid change. The proposals in our memorandum of 1943, expressing ideas exchanged between ourselves and government officials locally, could be implemented to a certain degree, and a directive on devolution policy, issued jointly in 1945 by Bredin as Governor of the Province and myself, who had just taken over the post of Manager of the Syndicate,[5] was an expression of our continued co-operation to that end. But while this could enjoin on Government and Syndicate staff a combined operation to develop village councils and a joint interest in maintaining agricultural efficiency at the same time, the substance of a new policy, namely finance and an agreed plan of wider intentions, was beyond us.

Bredin attempted to keep the initiative and, harking back to discussions on the eve of the war which had envisaged the creation of a local management board, suggested that one should be set up forthwith as the forerunner of management after 1950.[6] But the proposal conflicted with the Gezira Advisory Board in Khartoum as the supreme body formulating government policy, and with the London Board of Directors of the Syndicate. It was difficult to expect the central Government, and particularly the Financial Secretary, to come to any decision yet as to the form of management after 1950, and all that Bredin could get was permission to set up a subordinate Gezira Local Committee with power to initiate proposals to the Gezira Advisory Board 'taking due account of the lines of policy laid down by that Board' and with no power to discuss any matter affecting the agreement with the Syndicate without the prior authorization of the Gezira Advisory Board.[7] It was all rational, correct and safe, and thoroughly deadening to a quick, progressive policy.

It will not have escaped the reader's notice that all the social planning was still being made for the tenants, not by them. Syndicate personnel in their more cynical moments were apt to speak of the tenants as their sleeping partners, and in 1938 Rugman had written of the Gezira Scheme, 'One partner (the Company) is active, one (the Government) is largely dormant, and the other (the tenant) is active but, for the present, dumb.'[8] It is true that the village council system was intended to give them a more responsible role in the locality while, when the Gezira Local Committee was created, two tenant representatives were appointed to it by Bredin as a first step to association in policy at the centre. But these two were well-esteemed members of the local government. Nothing as yet disturbed our unruffled assumption that the Government and Syndicate would lay down the course of progress and knew best what was good for the tenants.

1946 will always be remembered in the Gezira as the year in which the tenants awoke. Ignoring somewhat rudely the plans arranged for their social progress, and rejecting outright any claim that they could be represented through local government, they made clear at once that their major interest was more money. A variety of circumstances impelled this new irruption into the stream of the Gezira story.

The most important of these circumstances was the change that the Scheme itself had brought. A generation ago local society had been simple and isolated. Transport was by donkey and camel and visits seldom extended beyond the neighbouring villages. Education consisted in learning the Koran by heart, assisted by a rap on the knuckles if attention wandered. For health service the people turned to the local religious teachers. Most wants were satisfied by local products and conditioned by custom which was itself the outcome of years of harsh experience. Money was a rarity. Most villages were made up of the descendants of a few heads of families who were often still alive. Respect was engrained in such a family circle for, apart from natural affection and a sense of honour, individual livelihood was not easily obtainable outside it. Obedience was expected and accepted, and no one hesitated to suggest a whipping for transgressors.

Now all was changed. It was rather like the change in English society in the nineteenth century but it happened much more quickly. Our direct administration had been naturally accepted in the early days and we were slow to see how paternalism was getting out of date. In contradiction with the past villages were no longer isolated. Cars and lorries plied everywhere and people paid regular visits to growing market towns. Trade began to boom, stimulating new wants and creating new concepts of a tolerable standard of living. Urban sophistication entered.

Education came into universal demand so that sons could get better-paid, more influential jobs. It was no longer a matter of memorizing the Koran but rather a door opening to the world's lay knowledge, encouraging a challenge to accepted belief and beginning the development of individual critical judgement. Newspapers began to bring, and create a desire for, news of happenings in other parts. They also gave, for the first time, a forum for anonymous criticism of a general nature, in contrast with personal petitioning in the past. Such influences caused people to question the virtue of obedience. It was becoming a society of half-knowledge, less cohesive than in the past and restless, increasingly resentful of nursery orders yet with little mechanism to understand the complex technical background to such orders and with none of the responsibility of association with decisions.

Basically significant also was the character of the tenants themselves. They were tough, warm people, and when their own covering of dignity and good manners was drawn back by some emotion they were liable to fanaticism and violence. Shrewd in intelligence, they were suspicious of motives yet credulous of rumours. They gave their confidence rather to persons than to ideas.

They were proud, and responded best to challenges which suddenly demanded the best of them and then suddenly subsided. They were not naturally attracted by a steady routine. Delighting in ostentatious show and despising the miser they were impatient of all arguments in favour of thrift. And in the end they were lazy, as was to be expected in such a climate. It is hardly an accident that slavery flourished most in the world's hottest spots, and in the northern Sudan for generations work had been associated with slaves. However much others might be planning the future society as one of hard-working peasant proprietors they showed a marked preference themselves for a future as gentlemen farmers, and one of the first uses to which they put the additional money which the Scheme brought them was to hire others to do all the work.

Significant also were the changes of fortune they had experienced. The depression years broke on them before the traditional flavour of past society had entirely evaporated. Fortune and misfortune had often alternated in the past and it was no novelty then to tighten belts until the lean time was over. It was, however, bitterly disappointing. Investments from the profits of the first four good years in animals, in gold and silver ornaments on women, or in land, had gradually to be sold. Even though the irrigated food crop and the regular loans had seemed to outsiders to be advantages which they would be glad of, the increasing discipline of the Scheme, the constant attendance, the need to find labour or work oneself, the difficulty of getting off for any length of time, and with all this drudgery the absence of any profit, made the depression years a period not easily forgotten. It might be accepted philosophically at the time but the memory persisted as of a duty done to the community, and certainly as of a good turn in steadfastness to the Government and the Syndicate, which deserved recognition.

As in so many historical parallels, it was not at the nadir of their fortunes that the people of the Gezira became vocal, but when a change for the better had made acceptance of past attitudes seem obsolete, and particularly when a check in expected improvements caused a sense of frustration.

The check was due to the war. It was not, this time, a matter of falling yields and prices. On the contrary, book profits were increasing, which was in one sense annoying to the tenants because everyone assumed that they were better off, whereas in reality everything was getting more and more expensive. Consumer goods were in terribly short supply which created a black market. Labour was finding all sorts of alternative openings created by the war, and the very additional money in everyone's hands, chasing the scarcer goods and shorter labour, added to inflation.

A kind of coffee-house grouse got around the tenants as a community. It was all very well for the Government and Syndicate to talk about doing without, and saving, and working harder as a solution to inflation, but all this was particularly galling just when there was a chance of better living and more leisure. And had everyone forgotten what the tenants had been through in the depression years? It was all very well for the local government bosses and the merchants. One lot arranged the ration lists and the other lot distributed them and neither went short. Anyway, were the tenants getting their rights? Some people said that the cotton sale prices were a put-up job, and there was this rumour of a lot of money being tucked away in a reserve fund, or was it a welfare fund? If there was any welfare going it had better start right at home. A tenant could go down to his local office and get his personal account explained if his block inspector was in a good temper. But they could not tell you there about the joint accounts and sale prices and merely referred you to Barakat Headquarters, who never published anything except their company accounts, and to deal with whom there simply was not any organized tenants' body.

This kind of grouse touched a chord in the hearts of another section of the community. After the rejection of their demands by the Government in 1942 the Graduates' Congress split into two. All were disappointed but while one section (which later developed into the Umma Party), most of whom were in positions of responsibility in government service, decided to co-operate with the authorities in progressive political advance, another section (which later developed into the Ashigga Party), distrusting that the British would ever surrender political power, went into opposition. They had been told that they represented but a small urban element in the nation, which was mainly tribal and rural. The spectacle of countrymen in the economic heart of the Sudan dissatisfied with their lot and with tribal representation, and similarly seeking as a class a bigger say in determining their livelihood, evoked at once a natural sympathy and an access of strength. It was not long before the Ashigga Party was assisting certain of the tenants to make an organization of their own, and before an incident presented them with occasion to put it into use.

It will be remembered that the Government had generously set aside the balance of the debt, due to it from the tenants on account of the years 1930–1, as capital for a Tenants' Welfare Fund. Interest had been accumulating and Bredin felt that the tenants themselves should be consulted as to the spending of it. But the only machinery for consulting them was the local government, the chief men in which were, of course, also tenants. The representative of the southern Gezira, one of the two on the new Gezira Local Committee, accordingly called a meeting of local councillors which was attended by a large crowd of spectators. While councillors vied with each other in apportioning the welfare revenue for mosques and schools in their own villages, the cry went round the spectators that they were carving up the Tenants' Reserve Fund. Pandemonium ensued, and it was brought home very forcibly to the authorities what a dubious ally ignorance had been.

Bredin and I myself, as Manager of the Syndicate, felt it essential to reassure the tenants and had to reveal that £E1,300,000 had been prudently and paternally tucked away for them in the Reserve Fund and was intact. The result was electrifying. Within a week, and on the eve of sowing, 90 per cent of the tenants had sworn an oath not to plant the cotton crop until they had had all the money out. It was the Gezira's first strike. Few of the organizers were people of any previous known importance.

The strike was settled through the mediation of a Sudanese Committee of the new Advisory Council for the northern Sudan, which recommended the payment of £E400,000 out of the Reserve Fund to supplement the year's profits. There was justification for some rebate when regard was had to the large sums transferred to the fund during the war. Economically it was more difficult to be happy about the pay-out, for inflation was bound to swallow up much of its value. But economic autocracy was going out of fashion. To have set up the Advisory Council implied a wish to associate the people with policy decisions, and if the first act was to reject their recommendation how would they learn responsibility? How indeed? And not the Advisory Council only, for clearly some central tenants' organization must henceforth be created or admitted.

As 1946 drew to a close it was clear that the nursery days were over. With the termination of the Syndicate's concession and the problem of the future pattern of society there were difficulties enough gathering for decisions, and decisions in which from henceforth two new forces were probably going to share—politicians and tenants. The Gezira river was moving out of the plain into the cataract. And we, the managers, who were justly proud of our technical and financial success, were finding that the biggest problem ahead, just as in industry at home, was going to be human relations.[9]

Chapter 18

DOWN TO EARTH

Conflicts of ideas among the principal actors have occupied the centre of the stage in a great deal of this story. It is necessary to fill in, now, more detail of the crowd and of the background scenery. Some detail has already been given, more particularly in Chapter 8, but it is desirable to amplify this in order to convey a sense of the continuous importance of relationships at the tenancy level.

On those relationships, whatever the stress at higher levels, the Scheme's morale depended.

Once, when old staff were asked to define for newcomers the essence of this relationship, they set down the following precepts:

1. The tenant is a tenant and not a labourer.
2. Patience pays. Don't lose your temper. Don't swear at tenants or labourers. Never strike anyone.
3. Always insist on a high standard of work and stick to your word.
4. See for yourself and don't take too much for granted.
5. Try and take an interest in the individual.
6. Get to the bottom of every grievance.
7. Apart from your work, develop as many interests as you can in the Gezira Scheme.

A critic of paternalism may smile at such simple homilies, with their faint suggestion of fraying tempers. But he would be wrong to sneer. As long as a father-figure was important, these were the conditions of confidence. On the practice of these precepts depended in large measure the secret of success, and one of the dangers of devolution was the risk of their disappearance.

The newcomer to the field staff in later years, and the newcomer to a tenancy, came into an atmosphere different from that of the pioneering days. Something of charm was lost, for all simple societies seem attractive by contrast with the tensions which development brings. But something of vitality was gained, as every week in the calendar brought field officer and tenant together in the practical problems of production.

June now was the only month of relaxation in the field. While in the offices accountants worked overtime to tot up the results of the past season the parched, bare land awaited the blissful rain. The farming calendar started in July. This was the month of final preparation for the hustle which began when the water arrived in the last ten days and continued, with short lulls, until irrigation ceased at the end of March. The rainy season from July to September typified the hustle at its most exacting period.

First the field-channels had to be dug out to an adequate section to carry the water, without breaking, to each ninety-feddan unit of cotton and dura. Within the units each ten-feddan tenancy required subsidiary preparation. At every thirty yards smaller supply-channels had to be made right across the tenancy. Parallel to these and evenly spaced between them lines of small containing banks had to be raised, and at right angles to them again every fifteenth ridge in the furrowed land had to be strengthened and connected. Transformed in this manner the surface of each tenancy was divided into a regular pattern of 192 tiny plots, to each of which the water could be evenly distributed, the whole field resembling from the air a gigantic piece of squared paper.

Water went first to the dura land but there was barely ten days for a tenant to water and sow his dura before he must hurry to water and sow his cotton. Blackarm danger precluded cotton sowing before the 10th of August but it had to be completed by the end of that month to avoid a fall in yield and especially in grade. Looked at from the central organization, the sowing-season calendar meant that 100,000 feddans of dura had to be watered and sown between the 25th of July and the 10th of August and 200,000 feddans of cotton between the 10th and 31st of August. Broken down at the block level these figures meant a programme time-table for every field unit, and within the field for every tenancy, for the canals were not designed to water all the land at once and then close down. They were designed not for an uneconomic peak but for a constant flow, and that meant a regulated rotation.

Planting was done by hand. An adult worked in front opening, with a traditional sowing stick, little craters in the moist soil at two-foot intervals along the ridges. A child followed behind and threw a cluster of seed into the craters with supposedly unerring aim and buried the openings with his foot. Hardly was planting finished before weeding was at hand. It was usually done with a long Dutch hoe. Stimulated by the watering, the weeds required instant removal and, as each tenant faced the prospect of cleaning five feddans of dura and ten of cotton as quickly as possible, the call on labour was tremendous. At three weeks after planting the cotton needed thinning down to three plants per hole. Thinning was followed by reridging, a process which broke through the small water channels and containing banks within each tenancy and had to be followed in turn by their reconstruction. Once again these operations were up against time for by now the cotton needed its second watering. Weeds then grew again and had to be hoed a second, third and fourth time, after each watering, until the cotton plants were big enough to cover the soil. Similar repetitions of weeding were needed until the dura crop was established.

In the midst of all this hustle, regular days had to be set aside for inspecting last year's cotton numbers and destroying seedling and ratoon cotton which might have sprouted in the rains, and would expose the district to the dangers of the blackarm and leaf curl diseases. Lubia had to wait its turn, with everyone preoccupied by dura and cotton, but then this crop too had to be hurried forward. If it was not established by September a short fodder crop was certain, for it could get no water after the end of December when the precious storage water was needed for cotton.

The rain season was thus a period of immense vitality and, if all went well, of immense satisfaction as the bright green of the growing crops emerged from the weeds and covered the chocolate earth with neat rows of strong, healthy plants. They were the days when men sang at their work, full of hope as the clouds gathered in the great panorama of sky and the cool wind blew.

But there were other days when nature, both human and celestial, was less accommodating. These were the ones that tested the character of field officer and tenant. Devastating rain, beneficial if it came early and harmful if it came late, always upset the programme. Morning light, for the storms came usually at night, would often disclose anything but a pretty picture. Creeping along the edge of the canal banks in his Morris Eight car, in contrast with the horse of former days, the field officer would survey the scene. The neat rows of healthy plants would look blown and bedraggled in the mud, the end tenancies in the fields submerged by great lakes of water. Quick decisions were needed to adjust the programme. How much should the water indent be cut in each canal? Where could the water be put in the meantime, for the canals would burst unless some fields were opened? Which tenants would have to resow all their crop? Which others must take advantage of the rain and sow unexpectedly, out of programme? All must turn out to drain away the water. The interruption would catch out the laggards who had not taken time by the forelock and cleared their weeds in the previous dry spell. Unless they got a move on this time weeds would smother their crops, push up their costs—and seriously reduce their yields.

The field officer must contact the villages to get all this rearrangement under way, and get on to the Irrigation Department to put his water cuts through as soon as possible. Even on the way there one of his canal control squad might meet him with news that his canal had burst in the night, and he must find labour to repair it. Meantime the villages themselves would often be flooded out, and the tenants too preoccupied with the discomfort of a leaking house, or the death of animals in the cold of the storm, to pay much attention to their tenancies.

Always the laggards had excuses. Gaballa had not drawn his seed— he had been going to tomorrow—and now how could he get it from the store in this sea of mud? Mohammed had no money left to hire urgent labour for those weeds. His profits had gone in settling debts. He would have to start in stages and be financed in driblets of loans as he completed each portion. Abd el Bagi had got married in June to a girl outside the Scheme. He had not been back since, relying on his brother to get things going for him but giving him no money to do so. The sheikh would have to be seen about his tenancy. If there was not an uncle prepared to bring it up to date quickly the village council had better send the boy a warning that they were recommending that the tenancy be reallotted to someone else. Finally there was old Ayesha, whose husband had died last year. She had no children but the council had persuaded the field officer to leave her as the tenant. Of course she could not manage it and he would have to find the labour for her and debit her account and, when it was established, have another go at the council to put in some villager as a manager for her.

And then, he had almost forgotten, there was Abd el Aziz. They had said he was sick. His cotton land had been watered but, when it was due to be sown, no one had turned up and nothing had been done. It had thus got too dry to sow. Now, with this rain, there was a chance to do it. But was he sick or what had happened? The field officer's memory went back to the earliest days in Teboob block. A young man had been sick on just such an occasion. His fellow-tenants had kept on saying he was sick so he had gone down to the village to see him. He remembered the sight to this day; the boy lying there in a trance. He had asked them what was wrong with him and they had replied that a man from Wad Shama had put the evil eye on him and they feared he would die. Could

'Planting was done by hand with the traditional sowing stick'

PLATE IX

'Weeding was usually done with the long Dutch hoe'

PLATE X

'Spraying against jassid fly came to be a routine operation'

PLATE XI

'The miracle of irrigation at its brightest'

(i) Rain-grown dura in a poor year

(ii) Irrigated dura

PLATE XII

nothing be done? Perhaps, if the field officer brought pressure to bear on the man to remove the spell. The field officer had done so, the man had removed the spell and the boy had at once recovered. It had been a curious story. But people did not go sick with the evil eye nowadays. It was probably malaria. Thank goodness, at last, the new technique of spraying every village house in the region twice a year seemed to give a chance of tackling malaria. It was one of the good things the social-development fund had handled. But meantime he must find someone to sow Abd el Aziz's tenancy.

Encumbered by such typical vicissitudes, momentum would get going again in dawn to dusk activity and gradually, as the days got drier in October, ease off into the first lull. By then slovenly sowing, careless thinning and delayed weeding had left their mark, too late now to be corrected, on the various crops. It was a time to bring order out of chaos, to shorten and regulate the water intervals to ten days for cotton and twenty days for dura, and to balance the watering rotations, to get the tenants on to clearing the weeds from water channels, roads and drainage lines, to make a final clearance check on ratoon cotton, and to cheer everyone up with another profits pay-day.

The next job was the spraying and, once again, it was up against time. Counts of jassid-fly, to determine the degree of infestation, had been going on weekly since mid-September, and to make the spraying most effective the object was to complete the whole Scheme in a month at the peak of the jassid onslaught. By aerial spraying this was easy but, as a check on cost and efficacy, much of the work was done by tractors. These worked day and night, and an exact programme had to be made for each machine, so that none were standing idle, unable to enter a wet field for lack of dovetailing with the watering rotation. Absentee tenants, who flooded their land too heavily or let water flow on their tenancy out of turn, had to be checked for fear of stalling the programme. Watch had to be kept on blocked nozzles, on the mix of D.D.T. in the tanks and on the tendency to shirk headlands, for the drivers operated with a bonus on output. A finicky but indispensable preparation was for a bull-plough to cut through the water channels and containing banks in each tenancy along the exact ridges due to be used by the tractor, to ease the passage of its wheels and obviate bumping of the sprayer-booms.

Another task as soon as the rains were over was the ploughing pro-gramme for the following season's crops. Each field had to be inspected. Land infested with seid grass had to be scheduled for deep ploughing by D.7 tractors, heavy land earmarked for separate operations of cultivating

I hope that a picture is beginning to emerge for the reader of the scenery of the plain in full production, and of the manner in which a hundred or so field officers, scattered over the Scheme, became absorbed, at so many daily contacts, in the lives of the twenty thousand tenants and their families and through them impinged on most of the population in the region. It left little time for any thought except of some direct executive problem on the spot and for any contact beyond the horizon of the local parish.

It was a relationship filled with the constant interchange of human characteristics and emotions. Simplicity and shrewdness, exasperation and patience, gloom and laughter were displayed every day on both sides. What really made it work? Integrity was important, of course, but primness rather repelling. A certain masterfulness in decision mattered, sometimes better attained by the quiet speaker, sometimes by the parade-ground voice. Mutual respect was necessary also, but, curiously enough, almost as significant was a mutual allowance and liking for the other's weaknesses. Napoleon's specific 'Activité, vitesse' topped all other virtues in importance and a sense of drive, a zest and enjoyment for a life of action, was the best asset in field officer and tenant alike. Closely behind it came the capacity to organize and control detail. To temper both qualities to the idiosyncrasies of others a covering of good humour made an invaluable catalyst. But it was not all work.

The arrival of winter gave everyone a new lease of life, and a feeling of well-earned leisure largely impossible in the strenuous days just passed. The symbol of winter was the arrival of the blue cranes. They would come in on the first north wind, flying in V formation like a bomber fleet, and often their harsh cry, 'Rahoo, rahoo', would be the first sound to startle a sleeper from his blankets as the sun rose and they passed over him, seeking the gleanings of the dura harvest over the land.

It was a sign among some of the British staff to look out their guns and plan a sand-grouse shoot next Sunday. Others would aim to search for gazelle, and perhaps leopard, round the stony hills of Gebel Segadi, south of the Scheme. Some would be content with a day far up the river away from everyone, fishing at the dam or with a gun handy for crocodiles, but seeking mainly the contrasting sense of immemorial peace which life on the river seemed to reflect. Others would take out their polo sticks, harden up their ponies, and fix a team of friends to play together through the season's tournaments. Wives would reach for their tennis racquets, clubs would open for the Monday afternoon and Friday that could now be enjoyed as a genuine weekly holiday. Dinner parties and bridge, the arrival of children from Britain, and an occasional dance completed the British scene of relaxation in the cold weather. Among the villagers, too, it was a time for social enjoyment, and drums would beat far into the night for weddings and circumcision parties. It was the lull before the next period of hustle in the field—the cotton-picking season which began in January.

Winter was also the favourite season for a visitor, and the sights he would see in a day's drive in picking time would give a good cross-section of life in the Gezira at this period of the year. A visitor approaching the Scheme from the outside in January would get the best impression of what it meant to the country. Dozing as his car ran through the great expanse of dusty earth and sere grass south of Khartoum, the home of a few scrub trees, an occasional nomad tent and a scattering of goats, he would be suddenly confronted, after thirty miles, with a complete contrast. The wall of green mirage filling the horizon ahead would disintegrate into fine crops of cotton, grain and fodder. Behind him was an empty wilderness, ahead of him for 120 miles southwards and twenty miles across lay mile after mile of ordered fields teeming with people, activity and animals. It was the miracle of irrigation at its brightest. Nostalgia for the past had to give way at such tangible proofs of progress.

Characteristic vignettes would imprint themselves on his mind at this season as he motored on through the Scheme, suggesting once again an intricate organization with elaborate attention to detail: the people picking the cotton fields in orderly lines just ahead of the water; the packing squares on each tenancy, with great white piles of cotton being shaken up, weighed on a spring balance, and stamped down into man-high sacks; the haughty camels walking ponderously with a sack on each flank to the collecting station; a weigher there shouting the folio number, name, and weight to his assistant for entry on the tenant's receipt; behind them a gang of porters loading the local cotton train to the chant of a bawdy song.

The visitor might stop at the block office and watch the white-robed tenants tethering their donkeys, drawing their picking loans against the receipts for sacks delivered, paying their pickers, dodging their creditors, and moving on to the store to collect new sacks, stamped with their folio numbers by the storeman, ready for next week's pick.

Every few miles also would reveal the tenants' homes, the villages swollen with new houses since the start of the Scheme. Some have spread into little market towns with a hollow square of merchants' shops and a new school. A few red-brick houses overtop the rest and reveal the homes of the most prosperous. A fine mosque, whose minaret is a beacon from afar against the morning and evening skies, will also be a sign of new prosperity, bringing to mind the churches built in Britain when new wealth from our first textile export, wool, led our ancestors also to express their gratitude in spiritual tribute.

One more sight on the way home is a sudden fire by the roadside. It is a ploughing team, and the little groups, their machines in the background, are huddled round the firelight, cooking their evening meal over a few rags soaked in paraffin, before turning in in the open after their regular sunrise-to-sunset day. It is the last vignette our visitor will remember as he too closes his eyes sleeping on the flat roof under a sky of sparkling stars.

April was trespass time. The water had stopped. The lubia and the dura stalks had been eaten down. Outside the Scheme grazing was finished and all along the edges huge herds of cattle, sheep and goats were collected, waiting for permission to close in on the 200,000 feddans of cotton, a bite of which would make all the difference to their survival until the next rains. The wind had swung to the south, bringing hot, lifeless days. Winter was over. Picking was nearly over but not quite and not everywhere. Tenants were tired of it, however, and getting in the last few bags was a fight against inertia and animal damage. Home-leave season had begun and the few field staff remaining waged battle with the stock. Owners drove them into the cotton at night and during the day ran a system of tic-tac boys to warn them to pull out before a field officer arrived. It was a good-humoured but sharp war, and owners were ready to pay a handsome fine if they were dim-witted enough to get caught. In the end a zero date was fixed and the whole Scheme was opened to an animal free-for-all, a mutual benefit then, for the stock cleaned up plants and ground and made the next process, pulling-out, easier.

May was the month for pulling-out, and it was the most disliked job of all. By eight o'clock in the morning the sun was hot and by midday the temperature might be 116 degrees in the shade. Little whirlwinds of dust were a common feature of the landscape, and even at night sleep was made difficult by myriads of sand-flies disturbed by the removal of the cotton. Theoretically it should have been easy for any tenant to pull-up, sweep and burn six little plots a day and complete his ten acres in a month. But the initial prospect of pulling up 110,000 plants by hand in the blistering weather was daunting, and days were always

238

wasted trying to hire someone else to do it before the process got under way. Once again the supervision had to be strict. Plants broken off instead of pulled out meant a risk of leaf-curl infected ratoon next season, while slovenly execution of the tedious sweeping and burning risked the carry-over of blackarm.

When the last days of the month approached, and the season ended, there was a quiet pleasure in sipping a whisky and soda on the flat roof at sunset and watching the whole surrounding plain pinpointed by bonfires. As dark came on and shadowy figures stoked them into sudden flame they conjured up for the watcher a suggestion of Dante's Inferno. At such a moment a man might wonder why he had put his life into such a strange and narrow compass. He had often intended to give it up and look for something else. What was it that always brought him back? The tenants had a saying that he who drank the Blue Nile water would always return. It was a hard country for a wife and children, but for a man it had a curious fascination. Was it the open-air life? One couldn't get anything much more open than the Gezira. Was it the people? The daily struggle together that made one either fall out and go, or share a tough respect and friendship for each other? Or was it the bond with the rest of the British staff? There were enough queerly conflicting characters among them. Yet there was the sense of sharing the same frustrations and achievements which brought all together in friendship, too. Perhaps there was something of all these features, and wrapped around them all a sense of creative pride. It might be a tiny corner of the earth in a distant land but, among all the blueprints for development in the world, it stood out as a practical success, full of the elemental satisfaction of producing two plants in the soil, and two ideas in the mind, where one grew before.

Part 3
THE CATARACT
1946–50

Chapter 19

MAKING A NEW PLAN

Once it had been decided in 1944 that the Syndicate's services as managing partner would not be required after its concession ended in 1950, arguments began to arise as to the best future organization. The London directorate of the Syndicate, so long a dominant influence, began to concede the planning of the future more readily to its local staff, who might be needed for the Scheme's continuity. Between ourselves as commercial administrators of the Scheme and the local officials of the political service there was considerable agreement as to future policy. As has already been shown, we were anxious to graft on to the economic efficiency of the Scheme a social policy which would encourage democratic development in place of the authoritarian régime which had been necessary at the start.

We were very greatly encouraged by the publication at that time of descriptions of the Tennessee Valley Authority in the United States. We could see analogies in our own projects with the principles enunciated by Mr. Lilienthal* as basic to the T.V.A.[1] Many of the principals, quoted as the reasons for its success, seemed to us appropriate for the future of the Gezira. Investment of government capital, not in all business as an ideology, but in a specific undertaking, so that the profit therefrom could be used deliberately to widen the life of a whole community and region, seemed as applicable to our case as to the Tennessee Valley. A generous decentralization of control, encouragement of a democratic rather than bureaucratic method of administration, consultation and co-operation with local councils and institutions in the execution of policy, seemed to us the right objectives in the future.

* D. E. Lilienthal. Lawyer: member Wisconsin Public Service Commission, 1931: Director of T.V.A. since 1933: Chairman, T.V.A. 1941: Chairman, U.S. State Department Board of Consultation on International Control of Atomic Energy, 1946: Chairman U.S. Atomic Energy Commission, 1946–50: Chairman and chief executive officer of Development and Research Company, 1953–: adviser to President of Republic of Colombia, 1954.

Planned on these lines future policy in the Gezira might contribute to a new outlook on colonialism and backward agricultural countries. Paternalism had been a great motive force in development but its days were numbered and we had to find a new one.

The contact of the future was surely not Imperialism or even Trusteeship, both of which contained elements of interested patronage, irritating to the protégé. Their place should, we felt, be taken by a sense of working together and demonstrating how, in a dependent country, the people could move forward to independence, equipped to make their own contribution to modern free civilization.

With this concept of regional development in mind we favoured for the future organization a Gezira Authority. This form of management, while maintaining responsibility for efficient cotton production, as the T.V.A. maintained responsibility for efficient power supplies, could use part of its profits to carry through the kind of social development programme which we had advocated in 1943. The Gezira Authority, in our view, needed to be as interested as ever in profit and efficiency, but would differ from the Syndicate, in that it could apply its profits not to shareholders but to stimulating new services to the community. The difference lay not in the profit motive but in the application of profit to a policy which neither private enterprise nor the ordinary departments of government were carrying out in such a poor country.

We who operated in the Gezira were not the only ones concerned with making a new plan. The special Sudanese Committee of the Advisory Council, which mediated in the tenants' strike in 1946, had originally been set up by the central Government to study all problems relevant to the future of the Gezira Scheme. Their report,[2] presented later in 1946, made the first base-line for discussion on the future. They shared our view of the need to co-ordinate plans for agricultural, educational, social and public health developments, but differed from us in believing that this co-ordination could be attained by ordinary departmental processes, reflecting in this respect the attitude of many departmental officials in the United States to the creation of the T.V.A. They proposed that a Gezira Scheme division of the Department of Agriculture should take the place of the Syndicate. This division was, however, to be under the control of a Higher Board of Management consisting of all the departmental directors, with additional members to represent the interests of the public of the Sudan as a whole, and of the tenants in the Gezira.

This proposal to harmonize the claims of Government, tenants and public in the management was accompanied by the following statement which gave a revealing picture of the prevailing attitude to development among Sudanese leaders:

> We shall only be saying the truth in stating that the nation as a whole will not consider the action of the Government in taking over the management of the Scheme as worthy of the joy and approval with which the decision has already been met throughout the Sudan, if it be not followed by a general revision of policy for attaining better organisation and management. The aim should not be confined to financial benefits only as was the case with the foreign commercial management. A basis must be found to cater for the welfare of the country as a whole and in particular of that community which lives within the boundaries of the Scheme. Such aims will not be attained if we do not give the Scheme general consideration not only from a humanitarian point of view, by utilising a part of its resources for the benefit of the community on which the whole Scheme is founded, but also by improving the social, educational and health conditions of the people. We must always remember that these things are part of the fundamental ends at which the construction of all such schemes should aim.[2]

The report of this special committee of the Advisory Council was referred to the thirtieth meeting of the Gezira Advisory Board. There the Financial Secretary, Sir Edington Miller* (who had succeeded Sir Francis Rugman in 1944), revealed some alarm lest the policy of the Scheme should pass outside the bounds of financial prudence. While accepting that general policy should be considered by a full board representing all interests, he insisted that the management should be controlled by a small committee under the chairmanship of the Financial Secretary and consisting of those members whose interests in the Scheme were primarily with the business and technical aspects. In making this recommendation, he pointed out that at least until 1974, when the servicing of foreign loans would be completed, the overriding consideration was finance.[3]

This reiteration of finance as the only arbiter of appropriate development in turn raised anxiety among us in the Gezira. Government and Syndicate officials had been trying to work towards a combined economic and social policy ever since the introduction of Schedule X on the eve of the war. Our co-operation had begun in anticipation of a new agreement between the Syndicate and Government. The decision not to renew the Companies' concession had already broken the continuity of this policy, which was faltering for lack of funds and decisions. Now

* Sir J. W. E. Miller (1894–1956), K.B.E., C.M.G. Joined Sudan Political Service 1920: Financial Secretary, Sudan, 1944–8: Secretary-General, Iraq Development Board, 1950–4.

it appeared that even after 1950 no definite plan to wed social and economic policy would emerge. The prospect of the dry hand of the Treasury in sole control was not inspiring.

James Robertson,* who as Acting Governor of the Blue Nile Province during the war had been particularly concerned with future policy in the Scheme, was now Civil Secretary and head of the political service in the Sudan. In September 1947 he sent a private memorandum[4] to Sir Edington Miller, which largely expressed our own viewpoint. 'I do not expect', he added, 'that everyone will agree with these ideas, but I feel strongly that we have a magnificent chance still of making something unique out of the Gezira if we can capture the imagination and enthusiasm of British and Sudanese. I think the present is the critical moment, and if we lose it in the next six months it will be impossible to recapture it.'

He pointed out that the board representing all interests, proposed by the Committee of the Advisory Council, would not come into being until 1950 and valuable time until then would be lost. Furthermore the proposal to control management by a small committee concerned with business and technical aspects suggested that the social needs were to be subordinated to purely materialistic aims. 'The Gezira Scheme', he continued, 'is not just a machine for the production of cotton and money: it might be the scene of a real experiment in mass education, in social improvements, in co-operative enterprise, in democratic control of local administration, as well as being an agricultural scheme of great importance to the Sudan.'

Robertson went on to emphasize the immediate political importance of presenting the Gezira Scheme afresh in such a way as to attract greater co-operation from the Sudanese. There was, he felt, an increasing tendency among elements hostile to the present administration to make the Gezira a political target in which the tenant was represented as the innocent countryman exploited by British companies in league with the British administration. Individual British officials and foreign personnel were pilloried as getting the best houses and high salaries at the expense of the poor peasant whose work supported the whole structure.

To counteract such a picture it was not enough to restate the truth about the original Gezira agreement and enumerate the evident benefits which had accrued to the people from it. What was required was a

* Later Sir James Robertson, K.C.M.G., K.B.E. Joined Sudan Political Service 1922: Governor Blue Nile Province, 1940–1: Civil Secretary, Sudan, 1945–53: Governor-General of Nigeria since 1955.

recognition of the disadvantages of losing freedom and being forced to be a socialized farmer. In other words, special attention in the Gezira Scheme should be paid to better housing and water supplies, better diet and health, more education, technical and academic, better recreation, more enlightenment (which meant a local newspaper and adult education), more economic and social development by co-operative planning than in the rest of the country, and the active assistance of educated Sudanese in furthering these objectives. He went on:

Elements of democracy now exist in the village councils, but these will soon deteriorate into places for talk and application for assistance, instead of becoming organs of joint management. This is because there is nothing at present for them to manage, as the existing Gezira agreement was designed only to split up cotton costs and profits.

In my opinion we cannot afford to postpone consideration of these needs until the agreement expires in 1950. It is most unlikely that these varied aims can be integrated into one plan unless one authority is created to administer the Scheme as one, and unless adequate legal and financial power is given to that authority to cut across departmental red-tape and lack of interest. A man with ability and personality might build up an organisation in the Gezira which would fire the tenants, villagers, school-masters, petits-fonctionnaires and other Gezira inhabitants with a joint enthusiasm to create better social conditions and greater economic prosperity than they have ever known. But the time will soon pass and the chance will be lost.[5]

The Gezira Advisory Board met in April 1948 to consider Robertson's memorandum. In spite of his plea for urgency it was difficult to take a decision quickly. Although Robertson was head of the political service, the initiative in Gezira matters lay traditionally with the Financial Secretary, and it was not as if anything was going wrong. The Syndicate was still running the Scheme quite satisfactorily. Robertson's call to take time by the forelock was political in objective, and although his memorandum was supported by a programme (designed jointly by Bredin, the Governor of the Blue Nile Province, and myself as Manager of the Syndicate), setting out in detail what was needed in social development and elaborating from our experience the need for one co-ordinating authority, there was by no means agreement in Khartoum on this solution.

Miller, the Financial Secretary, was not opposed to social development nor insensitive to the political tempo, but he doubted the Gezira's claim to special social attention. He had excellent reasons. The Government had sunk approximately £E14 million in the Scheme. Some £E2½ million of this had been advanced from its general reserves, and on this sum no interest had ever been paid. Up to 1939 the progressive result of the Scheme had involved a deficiency of £E2½ million. On this again no interest had been charged. The taxpayers elsewhere had underwritten the Scheme at the expense of their own needs. It was true that by 1947 the deficiency had turned to a total surplus of £E2½ million, but it was important to remember this history when an increase in annual costs in the Scheme was proposed on the grounds that expenditure on social services there was low relative to the revenue produced.

He concluded that any money for betterment would have to come from what would have been available for Syndicate shareholders. In 1950 the Government would assume the functions of the Syndicate and receive its 20 per cent share of the profits, but until it had experience it was impossible to tell how far that share would cover the annual expense and leave a surplus.

Miller also doubted the need for a special authority and other members, especially the Director of Agriculture, shared his doubt.[6] They feared that the new authority would try to overrule the other departments, but they were also convinced that the management and tenants of the agricultural enterprise should not be involved in local government. We, on the other hand, felt that local government was as yet very weak, and that our trained, resident field staff were in a providentially useful position to encourage the people to participate actively in the new decentralization of authority.

It was not easy to reconcile these views and there were other problems. One of these was the interesting recommendation of the Special Committee of the Advisory Council to include in the Higher Board of Management representatives of the public and of the tenants. In this way all interests could have a sense of sharing in the control, but on the other hand direction of policy might be confused by a multiplicity of authoritise.

An agreed quick decision on the issues could not be attained. Time could not be by-passed and in the end it was a new Financial Secretary, Sir Louis Chick,* who succeeded Sir Edington Miller, who had the duty of producing a plan in time to carry on the Scheme when the Syndicate's concession terminated on 30th June 1950.

In our arguments about a new plan for the Gezira, we were struggling with several of the problems of society common to this age of increasingly large units of management. The Gezira Scheme was by now one

* Sir Louis Chick, K.B.E. Joined Finance Department, Sudan Civil Service, 1930: Financial Secretary, 1948-53: Chief of Mission, International Bank Mission to Malaya, 1954: Chairman White Fish Authority since 1954.

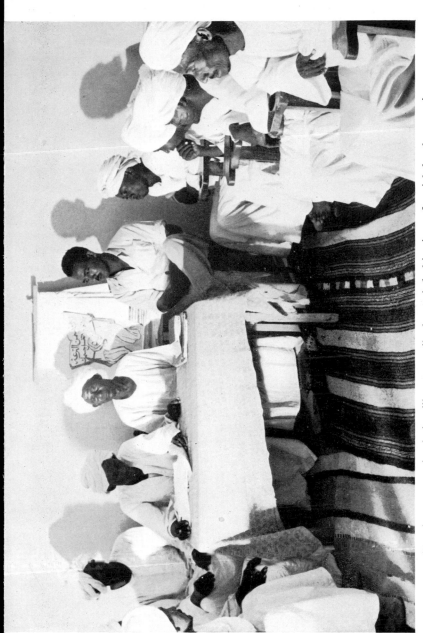

'Passing over patiently in village councils the varied objectives of social development'

PLATE XIII

Picking the cotton fields

PLATE XIV

'With great white piles of cotton being stamped down into man-high sacks'

PLATE XV

'The haughty camels walking ponderously to the collecting station'

PLATE XVI

of the largest agricultural estates in the world under one management yet with a large peasant society dependent on it. As so often in large-scale industry, and unlike most peasant societies, it was precisely the standardization of routines and the centralized organization which accounted for its efficiency. But on the other side a penalty was paid in human relations. As managers, our greatest problem was to humanize the undertaking without jeopardizing the efficiency. We needed to give to all the human beings connected with the Scheme a greater sense of participation in it and of wider social purpose from it.

Under the original agreement between the Syndicate and the Sudan Government there was no provision for such social investment. In one sense the cry for nationalization was connected with this fact. Management under private enterprise, it seemed, would give priority to profit loyalties and be unable to do anything about it. The belief arose that the State could and should operate with these wider social objectives. The Special Committee of the Advisory Council, whose remarks on the subject I have deliberately quoted, insisted on this.

Yet they were under something of an illusion. Miller's attitude made clear that the State would not necessarily take this view. It had to consider the claims of others in the country. And whether the capital came from the State or private enterprise there had to be a criterion of financial efficiency, and the test for this in both cases was the available profit. The State was not an isolated entity. It operated in a trading world. Whatever it might decide as to the distribution of profits between different groups in the country, it had to be careful that the social expenditure was a productive investment generating additional profit, and not a liability endangering the profit itself. If a strict view was taken of these limitations then the mere act of nationalization could hardly usher in the new era expected of it.

In the end Chick's proposals for the future were a cautious compromise. The emphasis was not on change but on absence of change. The triple partnership was to continue, except that the Syndicate's place as manager was to be taken by a new Gezira Board. Chick was anxious to establish in the public mind that the Board's primary function would be to manage a large agricultural undertaking in a businesslike manner. But he accepted the Gezira group's special social needs and the Board was to have special duties and special funds allocated for this purpose.

There had in the meantime been a major constitutional change in the country. The Advisory Council held its last session in June 1948, and the

With regard to the argument that the taxpayer, having provided the money for nationalisation, is entitled to reap the financial benefit, your Committee have come to the conclusion that, after the reserves have been built up, the tenants should share equally with the Government, representing the tax-payer, in any such surplus, because, had it not been for the hard work of the tenants and the patience with which they faced the lean years, the Scheme would have proved a failure and there would have been no Scheme to nationalise.[10]

The new proposals looked a sensible compromise. There was to be independent management, a generous and definite provision for social development, and a splitting of any surplus, after management expenses and reserves, between state and tenants. But in certain respects they were destined to bring difficulties.

The fixing of a limit rate to the cost of management was partly to discourage extravagance by the Board and partly to present the tenants with a real prospect, from the surplus, of something additional to the 40 per cent they had enjoyed before nationalization. But in an age of rampant inflation the limit quickly became a strait-jacket for the Board. So also with the reserves the fixing of the ceilings at £E3 million, which at the time seemed adequate relevant to crop values, was totally inadequate when prices soared. Moreover, the complicated financial allocations blurred the fact that the tenants did as a result get a substantial rise in their share. The uncertainty of the rise forfeited the co-operation which a definite increase in the percentage share would have fostered.

Prospects of co-operation from the tenants were also affected by the decisions taken as to the participation in management. The Scheme had always been spoken of as a partnership. Schedule X had suggested an ultimate aim of self-management by the tenants, and in the report of the Advisory Council committee, tenants' representatives were to be in the proposed Higher Board of Management.[11] The tenants themselves had by now become acutely desirous of having a proper say in their affairs. Their attitude was analogous to that of the educated classes to politics. They wanted to be treated as equal adult partners with a right to determine policy. They pictured Government and tenants splitting the profits and hiring management as a paid agency.

Chick and the Executive Council thought that the time for this had by no means arrived and that the small management board, independent of both politicians and tenants, was essential to the maintenance of efficiency. The Board was to be responsible to the Executive Council, and matters of policy between the state and the tenants were not to be decided by the Board but at the national level by the Executive Council in consultation with the Legislative Assembly.

From past experience of disputes in the Gezira, some of us thought that this was not enough and that there ought to be some machinery for bringing together more regularly the Government as provider of land and water, the tenants as cultivators, the Board as managers, and the public as beneficiaries from the revenue, in a Gezira Advisory Council. But the Select Committee of the Legislative Assembly advised against this as detracting from the authority of the Executive Council, and decided that the Gezira Local Committee could perform this function.[12]

This quite underestimated the nature of the problem of participation. Apart from an emotional resistance to being treated merely as the 'managed', the kind of subjects upon which the tenants really felt strongly were the marketing policy, equity in the current allocation of certain costs, the dates of payments of profits, and withdrawals from the Reserve Fund. These were not matters amenable to settlement by the Gezira Local Committee. They were not even matters for settlement between the Board and the tenants. They were matters affecting the national economy (in an age of inflation even the dates of large payments had a critical effect) in which all three partners and the public were involved and often at variance.

The result of these difficulties was that in the paramount problem of human relations, the Board still remained 'We' and the tenants 'They', and 'They' were suffering from disappointment both on the score of their share and on the scope of their participation.

The Gezira Ordinance had added an additional duty to the Board: 'The fostering of tenants' consultative bodies and consultation therewith.'[13] It was a duty which had already given a lively time to Bredin, the Governor of the Blue Nile Province, and myself as Manager of the Syndicate. It was destined to give an even livelier one to the Board. But there was one mitigating circumstance which greatly assisted the passage of the Gezira proposals. Ever since 1946 the price of cotton had been rising, yields had been steady, and profits vastly greater than ever before. The old partnership was ending in a blaze of white gold.

Chapter 20

WHITE GOLD

The marketing story of the Scheme has been described up to 1946 in Chapter 15. After the war the problem of how best to sell the cotton arose again, and this time there was the additional complication of attention to the rising claims of both tenants and public to influence the disposal of the crop.

The war itself had brought the Sudan Government much more definitely into the board room with the Syndicate in determining sales policy, for the bulk contract with the United Kingdom Cotton Control had applied not only to the Gezira but to all cotton grown in the Sudan. In this sense, apart from the technical details supplied by the Syndicate's London Board and Sir William Himbury, the bulk contract was a Government to Government business. The Manager of the Syndicate (myself since 1945) also began to come a little more into the board room, for he had the task of explaining the sales problems to the tenants.

The bulk contract ended with the 1946 crop and it might be thought that the Sudan Government would have reverted to its desire for local auctions. But the position had entirely changed. The bulk contract was now providing the quick sale and security of offtake sought in vain before the war, and it seemed difficult to better as a system of sale, provided that the price was fair. Moreover, the Cotton Control, with large financial resources, had been able to act like the B.C.G.A. on a bigger scale, and keep a large stock of different grades of Sudan cotton available for spinners to choose from. The Cotton Control had also persuaded many spinners who had hitherto not used Sudan cotton to change to this growth. This policy was of real advertising value to the Sudan and had widened the market in Britain.

The 1947 crop was nevertheless free for sale as seemed best, but there were difficulties facing its disposal. There was a large crop carry-over in America and Egypt. The European market had not recovered from the war. Eastern Europe, under Russian influence, was cut off from world trade. International commodity exchanges were still closed, and in the two traditional markets for Sudan cotton, the United Kingdom and India, the Government was still the sole importer.

In these circumstances bulk contracts were continued, and two were negotiated at an early date with the United Kingdom and India, at new fixed prices, covering the whole 1947 crop. But, as a check on these prices and to explore alternative markets, 10,000 bales were retained for sale by auction. The outcome was heartening. Whereas the 1946 crop had averaged 10 pence per lb., the 1947 crop averaged 19 pence. The prices obtained at auction, for 8,500 bales taken up, were slightly higher but not so much higher as to suggest that it would have been preferable to forego the safety of the bulk contracts and run the risk of the open market.

The financial results compared with 1946 as follows:

	1946	1947
Yield in kantars per feddan	3·4	4·0
Net divisible return (all partners)	£E2,605,000	£E6,789,000
Net divisible return per feddan	£E13·4	£E33·5
Tenants' profits (after repaying loans)	£E563,000	£E1,984,000
Tenants' profits per tenancy	£E29	£E96

The net divisible return, at £E33·5 per feddan, was the highest yet attained, exceeding even that of 1927.

The satisfactory results of bulk purchase in the sale of the 1947 crop made it seem reasonable to repeat the formula for 1948. The Raw Cotton Commission, which succeeded the Cotton Control in 1948, was anxious to take the whole crop, but agreed to accept 150,000 bales, an estimated 60 per cent, so as to leave 60,000 bales for a possible bulk contract with India, and 20,000 bales for auction. Alexandria futures market was now open again and reflected prices a little up on the previous year. The contract with the Raw Cotton Commission was fixed in November, as in the past, on prices current at that date which represented a rise of up to 6 pence per lb., according to grade, over the previous year. Looking back over the last twenty years it seemed a very satisfactory contract.

There now took place, however, one of those devastating events in the history of commodity markets which tend to defeat all those who try to find some perfect or stable system of selling or buying their crop. Owing to a great shortage of dollars it became more and more difficult for manufacturing countries to pay for American cotton, and as this situation developed it created a rapid premium for alternative growths.

Alexandria was the only futures market open in Egyptian-type cotton, and shortly after the signing of the contract with the Raw Cotton Commission (R.C.C.) the price in Alexandria began to rise steeply to levels not seen since 1919. In these circumstances the Indian negotiators refused to conclude a bulk contract.

By March 1948 it became clear that the bulk contract with the R.C.C., which had seemed so satisfactory in November 1947, was going to appear to the tenants and public in the Sudan as an incredibly cheap bargain to the United Kingdom. There was already criticism that, whatever the security to the Sudan, the bulk contract during the war with the Cotton Control had been unduly favourable in price to the United Kingdom over so long a period. An unintended benefit to Britain now, most open to misconstruction, might do a great deal of harm in terms of confidence both to future supplies as far as Britain was concerned and future off-take as far as the Sudan was concerned. The R.C.C. had originally wished to buy the whole crop and had only accepted 60 per cent to enable us to supply Indian and other markets. India had refused her chance. Could the R.C.C. be persuaded, in return now for a guarantee of the whole crop, to cancel the November contract and renegotiate a new price for the lot?

It fell to Sir Louis Chick to negotiate this awkward corner and he flew to England for the purpose in April 1948. The R.C.C. was remarkably magnanimous and agreed to strike a new bargain, which ended in a flat increase of 16·3 pence per lb. on all grades. It meant an average price a little below the level then current, but which worked out at 38·5 pence per lb. The yield of the 1948 crop had been below average at 3·4 kantars per feddan but at this price the net divisible return rose to £E11¾ million, nearly double the previous year, itself a record. After deducting loans, the tenants' profits came to just under £E4 million, or £E189 per standard tenancy compared with £E96 the year before.

What did the R.C.C. get in return? Fundamentally what it was looking for more than anything else at that time: certainty of continuous supply. For the R.C.C. regarded itself rather as an agent buying on behalf of Lancashire spinners than as a merchant operating for profit. Mr. Hugh Arrowsmith,* who so often represented both the Cotton Control and the R.C.C. in negotiations with the Sudan, was an interpreter of wide and wise vision in the long-term policy. By foregoing his pound of flesh on the price issue he obtained a lien not only on all the

* Hugh Arrowsmith, C.B.E. Cotton broker, 1910-40: assistant Controller, Ministry of Supply, 1940-6: member Raw Cotton Commission, 1951-4.

1948 but also on 60 per cent of the 1949 crop. This Chick conceded, for continuity was a two-way need. The bulk contract then, desired by both sides, was to continue, but this episode had revealed one weakness. It was difficult to operate on a fixed price. Some new system of pricing would have to be found for the future. After some argument it was hoped that this difficulty could be surmounted by relating Sudan qualities to Egyptian types quoted in the Alexandria market and taking the average price of these over an agreed period, and this was arranged for the 1948 crop contract.

Wooding, who had negotiated the November contract and blended his conservatism with a Victorian punctiliousness, added a characteristic comment when informing me of the results of the renegotiation.

I intensely disliked having to take part in these discussions since we have always held that a contract is a contract, and if the price had gone the other way we should certainly not have considered it reasonable for the British Government to ask us to take a lower price than had been fixed by the contract. I did not want to take part in any further bargaining, and I consider the whole thing rather disreputable. . . .

I do not know what effect this huge increase of price will have upon the tenants. They are due to receive a large appreciation from the 1947 crop in July. They are to receive £300,000 out of the Reserve Fund at the same time, and they will get a huge profit payment when the Pro-Forma prices are fixed, also about the same time. The tenants are already gentlemen farmers and it looks as if next year they will be gentlemen loafers.[1]

He was right; and attractive as this new wealth appeared it introduced an increasingly serious problem of inflation in a country where little opportunity for or knowledge of private capital investment, except in retail trade, existed. The predominant position of cotton in the country's economy became even more marked and rose to 80 per cent in value of all exports. The cost-of-living index for low incomes, taking 1938 as 100, had risen by mid-1948 to 305, and the principal factor in this was the greatly enhanced income of the cotton cultivators. The Government was the chief employer of labour, outside the Gezira, particularly in its public works and railways. There had already been considerable labour unrest at the continual rise in the cost of living and if these payments to tenants set off the spiral once again, especially in grain prices, the national interest would suffer.

These circumstances made it particularly important that the relationship between the management and tenants should be harmonious and it is time to turn to this subject again. After the tenants' strike in 1946 it became obvious that there ought to be some machinery for the representation of the tenants as a body. In each block there were the village councils and the block councils and the personal contacts between our field officers and the individual tenants. These relationships built up the local morale. What was missing was some point of contact at the top where the decisions affecting the tenants as a body were taken. The reasons for adopting a certain sales policy, the allocation of receipts and expenses in the very complicated joint accounts, the transfers to the Tenants' Reserve Fund, had never been discussed with the tenants as a whole or explained to the public. There was nothing to hide. There was nothing crooked about this reticence. It was just a projection of the paternal attitude. But as a result there was not only a great deal of ignorance; there were also a great many rumours about these matters which were quite untrue. A growing atmosphere of mistrust was generated by this situation.

And so Bredin, the Governor of the Blue Nile Province, and myself, the Manager for the Syndicate, who had already felt the need for getting ahead with social development, as described, felt also the urgent need for getting across to tenants and public the truth about all aspects of Gezira policy. As a start, on our joint initiative the Tenants' Representative Body was created. The tenants in each 'samadia' (the village agricultural unit) elected one of themselves to a block electoral college which then elected one of its number to represent the block. The forty block representatives formed the Tenants' Representative Body. The first elections were held in April 1947 and were the first elections ever held in a rural area of the Sudan.

As part of the policy of training the tenants towards management of their own affairs we had thought it essential to concede to the Tenants' Representative Body, in its original terms of reference, the right to advise concerning the administration of its own reserve fund and also concerning the timings of profits payments—matters hitherto arranged without reference to the tenants. This was deliberately heading for a squall and we knew it.

The belated setting up of the Tenants' Representative Body, and the circumstances of its creation following a demand for payment out of the reserve fund, started it off with a flavour of truculence. Wooding, approaching his seventies and with a Naval Commander's attitude to mutinies (he had served thus in the 1914–18 war), warned me that we had set up a monster liable to destroy rather than create confidence, and the early meetings seemed to confirm his view. Many blocks had elected those prominent in organizing the strike and all members arrived with a simple mandate from their constituents to get all the reserve fund paid out as soon as possible. At the second meeting in July 1947 they had been persuaded of the need to leave some cover for loans but not of the justice of the communal nature of the fund, and they recommended that it should be divided among existing tenants and replaced by small individual reserves to cover loans. Their advice was rejected and there for the moment the matter rested, assisted by the good results of the 1947 crop.

We had expected a good deal of political undercurrent but before long it appeared that the new institution was welcomed by the tenants above all as a focal point for their common interests. The members resisted an early attempt by Ashigga Party elements to form a caucus, and soon declared as a matter of principle an opposition to being dominated by any political or sectarian group.

They were in fact a fair cross-section of tenants, unconfined to one sect or party. Some, like Sheikh Mubarak Obeid from Talha, with a half-size tenancy on poor land, represented the younger generation impatient for a better standard of living. Disappointed with an income below average they easily found affinities with political discontent in the towns. Other blocks had elected more traditional leaders from well-known families. Such men were really conservative aristocrats, ready enough for a bargain but with little sympathy for new-fangled views. Yet another group was represented by men like Sheikh Ahmed Babikir El Izeirig, of Wad el Naim and Wad Medani, with a house in the country and a shop in the town—thoroughly successful men who had made full use of the Scheme's opportunities and turned the resulting profits into trade. Such men knew the latest quotations for commodity prices, and their coffee shops and they themselves became contact points for new leadership amid great diversity of personal interests.

In our accounts and reports the tenants used to appear as a colourless collective body. Nothing could have been farther from the truth. There were rich and poor, intelligent and stupid, genial and sour, like any other human society, and so they appeared in the Tenants' Representative Body. What united them was that they were tenants of the Gezira Scheme, meeting for the first time to exercise their influence and express their views as a group.

The creation of a formal body to talk to was not, in spite of Wooding's gloomy warnings, without its value to the management. For the first time in our history I made out for the tenants' representatives a breakdown of the receipts and expenses, and of the destination of sales, as these had transpired for the 1947 crop. Their answering questions revealed just those points in the accounts or the administration on which public confidence was not being obtained. My breakdown was not detailed enough. Where was the credit for the 'scarto' cotton, a by-product of ginning, which it was rumoured was taken as a perquisite by the ginnery manager? If the sales had all been made by bulk contract why had not the whole purchase price been received so that profits could be all paid out at once? Why was all the cotton sold to the United Kingdom and India? Were there not better markets? It was a very long way from an ordinary shareholders' meeting in London.

Meetings of this kind continued from time to time and covered all aspects of the Scheme's administration. They proved of good value in getting among tenants and public a better understanding of economic problems and of some of the difficulties we encountered in trying to sell the country's most important crop to best advantage. There may be astonishment that we had no organization of this kind before. This was not only due to a prolonged paternalism. There was always a fear by those in authority that the stupid tail might wag the intelligent dog and that if self-expression was conceded to people hitherto regarded as too ignorant to have a view, unwise policies would result. We had now to experience this consequence both in regard to the reserve fund and to the problem of inflation in general.

The tenants' representatives returned to their attack on the reserve fund at their fourth meeting in February 1948. It was abundantly clear that they would not voluntarily contribute from their annual share to a communal fund. The problem was to persuade them not to dissipate the whole of the existing fund as demanded by the express mandate of their constituents, who still regarded it as property which had been filched from them. Eventually the members agreed to a compromise by which we approved a further withdrawal of £E300,000 against acceptance by them of the necessity for keeping a minimum figure of £E4 per feddan in the fund as a guarantee for bad debts.

A withdrawal from the reserve fund on top of the best-ever 1947 crop profits was ridiculous enough. When in addition it became evident that the 1948 crop would produce far larger profits yet, a more serious problem of inflation began to confront us. War-time controls and rationing had ended, amid popular relief, in 1947, and other measures had to be taken to meet this situation. Export duty on cotton was raised to 5 per cent and government expenditure deferred but it was not enough.

Something would have to be done to spread the payment of tenants' profits over a longer period. This was an example of the kind of problem for which some of us had felt a higher advisory council for the Gezira would be useful, where representatives of the Government, the public and the tenants could sort out and try to reconcile the issues involved. But no such body existed. The tenants were legally entitled to their profits. After many years of only average earnings they wished to make the most of the present high prices and their representatives were primed to give nothing away. But the national interest lay in the other direction. What was the best thing to do?

Rather than have the tail wagging the dog, Chick decided temporarily to revert to a dose of paternalism. He instructed the Syndicate, which lacked the power to do this on its own authority, to spread the payment of profits immediately due from the 1948 crop over four equal instalments until April 1949, and to withhold appreciation payments (one-third of the total) until further notice. In the general affluence the tenants accepted this order and Chick hoped that they could be persuaded, when April came round, themselves to extend forward the appreciation payments still due on the 1948 crop. But it was like persuading Australian sheep farmers to postpone payment of their wool clip. They clamoured for their appreciation payment and it was granted.

Immediately afterwards, by July 1949, the results of the 1949 crop were to hand and disclosed an even more successful year financially. The average price of certain types in the Alexandria market, during the period January to May, had been agreed as the price criterion for Sudan cotton in the R.C.C. contract, and the R.C.C. had wished to include in the contract any cotton not taken by India or elsewhere. India had expressed a wish for a bulk contract but would not accept the price link, and once again negotiations there had proved abortive. 25,000 bales had been sold by auction as a check on the R.C.C. price links, and although the prices at auction had proved better for some grades, for others they had proved worse than the R.C.C. average and a relative loss of £E150,000 had been incurred in this test. Once again the bulk contract with the United Kingdom had proved very fair value. By a curious coincidence the average price realized was the same as in 1948, 38·5 pence per lb., but the yield had risen to 4·3 kantars per feddan. The resulting net divisible return was nearly £E14 million, and tenants' profits, after deducting loans, would amount to just over £E4½ million, or £E221 per standard tenancy.

The Blue Nile Province now presented an economic paradox such as can rarely have been paralleled. The Gezira area, in addition to unprecedented profits, was producing excellent grain crops, but across the river on the east bank, where rains had failed, famine measures were in progress. So far from any need to sell their spare grain, Gezira tenants were buying up grain from outside as an investment, and an indication of the amount of money loose in the Gezira was given when in August 1949 the premiums offered for eight flour-mill sites amounted to £E135,000.[2] The public attitude to the tenants began to alter from sympathy for the hard-used farmer to jealousy of the idle rich.

Meantime what was to be done about inflation? Chick had stepped up the export duty to 10 per cent. Was he to repeat the paternal order method of spreading profits? We persuaded him to let us try the democratic method first. After all, this was what we were trying to inculcate. The onus of getting the tenants' representatives voluntarily to take a more responsible attitude fell particularly upon two men, C. W. Beer,* the deputy-governor of the province, and Sayed Mohammed Awam Nimr† of the Department of Agriculture. They had been nominated by the Governor to help the tenants' representatives to get their organization going efficiently and, in the absence of any previous experience, their help had been welcomed by the tenants. The task of these officers was anything but a sinecure for they had to sympathize with a frustrated desire to get their own way on the part of the representatives and the 20,000 tenants behind them, but to temper the one-sidedness of these views to the needs of the country. Beer was an indefatigable enthusiast, with a passionate devotion to the building up of a people's own initiative combined with a shrewd ability to prick conceit and prod inertia. Sayed Awam worked more quietly. Essentially a countryman, he had a genuine interest in stimulating a better farming community and his influence was exercised more in private conversation than in public speeches.

The scene on this occasion was a vignette of many others. The forty representatives had collected in the province town, Wad Medani. They had as yet no meeting-place of their own and the meeting was held in a public building because the only room big enough to hold them, the Governor's office, took away their sense of independence. Argument and counter-argument went on while delegates, though appreciating the country's need, expanded on the difficulties of their own cost of living

---

* C. W. Beer. Afterwards Social Development Officer, Sudan Gezira Board: Membership Officer, Duke of Edinburgh's Study Conference, July 1956.

† Sayed Awam Nimr. Afterwards a director of the Sudan Gezira Board.

and the heavy labour costs of their own region. At last, as Beer recorded it, 'after being left alone to shout it out for twenty-five minutes', the representatives agreed not only to a time-table spreading the payments at regular intervals over the coming year but also to their profits being earmarked instead of loans and paid out against work done and cotton picked.

It was not the answer which a good paternalist would have liked, that is, a large appropriation to the reserve fund and no argument. But it was some achievement in voluntary democratic procedure and as such it evoked the congratulations of the Financial Secretary. And it set a useful precedent in a new routine of spreading payments and self-financing which effected some reduction in the weight of money, even if it made no contribution to savings.

Fortune continued to smile upon the last crop with which the Companies* were connected. In the 1950 season the yield went up to 4·6 kantars per feddan. The grade was excellent and the average price, the same sales procedure being continued, worked out at 41·3 pence per lb. The net divisible return rose to over £E16 million, equivalent to £E78 per feddan. The tenants' profits came to just under £E6 million, a matter of £E281 per standard tenancy.

Looking back to twenty years before, when Financial Secretary Schuster had taken such a big risk in pushing up the Scheme's area to break even at a net divisible return of £E10 per feddan,† the last four seasons of the old partnership, when seen in summarized form, gave a heartening finale, and the liquid assets of the country had gone up from their highest yet figure of £E12 million in 1945 to over £E30 million in 1950.

Season	Yield	Net Divisible Return £E	Per Feddan £E	Tenants' Profits £E	Per Tenancy £E
1946	3·4	2,605,760	13	563,419	29
1947	4·0	6,789,675	33	1,975,052	96
1948	3·4	11,753,038	57	3,904,026	189
1949	4·3	13,819,832	67	4,576,516	221
1950	4·6	16,118,155	78	5,820,630	281

The tables at the end of this chapter show the record for the whole period of the partnership from 1926 to 1950 in comparison with the

* As mentioned originally in Chapter 11 there were really two companies connected with the Gezira Scheme, the Sudan Plantation Syndicate and the Kassala Cotton Company. I have used the word Syndicate all the time in the text for abbreviation, because the policies of the two companies were in practice identified.

† See Chapter 11.

position at the end of the first twenty-one years already discussed in Chapter 13. It will be seen that the last four years:

1. Put on for the partnership as a whole almost as much profit as the preceding twenty-one years, making the total net divisible return just under £E100 million (Table 1).

2. Raised the Government's direct surplus from the Scheme from under £E1 million to over £E16 million (Table 2).

3. Raised the average annual tenancy profit from around £E30 to nearly £E300 (Tables 3 and 4).

4. Raised the Companies' (S.P.S. and K.C.C. combined) total of initial profit from £E7½ million to over £E16 million (Table 5), and the Syndicate shareholders' average dividend (before tax) on the nominal capital to 15 per cent, and on the nominal capital plus the share premiums to 9 per cent (Table 6). It will be noted that these particular percentages are not very much higher than at the end of the first twenty-one years. This is because dividends were limited in the last four years to 25 per cent. The Syndicate's reserves were however substantially increased in this period and when, on liquidation, the reserves were distributed, the shareholders received, in addition to the repayment of the share capital and premiums, a capital profit equivalent to 25 shillings for every 20 shillings of capital and premiums subscribed.

There might be argument as to which of the partners had done best. An overall judgement might be that the tenants' profit figures, except in the last years, were disappointing, especially with their five empty years in the depression (1930–4). On the other hand the Government was hopelessly in the red at this period, and of the three partners the thin time was shortest for the Companies. A glance at Table 5 will show that the Companies' interest revenue (which was mainly derived from interest on capital expenditure at 6 per cent) was a godsend to them in the depression years which the other partners did not enjoy, and the £E16 million balance in Table 5 appears at first sight a big price to pay for private enterprise participation.

On the other hand when this is broken down to the shareholders' average return in Table 6 it could not be called excessive. Moreover both Government and tenants had two advantages not applicable to the Companies and not noted in the tables. Firstly they each enjoyed a subsidiary benefit—the Government the large indirect revenue, and the tenants the irrigated food crop—and secondly they were the permanent inheritors of the Scheme while the Companies had only a temporary connection. And this at least could be said of the value of that connection. Without the Companies' capital and without the personal spirit of enterprise with which they spurred on the start of the Scheme, the Scheme might never have existed, and when they went they left their partners behind in prosperity and bequeathed to the country an economic backbone of its own for its coming political independence. If the same could be said of all foreign investment one of the world's most disputed problems might be on the way to solution.

It would be sterile to pursue argument further, for inevitably when the original percentages of the profits were agreed it was a matter of bargaining on an estimate of future fortune and, looking back, at least no partner could be said to have done badly. Indeed when 30th June 1950 went past a general feeling of satisfaction prevailed. The Scheme, after many vicissitudes, had in the end justified the hopes of its founders. It was beyond question a considerable economic success.

Just what aspects of it had enabled us to pull through the difficulties, what value its history as an example of development might be to others, both in what we had done and left undone, is worth analysing and I make some attempt to do this in the next chapter.

In 1946 a foreign visitor, Sayed Mohammed Afzal, later Director of Research of the Pakistan Central Committee, had paid us this compliment.

The Gezira Scheme is one of those outstanding experiments on socio-economic problems of the current century and its success is so great that it deserves to go down in history as a great romance of creative achievements. The rich fields and smiling faces of the workers on the land, who were till recently nomads of the deserts, going back and forth eking out a miserable existence from an unhospitable country, are a running commentary on this great experiment, and anybody who visits the Scheme cannot but be strongly impressed with the success of it. . . . I am taking this opportunity of describing the Scheme in the hope that it might be useful to the dwellers on the Indo-Pakistan sub-continent.[3]

He was exaggerating. The past had not been quite so bad nor the present so good as he painted it; but his indulgent comment encouraged our own belief that the story of the Gezira had an interest for the rest of the world as well as the Sudan.

Meantime, as the Companies stepped out of the partnership, generous appreciation of their contribution to the enterprise was shown by many Sudanese in public speeches in the Legislative Assembly. But perhaps the most pleasing conclusion, to many of us who had worked long in the Gezira, was a resolution of the Tenants' Representative Body. At its first meeting after 30th June 1950 a vote of thanks was passed to the Sudan Plantations Syndicate and the Kassala Cotton Company 'for their excellent work during the period of their concession and their valuable services to the tenants and the country, the result of efficient and high standards of agricultural management'. Coming from the one-time child to its foreign nurse it gave us a special kind of satisfaction.

TABLE I

The Economic Results to the Partnership from 1926 to 1950

1 Crop Year	2 Cotton Area in Feddans	3 Yield in Kantars per Feddan	4 Price in Pence per lb.	5 Net Divisible Return i.e. Net Crop Proceeds after Deducting Marketing Expenses	6 Net Divisible Return per Feddan of Cotton Area
				£E	£E
1925–6	80,031	4·8	18·0	2,340,616	29
1927	100,058	4·7	18·0	3,356,629	33
1928	100,768	3·3	19·7	2,563,402	25
1929	131,292	3·6	18·4	3,269,162	25
1930	174,164	2·3	7·9	885,905	5
1931	196,799	1·4	6·4	393,940	2
1932	194,935	4·1	8·5	2,270,988	12
1933	195,941	1·9	8·1	875,347	4
1934	175,834	2·3	8·6	1,025,324	6
1935	176,150	4·5	8·2	2,187,920	12
1936	185,758	3·7	7·9	2,077,858	11
1937	199,770	4·5	8·6	2,908,401	15
1938	207,242	4·6	5·9	2,091,913	10
1939	206,274	4·5	6·2	2,252,945	11
1940	206,880	3·8	9·6	2,722,407	13
1941	207,594	4·0	8·9	2,952,244	14
1942	207,121	4·0	9·1	2,922,591	14
1943	206,486	4·8	9·3	3,697,480	18
1944	206,571	3·1	10·6	2,614,936	13
1945	206,578	4·9	10·6	4,280,156	21
1946	196,541	3·4	10·3	2,605,760	13
				£E50,295,924	
1947	206,176	4·0	19·2	6,789,675	33
1948	206,346	3·4	38·5	11,753,038	57
1949	206,778	4·3	38·5	13,819,832	67
1950	206,737	4·6	41·3	16,118,155	78
				£E98,776,624*	

* This total includes £E198,912 credited to Wad el Nau Reserve Account in 1926 and 1927, and £E154,633 credited to the Seed Farm Running Account over the years 1926 to 1950. These were to meet special commitments and are not reproduced in the individual totals of the partners in the other tables.

TABLE 2

The Economic Results to the Sudan Government from 1926 to 1950

Direct Revenue compared with Direct Expenditure

1 Crop Year	2 Government Share of Net Divisible Return	3 Direct Expenditure	4 Surplus	5 Deficiency	6 Cumulative Surplus	7 Cumulative Deficiency
	£E	£E	£E	£E	£E	£E
1925–6	713,347	718,925		5,578		5,578
1927	1,150,191	721,412	428,779		423,201	
1928	958,835	814,009	144,826		568,027	
1929	1,256,076	970,504	285,572		853,599	
1930	337,785	1,027,245		689,460	164,139	
1931	150,016	1,023,103		873,087		708,948
1932	863,066	992,539		129,473		838,421
1933	330,267	896,219		565,952		1,404,373
1934	385,850	892,907		507,057		1,911,430
1935	836,444	952,483		116,039		2,027,469
1936	790,104	930,526		140,422		2,167,891
1937	1,120,093	956,217	163,876			2,004,015
1938	800,350	1,027,844		227,494		2,231,509
1939	862,314	1,032,313		169,999		2,401,508
1940	1,045,236	714,654	330,582			2,070,926
1941	1,147,076	696,740	450,336			1,620,590
1942	1,133,933	698,365	435,568			1,185,022
1943	1,434,824	716,792	718,032			466,990
1944	965,002	737,323	227,679			239,311
1945	1,559,636	752,519	807,117		567,806	
1946	939,481	773,543	165,938		733,744	
	18,779,926	18,046,182	4,158,305	3,424,561		
1947	2,696,510	855,843	1,840,667		2,574,411	
1948	4,703,604	918,832	3,784,772		6,359,183	
1949	5,523,844	966,628	4,557,216		10,916,399	
1950	6,455,609	1,134,693	5,320,916		16,237,315	
£E	38,159,493	21,922,178	19,661,876	3,424,561		

The direct expenditure includes the rent of the land, the interest and amortization of loans for the Gezira, and the cost of maintenance of the dam and the canal system.

TABLE 3

The Economic Results to the Tenants as a whole from 1926 to 1950

1	2	3	4	5	6	7
			DISTRIBUTED OVER			
Crop Year	Tenants' Collective Share of Net Divisible Return	Tenants' Cultivation Loans. Cost of Ploughing, Seed and Interest. Certain Collective Expenses	Transfers to the Tenants' Reserve Fund	Profits and Appreciations	Add Transfers from the Tenants' Reserve Fund	Total Profits Payments
	£E	£E	£E	£E	£E	£E
1925–6	936,246	400,045		536,201		536,201
1927	1,342,652	502,148		840,504		840,504
1928	1,025,361	440,895		584,466		584,466
1929	1,307,665	582,585		725,080		725,080
1930	354,362	592,144		Nil		Nil
1931	157,575	531,360		Nil		Nil
1932	908,395	604,283	8,064	243,366		243,366
1933	350,139	431,068		Nil		Nil
1934	410,130	404,409	5,689	84,825		84,825
1935	875,167	506,995	96,258	271,914		271,914
1936	831,143	441,782	116,597	272,764		272,764
1937	1,163,364	529,098	134,165	500,101		500,101
1938	836,765	558,784	38,937	239,044		239,044
1939	901,178	534,053	138,639	228,486		228,486
1940	1,088,963	487,161	243,217	358,585		358,585
1941	1,180,897	509,374	231,135	440,388		440,388
1942	1,169,037	506,495	173,835	488,707		488,707
1943	1,478,992	651,305	134,463	693,224		693,224
1944	1,114,915	525,144	43,497	546,274	32,426	578,700
1945	1,876,536	721,593	43,252	1,111,691		1,111,691
1946	1,148,658	529,293	55,946	563,419	400,263	963,682
	20,458,140	10,990,014	1,463,694	8,729,039	432,689	9,161,728
1947	2,715,870	717,005	23,813	1,975,052	8,961	1,984,013
1948	4,700,999	717,204	79,769	3,904,026	309,519	4,213,545
1949	5,527,933	932,470	18,947	4,576,516		4,576,516
1950	6,447,262	626,632		5,820,630		5,820,630
£E	39,850,204	13,983,325	1,586,223	25,005,263	751,169	25,756,432

See Table 4 for the results per standard tenancy.

TABLE 4

The Economic Results to the Tenants per tenancy from 1926 to 1950

1	2	3	4	5	RESULTS PER STANDARD TENANCY				
					6	7	8	9	10
						Deduct		Add	
Crop Year	Yield	Price	Tenants' Collective Share of Net Divisible Return	Equivalent to Average Credit per Tenancy of	Average Tenants' Loans	Transfers to Tenants' Reserve Fund	Balance being Average Profits Paid	Transfers from Tenants' Reserve Fund	Net Average Profit Paid
			£E	£E	£E	£E	£E	£E	£E
1925–6	4·8	18·0	936,246	117	50		67		67
1927	4·7	18·0	1,342,652	134	50		84		84
1928	3·3	19·7	1,025,361	101	43		58		58
1929	3·6	18·4	1,307,665	100	45		55		55
1930	2·3	7·9	354,362	20	34		Nil		Nil
1931	1·4	6·4	157,575	8	27		Nil		Nil
1932	4·1	8·5	908,395	46	31		12		12
1933	1·9	8·1	350,139	18	22		Nil		Nil
1934	2·3	8·6	410,130	23	23		5		5
1935	4·5	8·2	875,167	50	28	5	17		17
1936	3·7	7·9	831,143	49	27	6	16		16
1937	4·5	8·6	1,163,364	58	28	6	24		24
1938	4·6	5·9	836,765	40	27	2	11		11
1939	4·5	6·2	901,178	44	27	6	11		11
1940	3·8	9·6	1,088,963	53	24	12	17		17
1941	4·0	8·9	1,180,897	57	25	11	21		21
1942	4·0	9·1	1,169,037	57	25	9	23		23
1943	4·8	9·3	1,478,992	71	32	6	33		33
1944	3·1	10·6	1,114,915	54	26	2	26	2	28
1945	4·9	10·6	1,876,536	90	34	2	54		54
1946	3·4	10·3	1,148,658	58	26	3	29	20	49
			£E20,458,140						
1947	4·0	19·2	2,715,870	132	35	1	96		96
1948	3·4	38·5	4,700,999	228	36	3	189	15	204
1949	4·3	38·5	5,527,933	267	45	1	221		221
1950	4·6	41·3	6,447,262	312	32		281		281
			£E39,850,204						

TABLE 5

The Economic Results to the Companies from 1926 to 1950

1 Crop Year	2 Companies' Share of Net Divisible Return	3 Companies' Share including interest charged to Joint Account and Tenants	4 Companies' Expenses	5 Balance
	£E	£E	£E	£E
1925–6	582,281	622,008	215,763	406,245
1927	759,319	821,487	278,888	542,599
1928	573,954	632,979	223,557	409,422
1929	699,630	771,666	237,226	534,440
1930	192,702	293,779	188,060	105,719
1931	85,552	211,653	226,237	14,584 (Loss)
1932	495,807	647,178	190,348	456,830
1933	193,299	309,867	214,288	95,579
1934	226,841	329,317	220,407	108,910
1935	470,425	574,742	250,355	324,387
1936	451,386	556,506	280,524	275,982
1937	618,832	715,201	311,647	403,554
1938	451,104	527,148	290,667	236,481
1939	485,285	568,195	274,878	293,317
1940	581,958	659,806	240,528	419,278
1941	621,993	709,871	217,809	492,062
1942	616,261	693,687	214,870	478,817
1943	776,878	847,266	221,545	625,721
1944	533,584	608,303	237,131	371,172
1945	837,611	912,602	260,047	652,555
1946	516,938	584,692	270,189	314,503
	10,771,640	12,597,953	5,064,964	7,532,989
1947	1,372,042	1,465,512	301,716	1,163,796
1948	2,339,120	2,447,716	336,423	2,111,293
1949	2,741,206	2,861,206	401,243	2,459,963
1950	3,189,374	3,319,374	541,108	2,778,266
	20,413,382	22,691,761	6,645,454	16,046,307

TABLE 5—*continued*

1. The Companies' expenses in column 4 cover the running costs of directing and managing the project. They do not include provision for the recovery of capital expenditure not repayable at the end of the concession, such as clearing, levelling and minor canalization. Nor do they include provision for reserves or taxation. These commitments had to be met each year from the balance in column 5 before payment of dividend.

2. Unfortunately, since the Companies have been liquidated, detailed books of account are no longer available. For this reason the interest revenue has had to be estimated for the last two years, and it is not possible to give such interesting detail as, for instance, the amount of tax paid to the Sudan and the United Kingdom respectively. Only a general picture can be attempted, and an approximate breakdown of the disposal of the £E16 million balance is as follows:

	£E
Allocated to amortize capital expenditure not recovered	725,000
Allocated to taxation (United Kingdom and Sudan) exclusive of tax on dividends	4,000,000
Allocated to dividends (gross)	9,350,000
Retained as reserves, and paid out to shareholders on liquidation	1,925,000
	£E16,000,000

3. The above gives the position for both companies. What the individual shareholder got out of it, both by way of dividends and by payment out of reserves on liquidation, is illustrated by Table 6 which gives the position for the Sudan Plantations Syndicate. That of the Kassala Cotton Company would be roughly analogous.

4. The reserves referred to in paragraph 2 above, and paid out on liquidation, were added to by the realization of Zeidab estate and other external investments. Together these enabled a capital profit to be paid to shareholders, on liquidation, amounting to 25 shillings per 20 shillings subscribed, in addition to repayment of capital and premiums.

TABLE 6

*The Economic Results to the Shareholders of the Sudan Plantations Syndicate
from 1926 to 1950*

1	2	3	4	5	6	7
Year ending 30th June	Nominal Share Capital Ranking for Dividends	Premiums Received Thereon	Total Share Capital and Premiums	Rate of Dividends Paid on Nominal Share Capital	Rate of Dividends Calculated on Share Capital and Premiums	Amount of Dividend before deduction of Sudan and U.K. Tax
	£	£	£	%	%	£
1926	1,500,000	565,047	2,065,047	25	18	375,000
1927	,,	,,	,,	30	22	450,000
1928	2,250,000	1,690,262	3,940,262	25	14	562,500
1929	,,	,,	,,	25	14	562,500
1930	,,	,,	,,	10	6	225,000
1931	,,	,,	,,	Nil	Nil	Nil
1932	,,	,,	,,	Nil	Nil	Nil
1933	,,	,,	,,	4	2	90,000
1934	,,	,,	,,	6	3	135,000
1935	2,475,000	1,703,968	4,178,968	8	5	198,000
1936	,,	,,	,,	10	6	247,500
1937	,,	,,	,,	12½	7	309,375
1938	,,	,,	,,	10	6	247,500
1939	,,	,,	,,	8	5	198,000
1940	,,	,,	,,	8	5	198,000
1941	,,	,,	,,	8	5	198,000
1942	,,	,,	,,	10	6	247,500
1943	,,	,,	,,	12	7	297,000
1944	,,	,,	,,	20	12	495,000
1945	,,	,,	,,	22	13	544,500
1946	,,	,,	,,	25	15	618,750
Average Dividend				13·24%	8·12%	6,199,125
1947	,,	,,	,,	25	15	618,750
1948	,,	,,	,,	25	15	618,750
1949	,,	,,	,,	25	15	618,750
1950	,,	,,	,,	25	15	618,750
Average Dividend				15%	9%	8,674,125

1. The average dividends paid on the nominal capital amounted to 15 per cent.

2. The average dividends paid on the nominal capital plus the share premiums amounted to 9 per cent.

S 273

TABLE 6—*continued*

3. These figures are before the deduction of Sudan business profits tax and British income tax which amounted to roughly 36 per cent of the dividends declared. The average net dividend return to the shareholder, who had been a shareholder throughout the twenty-five years, thus amounted to 6 per cent assuming that he paid tax at the standard rate.

4. Apart from the above dividends, on the liquidation of the Syndicate a capital profit was paid to shareholders. This amounted to 25 shillings per 20 shillings of capital and premiums subscribed.

5. The figures for the Kassala Cotton Company are roughly analogous.

TABLE 7

Summary of the Tenants' Reserve Fund at 30th June 1950

Paid into the Fund	£E
Transfers from the Tenants' Collective Accounts	1,586,223
Surpluses on review of Depreciation Funds	157,827
Dividends on investments	372,404
Tenants' unclaimed balances	7,388
Sundries	3,957
	£E2,127,799

Less—Paid out of the Fund		
Towards repayment of the £600,000 Loan Debt	384,170*	
Transfers to supplement profits	751,169	
		1,135,339
Balance of Tenants' Reserve Fund at 30th June 1950		£E992,460

* The final account of the Loan Debt was as follows:

	£E	£E
Total amount charged on Tenants' Reserve Fund		601,358
Less Repaid through the Tenants' Reserve Fund	384,170	
Remitted by the Companies under conditions	119,553	503,723
Balance: remitted altogether by Government and Companies		£E97,635

The conditions under which the companies remitted the £E119,553 were that, in exchange, they would charge interest at 5 per cent on the capital cost of the ploughing machinery in the ploughing account from 1940 onwards up to a total of £E12,000 per annum.

At the same time the Government set aside £E119,553, out of the £E384,170 which the tenants had repaid, as capital for a Tenants' Welfare Fund so that in the end the effective sum which the tenants repaid of their £E600,000 Loan Debt was £E264,617. No interest had been charged on the debt since 1932.

Chapter 21

APPRAISAL

Before estimating the relevance of the Gezira story to other parts of the world, it is wise to recall that a number of natural advantages played a large part in the technical success of the Scheme.

The first of these advantages was the irrigation site. The Blue Nile river afforded huge quantities of water alongside huge areas of irrigable land. The slope of the river enabled the dam at Sennar to operate both as a barrage and a storage reservoir at a point where it could command most of the Gezira plain by gravity flow. This location and the gentle incline of the land from this point northwards had a basic effect on costs, for the heavy capital expenditure on one single dam could be spread cheaply over a large paying area. Thanks to this site advantage, the total capital investment for supplying the water could be reduced in the end to as low a figure as £E15 per feddan.

A second advantage affecting the irrigation capital costs lay in the relation of river to soil. While the dam at Sennar could command the plain from upstream, downstream of the dam the level of the land was much higher than the level of the river even in full flood. This site relationship has enabled the Gezira to escape the waterlogging from a rising water-table which has proved such a problem in many other irrigation schemes. As a result, expensive drainage has been avoided and only shallow surface drains have been needed to carry away the flood water from rain. The high clay content (and the exceptional depth) of the soil seems also to have played a part in reducing uptake of salts by capillary attraction from below. It has also proved economic, for thanks to the clay the canals became quickly impervious to seepage and required no lining with brick or concrete.

Next in importance to soil came climate. Beginning where the first rainfall began so near to the great dry region of the Sahara, the Gezira plain presented no very costly problem of forest clearance. Only in the southern blocks was there a heavy growth of trees. But of greater importance than low development costs was the advantage which irrigation could bring in the Gezira relative to the economy which preceded it. Because it was in a region where rainfall was sparse and erratic it brought a dual benefit. It enabled an entirely new cash crop to be grown and it raised the yield and removed the hazard from the customary food crop. This latter advantage, increased by the irrigated fodder crop where this was obtainable,* was of the greatest significance, for even if the cash crop produced little profit tenants in the Scheme had a greater security in food than anyone outside it.

The particular cash crop which could be grown in the region was another advantage. Not many parts of the world are climatically suited to fine, long-staple cotton. It is true that excessive dependence on one cash crop was, and is, a continual anxiety in the Sudan as in many other countries. As a hedge against the dependence, experiments were made at the research station which indicated that a number of other fibre, grain and oil-seed crops could be grown in the Gezira if need be. But long-staple cotton, with its combination of a valuable fibre and valuable oil seed on one plant, far outstripped any alternative as an export crop as long as yields were satisfactory and world demand for it continued. There was a great practical gain in specializing in a particular product with unusual advantages and using the profit as capital to diversify the economy in the rest of the country.

The very aridity of the climate was another advantage. The hot, dry summer months, when every plant not irrigated shrivelled and died, acted as a free quarantine period against the carry-over of pests and diseases by insect, bacteria or virus and reduced costly spraying and eradication routines against these constant dangers. Contributing to cut costs in another way, the dry climate over nearly nine months of the year enabled a very full use of agricultural machinery. That first step in evolving from a subsistence economy—the use of machinery to break up and prepare a larger area of land than customary for each individual family—is often made difficult by the shortness of the possible working season. Often a large number of machines are needed because they can only be used for a short time, which adds greatly to the cost. The Gezira

---

* Although five feddans of lubia per tenancy was theoretically provided for in the rotation it was in practice, after the depression years, limited to clean land and competent tenants. This restriction, originally imposed in the interests of better husbandry, was in later years retained of necessity owing to water shortage as the Scheme area extended. In the peak season when all three crops needed water at once, the demand for water exceeded in the end the carrying capacity of the main canal. Lubia, being the least important crop, had in these circumstances to be rationed.

climate enabled a minimum of machines to be used for a maximum number of days per annum.

Finally, in the Gezira irrigation could be brought to the people. There was no need for migration—often an expensive undertaking and difficult to get started because of innate conservatism. The potential tenants were already there, in their own houses and in their own established society. They already had an attachment to the region. It was probably a vital factor, encouraging perseverance through disappointing years and tolerance of the new, ordered form of agriculture.

This combination of natural advantages might not all be necessary to other crops and other regions but they would be worth noticing in any imitation of the Gezira Scheme. And this might well be undertaken, for the Gezira had one rather rare value in an underdeveloped country. Often a higher standard of living, in the sense of a cash income on top of subsistence, is not easily obtained in primitive communities except by working away from home. This raises considerable social problems, for the men go away to earn but leave their families behind on the homeland subsistence plots. If they take their families with them their wages can seldom keep them and they face the hazard of starvation if they lose employment. Underdeveloped countries can seldom afford either a family wage or unemployment insurance, so the men tend to keep one foot at home in the land and one foot in a job outside. The result is often a restless class of employees with a high turnover in industry and man-starved primitive agriculture. To get out of this predicament a more organized system of profitable agriculture with increased purchasing power is the complement to industrial production. In many countries the need for organized productive agriculture goes deeper, for an export crop is often the first, and for years the main, earner of foreign exchange, without which the next step in raising the standard of living—imports from other countries—is impossible. In such a situation the Gezira project is of more than passing interest, for it brought both the opportunity for a higher standard of living and greater security in food crops to the people in their homelands. It was also the major contributor to foreign exchange.

Apart from the natural advantages of site and climate, what were the features of the Gezira project which made it an economic success?

First of all, concentration of resources on one really large, promising area turned out in the end to be wise. There were times in the depression when this view was criticized and when it seemed that too big a risk had been taken at the expense of smaller advances in the rest of the country.

But at the end of 1950, with this great dynamic area pouring current into the heart of the Sudan's economy, it became obvious how much less valuable would have been a dissipation of all resources into a number of local schemes. The point is important, for provincial prestige and financial autonomy sometimes militate against the development of a project or of a region more able than any other, given the priority, to raise the general standard of living.

Concentration, in the project itself, on a definite economic objective was another major factor in success. The partnership was formed to make money. The claims on the profit by each partner were related to yield, giving a joint incentive to production. The inclusion of private enterprise capital in the risk encouraged a business outlook, which might have been lacking in a government department where actual loss or gain seemed less significant and where other qualities than business acumen are often desirable. Private enterprise, entrusted also with management, provided an element of drive and efficiency and started off staff and tenants with high standards of effort. Consideration for social welfare may have been postponed for too long, a matter referred to again below, but it cannot be denied that the priority given to economic efficiency was wise. Sometimes the welfare cart is apt to be considered before the economic horse.

The experimental approach by pilot schemes was valuable. The long experience at Zeidab, and later at Tayiba and Barakat, helped to evaluate not merely the most suitable crops and their treatment but all the details of a workable arrangement with the people, and these early schemes, and the later pumping stations, were educative influences to field staff, tenants and government officials in human relations, and helped towards the acceptance of the great changes which the main project brought. Another virtue of gradual development lay in accustoming the user in the market to have confidence in a new competing product.

Encircled by these attitudes, the core of Gezira success lay in the form of planned agriculture and the policy of control and help associated with it. The overall administration, a kind of imposed co-operative, eliminated the weakness of an individual striving alone. It brought to him the advantage of organized supplies and services, pure seed, fertilizer, sacks and other needs, and machinery for ploughing and spraying. It gave him the immense advantage of grading, processing and marketing at cost. He was not at the mercy of middlemen. It also gave him close contact with an efficient research station.

This was the superstructure. More important was the planned family holding, the decentralization on to an individual tenant-manager in each unit with a personal stake in success. It is around him that the most interesting features of the project revolve. He had to follow a prescribed rotation. He had to obey the reasonable orders of his agricultural adviser. He was personally responsible for production. He was not allowed to assign, mortgage or subdivide his unit. These controls provided a stable foundation of productive land usage, more fundamental to success than the co-operative superstructure. But they were designed not to suppress but to support the individual. The control was one side of the equation, and served as a collective protection against anti-social action or inaction. On the other side was the help given to each tenant to reap the maximum benefit from his own production.

These principles undoubtedly gave the Scheme great strength. They differentiated the Gezira from a pure collective in which all profits are pooled. The risk of falling to the lowest common multiple of effort, of not working if the neighbour has not turned out for work, was experienced and discarded in the Gezira when the baling out of water from each field-channel (for mosquito control) was organized as a collective duty of the tenants in each number. It was continually shirked until it was changed to an individual task.

The way in which help was given was as important to success as the controls. There is sometimes a danger of believing that all that is needed to raise the standard of living in areas which are primitive economically is money—as if a great release of latent private enterprise will then bring about the desired end. In practice, conservative inertia is usually far more prevalent than initiative, and one of the reasons for success in the Gezira was that this phenomenon was recognized as basic and methods of help were specifically designed to face it. Loans at a reasonable rate of interest were not merely made available, but related to each specific task. The financing of work in this manner, so that a man's horizon of effort need not be extended far in time or scope, made it easy for the general level of tenants to adopt the pattern of a new routine.

The high ratio of supervisory field staff, which the Companies employed and paid for, completed the pressure against inertia. Every 250 tenants had a local adviser to whom they had immediate access and whose job was to spur them on. Continuity of staff in the same place was less of a problem in the Companies than with government officials liable to transfer all over the country, and the contact between tenants and field staff, accustomed to each other, was a vital factor in success.

In difficult times, or with unsympathetic people, the system might be reduced to an autocratic bureaucracy, but in general it provided two essentials for the starting needs of a large number of people: an ordered and easy method of advance and someone nearby, of integrity and with a life interest in the job, who could be turned to as a father-figure in that advance.

Lastly there was the advantage which a properly organized system of agriculture, applied to smallholders, had over the alternative of plantation management by direct labour. This had a dual aspect. Socially and politically it encouraged the growth of a community with thousands of individual personal stakes in the undertaking. The economic aspect was as important. It provided much greater resilience in adversity. Syndicate experience in the early days of Zeidab revealed that the chances of profitable development under direct labour were much more marginal. If every hour of a tenant's time had had to be charged up, the Scheme could certainly never have survived the depression years. Yet even at that period, a tenant with his irrigated food crop was relatively better off than others. There might be empty pockets but there were not empty bellies, nor unemployment nor bankruptcy. In the uncertainties of world trade this factor of resilience was invaluable to an emergent country.

What were the weaknesses? In most cases they were the obverse side of the very factors which made for success.

If economic success was due to creating an organized system of control and help for a peasant society, the greatest technical problem was that of security for recovery of the costs involved. The common method —the pledging of land—was deliberately ruled out. The Gezira system was designed to frustrate the historic evils of this method and to stop the transfer of land or upset of the peasants' usage of it, on account of debt. Yet apart from land a peasant had only his domestic animals and a hut in the village; worthless as security and essential to his continued livelihood. There was therefore only one real security: the cash crop against which the very loans and costs to be recovered were being incurred. One of the big weaknesses of the Scheme was that there was never real agreement as to how the cash crop could best be used to cover the risk.

One method—for the lender to cover it himself by charging a higher rate of interest, or getting a larger share of the profits—was used in the early days of the Syndicate. This was found to be unsatisfactory if it greatly exceeded or fell short of the risk involved. Later it was thought better to put the risk on to the borrowers as a whole by charging individual debts against the tenants' collective share.

The advantage of this method was that it covered the exact amount involved, but it had two grave disadvantages. When debts occurred on a large scale and tenants who had not incurred them were expected to pay them off, the equity of the principle was hard to establish. The second drawback was that in a bad year the security of that year's crop alone was useless. There had to be a reserve fund. If this was an individual fund, as some favoured, there was a risk of constant pressure to draw it out for private affairs, and there would be poor tenants and new tenants whose reserve might not be enough. A communal fund avoided these drawbacks, and also covered the mischance of an overvaluation of the tenants' share as a whole, but in spite of Lord Lugard's* letter there were many who doubted the equity of a communal reserve fund.

The upshot of these arguments and counter-arguments was a general atmosphere of suspicion which confused the merits of the second objective of the reserve fund: the equalization of profits. In the end it became impossible to persuade the tenants to agree voluntarily to set aside to a communal fund sums from good years for supplementing bad years.

Security for loans and costs is one of the most difficult but essential problems in financing the evolution of a peasantry, and Gezira experience suggests that it would have been better to make a special charge against all tenants for the sole purpose of setting up a security fund until that object had been achieved, and to keep the question of a profits equalization fund entirely separate.

In fact, the second great technical weakness in the Gezira story was the failure to create a really adequate profits equalization fund for the tenants and to persuade them of its necessity. Just as the obverse to providing a system of loans should have been a security fund, so the obverse to concentrating development in one major area should have been protection in that area against excessive fluctuation and inflation. The tables at the end of the last chapter have shown the great variations which differing yields and prices made over the twenty-five years to the annual profits. As far as the tenants were concerned, the uncertainty of income had a disturbing effect on households only recently introduced to wealth, when the luxuries of one year became the necessities of the next, only to be cut off in the following year. Instead of the steadiness which a regular income might have induced in the family budget, a sudden flush of money caused everyone to compete for the first luxury—hiring someone else to work. As a result labour rates soared when large sums were paid out, and real profits diminished. A subsidiary effect was

* See page 167.

281

a buying urge on most merchant houses in the country, a flood of import goods and a sudden claim on the Sudan's foreign balances for payment. With the country's resources largely concentrated in the Gezira, the resulting inflation was relayed throughout the northern Sudan. The same process operated in reverse and then deflated the whole economy. A much more level spread of cotton profits would have been of universal benefit.

But there was another and, in the long run, more important national weakness in the absence of strong tenants' reserve funds. It had always been the custom to pay the tenants, at the beginning of the crop year in July, the *pro forma* profit of the past crop based on a valuation. This was easy as long as trade was normal and enough bales had been sold. It was much more dangerous and difficult in bad times. Overvaluation in the depression years contributed to the debt. The customary profit payment had then to be delayed and even suspended, leaving considerable doubt whether the tenants could and would carry on. A profits equalization fund would have obviated all this danger. But there was another point in it. In the absence of sums ample enough to make a profits payment the marketing of Gezira cotton in times of difficulty always fell under additional pressure. Buyers knew that the sellers would need money badly at the start of the new season to finance the tenants. If they held off their bids there was always a hope that price reserves would have to be dropped. A strong equalization fund able to finance tenants' profits payments would weaken the buyers' hope and strengthen the country's marketing position.

Bulk contracts and a stable price for their primary products are often felt to be a great need of emergent countries, in order to get continuity of steady development. Gezira marketing experience revealed some of the difficulties of bulk contract sales and this is a convenient place to appraise it for, as will be seen, it had some relevance to the question of reserve funds.

The pre-war arguments between Government and Syndicate had revealed that the country had three main marketing needs, as high a price, as quick a sale and as wide a market as possible, and that it was not easy to satisfy them all at once. The war-time bulk contract seemed miraculously to answer the maiden country's prayer: no alternative price offer was better, payment was quick and the whole crop was taken.

Did it prove a permanently good solution? To answer this some anticipation must be made of the Epilogue section of this book, which deals

with events after 1950, although for the reader this must mean an interlude of description in the appraisal theme of this chapter.

The first difficulty arose over price. As soon as Alexandria market was
reopened after the war an alternative price was quoted for comparison.
This did not seem to matter when the first bulk contract negotiated after
the war (1947 crop) was related to this price and it seemed stable. But
in the following year, when prices in Alexandria market rose steeply
just after a new bulk contract price had been fixed, comparison became
so odious that the Sudan had to request a renegotiation, which it was
lucky to get. It had to give a *quid pro quo* and promise another bulk contract. The price basis was changed from a fixed price to an average over
five months of Alexandria market prices. The difficulty about stability
seemed to be surmounted by this device, but Alexandria market became
a prey to speculators, and prices there at times became fictitiously high.
To try and keep the contract equitable the averaging period was cut in
1951 to three months and in 1952 to days of real sales only. Owing to
Egyptian Government intervention it finally became impossible to use
Alexandria market as a fair yardstick at all.

Meantime, for the 1951 crop a proposal to break away from the averaging period arrangements and hark back to a fixed price for half of the
crop was put forward by the tenants' representatives themselves. The
current price on the eve of harvest that year was very high. Cotton
growers on the White Nile estates had taken a chance and sold their
crop forward. Would Gezira do better or worse by waiting for the
average of the coming three months? Why not ask the Raw Cotton
Commission to close on the current price for half of the crop and leave
half to run on the average? The R.C.C. agreed. But the Financial
Secretary, Sir Louis Chick, disagreed on the principle that having
instituted an average to avoid the danger of a fixed price it was irrespon-
sible to discard it. The Gezira Board (half Sudanese, half British directors) agreed with the tenants, and a half-fixed, half-average price basis
was contracted. In the outcome Chick turned out the wiser. The Sudan
would have done better to stick to the average. But this was not his
object. He was concerned to follow a consistent policy and the story
reveals just how difficult it was to do this.

This difficulty became illustrated in 1951 not merely over price but
over quantity. The R.C.C. had been ready enough for some years to
take 60 per cent of the crop and in a sellers' market to take up further
unsold cotton as well. But this attitude was related to an average crop.
The 1951 crop, instead of the expected 220,000 bales, had turned out

367,000, and most of them, for lack of competitive buying, were delivered to the R.C.C. under the contract. It was two years' supply all at once and, as the Korean war drew to a stalemate, demand slackened. So for the 1952 crop quota the R.C.C. was not particularly keen. By contrast the Gezira Board became keener than ever to make a hedge on the future.

It had an additional reason for doing so owing to the situation in India, its second-biggest market. Here sales had been declining. Investigation revealed that the whole textile trade there was subject to government-controlled prices, and that the price which the Indian manufacturer using Sudan cotton was allowed for his finished product was considerably less than that of the manufacturer using Egyptian cotton. Naturally Indian buyers of Sudan cotton could not in these circumstances offer bids competitive with R.C.C. prices, which were linked to those of Egyptian cotton. There were vested interests involved in this state of affairs and, just when the Indian Government was persuaded to overrule these and change its price-fixing policy, large supplies of American cotton were suddenly made available to India on a government to government basis, which once again reduced Indian interest in Sudan cotton.

The difficulties over prices and quantities led to two conflicting states of mind. On the one hand was the desire for security. This desire led the Gezira Board in 1952 to try to negotiate with the R.C.C. for a longer-term contract for a definite quantity of bales each year. In this way the bulge of the 1951 crop might be spread. The R.C.C., with the same desire for security, was prepared to negotiate. But on the other hand public opinion in the Sudan, of which the tenants' representatives were usually a fair mouthpiece, was growing increasingly doubtful whether the bulk contract with the R.C.C. was not favouring one client and contracting the market just when it was necessary to widen it. The demand to sell the whole crop by auction began to increase once again. At the same time, in the United Kingdom, public opinion was increasingly doubtful whether bulk buying had not unduly favoured primary producers. As far as the Gezira story was concerned, this mental conflict was resolved by the return of the Conservative party to power in the United Kingdom, the closure of the Raw Cotton Commission, and an end to bulk purchase.

This particular difficulty in the bulk contract system was more intractable even than the problems of price and quantity, for it was the problem of carrying public confidence for any length of time. The bulk contract system always seemed more secretive, more dependent on the judgement and integrity of a few individuals, whether in the United Kingdom or in the Sudan. By comparison an open auction system and an open Liverpool market were always inclined to appear to the public in the respective Countries as a more genuine reflection of trade possibilities—whenever trade looked good. The truth seems to be, for both producer and consumer, that as long as they are worrying about security more than anything else they readily incline to a bulk contract, but as soon as this anxiety eases they will look over their shoulders for alternative prices and alternative markets and hanker for a freer system. After 1952 the Gezira Board swung over, with great popular acclaim, to an open auction system. But just as easily in 1957, when sales by auction faltered, it might have been attracted to a bulk contract behind the iron curtain. The moral seems to be not that bulk contracts are bad but that they are not at all an easy permanent remedy for instability. For this objective adequate internal equalization funds are an indispensable priority. Certainly without them no Gezira managing director or Sudan finance minister can sleep peacefully at night for long.

Mention of public confidence introduces the biggest weakness in the Gezira story: inattention to public relations. At first the needs of the Scheme demanded careful supervision from the officials and obedience from the tenants. This, however, did not encourage initiative or lead to maturity. The routine of managing other people, who were ignorant of the techniques involved in a process, became hallowed with an air of permanence and our attitude to public relations tended to be a mixture of aloofness, touchiness and conviction of rectitude. It was not easy to disengage from paternalism and replace it by a new tie of genuine participation. There were always many on the managing side who had got used to giving orders and feared that change might lead to rebellious attitudes, and many on the managed side, equally used to routine, who interpreted change as weakness. The great problem was to get these attitudes altered so that methods were accepted, not because they were the orders of some personality or institution but because they were the condition of economic and social progress, of which people had been genuinely persuaded, and in deciding which they had participated.

This transitional situation in public relations was not something peculiar to ourselves. It was in all the world around us. It could be seen as a central problem of the demise of colonialism and facing the government of a newly emergent territory. It seemed a dominant factor in industrial relations in our own country and a major dilemma of communist countries if tyranny was ever to be dethroned. In all these

285

spheres we could see reflected our own pattern of experience, an ebb and flow; an ebb towards reassertion of authority, a flow towards greater participation by the people concerned.

We tried to solve the problem by social development. I have mentioned the affinity we felt for the principles of that much greater regional development of our time—the Tennessee Valley Authority. Expressed in the 1949 report of the T.V.A. they set an objective to which we turned our own sights.

In its approach to the full development of resources, two governing principles have been followed by T.V.A. The first was that the way to lasting success was through education, through technical assistance . . . available to those who worked the farmlands in a form easily understood. It was an approach diametrically opposed to the 'Thou Shalts' and 'Thou Shall Nots' of regulation. The second was the recognition that to the greatest extent possible the job was to be done by the people of the valley, individually as farmers . . . collectively through their county and municipal governments, farmer cooperatives and their business associations.

This to us was the right destination for our own hopes, but what a distance away it was! All we had done so far was to build up an economy by making 'technical assistance available to those who worked the farmlands in a form easily understood'. But all the rest was the complete antithesis of paternalism. We had at last, belatedly, a programme for encouraging new initiative in farming, for co-operatives, for more representative county and municipal government, for participation through village and block councils and a tenants' representative body. But had we the relationship with the tenants and with the public in the Sudan, particularly the influential newly educated younger people, which would make a new tie of confidence between us, or had we hung on to paternalism too long? That was the question.

Apart from its various advantages and weaknesses, the Gezira story had some other special features of interest to the development problems of our time. One of the most relevant features was the deliberate mixture of economic and social planning which went into its origin. Those who started the Scheme refused to take the view that a higher standard of living was all that mattered, irrespective of how it was obtained or how the benefits of it were spread. This led them to adopt deliberate policies, both outwardly in their attitude to external capital and inwardly in their attitude to what was equitable for the people among themselves. One of the most interesting results of this standpoint was that, in complete contrast to the assumption today that vast sums of money are needed in a great hurry everywhere to deal with the problem of underdevelopment, they were much more concerned to establish equitable and practical principles of development than to hasten its pace. In a capital-starved world their viewpoint is well worth consideration.

Externally, in their attitude to foreign investors the originators of the Gezira Scheme rejected the idea that the motive of private profit was, alone, the best determinant of development. To them of greater importance was the harmonious evolution of the people in their own society. They did not object to private capital as such: they fully realized the need for it and the difficulty of getting ahead without it. But they were determined that it was not to dominate or deflect the policy which they thought right as trustees of the people. It was this attitude which led them to resist the use of immigration and big business for raising the standard of living, judging that their objectives would be liable to clash with the ultimate self-expansion of the peoples in the country.

Today, when so much of the hostility to western civilization is centred around the clash of interests between immigrant minorities and immigrant enterprises associated with them, and the rising aspirations of underdeveloped peoples, this determination to safeguard their wards has an astonishingly modern relevance. For it was not a negative attitude to development. They did not view the alternatives, as many do today, as a choice between immigration, foreign capital and a higher standard of living on one side and stagnant preservation of an existing society on the other. They did not seek to build a future for people educated only to the needs of their existing lives. On the contrary they sought and found a bridge of common interest between the future free expansion of the people and the foreign capital indispensable to that expansion. In doing so they went to the heart of today's most difficult development problem. This attitude and the financial structure which resulted from it is a special feature of the Gezira story which claims attention.

What did this attitude lead them to do about the financial structure? In the first place it led them to demand, both for the purpose of exercising enough influence on policy and to get more money for the country, a large share for the state in the provision of capital and in the profit. The Sudan was poor, the Government desperately needed more revenue and the Gezira was the biggest development project in the country.

In passing, an important technical result of this attitude should be noticed. Before the Gezira could ever pay its way there had to be a railway to the coast. Railways in undeveloped countries have sometimes been built by strategic funds, sometimes by private enterprise in return for land concessions. In this case the former method was not available from Britain, while the latter implied the negation of the Government's basic attitude to development. The necessary money was obtained by appropriation from Egypt by a loan, undated and without interest, eventually paid back forty years later. It was a typical example of the unremunerative level of development, without which the remunerative level could not be embarked upon, but which a poor country could not finance on banker's terms. Looked at from the viewpoint of international aid today (and assuming that the Sudan Government would not be expected to alter its strongest convictions and give land concessions to private enterprise in order to finance the railway), it is interesting to see that the Gezira used three levels of finance in order to get going: an investment fund level (the Egyptian Treasury) to finance the railway, an investment bank level to finance loans to the Government for its stake in the undertaking, and an equity capital level from private enterprise to finance the superstructure. In any reappraisal of the function and purpose of capital (and communism surely makes this essential) this triple combination in one undertaking has a technical interest, for it shows what flexibility of outlook can contribute to development, if it is allowed to do so.

But the two most arresting elements in the Gezira financial structure were the triple partnership and the time limit to the foreign share in the ownership. Once again these features emanated from the attitude which the originators of the Scheme took as to what was equitable and practicable. It was not a question of aid. There was nothing commercially unsound about it. It was a business proposition, but suited to the wider principles of development already determined. In the partnership the state, the people of the region and the private shareholder had an identity of interest. They sank or swam together. At the end of the concession the private shareholders, who had provided the professional management, the extra capital and the commercial contact and know-how which the country had initially lacked, were repaid their capital with a bonus. When the few foreign loans outstanding are redeemed the whole successful project will belong without lien to the Sudan.

It would be difficult to devise a structure more suited to meet the aspirations of people in underdeveloped territories. But it offered equally profitable scope and pride to the private enterprise partners in it. The structure was made possible because they did not take the line that permanent ownership of a source of raw material was an indispensable purpose of investment. It was enough for them that they were stimulating expansion in the production of a commodity in world use and badly in demand in Britain. There was no question of exclusive claim to it, and if their enterprise could at the same time help forward the participation and progress of the Government and people of the Sudan and increase their purchasing power, so much the better. Nevertheless, it is right to point out that the Syndicate's capital was in the end forthcoming because the directors believed that the Sudan Government could be trusted to play fair. It would be idle to pretend that the same confidence could be as easily extended yet to all untried emergent governments. To meet this very real difficulty the world has still to devise suitable forms of mutual insurance and some kind of agreed investment statute.

In the great problem of finding a bridge, psychologically acceptable to both sides, between developed and underdeveloped countries these attitudes and the structure they produced suggest a pattern worth consideration, not for every undertaking but for key undertakings. They suggest also that it is attitude and opportunity, not generations or centuries—as is so often said as a result of European experience—that enable a people to develop.

Internally, in their attitude to what was equitable for the people among themselves, the planners of the Gezira Scheme produced equally interesting results. To some people mention of the word planning conjures up visions of petty interference with the divine spark of initiative and encouragement of inefficiency, extravagance and failure. In the Gezira they did not view it that way. With bitter experience of a rack-rented peasantry, an uncontrolled rise in land values and a most unequal distribution of wealth which followed the development of irrigation in Egypt, they planned to prevent these undesirable social effects in the Sudan. They could see how weak an individual was in a primitive society and how tempted to sell his source of livelihood for immediate cash without realizing its worth. So their first land laws were designed to stop the land passing into the hands of the richest and producing a very poor rural proletariat.

A peasant society may be preserved, and with it a sense of economic equality, but it may be the equality of extreme poverty with small fragmented holdings, low yields and no capital. Gezira planning was designed equally to prevent this extreme. The standard-size tenancy, the planned rotation, the restrictions on transfer, and all the other items of control and help, were designed to bring, and did bring, the advantages of large-scale management to a peasant society. But to attain this aim there had to be government control of land use. The long-term rental was an ingenious solution where suspicion and resentment might have been caused by nationalization, but more important was the fact that the landlord thereafter had no means of increasing rents against the cultivator.

Apart from his rental at pre-irrigation rates, the landlord was given priority rights to tenancies for himself and his children and nomination rights for his relatives and friends. He therefore shared fully in the new benefits, but he was not allowed to corner them. The rule that he got in his own name only what 'in the opinion of the Government' he could personally manage, and the rule that each nominee thereafter was an independent tenant and unconnected with him, prevented this.

In a country starting late in terms of material civilization there was great value politically, socially, and economically in this dual planning for efficiency and equity. The Sudan has, as a result, an economic heart where the wealth from the irrigated land is spread among 25,000 different families, few of whom have more than one unit holding but where, because of the planning, the individual income per unit has a relatively high level. One is tempted to speculate whether instability in today's world could not be significantly reduced if as much attention as the Gezira planners gave was paid to the outcome of development in economic equity at the same time as political self-determination.

An appropriate question is whether these measures of control, designed to make development equitable and practicable, were in the end acceptable to the people. The only yardstick for judgement is the attitude of the people themselves. In 1950 an extension of 100,000 feddans in the north-west of the Gezira Scheme (raising the gross area to nearly a million feddans) was made possible by water economies. To a Sudanese committee of the Legislative Assembly was entrusted the opportunity of recommending some totally new principles of development. It was an important moment for such a decision owing to the approaching end, within fifteen years, of the Government's leasing of the existing land in the Gezira Scheme. Should the land in the new extension be nationalized? Should the water simply be sold to landowners to use as they liked? The committee consulted much opinion both inside and outside the Scheme, and ended by recommending that the existing principles should be applied to the new extension: the mixture as before.[1]

A second answer came from the continual demand of those who lived east and west of the Scheme for it to be extended to their lands as soon as more water could be stored in the Nile. In 1957 began the first stage of the Manāgil extension intended, when a new dam has been built at

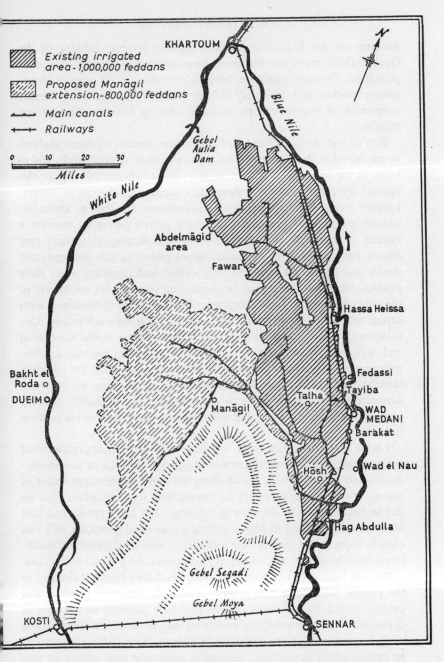

5. *The Gezira irrigated area 1953, with the proposed Manāgil extension*

Roseires on the Blue Nile, to add another 800,000 feddans to the Gezira. Once again the Sudanese have decided to stick to the same principles, the only alteration being a reversion to the original three-course rotation with its thirty-feddan standard unit, so that a higher proportion of tenants can be included and the benefits spread more widely.

Fear of state initiative and dislike of regimentation are more likely to be engrained in the western world than in underdeveloped lands, and to many in the west the principles of the Gezira Scheme will appear distasteful for one very good reason: they suggest an absence of liberty. Largely owing to the practices of communism, the state to them has become a symbol of tyranny. Conversely private enterprise conveys a symbol of liberty. There is a danger that this ideological concept may distort our approach to economic development in the uncommitted world and lessen the chances of a closer understanding with their peoples, for private enterprise to them often suggests not the liberty of the individual against political tyranny but the liberty of foreigners with capital and know-how to develop assets to their own advantage. Development, in such places, is no longer simply a matter of whether capital and skill from outside can see a profit, although this has still its contribution to make, but a matter of how the local people, as yet with few skills and little capital, can learn to acquire in agriculture, industry and administration the techniques to develop their own economy. It is by our contribution to this end that the value of western civilization is being judged.

I hope that the Gezira story will help towards truer appreciation of our mutual needs. Across the screen of history it reveals us as administrators and business men, drawn from the more conservative sector of our society, operating a project permeated with state initiative. That we did so had nothing to do with an ideology. We had experienced that often the state needed to play a part as partner and protector. We had equally experienced that private enterprise, with its commercial incentives, could be an ally, not an enemy, to national and individual freedom.

We had built up an economic project which now largely belonged to the people. We had in the process generated successful routines and capital. Could we now graft on to this base political and economic democracy? To that problem we felt we had an immense contribution to make with our western traditions of liberty. Many today are sceptical or cynical about democracy, judging it something that cannot be dissociated from its environment in western civilization. We saw it, rather, as the final contribution we could make, infinitely important and the real alternative to communism.

But, as the epilogue which follows this chapter will show, we had overestimated. It was not the importance of the theme which we had exaggerated. That remained, all the time growing greater. It was the importance of ourselves. In 1950 we were still thinking of ourselves as the leaders: still living in the past. Within five years any contribution we could make would have to be in a totally different context. The Sudan had become an independent country.

What we had underestimated was the importance in any true acceptance of leadership of a sense of experiences mutually shared. This was again a limitation from the aftermath of paternalism. Psychologically the situation was like that of the child of poor parents staying with rich relations. At first they are regarded as kind and it is good to enjoy the luxury of their house but it gives an inferiority complex and there comes a time when the strongest urge in the child's mind is to get away and make its own mark in the world. At this time there is almost a sense of resentment against the rich relations, a feeling in the child's mind that it does not belong to their world and a desire to seek the companionship of those in like circumstances. So it was with the Sudanese and our assumed leadership. There had to be a parting and then, if we were wise and did not lose all touch with each other, a new meeting-place, a club we and others could both join with a feeling of being equals. But we have not yet founded the club. It is the biggest task of statesmanship ahead of us.*

* It might be thought that the Commonwealth was the club, but this does not cover countries like the Sudan which, feeling that it had affinities elsewhere, did not wish to join the Commonwealth. All regional alliances, natural and useful as these are, suffer from the suspicion of separatism which they create outside them. This defect applies equally to the Commonwealth, the Arab League, the Afro-Asian axis, the Atlantic Community, the European Common Market, or Communism. It would appear that one of the most important considerations for the world is whether much more effort should not be made to use the United Nations machinery both for contact and for investment for development. A serious study of the practical difficulties which have been found to prevent this medium being effective seems to be overdue.

Epilogue

Part 4
FULL FLOOD
After 1950

Chapter 22

DEMOCRACY PLANNED AND UNPLANNED

For me, 1950 would have been the appropriate date to close this story. When the Gezira Board was created all the staff previously with the Companies were invited to stay on with the Board, and almost everyone did so, including myself as its first Chairman and Managing Director. But I left the Gezira early in 1952, after nearly thirty years with the Scheme, and the story of its progress after 1950 should be told by other people. But because some time may elapse before another recorder appears, and because the next five years were full of exciting events, leading to the independence of the Sudan, I have thought it right to include this epilogue.

I have set it out in four chapters although once again, in reality, the themes discussed intermingled. This chapter shows how the picture of harmonious co-operation in democratic development, with which we initiated the Gezira Board, did not develop exactly as we had visualized it. The economic history was as exciting as the political and the next chapter describes the effect on the tenants' lives of sudden violent fluctuations in income. The third chapter shows what a large part politics came in the end to play in the story and the last chapter contains deductions from Gezira experience relevant to the relationship between emergent countries and the western world.

Our task as the management under the new Gezira Board was to inspire confidence that the Scheme would not suffer through the break-up of the old partnership and at the same time to put into practice the new ideals of community development. Economy and efficiency had still to be primary objectives, but we had to show that we were not a super-authority interfering with the work of administrative and departmental officials and local government authorities. Our job was the initiative rather than the execution. Although some activities would fall to our responsibility alone, most of them would be in alliance with some technical department or local council. We had to be careful, too, that we were

297

not regarded as a milch cow. Our social development budget was for experiments in productive inventions and processes. We would sink the first bore well, or pay for the trial village-spraying experiment for malaria control. After that the execution and cost should be on others.

One difficulty facing us was that many tenants thought that the idea of social development was invented by the Government to cheat them out of the 50 per cent share which they thought they should have from the cotton profits when the Companies departed. They believed that in charging social development on the profits the Government was simply passing against the Scheme national expenses which it ought to bear itself. We had to prove to tenants that to invest in social development was really to invest in their own future and that if the Scheme did not provide the funds for it no one else was going to do so. There would be, of course, a degree of overlapping, and government departments and local government authorities would rightly be sharing some of the expenditure. The proposed Local Committee, where the allocation of social development funds was to be discussed regularly between representatives of the tenants, local authorities, government departments, the general public and the Board, was intended to work out this process in a common annual plan.

The first social development budget, which we put to the first Local Committee meeting, listed the aims, for convenience, under headings such as farming production, social needs, health, and self-management, but added together they meant democratic regional development.

Under farming production, two interesting projects were already in being. One was the first agricultural training school for tenants' sons. Here sixty boys went through an annual course showing how to produce the maximum benefit in variety of crops, and with attention to animals, from a standard tenancy. Selection was made with parents present, for the object was to get boys who were going back to the land, not to educate white-collar instructors. This school's history was an example of how much social development was intended to be a matter of co-opera-tion. Originally planned by the Companies, the pupils recommended by the tenants, the supervision undertaken by the Department of Agriculture, the headmaster and staff supplied by the Institute of Education, it was already a marked success and we were advocating a duplicate school as a next step.

A second item of interest in the farming programme was the single village experiment. Here one field officer was in charge of the complete development of one village. His instructions were to lift his sights to the horizon of 1975. He was expected to be farming with the attitudes of farmers in Europe and America, with pedigree animals controlled and related to the land's capacity, with maximum production of all crops, and every sideline like dairying, vegetables, fruit and poultry. The Tana dam was assumed to have been built and water available for any rotation. Everything possible was to be done by machinery and drudgery reduced to a minimum. As in previous Gezira history the concept was a concentration of resources and a free hand in ideas on a small pilot area, as a prelude to social and economic possibilities which faced the whole Scheme.

Under social needs, we already had women welfare workers teaching sewing and cooking, and a health visitor teaching child welfare. An anthropologist and dietician, Mrs. G. M. Culwick, had been checking over weights and heights and food health values in the daily diet of the people. Her reports had been so illuminating that we wanted her to go on to that general social investigation of conditions in the villages for which we, as managers, had long felt the need. For recreation, football had been organized with village and block teams and become universally popular, thanks to the joint interest taken by field staff, Sudanese clerical staff, schoolmasters and adult education men.

Under health we were engaged in two anti-malarial experiments, each extending over four blocks, and we were hoping that the posting of a special doctor, primarily for bilharzia research, by his very presence on the Local Committee, would add new stimulus to the local dispensaries. A proposal was also afoot to finance, jointly with the town council, a midwives' training school and clinic in Medani town.

Under self-management there were all kinds of allied activities, for ultimately it was to the build-up of the region to manage its own affairs that all roads led. In practice we had the new local government authorities, the block councils, the village councils, and the Tenants' Representative Body, all places where people could get a real voice in their own affairs. And so that this voice might become increasingly informed and intelligent we had adult education teams giving village courses on how things were run in the country and helping village councils to understand and stick to procedure. Mass literacy campaigns had been well attended. Our Gezira newspaper, in which we hoped everyone would feel a share, had been started, and it was intended to be a big influence in widening people's horizons. Linked in on the agricultural side was the whole policy of devolution, with village samads being trained by our field staff to manage the village agriculture for the people under the

299

village council. We felt that it was all training so that the best could go on to take a full share in national counsels.

We had made a start, anticipating the setting up of the Gezira Board. But there was plenty more to do. We had few co-operatives. We had no travelling libraries. We had yet to plant fuel forests and recruit a horticultural officer. We had not begun breeding and selection of animals although we had a nucleus at the research institute. We had not invented a cheap house nor started up technical training for village boys. But there was enough to show what we were after: improvement in land and mind and body, and a chance for young men with ambition to build up their country practically.

What happened?

Our attitude, as doubtless the reader will mentally have criticized, was still very paternal. In our social development plans we still visualized ourselves as the leaders, foreseeing what was best for the people. But the policy was no longer the 'thou shalt' of earlier paternal days. We had deliberately encouraged the expression of the people's own views through a variety of agencies and we soon found that their views on what they wanted by no means coincided with what we thought they ought to want. It was partly a reaction against paternalism, a desire to have their own way, and partly that their priorities were not ours. Some of it has already been foreshadowed in Chapter 20 describing relations with the Tenants' Representative Body, and these now became very much more difficult.

Broadly speaking, the people were uninterested in the more educative elements in our proposals and in the local build-up on which we set great store, but supporters of items which affected their own finances. For reasons which will be explained in the following chapter the tenants (and they dominated the Local Committee) were increasingly preoccupied with trying to alter the financial structure of the partnership and to pass on the cost of some of their traditional duties to others. Adult education was an example of these attitudes. After a few years of enthusiasm the Local Committee began to show reluctance to vote funds for the men's teams. The business of the latter was to explain duties not to advocate altering them, so they could lead to little but talk. By contrast the Committee was eager to support women's adult education. The cooking and sewing classes had practical application at once. Wives who could repair their own dresses and serve up a better meal at less cost suited the hour exactly.

Something of the same fate affected the Gezira newspaper. Never a house magazine, and intended to be a farmer's fortnightly encouraging argument and intelligent interest among the tenants, it had to steer between expression of the Board's or national views and those of the tenants. But a middle course in the effervescence of an emergent territory was never good for newspaper sales and the circulation began to decline. Rather similarly, after early enthusiasm, the Local Committee began to consider the encouragement of recreation too expensive a frill, and at the same time resolved that expenditure on health ought to be solely the duty of the Ministry of Health.

On the other hand the agricultural aspects of social development, the training farm, the single village experiment and the horticultural service, were popular and equally strong support was extended to projects dealing with village deficiencies, such as forests to provide fuel and a building research unit to discover how to make mud houses waterproof.

In this manner the social development budgets were modified from the sort of community initiative which we as planners had envisaged to an expression of what the people themselves desired, and the biggest example of this was in education. They were puzzled and lukewarm over items which we sponsored as educative and healthful to the region in a general way. But when it came to formal education, the means to lift their sons to a hoped-for career in a higher social and financial scale, they were on a subject which really interested them. They threw out health as a purely central government matter, but to accept such a principle for the building of intermediate schools threatened altogether too slow a pace, and they found in the social development budget a welcome opportunity for supplementing the central government in the financing of school buildings, while the tenants undertook to find and pay the teachers.

One of the most popular items was the sinking of tube wells in villages, but its very success brought us face to face with a difficulty which jeopardized one of our major principles in social development: that the Board was only the experimenter, leaving the people themselves, or their appropriate local authority, the duty of financing the continuation of any new service. A piped clean water supply on site, in place of a petrol can filled with the indifferent and sometimes stagnant water of the canal, often at a distance, was a very popular service. But the initial cost was high. The Board could help with engineers and materials but the appropriate financing agent was clearly the local government. Unfortunately there was a handicap. Local government revenues in the Gezira were practically confined to beer licences. Taxation of the tenants' crops and incomes was specifically precluded by the promises made to them, when the Gezira Scheme was started, as an additional inducement to entering it.* It had been envisaged that local government would be developing *pari passu* with the regional development initiated by the Board, and would be a main agent in the team. In fact, lack of revenue made it totally unable to play its part. This handicap was serious for it forced the Board to forgo the major principle of self-effort in social development and the people came to think of the latter as a fund for financing their particular fancies, and flocked to it as a kind of obligatory charity institution.[1]

While all these results might be judged disappointing from the planner's angle they were very far from disastrous. The problem of local government finance could in the end be put right by central government grants, and meantime the Gezira Local Committee and all the activities of the social development department were bringing into intimate association with the Scheme a great many intelligent Sudanese who had hitherto only viewed it as a foreign-operated affair. I can mention here only a few but they typify a wide range of new influences.

There was Sayed Mohammed Omar, from the Department of Education, the first organizer and pioneer of our adult education teams. He was sent by the Sudan Government to spend a year at Oxford, working under the direction of Miss Margery Perham, and he grasped, more than many of our British staff, the democratic ideals we were after at the grass roots—the village level. He had a delicate task, for at that level he and his teams confronted not only the highest common multiple of dead inertia and ignorance but all the grouses which individual tenants might voice against their individual block inspector in the light of their own fortunes. He had to preserve a balance between a suspicion among the field staff that his activities might undermine their authority and a feeling among the villagers that he was out of sympathy with their troubles, which would have been fatal to his object. He had also to convey his enthusiasm, and yet get this delicate relationship, to his team.

There was Suliman Bakheit from the Press. He had been on the staff of one of the best Sudanese newspapers in the capital and, as such, very much an outside critic of the Gezira. We persuaded him to be editor of our newspaper. He, too, entered with enthusiasm into the spirit of building up a rational judgement in the region. He too had to steer through a maelstrom of conflicting arguments.

There was Sayed Ahmed Yusif Algam, a tenant, and the chief voice

* See Chapter 7, page 87.

on the Local Committee. He was one of the new men thrown up by the Gezira Scheme. He had taken on additional tenancies when others had resigned and the land lay empty in the depression years and, with the better profits, was now reaping his reward. Although he lacked the social background of a traditional tribal authority the Government had made him chairman of a local government council in the central area. Equable in temperament and persuasive in personality he had consolidated a faction-ridden district of different tribes and then passed on to be a distinguished member and chief spokesman for the Gezira in the National Legislative Assembly.

There was Omar Mohammed Abdulla. For long we had regarded him merely as a good filing clerk. A strike among workshop personnel revealed by chance that he had many of the qualities of a good negotiator, with the patience to understand issues at stake and a reputation for integrity in judgement. After a period studying industrial methods in Britain, he became our first labour relations officer.

Of a different calibre from all these, both in education and in experience of the world at large, was Sayed Mekki Abbas, the Social Development Director on the Gezira Board. He had already had a career which had brought him into close contact with the Scheme. His exceptional ability had been developed by V. L. Griffiths,* a pioneer of modern rural education in the Sudan and a man of rare foresight in understanding the need for finding a new relationship to replace paternalism. Griffiths used him as one of his right-hand men when he founded the Institute of Rural Education at Bakht el Roda on the White Nile. From there Mekki Abbas had pioneered the first ideas of community development among tenants of the government pumping schemes. Experience of the difficulty of getting co-ordinated action from government departments had led him, like us, to believe that a single authority was essential, and firsthand knowledge of the people in the irrigated areas had inspired in him a sympathy with the ideals which we associated with social development. He quickly attracted the attention of the central government and was nominated a member when the Advisory Council for the northern Sudan was set up in 1944. He had completed his education at Exeter University in England and his fluency in both the Arabic and English languages and thought made him a natural choice in the Assembly as a

---

* V. L. Griffiths. Subsequently at the Department of Education, Oxford University, and engaged in a number of educational investigations in the colonies. See his book, *An Experiment in Education* (London, Longmans Green and Co., 1953), for a description of his work in the Sudan.

chairman or secretary of committees. He was a member of the Special Committee on the Gezira in 1946, but resigned shortly after from government service, on disagreement with government policy concerning the southern Sudan. After an interlude as proprietor of his own newspaper—an unsuccessful attempt to create a *Manchester Guardian* of the Sudan—he spent two years at Nuffield College, Oxford, working with Miss Margery Perham, writing up the tangled political history between Britain, Egypt and the Sudan since the condominium began.* He was about to accept the post of starting a new Institute of Education in Libya when the Governor-General invited him to return to the Sudan as a director of the Gezira Board, and we naturally asked him to take on the province of social development.†

Sayed Abd el Hafiz Abd el Mouneim, also appointed to the Gezira Board, represented another valuable new connection. He was a business man. Quiet in manner and very shrewd in judgement, he brought to the Board the experience of long family trading connections with Egypt and elsewhere in a whole variety of produce. In a field hitherto restricted by us to British commercial or government contacts, he linked the administration of the Scheme for the first time with the rising Sudanese mercantile community.

In all societies, democratic or otherwise, vitality depends on an *élite*. I use the word, not in a snobbish sense, but as indicating the importance of key men who, if they hold a common faith, enormously influence the attitudes of their colleagues. In Gezira society, emerging from a paternal background, they were doubly important. In such a case the mass of the country people were not normally interested in politics and principles. What really concerned them were their family affairs, the yield of their crops, the state of the grazing, the price of cotton and the cost of labour. In such a case there is always some danger of parties being formed and progress being associated, not with principles but with persons. That is why I have mentioned these men, for if someone asked 'What of the future?' the answer depends in large measure on how far these types from such different backgrounds, and others like them, preserve the cohesion of a common objective. It was good for the Gezira that by 1950 we had got these men operating with us. It was bad that we had been so slow in doing so.

---

* *The Sudan Question* (London, Faber and Faber, 1952).

† Sayed Mekki Abbas later became Managing Director of the Sudan Gezira Board. In 1958 he was designated as first Secretary-General to the United Nations Commission for Africa.

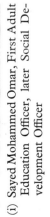

(i) Sayed Mohammed Omar, First Adult Education Officer, later Social Development Officer

(ii) Suliman Bakheit, first editor of the Gezira newspaper

PLATE XVII

(iii) Sayed Omar Mohammed Abdulla, first Labour Relations Officer, later Assistant Manager

(i) Sayed Mekki Abbas, Social Development Director, later Managing Director

(ii) Sayed Abd el Hafiz Abd el Mouneim, Director, later Chairman

(iii) Sayed Mohammed El Awam Nimr, Tenants' Adviser, later Director

PLATE XVIII

Something of the alternative danger—the pursuit of a person rather than a principle—now took place on the other limb of social development, that connected with the Tenants' Representative Body. The Gezira Board had a duty, under the Ordinance, of fostering tenants' consultative bodies. It tried to interpret this duty on a basis of identity of interests, although it was aware of potential conflict. In the Board's first report in 1951, the problem was expressed as follows:

> Such a situation contains, of course, an inherent risk of dispute about who is the final arbiter of policy. The Board, while making clear that this must ultimately lie with the Board as responsible manager of the Scheme, believes that the intention of the Ordinance was that a reasonable atmosphere of compromise, and a firm faith in a joint spirit of cooperation, should be the true solvent of the problems of management. The Board believes that the intention of this machinery was to avoid a drift towards centralisation, a decline in voluntary effort and a divorce of the mass of the people from responsibility . . . and the Board intends to use it to encourage more and more people to do more for themselves. . . .
>
> A critical illustration of the problem is the cotton sales policy. There can be no question that some body in the end has to make the decisions on this important matter and that that body is the Board. Nevertheless it is perfectly reasonable that the tenants, with their big stake in the result, should wish to have some say in these decisions.[2]

The reader may remember that, after an initial period of conflict with Government and management, the Tenants' Representative Body had mellowed. This process continued until 1952, and joint consultations about marketing policy, and agreement to postpone for a year part of their 1951 profits, were encouraging examples of co-operation on the identity of interests assumption. But after a while this very success in co-operating with management began to tell against the Tenants' Representative Body among its own constituents. It was a new organization in which forty representatives were supposed to speak for a large and scattered electorate of over 20,000 tenants and, much more difficult, to convey back to them the results and reasons in its consultations with the management. Efficient local contact—a vital need—was not well organized, and the representatives got out of touch with the rank and file.

The system was reorganized in 1952 and the name changed to Tenants' Association, which was changed again in 1953 to Tenants' Union. These changes symbolized the urge to get altogether away from the paternal origin, and in the process vital differences were made in the constitution. The Tenants' Representative Body originated in government and management concepts and was allied to the theme of developing democracy in village and block councils under the guidance of our field inspectors and the local government officers. Although the machinery of election was indirect each tenant was automatically a member of the electorate.

The new constitution abolished all this. Membership was made voluntary and voting direct and individual. This was a natural evolution of thought parallel to the procedure of national political parties in the country but in the case of the Gezira, where the Tenants' Union was the recognized negotiating body, it became increasingly difficult to know how far the views expressed by the Union's officials were really representative of the tenants. In practice the change ushered in a contest for power and put a considerable strain on the Board's principle of co-operation on a basis of identity of interest. This became particularly prominent when, after an election at the end of 1953, Sheikh El Amin Mohammed El Amin, another hitherto obscure person with, significantly, only a half-holding, became elected as President. He was a Communist.

As such he did not propose any major alteration in the form of society. He concentrated on making himself the spearhead of grievances and promises and on aiming to alter existing arrangements so that they came under his control. Many of the grievances had some justification, especially in the economic circumstances which will shortly be described, and often it was more his intemperate manner than the subject-matter which made him objectionable to the management. The issue of power, however, was another matter and some of his demands illustrate how inevitable was a drift into conflict.

Before this election it had become clear that the Council of the Tenants' Association, just like its predecessor the Tenants' Representative Body, was unable to hold the allegiance of its constituents. Sheikh El Amin and his followers repudiated accommodation between the Association and the management and threatened to organize a boycott just as cotton picking was about to start. The management retorted to this extremist element by instructing the field staff that any direct refusal by a tenant to obey orders should be immediately reported and the tenant considered for ejection.[3] A mediating committee was set up to plan elections for a new council, to see who did represent the tenants, and the result was a sweeping success for the tenant-critics of the Association and brought Sheikh El Amin into power.

His first proposals aimed at consolidating this power by changing the constitution, so that a general council of members was to meet only annually while a small executive committee was to be the real authority of the Union. Elections to this committee were to take place only every two years, and control of the tenants' welfare fund and the reserve fund was to be vested in it. Finally, membership of the Union was not to be confined to tenants but open to anyone. The Sudan Cabinet, now composed entirely of Sudanese,* refused to approve these proposals.

A compromise constitution, confining membership to tenants, providing for annual elections to the committee and leaving with the Gezira Board control of the welfare and reserve funds, was agreed to,[4] and Sheikh El Amin then turned to other tactics.

The Tenants' Union had established branch committees of its members and now demanded that they should be the sole representative local body with whom the block inspector should discuss all matters. The degree to which these branch committees were under central control or were really representative was unknown (for by contrast with the original Tenants' Representative Body the Union now made a point of secrecy in its affairs), and the proposal ran counter to the whole machinery of village and block councils as the focus of local affairs.

Another demand reflected a claim not to treatment as an adult partner but to a controlling voice. The Union wanted representation on the sales committee and demanded that sales should be dependent upon the consent of the tenants' representative. They wanted the right to watch over cotton grading and weighing and access to auditing of accounts— legitimate enough as long as illegitimate interference was not implied— but they added a claim to have a say in items of management expenditure in the Scheme. Yet another demand was an increase in the tenants' share to 50 per cent and review of the tenants' liabilities with the object of reducing them. 'Now that the Scheme is nationalized,' they said, 'the inescapable conclusion is that the tenant's income should rise and his standard of living improve.'[5]

Some of these demands were matters for the Government, but a committee of the Cabinet asked the management to meet the Union representatives to discuss their complaints in July 1954.[6] A joint co-operative approach was hardly possible in the circumstances, and it is not surprising to see this in the comments of each side on the meeting. 'I regret to state', recorded G. R. H. Dew, the manager, 'that I found all the members most uncooperative in every way, and in my opinion it will be impossible to discuss anything with them in an atmosphere of

* The political evolution of the country is explained in chapter 24.

307

understanding and reciprocal confidence. Unless one gives in weakly to all their demands one is immediately accused of lack of cooperation and of being opposed to the Union.'[7] 'We believe', recorded Sheikh El Amin, 'that this attitude of the responsible authorities is not gratifying. The Union will never drop these demands and will continue to struggle for their realisation or otherwise be convinced that the tenants' demands cannot be realised without the tenants' force. The tenants realise this fact too and the day to day experience of the Union adds to their conviction.'[8]

One of the problems of the Union was finance. The running expenses of the Tenants' Representative Body, the cost of taxis and accommodation for members coming to meetings and so on, had been charged up to the annual income of the tenants' welfare fund, and there had been a good deal of free official help in buildings, secretaries, stationery, etc. This was no longer available to the independent Tenants' Union. There were also competing social claims on the welfare fund and the annual income was in any case inadequate for capital needs like staff housing and a new meeting hall. The Board had made a special grant to meet the capital expenditure in 1952,[9] but the running costs continually ended in a deficit and the Union took the view that while its finances were its own affair the Board ought to meet the deficit.

This was naturally unacceptable to the Board and they were anxious to encourage the Union to become self-supporting. The tenants' subscriptions were estimated at £E5,000 a year and early in 1954 the Board agreed to make a grant for the next three years equal to the contributions collected from the tenants up to a maximum of £E10,000 in any year. After this the Board would make no further contributions, and this grant would be conditional on the Union publishing audited accounts within a specified time and acting within its constitution.[10] In November 1954 the Union's secretary was arrested for failure to pay into the Union chest £E200 which had been paid over by the Board, and in March 1955 the Board decided not to make their contribution to the Union funds until audited accounts were produced. In any case the Board was unable to calculate the amount of its contribution since it depended on the amount of the tenants' contribution and this the Union refused to divulge.

In April 1955 the Union countered by publishing a statement purporting to prove that the average tenant was making a loss of £E136 a year. The reason for the publication was, according to the Union, to enlighten the public about the poor economic conditions under which the tenant suffered during the imperialist régime and up till now during the nationalist government.[11]

The Union followed up this statement in July 1955 by threatening to organize a strike at sowing time until their demands were conceded. The Managing Director (now Sayed Mekki Abbas) retorted by offering each tenant £E20 from the reserve fund, and a further £E10 later in the year, provided he individually signed an undertaking for responsible behaviour. In taking this line he pointed out that he was having regard to the interests of those members of the Union who might have paid their subscriptions but did not fully agree with the leader's policy, as well as those tenants who were not members of the Union and hence had no means of expressing their opinions at all.[12]

This tactic was successful. The Board was aware that many tenants distrusted the financial integrity and disliked both the politics and the power-grabbing tactics of Sheikh El Amin and his friends, even though they shared a common view about the tenants' financial position. When the elections for a new committee of the Union came up in 1956 Sheikh El Amin and his party were defeated, familiar faces like Sheikh Ahmed Babikir Izeirig returned to responsibility, and more harmonious relations were re-established with the Board.

This atmosphere of conflict was depressing for the work of encouraging democracy at the village council level. It had never been easy to get either staff or people away from the concept of the Scheme being run by a bureaucracy. The local villagers' first reactions to promptings towards responsibility had been 'You decide for us. We will only quarrel among ourselves.' Later they were apt to go to the opposite extreme and resent any interference or advice from the field staff. Local government, which had been meant to be an ally in this process of educating for democracy, had lagged behind for it had no funds to provide personnel for this purpose. Sometimes the village council's decisions reflected particular pressure groups and impaired both justice and efficiency, and the field staff tended to become both bewildered and bored by the whole objective.

The management had tried to clarify the policy in a new directive in July 1952:

In agriculture, just as in local government, the aim of devolution is to devolve on to the samad and village council varying responsibilities so that in the end they can completely manage most of their own agricultural affairs, and the long-term view is that the field inspector will very gradually shed his role as direct controller and emerge as an adviser.

This aim is not achieved by the field staff simply abdicating and leaving samads and village councils to make what decisions they like in agricultural matters, but by a conscious policy of training, guidance, and, when necessary, veto. The final word on agricultural matters must still lie with the Board's staff who must satisfy themselves that the samads' and councils' decisions are fair and sensible.

But while the need for agricultural efficiency must act as a brake on accelerated devolution, equally the aim is not achieved by direct control alone, which, however efficient for the present, builds nothing for the future. All staff are therefore required to pay just as much attention to this long-term problem as they are to the short-term need of efficiency. Ability to carry out this dual aim is an essential qualification for service with the Board.[13]

The conflict with the Tenants' Union at the apex made it difficult to carry out this ideal at the base. The field staff could not easily threaten direct action against disobedient tenants and at the same time encourage devolution of powers. As a result, in this period the system of block and village councils and samads developed more as a convenient medium for consultation and for circulation of official viewpoints than as a spearhead of self-management. It was not that the ideal was killed. A recent visitor to the Gezira found the village councils flourishing in some respects.[14] But until the validity of the tenants' grievances, as expressed by the Union, could be assessed and accommodation on them reached with more reasonable representatives than Sheikh El Amin, progress on building democracy in the villages was inevitably hampered.

In some aspects the story of the Tenants' Union had similarities with that of industrial relations in Britain. There was the difficulty of where to draw the line over managerial functions. There was the concept of consultation, with the management viewing the Union as a medium for giving the tenants a greater sense of sharing in the control of the undertaking, while the tenants' representatives often viewed it rather as an instrument to get control and to force their demands upon the management. There was the difficulty in the Tenants' Representative Body and the Tenants' Association of getting continuity in relations between the management and the tenants, because more extreme elements tended to repudiate their representatives and the latter then got out of touch with the rank and file. There was the suspicion in the case of the Union that Sheikh El Amin and his committee were more concerned to acquire power and cause disruption than to get a settlement. But there was, all the same, a sense of grievance there, which gave the opening to intractability in the negotiating room. The causes of this are examined in the next chapter.

Chapter 23

THE PARADOX OF POVERTY IN PLENTY

It is necessary now to turn to the economic background to get to the bottom of the tenants' sense of grievance. This is by no means self-evident for many of the tenants, according to book income figures, were doing much better financially than before the war. But there were the inflation, the rising cost of living and the demand for a rising standard of living, and the great difficulty of assessing how far the tenants were themselves to blame for their troubles.

June 1950 was memorable in the Gezira for the termination of the old partnership with the Companies. For the world at large it was memorable for the outbreak of the Korean war. The effect on the sale price of Gezira cotton was phenomenal. By a curious coincidence of favourable circumstances the average yield of the 1951 crop, the first season under the new Gezira Board, was also phenomenal, being, at 6·8 kantars per feddan, 37 per cent higher than any previous average yield obtained from the Scheme.*

The combination of high price and high yield produced in a single season a crop with an export value of over £E54 million. The net divisible return to the partners, after the Government had taken £E10 million in export tax, was £E44 million, of which the tenants' share was £E18 million, resulting in an average profit per tenancy of £E800. The wheel had turned full circle. Twenty years before, in 1931, from nearly the same acreage the export value of the Gezira crop had been only

* This exceptional yield was attributed primarily, once again, to the incidence of heavy rain prior to planting combined with light rain the preceding year (see Chapter 14, page 174 for discussion of the rainfall formula). Another factor was that fertilizer (mainly ammonium nitrate) was at last again available in quantity, after being restricted in World War II, and was applied to much of the area. The response to fertilizer was always best in a good rain year and higher cotton prices made its use more economically attractive than in pre-war years. A third contributing factor was the rotation history. Half of the 1951 crop fields had last been cropped in the 1948 season, one of low yield with little drain on soil nitrogen. All these factors appeared also to be favourable for grade.

£E750,000, the net divisible return only £E400,000, and the profit per tenancy nil.

An increase in the net divisible return of a hundredfold, compared with the nadir of fortune in 1931, was indeed exciting but, alas, this peak was short-lived. The 1952 crop fell back below average in yield and grade and the price fell also, returning the average tenancy profit to the £E300 level of 1950. For the 1953 crop a good yield was offset by further falling prices and the profit per tenancy fell below the £E200 level.

The diagram facing page 320 will give the reader a more striking impression than any words can convey of the astonishing result of the 1951 crop compared with the whole previous financial history of the Scheme and with the two years which followed. It will be remembered that the Gezira Scheme Ordinance of 1950 fixed the ceilings of both the Board's and the tenants' reserve funds at £E3 million respectively.[1] It also provided that the Board's 20 per cent share, after deducting costs, should be first applied to filling these funds. The financial value of the 1951 crop was so great that this objective was attained in the very first year with the result that the whole of the tenants' share of the profits, namely £E18 million, fell due to be paid to them. Although, by agreement with the Tenants' Representative Body, the payment was spread over more than one year, this huge sum of money dwarfed any previous problem of inflation. The payments from this crop, averaging £E800 per tenancy, were followed by the very steep descent to the £E200 level and this contrast formed the economic background to the tenants' grievances referred to in the last chapter.

To convey how this contrast came to suggest a sense of poverty rather than plenty I am going to draw liberally on an unpublished report by Mrs. Culwick entitled 'A Study of the Human Factor in the Gezira Scheme'. After making the dietary survey mentioned in the previous chapter, she was undertaking for the Board a social investigation to study what living conditions really were like in a village, and in particular how many people had to be supported from a tenancy, and on what the tenants spent their money. She made her study in three representative Gezira villages from 1951 to 1955, and to read her report is like looking through binoculars at a particular site as opposed to the distant general view. The result is a fascinating close-up of local society under the impact of the Scheme's advantages and disadvantages and in certain respects reveals the background to management-tenant relations in a way no official statistics could explain. A great deal of the following account draws on her own vivid description.

312

What Mrs. Culwick's survey brings out above all is the enormous influence which social attitudes were having upon the economic arguments. The divorce of landownership from the revenues of the Scheme had certainly prevented the creation of a rich landlord minority, but it had not exactly resulted in a classless society of hardworking peasant proprietors, such as might have been expected from the very wide distribution of tenancies. What, rather, had evolved in the twenty-five years of the Scheme was that the sentiment and prestige normally attaching to land-ownership was now connected with the possession of a tenancy. One of the tenants' complaints was an objection to being called 'tenants' at all. A large measure of this objection lay in the flavour of subordination that the word carried. Conversely their demand to be treated as 'partners' arose from the word's association with independence and social position; its implication that they were employers not employees. Within a village, ownership of a tenancy was socially as well as economically attractive, and from these social intangibles came a sharply felt class distinction between being a tenant and being a labourer. It would be hard to exaggerate the effect of these social attitudes on one of the Gezira's greatest problems—work.

In the sample villages about 45 per cent of the population were families of tenants and half-tenants, the latter as a result mainly of a split between heirs on the death of the original tenant, subdivision being permitted to this extent in the Scheme. In the upper social levels came the principal village shopkeepers, as well as the most prosperous tenants and the half-tenants most closely related to these. These tended to be the most prominent families for hereditary and other social reasons, and in these circles could also be counted those who had acquired any marked degree of education.

At the other end of the economic scale came casual labourers, herdsmen and the like, who included a large proportion of the racially darker elements in the village. Intermediate came the bulk of the half-tenants and the tradesmen, craftsmen and people who for one reason or another were in the process of moving up or down the scale either socially or economically. The frontiers were not impassable, although beneath the surface camaraderie of Islamic social custom the barriers of snobbery were much the same as in our own society. Lastly, and socially outside the pale of all these groupings, came the immigrant labourers from farther west, Sudanese or foreign, settled or migrant.* While the

* There was in the Sudan considerable antagonism to the degree of immigrant influx, particularly to the fact that immigrants were given tenancies in the Scheme

intermediate group came somewhere near the normal conception of working tenant, the upper group would be more nearly described as gentlemen farmers. Naturally they were the model of what any tenant wanted to be.

As a tenancy began to bring in money, so did families connected with the tenancy spend their money in satisfying their wants in ways which differentiated them socially still farther from their neighbours. The percentage of tenants married at the time of the survey was 91, compared with 58 of the non-tenants. Fifty-four per cent of the tenants had married two wives in their time, compared with only 20 per cent of the non-tenants. A listing of animals present in two of the villages gave the following totals as owned by tenants and non-tenants respectively.

	Tenants	Non-tenants
Cattle	225	6
Sheep	136	2
Goats	458	87
Donkeys	141	33

The traditional local house had been the single-roomed hut with its pointed thatched roof, which still characterizes the villages outside the Scheme. The first step ahead was to a square mud-brick room with a flat mud roof. In the survey only 2 per cent of tenants' houses were still of the old round type, compared with 16 per cent of non-tenant houses, and living in a round hut was something to be spoken of deprecatingly and with humility.

One of the first uses for more money was a better standard of feeding, and the diet in the tenants' homes was characterized by more meat stews, tea, coffee and sugar than those of their neighbours. A quick follow-on was getting rid of the chores, and tenants' housewives could be socially differentiated by whether instead of collecting dried dung for firewood they bought charcoal; instead of grinding flour themselves they sent grain to the mill to be ground; instead of drawing water themselves from the well they bought it and sent their washing to the

in the depression years in default of local application at the time. The immigrants were not Europeans or Asiatics. They came mainly from French Equatorial Africa and Northern Nigeria. At one time they held nearly 20 per cent of the tenancies but by 1951 this figure had fallen to 12 per cent. The fact that they did not mix socially, and that they held any tenancies at all when these were increasingly desired as local population increased, gave rise to tension. On the other hand the tenants were very glad to have their services as casual labour, and some settlements, and even the allotment of a few tenancies, were welcomed as they formed gathering points for this purpose. The subject of immigration into the Sudan had ramifications outside the Gezira and a full discussion of it would go beyond the confines of this book.

laundry. They had new standards of dress and with them new expenses in soap and toilet requisites. They began to have new standards of health. They needed new medicines and took a taxi to get to the doctor. Private practice flourished as they sought to avoid the queues at the hospital. And they wanted their children, both boys and later girls, to be better educated than they were, educated away from a background of labour. In all these ways ownership of a tenancy had come to carry an objective of—almost an entitlement to—a different standard of living.

The village survey revealed that the average number of persons being supported by a standard tenancy was 6·6. It might be thought that while the income from a tenancy had to be regarded as distributable among these numbers, they had the advantage of providing an additional labour force. It was precisely here that the social attitude to work made this argument invalid.

As far as women were concerned, apart from those who were actually tenants, there was a strong reluctance to go out to the fields to work at all. This was partly a matter of a loss of face: it implied need of money or the failure to secure a prosperous husband. Mrs. Culwick found that those who did admit to doing such work were loud in self-pity about it, while others present were equally loud in their sympathy. The men themselves felt that a wife's place was at home unless times became very bad indeed, and it was with pride that one would say 'My wife has never set foot in my tenancy. She only knows by hearsay how you pick or how you sow.' All alike considered it highly improper for younger women to appear in the fields unless the money and labour situation became really desperate. All this was admitted to be in great contrast to the days before the Scheme when everyone used to turn out quite happily for sowing, weeding and harvesting. But that had been for a short period at a time and was in days when fellow-workers were mainly people from their own village. It was a very different matter to expect women to work the much longer periods demanded by the irrigated crops and among the motley crowd of strangers who filled the Scheme today.

While attitudes of this kind restricted half of the potential home labour force, there was also a good deal of resistance on the male side of the family to becoming an agricultural worker even on the family holding. This attitude was connected of course with the aspiration to be a gentleman farmer on one's own holding. Fathers were finding it increasingly difficult to keep their sons. To be a tenant's son and not to get a tenancy was to be unemployed, and to seek escape into some occupation away from the family holding. A tenant-member of the national Senate who pleaded in all earnestness for a change to a closer rotation giving more individual holdings, to relieve 'serious unemployment' in the Gezira, was reflecting the popularity of this attitude.

In any argument as to whether the tenants were doing well or badly, the survey thus reveals how instinctive was the tenant's feeling that his income was always required to feed more mouths at better standards, while his costs of hiring outside labour for every operation were continually going up. Increasing money in circulation and increasing aversion to work were all the time increasing the scope and the price of those who would work. The remedy—that those whom the tenancy supported should do more of the work themselves—ran counter to all the prevailing social attitudes in the village. Estimates made by the management as to tenants' income were based on the assumption that labour was only hired for marginal periods when the family could not do all the work themselves, and always assessed from what income the Scheme could produce, not from what standard of living the tenant was entitled to expect. These differing viewpoints of tenants and management were bound to put human relations under considerable strain.[2]

Moreover, the tenants could hardly be expected to be money managers. With female literacy at nil and male about 45 per cent it was difficult for most tenants to have any idea where they stood financially. Each tenant's account in the Board's office might be clear and correct, but few knew really what additional money they spent on their tenancies on top of the loans they received from the Board, particularly in the prosperous years when loans were reduced to a minimum and tenants were expected to finance extra hiring from their profits in order to reduce inflation. In the early days, when every operation had carried, on completion, its appropriate advance, it was easier to know exactly how one stood—and indeed the loans system was a major attraction. The metamorphosis from the tenant supported step by step through the year, by such cash loans, into the tenant almost entirely managing his own finances might be rightly claimed as a wise evolution from paternalism and an essential step against inflation but, as Mrs. Culwick neatly noted, was an achievement which appealed more to the administrators, economists and social developers than to the object of their interest himself.

The tenant's great anxiety was to have money to attract labour for the peak periods of weeding and picking and if he had to finance this from his own income it led him in turn to ask for definite dates of payments for such income. It had been agreed between the management and the

Tenants' Representative Body that there should be six such dates spread over the year for payment of profits and appreciations, but even this did not help a tenant to be chancellor of his own exchequer so well as the monthly payment of wage-earners in the Sudan, let alone the weekly payments in our society. Under the old system, with loans which had eased him along through the season's work, the profits, though they might have been small, did really seem like profits, to be spent on his private affairs and not on his running costs. But in the prosperous years, with their self-financing and the inflation, although people kept telling him how well off he was, it often seemed to the tenant that the more he drew the more he paid out on the running of his holding. This led him to feel that he was being made to carry more than he used to and, as they said to Mrs. Culwick, 'The tenancy eats it all. It comes. It is gone, and I am left with an empty pocket.'

Here then was the tenants' social situation at the time of the Gezira's *annus mirabilis*, 1951, and of the catastrophic fall in income which followed it. It was compounded of a number of ingredients: the genuine outgoings on the tenancy; the use of hired labour beyond the necessary minimum because of the high social value set on freedom from manual work; confusion between what was wanted and what was needed, created by the rapid expansion of his spending powers; clamorous demands from a family with only the vaguest understanding of the realities of the situation; determination to keep up with the neighbours; and all the time the costs of everything inflated under these social conditions by the very revenue, which therefore became disappointingly evanescent.

The sudden rise to the great affluence of 1951, averaging £E800 profit per tenancy, naturally accentuated all these social tendencies. The model of gentleman manager rather than peasant worker suddenly became possible for every tenant. Both income and expenditure rose to a scale hitherto unknown, and everyone engaged in a vast spending spree. After the satisfaction of priorities in food and clothing, social occasions stood out as pre-eminent in the scale of values. In the general prosperity thousands of pounds went in the pleasures of social display, thousands more in wild competition for goods and services in limited supply,—a scramble in which prices soared and money went to waste like water. Innumerable wedding feasts filled the night with the rhythm of drums. Taxis crammed with well-dressed tenants sped from village to village. Scores of lorries carried the less opulent on their social errands. The markets were crowded with eager customers for goods of all sorts, the beer shops crammed with eager patrons. Many more people than before took out trading licences; competition for flour-mill sites, ferry rights and the like sent auction prices soaring to fantastic heights. When it came to the pilgrimage season large parties set out for Mecca, quite a number by air. Later the returning pilgrims were fêted on an unprecedented scale.

Large numbers of tenants sought the opportunity to build themselves better houses, this time in the next upward transition from mud brick to red brick. The resources of the kilns along the Blue Nile bank were strained to the uttermost. The price of bricks and transport soared in the scramble to obtain possession of every batch burnt. A similar scramble went on for the services of anyone who knew how to build. In the house standards of feeding, dress and personal toilet rose. The general prosperity gave wide opportunity to traditional customs of ceremonial giving, since generosity was greatly esteemed and socially admired, and hundreds of pounds were collected in public subscriptions for projects with local appeal, such as mosques and schools.

Accompanying this scene of prosperity was a phenomenon which seems at first sight a little out of place. Debt is often thought of as a symptom of need, but in the Gezira, as in the Punjab according to Sir Malcolm Darling,[3] it was equally a symptom of prosperity. The profits of 1951 indeed eliminated much debt arising from need, but equally stimulated an immense extension of credit. There was nothing unusual in this. It was merely another example of the hire-purchase system so prevalent in our own and American society. When Mrs. Culwick's investigation started, it was no exaggeration to say that debt was a joke. The man to be pitied was the poor chap who could command no credit, the unfortunate who could not get into debt. And an average debt of £E50 was a laughing matter, not a burden, when one's income was £E800 a year and one hoped it was going to continue like that.

That, however, was just the point of danger. There is a great difference between the intensity of economic risk in our societies—spread over so many activities and products—and that in societies like the Sudan so dependent on one dominant crop.

The £E50 debt became no laughing matter at all when the income began to fall in 1952 to £E300 and in 1953 to £E200. Then indeed a change came over the tone of the discussion. Laughing optimism gave way to groaning. The whole scale of values, of needs and wants, had been thrown upwards by the simultaneous flood of money and consumer goods. It was a most unpleasant reality on top of this to be flung down the waterfall, to be faced with a horde of importunate creditors, to have to cut down the expanding instincts of all the family towards a pleasanter standard of living and throw them into reverse, to have to give up the short-lived ideal of managing and get back to working a tenancy. In such unpleasant straits it was natural to look for any mitigation, by demanding a larger share of the proceeds, by raiding the reserve fund, by challenging the expenditure of the Board that was outside tenants' control and might be extravagant, and by questioning whether the proceeds were as much as could be obtained by different methods of sale. It was natural that hope should line up behind any leader who promised to win something from these alternatives, and to feel that there was some truth in his assurance that Gezira tenants were among the worst remunerated cultivators in the world.

In such an atmosphere, when few were inclined to accept the truth that any redivision of rewards could be of negligible effect compared with the influence of yield, grade and price, there was demonstrated the great value of two features peculiar to the Gezira. The first was the accepted routine of planned agriculture. Whatever the arguments about splitting up the cake, the solid habits of the Scheme, hammered out in earlier years, went steadily on underneath the surface with the accustomed rotation and the framework of rights and duties. To each tenant in his personal capacity there was still every year the water for his food crop, the machinery for his ploughing, the organization providing him with seed, fertilizer, spraying, and supervision, and offering him perhaps another lucky year. One of the most astonishing facts of this period was that, ever since the management was taken over by the Gezira Board in 1950, the tenants had carried on without signing the annual tenancy agreements. They had refused to sign them because the Government had refused to alter their legal nomenclature from tenants to partners. So legally they had no security whatsoever. The trust, after twenty-five years, was not in the legal document but in the treatment they had come to experience and expect from the managing staff.

And, guardian in this dangerous hour when all might have been made peons of the moneylenders and the astute, stood the protecting rule: no mortgage permitted against a tenancy; no debt valid in a court of law against the crops except for agricultural work done on them.

These two features kept the foundations of social stability firm. It was exceedingly disappointing that this great current of wealth should have passed through the Gezira so unproductively. It would have been better to have seen it canalized into sensible investment, or put into an equalization fund and spread over a much longer period. But that it was not disastrous was an unnoticed tribute to paternal planning. And yet there is another side to it. The spree ended. The taxis faded away, the spate of festivities died, the markets grew quiet. Visible signs of it all remained in the form of new houses, many of them in burnt brick but many badly built, radios, sewing-machines, pressure lamps, a few refrigerators, and quite a lot of furniture and furnishings. Within were young women with golden treasure stowed away. Without were animals, bicycles, cars. Little enough really, considering the purchasing power that had been available. And of course it had upset everybody psychologically. But how many tales of giving and receiving like merchant princes will now regale Gezira families for years, inspiring listening children with nostalgic hope for another year like 1951 in their time? For to them still, perhaps in lucky contrast with ourselves, everything in life has not yet come to be arranged like arithmetic. And who can say that the urge for a higher standard of living in such lands—the road, after all, to our own prosperity through international trade—does not derive enormous stimulus from such experiences and such dreams?*

* This is not just a flight of imagination. The year 1919, when the price of cotton rose to a peak of 100 pence per lb., was the nearest analogy to 1951. Profits in 1919 were in the region of £E1,000 per tenancy in the two pilot schemes at Tayiba and Barakat, and the memory of this prosperity was a considerable factor in encouraging the surrounding people in the Gezira to accept the irrigation scheme and the economic change which it implied.

(i) Sayed Ahmed Yusif Algam, member of the Legislative Assembly

(ii) Sheikh Ahmed Babikir Izeirig, Chairman of the Gezira Tenants' Association and later the Gezira Tenants' Union

(iii) Sheikh El Amin Mohammed El Amin, first chairman of the Gezira Tenants' Union

PLATE XIX

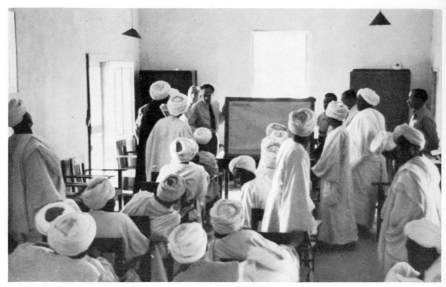

(i) The Tenants' Association discussing marketing policy

(ii) Typical Gezira crowd at an agricultural show

PLATE XX

Chapter 24

TRANSFER OF POWER

Interacting all the time with the social and economic currents just described was the problem of politics. The British paternal administrators were proud of their virtues. They had brought order, justice, some economic advance and a foreign civil service with a very high code of integrity to a country which had not experienced these benefits before, and when the small educated class first pressed for political independence, the British were genuinely doubtful whether these benefits, so important to the bulk of the population, would continue. They rejected as untrue and prejudicial to their wards the claim of the educated classes to represent the whole country.

This attitude arose from a mixture of mental habits and beliefs. There was, for instance, the heritage of indirect rule. For a long time many British believed that for most of the people the tribal leaders were more truly representative than the educated minority and that their customary methods and loyalties reflected the people's own desires. It had been a dictum of the Sudan Government, in the period of indirect rule, that there was no future in politics for the educated classes. They were supposed to confine their interests to technical service. Parallel with indirect rule there was, however, a growing belief that there must be a gradual change towards more democratic representation but this, it was felt, was bound to be a slow process and ought to operate simultaneously in local government and central government, not to be rushed through at the apex alone or for the educated class alone. There was also a feeling that in introducing the concept of democracy, fine as this ideal might ultimately be, the Government was ahead of the people. To work successfully there had to be adequate standards of performance and understanding, as much concentration on the executive side of the process as on the conciliar. Although everyone could talk, without experience few could act.

Even on the conciliar side there had to be time for cohesion to develop and for members to think of themselves as representatives and not merely delegates of their tribe or region. Time was needed also to understand the value of having a peaceful method of changing a government. Without such understanding there was the danger of party rule disregarding minority feelings. There was also the danger of political advance evolving not through party policies based on national programmes but through the power and prestige of an individual, of democracy degenerating into dictatorship. These were not imaginary dangers. They could all be seen happening in Egypt. On the executive side there was the great risk of nepotism and graft, and the difficulty of finding personnel of sufficiently high quality, especially for local government services. In the long run these problems might be solved by the spread of education and experience, by the provision of finance for local government and of a school of administration to train competent and reputable candidates. But inevitably all these demanded time.

Apart from these considerations, which slowed the pace of those British who genuinely believed in a democratic destiny for the country, there were rumours that certain British officials favoured, instead of democracy, an aristocratic evolution associated with a kingship in the person of Sayed Sir Abd el Rahman El Mahdi, one of the two big religious leaders whose influence was greatest in the country areas of the central and western Sudan—and Sayed Abd el Rahman himself was at one time suspected of encouraging this suggestion. There was in fact little prospect of such a policy being developed without splitting the country in two, for it raised profound apprehension in the mind of the other great religious chief, Sayed Sir Aly El Mirghani, who had an extensive following, mainly in the towns and in the northern and eastern Sudan.

But all these factors aroused in the educated classes considerable suspicion of the sincerity of British policy and increased their pressure for political independence.

Before long it became clear that in calling for independence they could easily rally support in the countryside by asking such simple questions as why the British should get all the high pay and live in the best houses. Older people might offset this by remembering the benefits brought by British rule, but to the younger generation, who had no experience of the poverty of the country in the past, these contrasts seemed unfair in the present. There was also the call to patriotism. Why should foreigners run the country when all around in the Middle East their neighbours were managing their own affairs? Not only was this a very fair question (the only logical answer being 'Would you not do a bit better than them by waiting a little longer?'), but it was the sort of sentiment no man worth his salt, or with a shrewd eye on his future, would like to stand out against. Amidst these pressures it would have been strange if many of those in the Civil Service, and the growing educated section of the younger generation, had been as interested in learning to do their job well by slowly working up from the bottom as they were in getting rid of the foreigners and stepping into their shoes.

The Sudan Government's official policy all this time had been a typically British compromise. The setting up of the Advisory Council in 1944, and of the Legislative Assembly in 1948, was intended to give gradual but real experience in the parliamentary and ministerial machinery of a democratic form of government prior to self-determination, and there can be no doubt that they made a great contribution towards a sense of national cohesion. As a parallel part of this policy, the training and promotion of educated Sudanese to responsible posts was stepped up through all the government services. All the time, however, the assumption remained that the Sudanese, like his British predecessor, should work his way up from the bottom, and all the top posts in the services remained in British hands.

The Gezira should have been in the forefront of these Sudanization plans but, as I have already shown, after 1944 when the Government decided not to renew the Companies' association, these general issues were shelved until the formation of the Gezira Board. Bredin, when Governor of the Blue Nile Province, and I had advocated the recruitment to our field staff of certain Sudanese officers demobilized from the Sudan Defence Force in 1945, but the Syndicate Board had feared that this policy might upset the British field staff and make them uncertain about their future; they also feared that it might unsettle the tenants. The Gezira was financially essential to the country and, with the opportunity for graft, the need for integrity in the field staff seemed overriding. Caution, therefore, became easier to believe in than foresight. This belief was all the stronger because the better men among the educated tended to look for careers in government service and it was feared that the Gezira would only get those who were left over. But as a result of all this caution, by 1949, when policy was at last fixed, we had to begin rapid recruitment of Sudanese to the field staff under considerable political pressure.

The Select Committee of the Legislative Assembly, appointed in 1949 to report on the future administration of the Gezira, reflected this pressure and made a particular point of the urgency for Sudanization. One of the ways, they said, to achieve this aim was by training a sufficient number of Sudanese as directors where they would share the responsibility for administration, agricultural management and social development, and at the same time gain experience from their non-Sudanese colleagues.[1] This was an eminently sensible suggestion and, as in the case of the Executive Council, the experience of working together continuously on common problems removed a great deal of the coldness and misunderstanding which had arisen through lack of contact in a joint responsibility.

Another suggestion of the Committee, which they pressed upon me personally very strongly, was that a selected Sudanese should be appointed Assistant Manager to gain experience alongside the British Manager with a view to taking over his job later. We were far less sanguine about this suggestion. There was a risk that it might cause uneasiness among the senior members of our British staff who had not yet signed on with the Board and whose experienced service was particularly needed. But our main reaction was that the proposal was unreal. It was not the sort of thing we had ever done with British personnel in the past. A manager, we felt, could not learn his job by starting as an observer at the top. His everyday decisions were based on experience accumulated over the years by working his way up and it was this method which moulded a man's capacity as manager and built up the staff's confidence in him. We felt that the process could not be short-cut.

We therefore pressed the Committee to drop this proposal and they deferred to our judgement, making their recommendation in their report as follows:

Your Committee strongly recommend that the Sudanese should have the maximum possible share in the administration of the Scheme . . . and endorse the policy, already begun, of recruitment of Sudanese for appointment as field officers. This should take place as fast as possible without lowering the standard of administration. In this respect it is essential that a sound tradition should be established from the start.

Your Committee have thought it expedient that a number of capable and well-educated Sudanese be appointed as field officers with a view that one of them will in due course, and after gaining experience from the bottom, climb up the ladder and be the assistant manager, to understudy the manager to enable him eventually to assume the responsibilities of manager, when the opportunity presents itself and he has fully qualified for it. . . . After serious thought, your Committee, while insisting that every effort should be made to train Sudanese for higher executive posts as soon as possible, support the principle that promotion should be strictly on merit, particularly in the Gezira where continued efficiency is so essential to the prosperity of the country.[2]

We could all subscribe to this view which at the time seemed wise. Subsequent events made it more doubtful whether our judgement was right and whether it would not have been wiser to accept the Committee's first instinct of appointing an understudy—and even extending the principle more widely than just to the post of Manager. This question will come up again for consideration later in this chapter.

At the time we had all the more confidence for our view because our programme for Sudanization from the bottom looked as if it was going through very rapidly. Our field staff comprised about one hundred British. We had not recruited many since the war and at the normal wastage and retirement rate half of the field staff would be Sudanese by 1956. This would not give them any excessive time to digest their experience, for in the following ten years, as individual British retired, the Sudanese would find themselves in the senior posts and take over the whole administration of the Scheme. There was also the prospect in the near future of large extensions in area, calling for an overall increase in staff.

The rapid recruitment of well-educated Sudanese could obviously not be made suddenly from the very small number who issued annually with agricultural degrees from the University College, where agriculture was usually the last subject chosen. But this did not worry us. In recruiting British staff we had always been far more concerned with character than technical qualifications. We applied the same principle to Sudanese recruits and increased the age limit. As a result the field of recruitment embraced the whole country. Application was wide and choice correspondingly greater. Character may be located anywhere and although we naturally did not attract men who were well placed for promotion in their existing careers our offer appealed to others who for various reasons felt frustrated. Many came from the Education Department, others from the Customs, the railways, local government service and private business. One of our best choices in the outcome was a public-health officer. We had taken care that on our selection committee the majority were Sudanese. We did not find that this involved us in bias and they were far shrewder judges of Sudanese character than we were and far more knowledgeable of the individual background of the candidates.

Such then was the kind of evolution to which we looked forward with some confidence even when I myself left the Scheme early in 1952. But events proved that we were still too cautious.

I have mentioned in Chapter 17* that when the Government rejected in 1942 the demand for a much bigger say in the conduct of affairs by the Sudanese educated class, the latter split. The broad picture which emerged was of two groups: the Umma Party co-operating with the Government and gaining the political experience of operating the Legislative Assembly and the Executive Council, and the National Unionist Party (N.U.P. for short; an amalgamation of the Ashigga and other non-co-operators) missing this experience and flirting with Egypt.

Until King Farouk fell from power in Egypt the Sudan had been regarded in that country as a province of Egypt (which of course it had been before the Mahdi's rebellion),† perhaps with an undetermined status, but always under the Egyptian monarchy. The professed aim of the British Government on the other hand was self-determination for the Sudanese, although it would fix no date or time-table for its realization. In these circumstances the Umma Party, while they had to avoid being identified as stooges of the British, could pose as patriots guarding the country against submission to Egypt, and there was no question that Sayed Sir Abd el Rahman El Mahdi represented such a figure for it was his father who had raised the patriotic revolt and driven the Egyptians out in 1885.

These circumstances were entirely altered when the revolution took place in Egypt in 1952. After the departure of King Farouk and the accession to power of General Neguib the attitude of the Egyptian Government to Sudanese aspirations changed. Neguib let it be known that Egypt was now willing to concede self-determination to the Sudan immediately, but on condition that all British personnel in the administrative service, police and Sudan defence force relinquished their posts to Sudanese, to enable the country to exercise self-determination in a free and neutral atmosphere. A transitional period not exceeding three years was suggested for this process during which there would be full self-government for the Sudanese as soon as a parliament had been elected. In the autumn of 1952 General Neguib, who incidentally had a Sudanese mother and had had part of his education in Khartoum, invited representatives of all the political parties of the northern Sudan to Egypt and concluded an agreement with them on the lines of these proposals.

In effect Neguib's offer accepted the British objective but advanced it to the immediate future. The creation of the Legislative Assembly and

* See page 227.
† See above, page 29.

326

Executive Council and the extensive Sudanization of government services had been preludes to this objective and, although such quick
elimination of British personnel had certainly not been in her plan,
Britain accepted the proposal as the logical outcome of her policy. Any
delaying tactics by then would have provoked the united hostility of the
whole northern Sudan.

When the elections took place the N.U.P. naturally stood as the
patriots who had got rid of the foreign yoke, while the Umma Party had
to defend themselves against the charge of collaboration. The N.U.P.
won the elections and there came into power in 1954 an all-Sudanese
Government of politicians, few of whom had any experience. Many of
the British had in the preceding ten years cast aside their aloofness and
formed friendships with those educated Sudanese who were working
alongside them in posts of responsibility. Although this association did
not go very deep socially—each race reverting for relaxation and recreation to its own community, and with the great difficulty which the
women on each side had in finding a common contact—it undoubtedly
created a closer sense of camaraderie. Unfortunately this was not the
case with the new Government which had just come into power. To the
British they were simply the agitators, suspected of being bribed by
Egypt, largely unknown and therefore probably incompetent. Their
leader, the first prime minister, Sayed Ismail El Azhari, who was of
course a national hero overnight and later displayed very considerable
powers of statesmanship, would then have been thought of by the
British mainly as a one-time rather mediocre schoolmaster. To the
members of the new Government, on their side, the British were simply
the imperialists. We were completely out of contact with each other and
this, once again, proved a critical factor in the situation. These events
naturally caused immense excitement throughout the land and quickened the appetite for shaking off the foreigner, while the advent of the
N.U.P. to power added a flavour of hostility to the process.

The Gezira was not technically included in the constitutional agreement under which the British officials were to leave the country within
three years and theoretically the Sudanization plan which we had drawn
up in 1949—of working up from the bottom—could have continued. In
practice, pressures from two directions made this impossible. The new
Council of Ministers itself, both leading and responding to popular
pressure, instructed the Gezira Board to draw up a much more rapid
plan of Sudanization, while the British staff, increasingly disliking an
atmosphere in which they were pilloried as undesirable, if not worse, felt

less and less inclined to stay. We had in 1949 given undertakings to British staff for compensation in the event of dismissal owing to Sudanization, although we had regarded this at the time as a distant possibility likely to affect only the younger men. With some adjustment these terms could be made to meet the new situation and by 1955 almost all the British staff had preferred to take their compensation and go. Very much the same thing happened at the Gezira Research Institute. The responsibility for the whole undertaking now fell upon the Sudanese, the first of whom, it will be remembered, had only joined the Board in 1950, and the first handful of whom had only been recruited to the field staff in 1949.

During 1954 and 1955 the Gezira Board, and particularly Sayed Mekki Abbas, who now became Managing Director, and Sayed Abd el Hafiz, the new Chairman, were anxious to persuade individual British to remain, particularly men whose ability they respected and those in key positions for which as yet no Sudanese had had time to acquire enough experience. In this they were only partially successful, for just as in the general excitement the emotion about national independence, and to a certain extent zenophobia, increased by geometric progression, so at the same rate did those circumstances disappear which had kept the British interested in the country. It was a situation compounded partly of the general change in the climate, engendering distaste and insecurity, and partly of the individual reaction of a man, and especially of his wife and family, to the total disappearance of a British social community. For the first time the prospect was of living not merely in the Sudan but with the Sudanese, and it was strange.

These circumstances left the Gezira in 1955 with a young and largely inexperienced Sudanese staff. People who visit it today will find, indeed, among them a pride like ours in the inheritance we passed on to them. They will find, too, a determination, evoked by the sense of real responsibility, to make the project as fine an achievement in their time as ever it was in ours. But our delay in the Gezira in associating educated Sudanese and, I believe, tenants, with the administration and direction threw an exceptionally heavy burden on those Sudanese who took over from us, and especially upon the Managing Director, Sayed Mekki Abbas.

One of the temporary casualties resulting from this was the very ideal we wanted to instil—the sense of regional democratic development. For inevitably, with a largely inexperienced staff and continuous disputes with the tenants, the need for efficiency and so for assertion of bureaucratic control was for the time being paramount. This might have been avoided if we had started Sudanization earlier and if we had picked and trained able men in more of the senior positions, double-banking them to do this—in other words, followed the instinct of the Gezira Committee of the Legislative Assembly, instead of being quite so insistent on working up from the bottom on the British analogy. The danger of not having done so is that while on the surface the routine of the Scheme continues with remarkable success with, in addition, a great expansion programme in the Managil extension, underneath the surface, as the Sudanese themselves are the first to fear, efficiency may fall. Had a policy of training in high executive positions been followed earlier the hope for the future would be all the higher. It is in the province of research, financial and cost control, and in engineering that the loss of foreign experienced personnel may leave the biggest hazards. For proficiency in these subjects, there was simply not enough time and opportunity.

Many readers may feel that there was really no need for us to stay as long as we did since as soon as a country acquires independence it can hire any advisers it needs from non-colonial countries and international sources. There is clearly some truth in this and doubtless many Sudanese preferred an independent expert under their control to a man who had been associated with the old régime of authority. Here, however, matters did not turn out as might have been expected. Neutral advisers hired by the new Sudanese Government proved in many instances disappointing, mainly because the short-term contracts appealed only to mediocre men and gave no time for acquiring a background knowledge of the country and the language and a real interest in its people. The truth was that, whatever its faults, the old régime had provided opportunity for this and if British personnel who had such a background could have remained as advisers after independence, with a mutually harmonious relationship, it would have been beneficial. Those very few who did remain, in finance, in irrigation, in the railways, and in the Gezira (often in the necessary position of watching Sudanese making decisions, of the wisdom of which they were doubtful, instead of making them for the Sudanese as in the past), were more valuable to the country than any others could be at a very critical time as, I believe, many Sudanese would now be the first to concede.

Other readers may feel on the contrary that we should have hung on to power in the Sudan until the Sudanese had more experience; but when the Sudanese were clamouring for independence we had to make a choice, either to enforce our stay against universal resistance, a course liable to prejudice the co-operation which alone could give the extra benefit of experience, or to conclude that the most important thing for the future was to preserve a good relationship and go. Either choice was bound to be a compromise with perfection.

At such a time, when more harm might have been done by staying than by going, everything that we had done to give the Sudanese experience in managing things themselves meant a better augury for their future. Anything that had made the pressure for independence more temperate and persuaded the Sudanese that time was needed for training and experience was of vital value. Looking back, then, our experience suggests that in a situation where risks have to be taken they are better taken by starting early to share responsibility and by ensuring that nothing impairs belief in the sincerity of our intentions.

One other conclusion may be hazarded from our experience. There came a time, and it was earlier than any of us imagined, when it would have been wise to look to the future ties which might preserve contact and to give these greater priority. It was not that we were hanging on to power and prestige, as many Sudanese thought, but we were hanging on to paternal leadership. We should have put more Sudanese into the saddle earlier and worried less about old bonds which were bound to disappear. For the local man had to have responsibility to make his own mistakes. It was the only way he could learn. The vital contact point of the future was, rather, the English language and all that it meant for access to common ideas. We should have switched our sights earlier to education, technical training and trade, for these were interests we would both need to share and to expand after independence.

We were too slow also to think ahead and create an atmosphere in which British and Sudanese could co-operate on the same status. We should have given priority to the need for a mutually harmonious relationship. In our imperial heritage, so linked to leadership training in our public schools, the tradition was of service to help on backward peoples. No impartial critic would deny that a great deal had been done in the Sudan to fulfil it. But it was a system training an officer class for positions of authority, not for everyday life among equals. It always left the Sudanese in doubt whether our objective really was their independence.

These were not fatal faults. Our parting was not unfriendly, in spite of the emotions of nationalism which make the period of transfer of power so liable to recrimination. But the result was that, once our position of authority was gone, we had at first no other relationship to fill the vacuum. This was a drawback at the end of a story of development so full of value. It was natural that the Sudanese should seek their closest connections in the Arab world, just as we in Britain seek them with those who seem closest to us. Yet the ties of interest and friendship between these regional alliances have seldom been more important to the world. May that between Britain and the Sudanese people become again a close one! To make it so we shall need to remember mutually one last proverb which the people of the Gezira taught us:

> To teach the old is like writing on water,
> To teach the young is like carving on stone.

One of our mistakes in the Middle East has been to forget that one of the strongest bonds of the future is the mutual contact of youth.

Chapter 25

THE WIDER RELEVANCE

The reader may feel that further comment is like jobbing backwards, shutting the stable door after the horse has bolted. But a post-mortem has a value and in closing this book it is pertinent to relate the story to the much wider field of western world relationships with the African continent. It may help to detect those elements which are liable in the end to be poisonous in the aftermath of colonialism and to reveal those which should be strengthened in order that a better relationship may be built.

Colonialism is not merely a relationship between European powers and their erstwhile colonies but equally often a relationship between the more primitive and the more progressive within the country itself. Certainly in the Sudan today the Arabs of the northern Sudan are in the same relation to the negroid races of the southern Sudan as were the British to them. But to many people colonialism means the relationship between the western world and hitherto dependent countries with a low standard of material living. This applies not merely to the relationship between an imperial power and another country which it still controls, but also to that between a European resident minority and the indigenous majority. The African continent is in particular permeated with these situations. For this reason the case history of the Gezira Scheme both economically and in human relationships may, I believe, have a wider interest than the mere telling of a past tale. For the story, so characteristic of the economic, social and political searchings of our age, leaves in the mind a last vital question, 'What does the western world stand for?'

There have always been two strains in British imperial history and doubtless this is true of many nations. There is a trusteeship strain, such as that embodied in the introductory text from India, which runs so strongly through this story and which aims ultimately at self-determination, and there is a power strain. Often European business interests and

European settler communities have been critical of the trusteeship strain and have voiced the virtues of the power strain. The power of the British Empire, the access to raw materials, the protection of trade interests, and immigration to increase settler communities have seemed paramount to them. Often they have had the economists on their side, confirming from statistics that a higher standard of living for all in the territory has been attained more quickly where encouragement is given to immigration, foreign private investment and a 'civilized' government. But always this method has been resented in the end by the indigenous people whenever education has given them a voice. The assumption that they are passive elements in the situation has time and again been proved an illusion.

The Gezira Scheme was planned in the spirit of the trusteeship strain. It was based on the belief that stability and permanence of economic investment will depend in the end on the contentment of the people and is unlikely to be attained merely by imposing on a country the quickest way to a higher standard of living irrespective of the political circumstances which accompany it. Governor-General Wingate was fully aware of these two strains when he wrote in his report for 1906 that it was scarcely an exaggeration to say that the whole future of the Sudan depended upon the treatment which the subject of private enterprise development received, and the story of the Gezira is an example of the building up of a dynamic indigenous economy on the assumption that trusteeship of the indigenous people's future was paramount even if the results in developing a higher standard of living were achieved more slowly.

In underdeveloped countries the need for an ordered plan to overcome poverty is extremely difficult to avoid. The problem is to get off the ground floor of mere subsistence, but also to see that the benefit does not remain merely in a few hands, leaving a great rift between enterprising rich and feckless poor. But as soon as planning is introduced there is the difficulty of avoiding an autocratic régime. Hence the importance of democracy, of a sense of participation by the people in the whole process. In our day in the Gezira, bringing civilization was bringing this sense of ordered liberty. It naturally led to a desire to be treated as free and equal.

American history reveals something of the same two strains, a trusteeship complex predominating at one time, at another a power complex. The trusteeship strain in both Britain and the United States, coinciding after the first world war, played an underlying part in the establishment of the League of Nations and again later of the United Nations.

This initiative evoked an immense response from countries which had hitherto formed parts of other nations' empires. The connection between trusteeship, self-determination and the United Nations was not fortuitous. It implied a belief that in foregoing the concept of power and supporting that of self-determination there would be less threat of war. The erstwhile colonial power would have no need to retain control of outside territories in self-protection if the United Nations became an effective medium for the settlement of disputes.

The two imperial strains of trusteeship and power have nevertheless continued side by side. The United Nations has not yet proved an acceptable medium for solving all disputes and the stark reality is that, in a world still liable to break into war, a policy of self-determination means that a hitherto dependent (and *a priori* reliable) country is now free to adopt, or not to adopt, alliances in its foreign policy of its own choice. The choice may depend on what mood prevailed before the transfer of power. It may be the choice of a small group or individual, or the choice of men experienced in responsibility. It may depend on slights remembered, on a sense of inferiority imposed or on belief in certain principles, or on a sense of solidarity with those of similar race or circumstances. The choice may be affected by what attitudes are taken, what contacts made, after the transfer of power. The choice may affect a great deal of the world, although it may be determined by the treatment and behaviour of only a few people. Clearly it may be no longer a local but a world problem.

These considerations conjure up doubts in many parts of the world about the wisdom of self-determination in all cases and about the safety of giving up control. They encourage the suspicion that while some nations renounce control others use the opportunity to extend their empire. They cause anxieties about defence and these in turn easily reawaken recollections of prestige. These are then supported by the fears for interests likely to be adversely affected by self-determination— the control of important raw materials or business interests or the status of European resident minorities. This complex of attitudes encourages a belief that colonialism has its merits, and the need for adequate time to prepare for self-determination is then often misapplied and used as a justification for qualifying the aim of self-determination itself. This retrogressive attitude provokes a reaction and quickens the fervour for independence among indigenous dependent peoples all over the world— irrespective of their need for time and technical competence.

As a result of this dual strain we face the world with a confused purpose at a time when singleness of purpose has seldom been more important. In contrast with the simple faith of the early administrators in the Sudan that they were doing good by bringing their interpretation of civilization to that country, and in contrast with the communists, the policies of the western world do not now reveal clearly what it stands for.

Many would answer 'liberty', and in recent months our Prime Minister and the British Ambassador to the United States have given expression to this answer by contrasting with communism the British practice of granting self-determination to hitherto colonial territories, as if this was the paramount objective. The President of the United States, at the meeting of the heads of Governments of the fifteen Nato powers at Paris in December 1957, voiced something of the same sentiments when he said:

This is a time for greatness. . . . We pray for greatness in the spirit of self-sacrifice, so that we may forsake lesser objectives and interests to devote ourselves wholly to the well being of all of us. . . . We have demonstrated a will for the spreading of the blessings of liberty. Within the last fifteen years our nations have freely granted political independence to twenty countries with populations totalling 800 million people.

The President went on to say:

The members of our community need to feel an increasing responsibility to help other free peoples to attain for themselves relief from what has been for them an age-old blight of direct poverty. We have, as I have recalled, been parties to the grant of political liberty to hundreds of millions of people. But that bestowal could be a barren gift, and indeed one which could recoil against us, unless ways are found to help less developed countries to achieve an increasing welfare.

If this is the context in which western world-policy is formed, the principles of the Gezira Scheme are, I believe, particularly suited to be one of the ways of carrying it out—especially if care is taken to correct some of the mistakes we made. It could be a pattern eminently well-fashioned both to our own and to an emergent country's need. It is investment in partnership with the people, with the aim of giving them ultimate ownership of their own major economic assets; consideration for social equity in distributing the benefits of development; the provision of competent managerial and technical experience on a businesslike basis, with earlier and more deliberate training of local people in posts of responsibility than we practised and a closer contact in terms of friendship and equality in place of the aloofness and authority with which we operated; it implies passing over to them, to the degree that they wish it,

335

the political, legal and administrative traditions which have helped us in the defence of our own liberties; and the pursuit of this policy not merely in politics and government administration but equally in business.

A policy of this kind might be both realistic and acceptable as a preparation for transfer of power in those territories still under colonial rule, and experience in the Sudan suggests that this would be all the more so if international institutions, after this prelude, could take on and continue this process, in which young men all over the world would surely find a vocation for creative service if given an inspiring lead.

Can the western world give such a lead, setting before the individual countries still dominated by individual European powers an unequivocal objective of self-determination after a practical period of control and help, and pooling their immense resources to this end? Can they follow this by working out, round the table as equals with the newcomer territories, in international context, the details of the process of development, the terms of an investment charter to attract private enterprise, the provision of investment funds for the unremunerative level, the extension of the International Bank for the fixed interest level, the interchange of technicians and training, and provision to safeguard the legitimate fears of European minorities?

Such a lead would be the logical outcome of the trusteeship strain in our imperial history. A great deal of western world initiative since the war implies such a policy. Aid in one form or another has proliferated from colonial powers to their colonies, from the United States, from non-colonial countries bilaterally, from the United Nations or from regional arrangements such as the Colombo Plan or the European Common Market. The idea is in the air but the multiplicity of agencies is confusing and the individual agency today is often not enough. More important, the aid is not specifically linked to the assumption of self-determination. Sometimes it conveys an implied string or a veiled continuance of the power strain.

These weaknesses confirm the impression that the western world is undecided about what it stands for. This is particularly the case in the continent of Africa where more than anywhere else in the world European powers still have a large measure of control and responsibility. Apart from the two ends of the continent, Algeria and the Union of South Africa, where self-determination for the indigenous people is no part of the present European programme, there are instances all over the continent where European policy is inconsistent. On the one hand the Sudan, Ghana and Nigeria illustrate the concluding phases of the trusteeship strain in British policy. On the other hand Kenya, Tanganyika,* and the Central African Federation belie this objective. Here compromises are suggested. Vague terms like multi-racialism and partnership are put forward in place of liberty, democracy and self-determination. These changes have been made, of course, because of the fears of small European resident minorities which are at present in dominant positions. They arouse in turn among the indigenous populations considerable fears either of permanent subjection to a minority group foreign to them or of being cheated out of national liberty. A policy that encourages the continuance of European immigration and economic development by private European capital, and gives no opportunity to the indigenous people to choose or reject it, has very little in keeping with the concept of trusteeship and the aim of independent maturity.

Something of the same uncertainty of aim applies to the inclusion of the overseas territories of the powers in the European Common Market. Economically this shows an advance from the days when each individual colonial power handled development on its own, with its own often inadequate resources. Now, at least the powers discuss the pooling of their combined strengths for development. But in taking this partial step there is a risk of creating a closed shop as far as other African territories are concerned. Moreover, the initiative came from Europe and runs as much risk of being interpreted by the indigenous people as a reassertion of colonialism, economic and political, as does the undefined policy in British East and Central Africa. The considerable Portuguese possessions remain outside the self-determination concept altogether.

A policy halting between the two alternatives of a trusteeship objective and a power objective may forfeit the strength of either. The right hand may defeat what the left hand is trying to do, and vice versa. To educate but not to associate is certain to alienate. To preach and encourage the practice of democracy as an objective for a country in which Europeans have no settlement and deny it as an objective where there is such settlement is certain to invite suspicion not co-operation.

If we are giving priority to the maintaining of our own power and control, then such a policy as we pursued in the Sudan is dangerous, for education in our own ideals implies sympathy with universal liberty. But if we are aiming to spread these ideals, then we cannot without detriment to our relations with the people adopt a policy which is inconsistent with them.

* The policy in Tanganyika has been changed since these words were written and is now more clearly aligned with that pursued in the Sudan and Nigeria.

Montesquieu in the eighteenth century, himself the precursor of so many of these very ideals, put the choice before us in these words:

If I knew something which was useful to me but which was prejudicial to my family I would throw it out of my mind. If I knew something which was useful to my family but was prejudicial to my country, I should try to forget it. If I knew something useful to my country but which was prejudicial to Europe and to the human race, I should regard it as a crime.[3]

It is clear that many countries all over the world are involved in the difficult choice between national and international objectives. All are tempted to identify patriotism with nationalism, and a country which has been dependent and under colonial rule has to go through a phase of nationalism to feel itself an equal of others in the international world. Whether such countries come up to join us as angry rebels or as helpful friends may turn on our behaviour in the fields where we are still responsible. The coolness of so much of the newly emergent world towards the west is not the result of the application of the democratic principles which we believe in and defend for ourselves but of our departure from them.

The heads of government of the fifteen countries comprising Nato, at their meeting in Paris in December 1957, made this statement in their subsequent communiqué.

We express our interest in the maintenance of peace and the development of conditions of stability and economic and political well-being in the vitally important continent of Africa. We hope that the countries and peoples of that continent who are disposed to do so will cooperate within the free world in efforts to promote these purposes. We affirm the readiness of our countries to cooperate for our part with the countries and peoples of Africa to further these ends.

Are these just platitudes or are they the prelude to a real policy in which the vast strength of Europe, the Commonwealth and the United States could be pooled to build up the true political and economic liberty of those peoples for whom we are still responsible? Will the European resident drop his fear and play his part, accepting his position as a vital minority? Will the administrator move over from his position of paternal authority to the humbler role of adviser? Will our capital build up their enterprise, not just our enterprises, in their lands? And, having set its wards on their way, will the western world keep contact with them as equals in the international field? These are the questions Africa asks. They challenge the western world with few tasks so difficult, yet so imperative and so honourable.

APPENDIX I

(a) Tenancy Agreement Form

Name of Block ....
Name of Rightholder....................................
Name of Cultivating Tenant.............................
Status of Tenant (Rightholder, Nominee, etc.)..........
Folio Number..
Date of Agreement.....................................
Season ....

AN AGREEMENT made between THE SUDAN PLANTATIONS SYNDICATE, LTD. (hereinafter called the Syndicate) of the first part and........................ (hereinafter called the Tenant) of the second part:—

WHEREAS the Tenant is desirous of taking from the Syndicate a Cultivating Tenancy under the provisions of the Gezira Land Ordinance, 1927, of.........feddans of land at.............. for the cultivation of cotton and other crops and the said tenant has seen the land specified and has a thorough knowledge of its boundaries.

AND WHEREAS the parties have agreed that the said cotton crop shall be grown and marketed and the proceeds of the sale thereof divided as set out in the 1936 Standard Conditions of Tenancy published by the Syndicate and posted at the Syndicate's Block Office at..............

NOW IT IS HEREBY AGREED between the parties:—

1. The Syndicate agrees to let and the Tenant agrees to take until the first day of June next the plot of land.........feddans in area above described.

2. The provisions of the 1936 Standard Conditions of Tenancy published by the Syndicate and posted in the Syndicate's said Block Office at.....................shall apply to and govern the Tenancy hereby created and the growth and marketing of the said cotton crop and the division of the proceeds of sale thereof in the same manner as if the same were incorporated and set out herein verbatim, and the Tenant hereby acknowledges that he has had the opportunity of reading and of having read to him the said Standard Conditions.

```
....................     ┌ The Tenant   ....................
              Signed ┤      for
....................   by: └ The Syndicate ....................
```

Seal or signature of Sheikh ⎫
(or responsible person) as ⎬
Certificate of Tenant's identity ⎭

339

I hereby certify that before signing the Agreement................
has had an opportunity of reading and having read to him the 1936
Standard Conditions of Tenancy posted at the Syndicate's Block Office
at......................................

Signed: Omda or Sheikh

MEMORANDUM OF RENEWAL

This tenancy has been renewed for the period stated below, namely:—

Period Ending	Signature on Behalf of Company	Signature or Seal of Tenant

(b) Standard Conditions of Tenancy (1936)

1. Tenancies are created under and subject to the provisions of the
Gezira Land Ordinance, 1927, certain of which, without prejudice to the
application of the Ordinance as a whole, are, for the information of
the Tenant, set out in the Schedule hereto.

2. The Tenant shall cultivate the land in a proper manner and according
to the scheme of Crop Rotation laid down by and to the satisfaction of the
Syndicate and shall in all things obey the reasonable orders of the Syndicate's officials in all matters relating to the cultivation, irrigation and
harvesting of the said crops. The said scheme of Crop Rotation shall allow
the growth by rain cultivation and subject to the prior requirements oi
the cotton crop by irrigation water on a portion of the said land of a crop
of durra sufficient for and restricted to the Tenant's own requirements.
Provided that the Tenant shall not sell any part of the said crop and shall
in no way neglect the cultivation of the Cotton crop for the sake of the
durra crop. Provided further that the Tenant shall not remove nor permit
the removal of any stalks of such durra from the said land but shall ensure
that they shall be entirely consumed on the land by animals, and if the
Tenant shall remove any part of such stalks or shall not introduce on to
the said land animals sufficient in the opinion of the Syndicate to consume
such stalks within a reasonable period the Syndicate may bring on to the
said land such animals for such period or periods as it thinks fit to ensure
the consumption of such stalks as aforesaid without prejudice to the provision of Condition 13 hereof.

3. The Tenant shall at his own cost make the field channels (abu sittas)
on his land and shall bear the cost of the work done by the Syndicate in
excavating the part of the feeder channel (abu ishreen) which abuts on his
land to an extent not exceeding PT.25 per chain (twenty metres) and shall
during the tenancy keep the same in sound repair and free from seepage
or leaks.

4. The Syndicate shall supply the ploughing and other machinery necessary for the cultivation of and shall carry out the ploughing of the said land and the cost of such ploughing and supply of machinery shall be apportioned between the Tenant and all the other cultivating tenants under the said Ordinance on a feddanage basis.

5. The Syndicate shall supply water necessary for the irrigation of the said scheme of Crop Rotation but if at any time by reason of breakdown of machinery, canals or other irrigation work or any other compulsory circumstances the supply of water to the said land is interrupted, the Tenant shall have no claim against the Syndicate for any compensation on account of the water not reaching the land under cultivation.

6. The Tenant during his tenancy shall comply with the Sanitary Regulations for the time being in force and shall deliver back to the Syndicate the said land free of all cultivation together with all Gadwells clean and in proper working order on the 1st day of June next.

7. Immediately upon harvesting the said Cotton crop the Tenant shall deliver it to the Syndicate at the Syndicate's collection station at . . . .

8. If at any time the Tenant is reasonably in need of an advance in money or kind in order to enable him to carry out his agricultural obligations hereunder the Syndicate shall, provided that it considers such a course businesslike and proper, make such advances on such reasonable terms and to such extent as the Syndicate shall in its absolute discretion think fit.

9. The Syndicate shall sell and dispose of the Cotton crop harvested and delivered by the Tenant as aforesaid together with that of all the other cultivating Tenants under the said Ordinance for such prices and in such manner as it may think fit.

The gross profits of the said Cotton crops shall be the sale price thereof realised as aforesaid after deduction of the cost of transport, ginning and other expenses of sale or incurred for the benefit of the said crop.

Of the said gross profits the Cultivating Tenants shall be entitled collectively to 40 per cent. while the Syndicate shall retain the remaining 60 per cent. as the share of the Syndicate and the Sudan Government in satisfaction of rent, land tax, and expenses of irrigation and management.

10. (1) There shall be opened for the said crop a Tenants' Collective Account to which shall be credited the Tenants' collective 40% of the gross profits and any other sums which from time to time may be transferred from the Tenants' Reserve Fund or which fall to be credited to the Tenants as a whole through the Tenants' Collective Account covering the said crop.

(2) There shall be debited to the said Tenants' Collective Account:

(1) The total of the sums from time to time credited in the individual Tenants' accounts kept by the Syndicate in respect of their share of the net divisible profits whether such payment be in anticipation of or subsequent to the realisation of the gross profits:

(2) The usual and proper Tenants' Collective Charges and Expenses;

(3) The total of the debit balances appearing in individual tenants' accounts kept by the Syndicate as at the 30th June in the year covered by the Tenants'

Collective Account in question. Individual debit balances so dealt with shall thereafter be deemed to be a debt due by the individual to Tenants' Collective Account.

(4) Any sum which may be transferred to the Tenants' Reserve Fund in accordance with the provisions of Condition 12 hereof.

11. The amount payable to the individual Tenant for the crop delivered shall be ascertained by dividing the sum available in the Tenants' Collective Account after the deduction of the items aforesaid among the Tenants pro rata to the number of kantars delivered by each the quality of such deliveries being taken into account as far as possible.

12. There shall be debited to the Tenants' Collective Account such sum as the Government and the Syndicate may agree should be so debited and paid into a Tenants' Reserve Fund to be used for the benefit of the cultivation scheme under the said Ordinance for which Fund moneys have already been temporarily provided in advance by the Government and Syndicate.

13. If the Tenant neglects or is careless in the cultivation of his crops the Syndicate shall have the right without the consent of the Tenant to take such steps as the Syndicate may consider proper for the safeguarding of the crops, and any expense incurred thereby shall be a debt from the Tenant to the Syndicate and may without his consent be deducted by the Syndicate from his share of the proceeds of the crops. Further, if the Tenant neglects or is careless in the cultivation of his crops or neglects to carry out the reasonable orders of the Syndicate's officials in any of the aforesaid matters or fails to comply with any of the other provisions of the Government or the Syndicate, the Syndicate shall have the right to terminate the tenancy forthwith without any compensation to the Tenant (except as hereinafter provided) and to hand over the land and cultivation to a new tenant who shall take over the land and cultivation subject to the debts to the Syndicate secured thereon but free from any claim by the old tenant (except as hereinafter provided).

14. If the Syndicate terminate the tenancy under Condition 13 hereof the Syndicate shall as soon as the proceeds of the cotton crop become payable to the new tenant pay over to the old tenant out of such proceeds the value of the labour and capital put into the cultivation of the said crop by the old tenant. Such value shall be assessed as soon as possible, after the termination of the tenancy by a Board composed of a nominee of the outgoing tenant, a nominee of the incoming tenant and a nominee of the Syndicate.

15. If in the opinion of the Syndicate the Tenant shall have committed a breach of these Conditions warranting the cancellation of the annual renewal of his Agreement, then the Syndicate will give the Tenant notice of the breach complained of and such notice shall be delivered to the Tenant not later than the first day of June in the current year of the tenancy.

16. The English copy of the Tenancy Agreement and of these Conditions shall together form the official Contract. The Arabic translation thereof is merely for the information of the Tenant.

SCHEDULE

THE GEZIRA LAND ORDINANCE 1927

Section 11 (1) Except as hereinafter provided in sub-sections (2) and (3) the owners of every plot of land which is acquired by the Government under this Ordinance and which is irrigated under the irrigation scheme shall have the right to take up within a reasonable period after the date when water is first available for the said land under the said irrigation scheme yearly cultivating tenancies of such areas as they themselves are in the opinion of the Government competent to cultivate subject to the conditions hereinafter set out and in other respects upon the usual terms and conditions upon which from time to time all cultivating tenancies within the area of the irrigation scheme shall be granted and they shall also be entitled to a renewal of the tenancies every season so long as they shall have duly performed and observed these conditions.

Section 13 (1) Every sale, transfer, assignment or other disposition of crops growing or intended to be grown on land comprised within a cultivating tenancy or of the proceeds thereof and every mortgage or charge by a cultivating tenant purporting to be secured or intended to be secured by such crops or the proceeds thereof shall, if made or created without the consent in writing of the Government be absolutely void and of no effect.

(2) Every transaction to which a cultivating tenant is a party whereby such tenant is or may become liable for the payment of any sum of money to be calculated by reference either expressed or implied to the value of any crops growing or intended to be grown on the land comprised within a cultivating tenancy shall, if entered into without the consent in writing of the Government, be absolutely void and of no effect.

Section 13 (3) No action shall lie for the recovery of any moneys claimed to be payable under any transaction made void under the provisions of sub-sections (1) and (2) whether the sale, transfer assignment or other disposition relates solely or only in part to the crops or the proceeds thereof or whether the crops or the proceeds thereof mortgaged or charged are alleged to be the sole security or only part of the security for such moneys or whether the value of the crops is the sole basis or is only partly the basis for calculating the amount of such moneys.

4. No execution under the provisions of Order XV of Schedule I to the Civil Justice Ordinance shall be granted by seizure and sale of the crops of any cultivating tenancy; and save with the consent of the Governor or the Commissioner appointed under this Ordinance no such execution shall be granted by attachment of any sum due to a cultivating tenant in respect of the proceeds or any part of the proceeds of the crops of his cultivating tenancy except in the cases following, that is to say (a) an execution of an order to pay maintenance alimony or other family allowances made by a Court of competent authority against such cultivating tenant; (b) an execution of a decree for the payment of a sum of money due by such cultivating tenant to a labourer for wages in respect of labour performed by such labourer on a cultivating tenancy; and (c) an execution of a decree for the payment of a sum of money due by such cultivating tenant in respect of any transaction mentioned in subsections (1) and (2) to which the consent in writing of the Government has been obtained.

343

EXTRACTS FROM AGREEMENT OF 1929 BETWEEN THE SUDAN GOVERNMENT AND THE SUDAN PLANTATIONS SYNDICATE

PREAMBLE AND CHAPTER I
concerns legal definitions

CHAPTER II

THE GENERAL OBLIGATIONS OF THE GOVERNMENT AND THE SYNDICATE

2. The Agreement dated the 17th day of October 1919 made between the Government and the Syndicate and the Supplementary Agreement contained in a letter of even date therewith from the Government to the Syndicate are hereby cancelled as from the 1st day of July 1926 save as regards any rights or liabilities of the parties thereunder accrued up to that date.

3. (*a*) and (*b*) *concern description of area to which agreement applies.*

During the continuance of this Agreement the services rights and functions in respect of the said area and the cultivation and crops thereof and the financing of the tenants and otherwise hereby entrusted to or undertaken by the Syndicate shall be exclusively rendered exercised and enjoyed by the Syndicate.

4. The Syndicate shall as part of the joint undertaking but at its own cost generally manage and supervise the letting of the said lands and the cultivation thereof by the tenants and the collecting storing and marketing of the cotton crops grown by the tenants and in particular:—

(*a*) Shall let the Concession Area on tenancies for one year or less under a form of agreement to be approved by the Government.

(*b*) Shall maintain an adequate and efficient staff to instruct the tenants and supervise the cultivation.

(*c*) Shall make loans for seeds implements cattle labour and other agricultural operations to tenants who reasonably need the same to enable them to carry on their agricultural operations provided that the Syndicate shall be free to refuse a loan in any case or cases in which it considers it would not be businesslike or proper to make it and shall have an absolute discretion as to the amount of any loan. Such loans shall be made at such interest and upon such terms as shall comply with any general regulations agreed upon between the Government and

344

the Syndicate the main object of which would be to ensure that loans should be advanced against work done on the land and implements and stock actually supplied. Such interest shall belong exclusively to the Syndicate.

5. The Syndicate shall do the following things at its own cost except so far as hereinafter provided to the contrary:—

(a) Provide and maintain all such storehouses, dwelling-houses, offices and other buildings, heavy farm implements and machinery, stores and supplies as are necessary to enable it to perform its obligations hereunder:

(b) Provide, on or in the vicinity of the Concession Area, maintain and work all such ginning factories, gins, baling presses and equipment as are necessary for the ginning and baling of all cotton grown on the Concession Area. The term 'ginning factories' in this Agreement is to be deemed to include workshops, loading banks, staff quarters and offices, workmen's quarters and other buildings required in connection with the factories and erected with the approval of the Government.

(c) Provide and maintain all works of subsidiary canalisation as defined in Clause 9 (a) subject to the provisions of Chapter IV hereof and such surface drainage as may be necessary together with the necessary bridges over subsidiary canals, such canals to be constructed in accordance with plans approved by the Government Engineers and to their satisfaction and such roads as may be necessary to afford reasonable means of transit such as have hitherto been provided in Area A available for the purposes of this undertaking and for persons requiring to cross the irrigated area, e.g. from one village to another or to get to the river.

(d) Clear and level all land in the Concession Area capable of irrigation by gravitation and proposed to be irrigated which requires clearing or levelling so as to bring it into a suitable condition for irrigation and cultivation.

6. The Syndicate shall not unless authorised by the Government carry on the business of an agricultural bank nor make agricultural loans except to the tenants of the lands let by the Syndicate under this Agreement and the tenants of other lands owned irrigated or managed by the Syndicate.

7. *Concerns £400,000 debenture advanced by Government to Syndicate.*

8. The Government will at its own cost obtain on lease or otherwise acquire the Concession Area and will give the Syndicate possession of the same as and when required during the period and for the purposes of this Agreement.

9. (a) The Government shall at its separate cost construct the irrigation works necessary for carrying into effect the said scheme not including works of subsidiary canalisation and shall maintain and keep the said works in good repair during the period of this Agreement. The system of canals to be constructed by the Government within the Concession Area shall be so designed that no part of the land thereof will be more than one thousand three hundred and fifty metres distant from a canal. All other canalisation for distributing irrigation water within the Concession Area and incidental works exclusive of any sluice pipes or other outlets from canals constructed by the Government shall be deemed to be works of subsidiary canalisation. The Government shall also at its own expense operate the irrigation works comprised in the said scheme except works of subsidiary canalisation as defined above.

(*b*) The Government and the Syndicate shall take all proper sanitary precautions in the execution of the works to be constructed by them respectively and the Syndicate shall within the Concession Area comply with the sanitary regulations for the time being in force (the Government taking all steps which are reasonably possible to prevent leakage from all canals constructed by them) and the Syndicate shall use its best endeavours to enforce the performance and observance of the same regulations by the tenants. The Government will consult the Syndicate before applying any new sanitary regulations to the Concession Area and the Syndicate is to have the opportunity of stating its views from time to time.

10. The Government shall not during the period of this Agreement grant to any other person or body of persons any concession similar to that granted by it to the Syndicate in respect of the cultivation of any of the land defined on the plan annexed hereto and marked 'Second Plan'* but the Government reserves liberty to provide for the cultivation of such land by direct arrangement with native tenants.

CHAPTER III

THE METHOD AND COST OF IRRIGATION

concerns method of irrigation

CHAPTER IV

THE METHOD AND COST OF DEVELOPMENT

18. All field channels (abu sittas) shall be constructed and maintained by the tenants of the holdings served thereby or at the cost of such tenants.

19. All feeder channels (abu ashreens) shall be constructed by the Syndicate and shall be maintained by it until handed over to the tenant as hereinafter provided.

20 and 21. *Concern recovery of part cost of feeder channels from the tenants.*

22. It is agreed that durra and forage crops shall be grown by the tenants upon ten feddans of each holding the area of durra not to exceed five feddans and the durra stalks and forage crops to be consumed on the holding by live stock. Water shall be provided therefor with due regard for the prior requirements of the cotton crop and in accordance with the arrangements contained in the Second Schedule.

23. The Syndicate shall subject to the provisions of sub-clause (2) hereof at its own cost provide the ploughing and other machinery necessary for the cultivation of the Concession Area and the cost of ploughing shall be deemed to be a loan to the tenant subject to the following provisions:—

(1) The cost of ploughing shall include the cost of maintenance and repairs and renewals of parts and the salaries (including annual bonuses paid to employees and amounts contributed by the Syndicate to the Staff Provident Fund

* Not printed here.

of such engineers engaged for supervising ploughing as would not otherwise be employed by the Syndicate and interest at the rate of 6 per cent. per annum or 1 per cent. above Bank of England Rate whichever shall be the higher on all annual running expenditure (including stock of spares) for the period between the disbursement and the recovery thereof but not interest on capital nor any charge for the services of the agricultural or general supervising Staff of the Syndicate:

(2) There shall be deducted by the Syndicate each year from the Tenants' share of the gross profits with the cost of ploughing chargeable to them a sum of $7\frac{1}{2}$ per cent. upon the capital cost of all machinery provided by the Syndicate necessary for ploughing ridging and similar operations incidental to the cultivation of the Concession Area. This sum shall be placed by the Syndicate to a special reserve fund to be held by the Syndicate on behalf of the Tenants to be paid over to the Government as hereinafter provided. As this special reservation is intended to create a fund which at the time when the economic life of such machinery is ended will equal the original cost thereof no withdrawal shall be made from such fund in respect of any repairs or general upkeep but the whole or any part of such fund may be used in purchasing new machinery in replacement of such machinery as is worn out or is agreed with the Government to have become obsolete. This special reserve fund shall be a separate fund but shall be subject to such review as is provided in Clause 33 (4) and the Fourth Schedule hereto. The Syndicate shall during the continuance of this Agreement have the right to use the balance standing to the credit of the fund for its own business by way of loan and shall pay into the fund interest or charge interest to the fund as the case may be in the manner laid down in Clause 24 (2) in respect of the depreciation funds. The balance at the credit of the fund at the termination of this Agreement shall be paid to the Government on behalf of the Tenants as provided in Chapter VI and Schedule 1 (a) hereof the Government paying to the Syndicate the initial capital cost of the said machinery pursuant to Clause 36 hereof.

24. (1) The balances standing to the credit of the special reserve Fund referred to in sub-paragraph (4) of Clause 33 and the depreciation Funds referred to in Clause 33 (2) and in Clause (6) of the Third Schedule are to be held by the Syndicate and paid over to the Government on the termination of the Agreement as provided in Chapter VI and Schedule 1 (a) hereof but the Syndicate shall during the continuance of this Agreement have the right to use such balances for its own business if it so desires.

(2) The Syndicate shall pay into each of the several funds referred to in sub-paragraph (1) of this Clause a sum each year representing interest at the rate of 5 per cent. on the amount standing to the credit of any such fund during that year and shall be entitled to charge interest to any such fund calculated in the same manner at the rate of 6 per cent. for any year during which the said fund is in debit.

25. The rights of the landowners whose land is included in the concession area to take up cultivating tenancies shall be as laid down in the Gezira Land Ordinances 1921 and 1923 and 1927.

26. Notwithstanding Clause 25 hereof but without prejudice thereto it is agreed that landowners who have large areas or are for any reason incapable themselves of cultivating shall be allowed to nominate as tenants such relatives as would normally inherit their land.

CHAPTER V

THE ASCERTAINMENT AND DIVISION OF PROFITS

27. The gross profits as defined below of the cotton crop in every season from each holding shall be divided between the Government the Syndicate and the Tenant as follows:

(1) To the Tenant 40 per cent.
(2) To the Government 40 per cent.
To the Syndicate 20 per cent.

This clause also includes provision for the sliding scale mentioned on page 127, from 1926 until the first extension of 150,000 feddans was completed.

Such gross profits shall be deemed to be the price actually obtained by the Syndicate for the sale by it of a like quantity of that season's total cotton seed and ginned cotton (taking grade into account so far as practicable) after deducting from the said price obtained by the Syndicate the expenses enumerated below together with interest payable to the Syndicate at the rate of 6 per cent. per annum or at the rate of 1 per cent. over Bank of England rate whichever shall be the higher on the working capital employed by the Syndicate in financing the operations in respect of which such expenses are incurred for the period between the disbursement and the recovery thereof:

(*a*) The cost of transport from the Syndicate's collecting Stations to the ginneries, and from the ginneries to the market including warehousing.
(*b*) The cost of ginning.
(*c*) Insurance.
(*d*) Usual and proper marketing expenses which have hitherto been paid by the Syndicate and deducted from the price obtained by it for the cotton seed and ginned cotton.
(*e*) Other expenses which it is agreed between the Government and the Syndicate are incidental to marketing.
(*f*) Any other expenses which it is agreed between the Government and the Syndicate were incurred for the benefit of the cotton crop.
(*g*) Export Tax.

28. If at any time it shall be agreed or decided under the provisions of Clause 32 that throughout the Concession Area the share of the said gross profits allotted to the tenants is to be increased above 40 per cent. on the ground that their share has become as a result of general conditions, economically inadequate, then the first 2½ per cent. of such increase shall be provided out of the share of the said gross profits allotted to the Government and the balance by the Government and the Syndicate in proportion to their respective share in the said gross profits.

29. If any increase shall be so agreed or decided to be necessary on any of the following grounds, viz:—

(*A*) Because the Government has increased railway rates above the levels now obtaining in such a manner as directly to affect the cultivators in the Gezira area (always excepting any general increase in railway rates necessary to meet a general rise in operating costs attributable to increased costs of labour, fuel, plant and materials) or

348

(*B*) Because the Government has increased taxation local or general above the levels now obtaining in a manner directly affecting the cultivators in the Gezira area or

(*C*) Because the Government has granted to tenants or cultivators of any of the land defined on the second plan terms of tenancy which are in its opinion in substance (and not merely superficially or in appearance) more advantageous than those prevailing in the Concession Area or

(*D*) Because of any other similar action by the Government then to the extent to which any such increase is so agreed or decided to be necessary on any such ground such increase shall be borne by the Government without any right to claim contribution from the Syndicate.

30. If the necessity for any increase so agreed or decided result from uneconomic or extravagant methods of cultivation introduced by the Syndicate or from negligence inefficiency or fault in the manner in which the Syndicate carries out its functions of management or from the effects thereof then such increase shall be provided by the Government and the Syndicate in proportion to their respective shares in the said gross profits.

31. Any such increase may be made in the case of lands which are of inferior quality or which are unfavourably situated without being made generally in the case of every tenant, but no decrease below 40 per cent. shall be made in the share of the said gross profits allotted to the tenants unless generally in the case of all tenants.

32. Subject as aforesaid if the Government or the Syndicate shall at any time be of opinion that the share of the said gross profits allotted to the tenants should be increased or decreased the Government and the Syndicate shall discuss the matter and attempt to come to some agreement but in the event of their failing to agree the matter shall be referred to an arbitrator or arbitrators to be agreed upon between the parties and in default of such agreement to the High Commissioner for Egypt and the Sudan whose decision shall be final, but otherwise no increase or decrease shall be made except by agreement between the Government and the Syndicate. Any decrease in the tenants' share shall accrue to the Government and the Syndicate in the same proportions as their respective shares in the said gross profits.

33. The cost of ginning shall include only such amount as may be necessary to cover:—

(1) The actual cost of ginning and baling in labour material repairs (including upkeep and repair of ginning factories) replacements (except repairs and replacements which may be provided out of the fund established pursuant to sub-clause (4) hereof) and other working expenses including salaries (in which shall be included annual bonuses paid to employees and sums contributed by the Syndicate to the Staff Provident Fund) and reasonable expenses of supervision:

(2) An allowance to provide for the depreciation of the ginning factories at the rate of $1\frac{1}{2}\%$ per annum on the capital cost thereof which shall be paid into a separate Reserve Fund to be constituted for the purpose:

(3) Interest payable to the Syndicate upon the capital cost of the plant and ginning factories incurred by the Syndicate at the rate of 6% or 1% over Bank of England Rate whichever shall be the higher:

(4) Payments to a Special Reserve Fund to be separately constituted for the purpose of repairs, replacements and general upkeep and renewals of such plant

and machinery at the rate of $7\frac{1}{2}$% per annum upon the capital cost of such plant and machinery. The state of such fund shall be reviewed on July 1st 1930, July 1st 1934 and 1st July in every fourth year thereafter in order to determine whether the said rate of payment should be increased or diminished. Such determination shall be made according to the principles laid down in the Fourth Schedule hereto. Any amount to the credit of the said fund shall be available for expenditure for the purposes aforesaid in any year at the Syndicate's discretion.

34. If at any time the Syndicate has in its hands any sum which is by virtue of this Agreement payable to any tenant (not being a sum payable to a tenant on his general account where such account is in credit and the sum is at the tenant's call and the tenant has not drawn it) the Syndicate shall pay to such tenant interest at the rate referred to in Clause 33 (3) upon the sum so payable. If any such sum is to be paid to the Government the interest on such sums shall similarly be paid to the Government. The Syndicate may deduct from any such interest or any other monies payable to the tenants an amount sufficient to provide a fair equivalent for miscellaneous expenses incurred by the Syndicate in connection with the remittance and distribution to the tenants of the sums so payable. The amount and manner of such deduction shall be fixed according to the principles laid down in the Fifth Schedule hereto.

CHAPTER VI

THE TERMINATION OF THE AGREEMENT

35. This Agreement together with the Gezira Light Railway Agreement of the 26th day of May 1923 between the Government and the Syndicate shall be in force until June 30th 1950 unless the Government exercise any of the rights conferred on it by Clause 38 or any of the events specified in Clause 41 occur.

36. On termination of this Agreement by effluxion of time the Government shall take over any ginning or baling factory or factories at any time erected by the Syndicate with the previous consent of the Government pursuant to Clause 5 (b) hereof including any fixed or movable plant or machinery installed or used therein and the machinery referred to in Clause 23 hereof at the initial capital cost to the Syndicate.

37. Upon such termination of this Agreement the Syndicate shall surrender to the Government the whole of its rights in the concession area and all canals drains roads and bridges constructed by the Syndicate thereon in a good state of repair without any payment therefor and shall also deliver over to the Government in a good state of repair all storehouses dwellinghouses offices and other buildings thereon or in the vicinity thereof erected with the previous consent of the Government and all such stores and supplies as are required for carrying out the functions of the Syndicate under this Agreement the Government paying for such storehouses dwellinghouses offices and other buildings stores and supplies at a valuation. Upon the termination of this Agreement the Government shall

pay to the Syndicate the amount of and take over all existing loans to the tenants and the accrued interest thereon provided and so far as such loans have been contracted within the period of twelve months before such termination, and the Syndicate shall pay over to the Government any unexpended balance of the special reserve funds for ginning plant and machinery, for the machinery referred to in Clause 23 hereof and for depreciation of ginning factories.

38. Upon giving not less than one year's previous notice in writing the Government shall have the right on June 30th 1939 or June 30th 1944 at its option to terminate the said Agreements and take over from the Syndicate the management of the concession area and the undertaking and assets of the Syndicate (other than assets unconnected with the said scheme) including the Gezira Light Railway as a going concern together with such amount of working capital not exceeding £700,000 as the Government may require.

39. If the Government exercise the right given by Clause 38 hereof it shall pay to the Syndicate the following sums:—

(*A*) On 30th June 1950 a sum representing the value of the Syndicate's assets on the date of termination such value being ascertained according to the principles laid down in the First Schedule hereto and in the Gezira Light Railway Agreement respectively.

(*B*) On 30th June 1950 the amount of working capital actually taken over.

(*C*) In respect of each working year (that is the period from 1st July in any year to 30th June in the year following) from the date of termination to June 30th 1950 an annual sum of money which will be the total of the following sums:

1st. The average annual value (for the five completed years preceding the termination of the concession) of the Syndicate's net profits derived from the concession.

2nd. A sum equivalent to 6 per cent. per annum on all working capital and assets of the Syndicate taken over by the Government in regard to which the Syndicate would have been entitled under this Agreement to receive interest.

Such annual sum shall be calculated in the manner specified in the First Schedule hereto such sum being payable as to one-half thereof at the termination of each working year that is on June 30th and as to the other half on the 31st December following. Should payment not be made at the due date interest to be added at the rate of 6 per cent. per annum until payment.

40. Further if the Government exercise the right given to it by Clause 38 hereof the following further consequences shall ensue:—

(1) The Government shall have the right (but not the duty) on giving the Syndicate 3 months' previous notice in writing of its intention so to do to discharge its obligation to pay the annual sum or any part thereof for the time being remaining owing by a lump sum payment representing the value at the date of payment of such sum or part at a discount rate of 6 per cent. per annum. Such payment may be made on the date of such termination of the Agreements or on the 30th June in the next or any subsequent year.

(2) The Government agrees that if it exercises the right given by sub-clause (1) of this Clause it will pay to the Syndicate at the same time as such lump sum as aforesaid the capital sums which are by it covenanted to be paid on 30th June

1950 under the provisions of this Agreement and the Gezira Light Railway Agreement such sums to be subject to discount at the rate of 6 per cent. per annum.

(3) The Government and the Syndicate shall co-operate in concluding an arrangement fair and reasonable to all parties for the Government to take on such of the Syndicate's staff and employees as the Government may desire to employ.

CHAPTER VII

CAPITAL AND MANAGEMENT OF THE SYNDICATE

41. The Syndicate shall not assign its duties or rights under this Agreement save with the previous written consent of the Government and the Government shall have the right to terminate the Agreement in the event of such assignment without such written consent or of the winding up of the Syndicate whether voluntarily or otherwise. But the consent of the Government shall not be unreasonably or arbitrarily withheld from an assignment by the Syndicate of its rights and duties under this Agreement to a new Company incorporated with the object of taking them over provided that the directorate or proposed directorate of such new Company shall comprise a majority of the Directors of the Syndicate and that the capitalisation of such new Company shall be subject to the reasonable approval of the Government.

42. The Syndicate shall raise sufficient funds by the issue of share capital to enable it to carry out the construction of the necessary works hereby imposed upon it and to provide adequate funds for financing the necessary advances to the tenants the ploughing of the land for cotton the ginning and the marketing of the cotton crop and the performance of its functions generally under this Agreement so that according to the standards of a prudent business policy the management of the undertaking will not be prejudiced by lack of adequate capital and shall in particular raise £1,875,000 by issuing sufficient of its authorised capital with payments in instalments to suit its requirements.

43. Whenever by virtue of the provisions hereof the Syndicate is entitled to charge interest the rate at which such interest shall be charged shall (unless expressly agreed to the contrary) be at the rate specified in Clause 33 (3) hereof.

44. For the purpose of this Agreement the Syndicate shall at all times have a responsible representative in the Sudan and such representative shall if the Syndicate so desire be vested with an honorary official position under the Government.

45. The Syndicate shall keep an office at Barakat or in such other place as may be agreed upon and shall keep there all necessary and proper books of accounts and vouchers and such accounts and vouchers shall at all reasonable times be open to the inspection of the Government.

46. The Syndicate shall submit to the Financial Secretary of the Government annually proper and adequate accounts showing the financial position between the Government and the Syndicate.

47. The Syndicate shall at the beginning of each year or at such other date as may be agreed upon submit to the Financial Secretary of the Government an estimate of:—

(A) The total area expected to be under crop in the ensuing year.

(B) The total gross profits for such year.

If during the course of the year they have reason for altering either of such estimates they shall at once notify the Financial Secretary of the Government.

48. The Syndicate shall consult the Government on all matters of importance affecting the said scheme with reference to the interests of the Government the Syndicate and the tenants respectively. The Syndicate recognise that in carrying out their functions of general management of the undertaking it is essential that this shall be conducted with due regard for and in a manner conducive to the general well-being and consequent contentment of the native cultivators as a whole.

CHAPTER VIII

THE SEED FARM AND ACCESSORY AREA

concerns the seed farm

CHAPTER IX

MISCELLANEOUS AND GENERAL CLAUSES

53. The Government shall not discriminate as regards railway rates affecting the concession area that is to say the rates on cotton or cotton seed exported from such area or on goods imported for use therein by the Syndicate or by the tenants shall not be increased above the levels now obtaining except as part of a general increase in rates throughout the Sudan.

54. *Concerns light railway material.*

55. The Government shall have the right at any time without payment of any compensation to withdraw from the concession area any land required for roads railway lines canals telegraph or telephone lines or for any public service whatsoever. In exercising such right the Government shall have full regard to the interests of the irrigation system and cultivation in the said area and shall repay to the Syndicate the cost of reinstating or replacing any works interfered with. The Government shall also if required by the Syndicate so to do provide an equivalent area of land to replace the area so withdrawn such equivalent area to be good average land suitable in the opinion of the Syndicate for cotton growing.

56. (1) In as much as the Syndicate is a British company at present liable to United Kingdom income tax and in order to avoid its subjection to a double burden it is agreed that so long as the Syndicate shall be liable

to pay United Kingdom income tax on the profits earned in respect of its operations in the Sudan or any part thereof any income tax or tax on profits imposed by the Government on such profits or part thereof shall not exceed the rate from time to time allowed by the United Kingdom legislation by way of relief against United Kingdom income tax paid or payable by the Syndicate the intention being that the Syndicate shall not in all pay more in any year than it would have been liable to pay for United Kingdom income tax only and that no income tax or traders profit tax in the Sudan shall be payable except to the extent that such relief is obtained and so that the Syndicate shall not suffer by having to pay any such Sudan tax from which it was exempt under the Agreement of the 17th October 1919. This Clause shall also apply to tax on any annuity payable hereunder.

(2) Save as herein provided no land tax or water rate or similar charge shall be levied against the Syndicate or any tenant in respect of any lands in or water supplied to any part of the concession area.

(3) No tax shall be levied upon cotton grown on any land in the concession area unless it is a tax applicable to all cotton grown in the Sudan and apparently of a permanent nature.

(4) If the Syndicate should become liable for any local rates in respect of any buildings erected with the previous permission of the Government in accordance with Clause 5 (other than ginning factories) such rates shall be paid as to two-thirds by the Government and as to one-third by the Syndicate.

(5) No animal tax shall be levied on draught and riding animals used by the Syndicate and its employees in the concession area.

(6) No motortax (other than a tax at the rate imposed by the regulations published in Sudan Government Gazette No. 451 of the 15th March 1925) shall be levied on any of the Syndicate's vehicles used in connection with the undertaking unless and until the Government provides an entirely different type of motor roads to serve the concession area.

(7) Save as aforesaid any rate or tax to which the Syndicate in the same way as any other person or corporation may be or become subject shall be payable by it in the ordinary way.

57. *Concerns calculation of interest.*

58. *Concerns freedom of government officers from personal liability.*

59. *Concerns legal interpretation of Agreement.*

60. *Concerns machinery for valuation.*

61. *Concerns arbitration in event of dispute.*

SCHEDULES

I. (*a*) *Method of valuing assets in event of early termination.*
   (*b*) *Method of calculating annuity in event of early termination.*

II. *Method of working Sennar Reservoir.*

SOME CARDINAL PRINCIPLES, SUPPORTED BY GEZIRA EXPERIENCE, IMPORTANT TO THE SUCCESS OF DEVELOPMENT PROJECTS OF THIS NATURE

Preliminary Principles

1. Economic growth, unless freedom is suppressed, calls for simultaneous investment of a dual nature: public and private, remunerative and non-remunerative, economic and social.

2. Underdeveloped countries depend, to a varying extent, on external assistance in capital, technicians and equipment, until the degrees of economic development, the volume of local savings, and the standard of education and vocational training at all levels are sufficient for the countries concerned to take full charge of their own future development.

3. The establishment of equitable and practical principles of development are more important than the pace. The sole motive of private profit is not the only determinant factor in development. An increase in the social product, and harmonious evolution of the people affected, are equally important.

4. For the reasons just stated, it is wiser to presume that an *a priori* situation of apparent incompatibility exists. On the one hand there is the desire of the governments of underdeveloped territories to control their own economies, and to reserve for their nationals the exploitation of natural resources. On the other hand there is the desire of foreign investors to safeguard their interests by powers of control and of management, and to obtain maximum profits for themselves.

Nevertheless, development is dependent upon cooperation between the two parties.

5. Cooperation may be made easier by specific arrangements to meet this situation, such as:

(1) Partnership between government and foreign capital, giving a sense of joint venture in the undertaking.

(2) Management entrusted initially to foreign capital, with the proviso of consultation with Government on all matters of importance.

(3) A time limit to the association with, and management by, foreign capital, with agreed terms for compensation on its maturity.

(4) Acceptance of nationals (indigenous cultivators or whatever they may be) as partners also in development, sharing in the profits, and, as soon as practicable, in the responsibilities, and not merely as paid labourers with no personal stake in what they are doing.

(5) An ultimate intention to withdraw the Government partner and to leave the undertaking to a cooperative, and adequate preparation for that objective.

z*

6. Successful operation of development is dependent upon mutual trust. A frank revelation of differences, followed by arrangements of the kind just outlined in an effort to overcome them, is more likely to engender trust than an imposed continuance of foreign investment without consultation on the one hand (so evident in Africa), or arbitrary interference with foreign investments by national governments on the other hand (so evident in Asia).

7. Acceptance on the investor's side further depends on confidence that an agreement freely entered into will be respected, and on belief in the stability of the government, the integrity of the personnel, and efficient public services. The establishment of mutual insurance facilities and a mutually agreed investment statute, and the provision of technical assistance on a regional or international basis may reduce these risks. Meantime the greater the risk, the higher the claim for profits, and the lower the desire to invest.

8. Acceptance on the local side can be enhanced and some of the aforesaid risks diminished, by

(1) Contact at all levels between the public opinion and society of the territory and the foreign personnel, management and directorate. Especially important is full explanation of the financial results both to working personnel and public.

(2) The training and advancement of local nationals to posts of responsibility.

(3) The sharing by local nationals in the direction.

Production Principles

1. Thorough preliminary exploration by means of pilot schemes.

2. An active external demand, and market contact, if the product is for export.

3. A planned system of land usage, based on scientific experiment and practical experience, and protected by a tenancy agreement.

4. A policy of control and help: control to ensure adherence to a productive system, help to make adherence at each point as easy as possible.

5. A vertical organization including initial processing within the country at cost, eliminating middle men.

6. The establishment of two separate funds for tenants, one to cover the contingency of debt when loans advanced can not be repaid, the other to provide a reserve for stabilization of profits.

7. A competent research station located in the development area.

8. Efficient, active and honest management staff, whose conditions of service offer, as far as possible, a long-term interest in and sympathy with the project.

Social Principles

1. The renting rather than the expropriation of land.

2. Attention to the equitable distribution of the benefits of development, in particular by

(1) Exclusion of landlords from any share, other than the initial rent, in the proceeds of development, as landlords.

356

(2) Inclusion of landlords and members of their families among the beneficiaries as priority entrants, but as individual independent tenants on the same footing as other tenants.

(3) Distribution of tenancies among as wide a circle of beneficiaries as possible, consistent with the retention of a standard size unit appropriate to the ability of an average family, and estimated to provide adequate food and enhanced income.

3. Legislation to protect the tenancy against subdivision, sub-letting, mortgage or foreclosure except by the management for a breach of the tenancy agreement.

4. Legislation to protect the tenant against any claim for debt on account of advances made against the crops, except those incurred to the management.

5. Provision, with due regard to the priority of economic efficiency, of funds, from the profits of the undertaking, to enhance the social development of the region, under the direction of a unified command but operating through, and in cooperation with, departmental and representative agencies.

REFERENCES

The main sources of information used have been:

1. (*a*) The *Reports by H.M.'s Agent and Consul-General on the Finances, Administration and Condition of Egypt and the Soudan* (London, H.M.S.O.) from 1898 to 1913.

(*b*) The *Reports by H.M.'s High Commissioner on the Finances, Administration and Condition of Egypt and the Soudan* from 1914 to 1920.

(*c*) The *Reports on the Finances, Administration and Condition of the Soudan* (Sudan from 1923) from 1921 to 1952.

All the above I have called the Governor-General's reports and referred to under the *symbol G.G.*

2. Files in the Sudan Government Archives in Khartoum, referred to under the *symbol S.G.*

3. Files of the Sudan Plantations Syndicate in the Sudan Gezira Board's Archives in Barakat, referred to under the *symbol S.P.S./S.G.B.*

4. Reports, Balance Sheets, Minutes, etc., of the Sudan Plantations Syndicate, previously at Cooper Brothers in London, now at the School of Oriental Studies, Durham University, referred to under the *symbol S.P.S.*

5. Letters among the Wingate papers, referred to under the *symbol W.*

All Command Papers, which are frequently referred to, are published in London by H.M. Stationery Office.

CHAPTER I

Authorities quoted:

Among the many books concerned with Sudan history, the following recent publications may interest the reader who wants a wider background: Mekki Abbas, *The Sudan Question* (London, Faber and Faber, 1952); Sir Harold Macmichael, *The Sudan* (London, Ernest Benn, 1954); K. D. D. Henderson, *The Making of the Modern Sudan*, The Life and Letters of Sir Douglas Newbold (London, Faber and Faber, 1953); and Sir Ronald Wingate, *Wingate of the Sudan* (London, John Murray, 1955)

1. Page 32   G.G. 1899, Cd. 95, p. 55.
2. „   33   G.G. 1898, C. 9231, p. 53.
3. „   33   G.G. 1900, Cd. 441, p. 75.
4. „   33   Ibid., p. 65.

CHAPTER 2

Authorities quoted:

The Governor-General's contemporary reports give a vivid commentary on the problems of this period, and the narrative draws on them liberally.

I am also indebted to an unpublished monograph, *Sudan Economic Development*, 1899–1913, by John Stone, in the library of the Institute of Commonwealth Studies in Oxford.

The two reports by Sir William Garstin, *Report as to Irrigation Projects on the Upper Nile*, Cd. 672 (1901), *Report upon the Basin of the Upper Nile*, Cd. 2165 (1904), give all the flavour of unexplored Africa.

1. Page 34 Governor-General's Memorandum for 1907 to Sir E. Gorst, H.M.'s Consul-General in Egypt, p. 1.
2. „ 34 G.G. 1904, Cd. 2409, p. 117.
3. „ 35 G.G. 1902, Cd. 1529, p. 73.
4. „ 36 G.G. 1900, Cd. 441, p. 82.
5. „ 38 *Report as to Irrigation Projects on the Upper Nile*, by Sir William Garstin, K.C.M.G., Cd. 672 (1901).
6. „ 38 Ibid., p. 14.
7. „ 39 G. Dupuis, 'Report upon Lake Tsana,' printed as an appendix to Sir William Garstin's *Report upon the Basin of the Upper Nile*, Cd. 2165 (1904).
8. „ 40 Cd. 672 (1901), p. 47.
9. „ 40 Cd. 2165 (1904), p. 166.
10. „ 40 G.G. 1904, Cd. 2409, p. 119.

CHAPTER 3

Authorities quoted:

The Governor-General's contemporary reports are particularly full of comment on the land policy. The work by John Stone, cited under Chapter 2, and *Correspondence respecting the Gezira Irrigation Project*, Cmd. 2171 (1924), are the other main sources used.

1. Page 42 G.G. 1899, Cd. 95, p. 48.
2. „ 43 *Sudan Government Gazette*, 1 April 1914.
3. „ 44 G.G. 1904, Cd. 2409, p. 144.
4. „ 44 G.G. 1905, Cd. 2817, p. 137.
5. „ 44 *Sudan Government Gazette*, 1 February 1914.
6. „ 45 *Correspondence respecting the Gezira Irrigation Project*, Cd. 2171, p. 46.
7. „ 45 G.G. 1904, Cd. 2409, Part III, p. 3.
8. „ 46 Quoted by J. Stone, op. cit., p. 7.
9. „ 46 Ibid.
10. „ 48 G.G. 1906, Cd. 3394, p. 123. This deals far more extensively with this particularly important matter, especially with reference to experience in India.
11. „ 49 Report printed in G.G. 1908, Cd. 4580.
12. „ 50 Referred to in G.G. 1911, Cd. 6149, p. 282.
13. „ 50 G.G. 1910, Cd. 5633, p. 89.

CHAPTER 4

Authorities quoted:

Apart from the Governor-General's reports, the important documents at this stage are the reports and balance sheets of the Sudan Plantations

Syndicate. The Board's minute books are of interest as well. The Syndicate's London Office was however destroyed by enemy action during World War II and very few documents have survived other than those at Barakat in the Sudan.

Interesting information is also available in the reports and memoranda of the British Cotton Growing Association, particularly its annual report for 1949 which contains its own appreciation of achievements in the Gezira.

1. Page 51   Referred to in G.G. 1903, Cd. 1951, p. 80.
2.   „   53   G.G. 1908, Cd. 4580, p. 77.
3.   „   53   Sir William Mather's speech was reprinted as a pamphlet by the British Cotton Growing Association.
4.   „   54   B.C.G.A. Memorandum No. 43 (confidential), November 1910.
5.   „   57   I am indebted for this story to Sir Ronald Wingate's biography of his father, *Wingate of the Sudan*, in which pp. 154–7 admirably illustrate the difficulty experienced in raising capital.
6.   „   57   *Report to the Council on the Possibilities of Cotton Growing in the Anglo-Egyptian Sudan* (B.C.G.A. Report No. 46, December 1912). *Cotton Growing in the Anglo-Egyptian Sudan*, report by Mr. Arno Schmidt to the International Federation of Master Cotton Spinners and Manufacturers Associations (1913).

CHAPTER 5

Authorities quoted:

Of particular interest in this chapter are the Wingate papers, and the personal recollections of Hewison and Davie, for the use of which I should like to make grateful acknowledgement.

1. Page 60   Schmidt's report, op. cit.
2.   „   60   G.G. 1912, Cd. 6682, containing report of Director of Agriculture.
3.   „   62   B.C.G.A. Report No. 53 (1913).
4.   „   64   Letter dated 10.4.1913. W.
5.   „   64   Letter dated 4.5.1913. W.
6.   „   65   Letter dated 11.4.1912. W.
7.   „   65   Letter dated 6.5.1913. W.
8.   „   66   Letter dated 10.4.1913. W.
9.   „   69   This account is based on letters written to the author by Davie and Hewison.
10.   „   70   The meeting took place on 4th June 1913. Those present were Kitchener, Wingate, Bernard (the Financial Secretary) and MacGillivray. This version of the offer is in the Wingate papers, and was the one sent to the Syndicate's Board in London. A slightly different version (omitting the percentage distribution) was sent back to Khartoum.
11.   „   71   Governor, Blue Nile Province to Director of Agriculture, 9.8.1913. W.

CHAPTER 6

Authorities quoted:

The Reports of the Sudan Plantations Syndicate and the Agreement between the Syndicate and the Sudan Government form the main background to this chapter.

1. Page 76 S.P.S. shareholders' meeting, 1911.
2.   „   79 Letter dated 3.9.1913. W.
3.   „   79 1919 Agreement, Clause 14. S.P.S./S.G.B.
4.   „   80 Record of meeting between the Syndicate Board and Kitchener in London, 21.7.1913. W.
5.   „   80 Wingate to Sudan Agent in London, 3.9.1913. W.
6.   „   82 S.P.S. shareholders' meetings, 1919–27.

CHAPTER 7

Authorities quoted:

The Gezira Land Ordinances and the Tenancy Agreement form the main background to this chapter. A useful source of information is a pamphlet, *Notes on the Gezira Irrigation Project*, published by the Sudan Government in January 1926. A most important document explaining the principles of the Scheme, and especially the policy towards landowners, is *Correspondence respecting the Gezira Irrigation Project*, Cmd. 2171 (1924). A special Sudan number of *The African World*, commemorating the opening of the Sennar Dam on 21st January 1926, has some excellent contemporary articles and photographs, available at the School of Oriental Studies, Durham University.

1. Page 83 Preamble to the 1919 Agreement. S.P.S./S.G.B.
2.   „   84 Sudan Government notice, 15.3.1920. The notice is also printed as a schedule to the Gezira Land Ordinance, 1921.
3.   „   87 This estimate is reproduced in *Notes on the Gezira Irrigation Project* (1926).
4.   „   89 G.G. 1904, Cd. 2409, Part IV, p. 44.
5.   „   91 S.P.S. shareholders' meeting, 1926.
6.   „   91 G.G. 1925, Cmd. 2742, p. 5.
7.   „   92 G.G. 1921, Cmd. 1837, p. 4.

CHAPTER 8

Authorities quoted:

The descriptions in the early part of this chapter are drawn from the author's personal recollections; in the later part from the Governor-General's reports, 1925–7.

1. Page 104 For a lighthearted description see E. Inge, 'A day in the life of a cotton inspector in the Sudan', *Empire Cotton Growing Review*, April 1935. For full technical details of the job, brought up to date, see *A Handbook for New Personnel* (Sudan Gezira Board, 1950).
2.   „   106 Letter, Schuster to Neimeyer, 16.7.1925. S.G.

CHAPTER 9

Authorities quoted:

The information in the early part of this chapter is derived from a private paper of Mr. W. N. Allan, irrigation consultant to the Sudan

Government, and from Sudan government files in Khartoum. I am greatly indebted to Mr. H. A. Morrice, adviser to the Ministry of Irrigation and Hydro-Electric Power in the Sudan, for certain suggestions, although he bears no responsibility for the text.

The report of the Nile Commission of 1925 is important, as it was the basis of the Nile Waters Agreement of 1929, which controlled the international use of Nile water throughout the Nile Valley up to the present day.

1. Page 110   The views of Sir Murdoch Macdonald are taken from his 'Note on water required and available for the Sudan Gezira Scheme', May 1918, S.G.
2. „ 112   The whole problem is reviewed in Schuster's 'Memorandum on the future financial position of the Sudan as it may develop in consequence of a resettlement of political status of the country and its financial relations with Egypt', July 1924, S.G.
3. „ 113   The ultimatum is reproduced in full in *Wingate of the Sudan*, p. 252.
4. „ 113   The whole of this episode is reviewed in the report of the Nile Commission, 1925.
5. „ 116   Nile Waters Agreement, 1929. Treaty Series No. 17 of 1929.
6. „ 117   Mohammed Mahmoud Pasha to Lord Lloyd, May 1929, clause 3, 4 (2), S.G.
7. „ 117   Nile Commission Report, 1925, clause 17.

CHAPTER 11

Authorities quoted:

Most of the references in this chapter are to letters and papers of the Sudan Government in Khartoum or Sudan Plantations Syndicate at Barakat. Descriptions at the end of the chapter are drawn from the author's personal recollections.

1. Page 127   Budget note in the Ministry of Finance archives. S.G.
2. „ 127   Schuster's Note for Council on the Draft Heads of Agreement dated 22.11.1926. S.G.
3. „ 129   S.P.S. papers. S.G.B.
4. „ 130   Letter dated 27.2.1927. S.P.S./S.G.B.
5. „ 130   This incentive was first suggested by Huddleston, Governor of the Blue Nile Province, in a note dated 2.3.1926, and was incorporated in the Heads of Agreement. S.G.
6. „ 132   G.G. 1929, Cmd. 3697, p. 31.
7. „ 132   A paper in the Ministry of Finance. S.G.
8. „ 133   G.G. 1928, Cmd. 3403, p. 51.
9. „ 136   S.P.S. shareholders' meeting, 1927.
10. „ 137   Quoted in G.G., 1903, Cd. 1951.

CHAPTER 12

Authorities quoted:

There is extensive scientific literature as the background to this chapter. The interested reader should refer to Tothill, *Agriculture in the Sudan*

(London, Oxford University Press, 1948), and to Knight and Boynes, *Agricultural Science in the Sudan* (Scotland, T. Buncle & Co. Ltd., 1950). The latter book is a bibliography of all scientific publications on the Sudan.

1. Page 141   Letter dated 17.12.1929. S.G.
2.   ,,   142   Note dated 1.6.1930. S.G.
3.   ,,   143   G.G. 1930, Cmd. 3935, p. 8.
4.   ,,   146   G.G. 1929, Cmd. 3697, p. 45.
5.   ,,   147   Taken from the Joint Auditors' Report for 1933. S.G.
6.   ,,   147   Letter dated 13.6.1930. S.G.
7.   ,,   148   Op. cit., p. 153.
8.   ,,   149   Letter dated 16.1.1931. S.G.
9.   ,,   149   Letter dated 2.2.1931. S.P.S./S.G.B.
10. ,,   149   Letter dated 4.2.1931. S.P.S./S.G.B.
11. ,,   149   Letter dated 1.10.1931. S.P.S./S.G.B.
12. ,,   149   Letter dated 18.2.1932. S.P.S./S.G.B.
13. ,,   150   Record of a meeting 29.2.1932. S.P.S./S.G.B.
14. ,,   150   Record of a meeting 13.6.1932. S.P.S./S.G.B.
15. ,,   150   Letter dated 28.7.1932. S.P.S./S.G.B.
16. ,,   157   G.G. 1934, Cmd. 5019, p. 94.
17. ,,   158   Letter dated 25.5.1934. S.P.S./S.G.B.
18. ,,   158   Memorandum dated 8.1.1934 forwarded to the Governor-General on 28.2.1934. S.P.S./S.G.B.

CHAPTER 13

Authorities quoted:

This chapter is very largely concerned with accounts, and most of the information is derived from papers of the Sudan Plantations Syndicate at Barakat and of the Sudan Government in Khartoum.

1. Page 161   G.G. 1933, Cmd. 4668, p. 99.
2.   ,,   167   Memorandum dated 30.10.1937. S.G.
3.   ,,   167   13th meeting of the Gezira Advisory Board 12.11.1937. S.G.
4.   ,,   168   Letter in the files of the Sudan Plantations Syndicate, S.P.S./S.G.B.
5.   ,,   169   Circular dated 31st December 1938, paras. 11 and 12. S.P.S./S.G.B.
6.   ,,   169   Letter dated 26.10.1937. S.G.

CHAPTER 14

Authorities quoted:

This chapter is concerned with scientific research and once again the reader who wishes to pursue it further is recommended to consult Tothill, *Agriculture in the Sudan*, especially chapters XIX, XX and XXI. The Annual Reports of the Research Institute give greater detail. For a short summary, Ferguson, *The Gezira Scheme*, reprinted from *World Crops*, Vol. 4, is useful.

The account given here is a personal interpretation by the author of the problems as they faced the management.

CHAPTER 15

Authorities quoted:

The main references in this chapter are to the files of the Sudan Plantations Syndicate in Barakat and of the Sudan Government in Khartoum. The loss of the Syndicate's London office files in the war has made it difficult to interpret the marketing policy at certain stages but I believe that the broad outline is correct.

I am greatly indebted to Mr. John T. Porritt of Combined English Mills Ltd. (through the courtesy of Sir Raymond Streat, late Chairman of the Cotton Board), and to Mr. Felix Carver, sales adviser to the Sudan Gezira Board, for certain suggestions, although they bear no responsibility for the text.

1. Page 180   Letter dated 2.3.1926. S.G.
2.   „   181   Issued 18.2.1926. S.G.
3.   „   181   Hewison to Schuster, 29.1.1926. S.G.
4.   „   181   Letter dated 23.2.1926. S.G.
5.   „   185   Letter dated 21.1.1936. S.G.
6.   „   187   S.P.S. shareholders' meeting, 1937-8.
7.   „   188   Minute dated 10.5.1937. S.G.
8.   „   189   Report dated 6.7.1937. S.P.S./S.G.B.
9.   „   190   Ibid.
10.   „   190   Report dated 4.5.1937. S.G.
11.   „   191   Minute dated 10.5.1937. S.G.
12.   „   192   Report dated 11.12.1937. S.G.
13.   „   193   Undated memorandum at Barakat. S.P.S./S.G.B.
14.   „   194   Report dated 21.3.1939. S.G.
15.   „   194   S.P.S. shareholders' meeting, 1939.

CHAPTER 16

Authorities quoted:

The main sources of information in this chapter are the Sudan Government files in Khartoum, and to a lesser extent the files of the Sudan Plantations Syndicate at Barakat.

1. Page 200   MacGregor to Schuster, 22.3.1926. S.G.
2.   „   201   Note by Schuster, 7.2.1927. S.G.
3.   „   201   Minute by Sir John Maffey, 10.2.1927. S.G.
4.   „   202   MacIntyre to Financial Secretary, 16.12.1928. S.G.
5.   „   202   Memorandum by W. P. Clarke, 16.1.1929. S.G.
6.   „   204   MacIntyre to Mayall, 19.1.1938. S.G.
7.   „   205   Mayall's memorandum, 15.2.1939. S.G.
8.   „   205   Rugman to Wooding, 27.4.1939. S.G.
9.   „   208   Newbold to Mayall, 5.2.1940. S.G.
10.   „   208   Discussion at Barakat 23.2.1940. S.P.S./S.G.B. Based on a memorandum by Mayall accepted by the Gezira Advisory Board, 6.5.1939. Subsequently embodied in a note by Governor, Blue Nile Province, to District Commissioners and Syndicate staff, headed 'Note on Hōsh experiment', 29.4.1941. S.P.S./S.G.B.

CHAPTER 17

Authorities quoted:
The main sources of information in this chapter are again the files of the Sudan Plantations Syndicate at Barakat and those of the Sudan Government in Khartoum, particularly of the Gezira Advisory Board. The summary of policy is taken from a memorandum by the author on 'The Future of the Gezira Scheme' in 1943, which was itself a synopsis of ideas expressed by a number of other officials, both in Syndicate and government service, in the Gezira at that time. Comments on the tenants at the end of the chapter are from the author's personal recollections.

1. Page 214 Note by Robertson, 9.12.1940. S.G.
2. „ 215 Note by Bredin, 7.9.1942. S.G.
3. „ 216 Memorandum by the author to S.P.S. Board, June 1943. S.P.S./ S.G.B.
4. „ 221 Newbold to Mayall, 5.2.1940. S.G.
5. „ 223 Directive on Village Councils, 24.2.1945. S.P.S./S.G.B.
6. „ 223 Note dated 1.8.1945 to Gezira Advisory Board. S.G.
7. „ 223 25th meeting of Gezira Advisory Board, 10.11.1945. S.G.
8. „ 224 Note by Rugman, 30.5.1938. (763-11-1) S.G.
9. „ 228 The strike gave rise to a great deal of controversy in the Arabic press as to the financial condition of the tenants, about which the public, owing to our previous policy of reticence, was generally ignorant. The management's contemporary view on this subject was therefore given in great detail by the author in a letter to the *Sudan Star* on 7th September 1946 headed 'Figures Talk', of which reprints can be found in S.P.S./S.G.B. and S.G. The article attempts to assess the annual worth of a tenancy at that date.

CHAPTER 19

Authorities quoted:
The important documents for reference in this chapter are the minutes and papers of the Gezira Advisory Board in Khartoum; the Report of the Special Committee of the Advisory Council of the Northern Sudan, appointed in 1944 to report on the future of the Gezira after 1950; the Report of the Select Committee of the Legislative Assembly on the Future Administration of the Gezira Scheme, 12.2.1950; and the Gezira Scheme Ordinance (No. 16), 1950.

1. Page 243 David E. Lilienthal, *T.V.A. Democracy on the March* (London, Harmondsworth, 1944). Reprinted as a Penguin Special, 1944.
2. „ 245 Report of the Special Committee of the Advisory Council of the Northern Sudan on the Future of the Gezira after 1950 (1946). S.G.
3. „ 245 Minutes of 30th meeting of Gezira Advisory Board. S.G.
4. „ 246 Robertson's personal memorandum was CS/SCR/2.Q.1, dated 24 September 1947. S.G.
5. „ 247 Ibid.
6. „ 248 Minutes of Gezira Advisory Board, 30th and 32nd meetings. S.G.

7. Page 250 Report of the Select Committee of the Legislative Assembly on the Future Administration of the Gezira Scheme (1950).
8. ,, 250 Ibid., para. 4 (*a*).
9. ,, 250 The Gezira Scheme Ordinance, 1950.
10. ,, 252 Report of the Select Committee (1950), para. 13 (iii).
11. ,, 252 The intention to have tenants' representatives on the Management Board was also in the mind of Sir Francis Rugman in 1938. See page 212.
12. ,, 253 Report of the Select Committee (1950), para. 7.
13. ,, 253 The Gezira Scheme Ordinance, para. 4 (S).

CHAPTER 20

Authorities quoted:

The main sources of reference for this chapter are the marketing files of the Sudan Plantations Syndicate at Barakat, S.P.S./S.G.B., and in the Finance Department of the Sudan Government in Khartoum, and the files on the Tenants' Representative Body at Barakat and in the Governor's office at Wad Medani.

1. Page 257 London Office letters, S.P.S./S.G.B.
2. ,, 262 G.G. 1949, Cmd. 8434, pp. 174–5.
3. ,, 265 Article entitled 'A note on the Gezira Scheme, Anglo-Egyptian Sudan', in the *Indian Cotton Growing Review*, April 1949.

CHAPTER 21

Authorities quoted:

This chapter is a personal appraisal. Short articles on the Gezira Scheme by the author can be seen in *The Times Survey of the British Colonies*, December 1950; in the *Journal of the Royal Empire Society*, September 1952; the monthly magazine of the English Speaking Union, *The English Speaking World*, October 1952; the report of International Days for African Studies of Ghent, 1954; the *Journal of the Royal Society of Arts*, December 1955; and in the papers prepared for H.R.H. the Duke of Edinburgh's Study Conference, 1956.

A short appraisal of the Gezira Scheme was given by William A. Hance in the *Geographical Review* (New York), Vol. XLIV, No. 2, 1954, and one entitled *The Social Aspects of the Gezira Scheme in the Sudan* by G. H. Van der Kolff (Amsterdam, Royal Tropical Institute, No. CXXIV, 1957).

1. Page 290 Report of the Select Committee on the Future Ownership of Land in the North-west Extension of the Gezira Scheme (1950). S.G.

CHAPTER 22

Authorities quoted:

Many of the events recorded in this chapter occurred after the author had left the Sudan, and must be regarded as a limited interpretation from correspondence and statements in the files of the Sudan Gezira Board at Barakat.

REFERENCES

The annual reports of the Sudan Gezira Board give the general background. Agenda papers of the Gezira Board, and the files on devolution, social development, and the Gezira Local Committee provide the main reference documents. Of particular interest are the files concerned with the Tenants' Representative Body and its successor, the Gezira Tenants' Union.

1. Page 302   See particularly a letter in the social development files, dated 26.10.54, from Rahma Abdulla (then Social Development Officer, later Ambassador to India) to Governor, Blue Nile Province, remarking on the practice of village deputations asking for assistance, and their difficulty in understanding where the Board's financial responsibility ended and that of local government began.
2.   ,,   305   S.G.B. First Annual Report, 1950–1, p. 15.
3.   ,,   306   Circular to field staff, 23.12.53.
4.   ,,   307   The Council of Ministers endorsed the constitution on 6th April 1954.
5.   ,,   307   These demands, and others, were submitted by the committee of the G.T.U. to the Gezira Board and the Government, who delegated three ministers to meet their representatives in July 1954.
6.   ,,   307   Minister of Social Affairs to Manager, 8.7.54.
7.   ,,   308   Manager to Minister of Social Affairs, 14.7.54.
8.   ,,   308   Circular to all members from committee of G.T.U. 14.7.54.
9.   ,,   308   S.G.B. to Gezira Tenants' Association, 22.11.52.
10. ,,   308   Agenda paper, S.G.B., 39th meeting.
11. ,,   309   Statement by G.T.U. on the economic condition of the tenant, 6.4.55.
12. ,,   309   Address by Sayed Mekki Abbas, broadcast to the tenants, 4.8.55.
13. ,,   310   Directive on devolution, S.G.B. 1st July 1952. This directive summarizes the purpose and history of devolution and explains the composition and duties of the various S.G.B. and local government councils.
14. ,,   310   See G. H. Van Der Kolff, *The Social Aspects of the Gezira Scheme in the Sudan* (Amsterdam, Royal Tropical Institute, 1957, No. CXXIV).

CHAPTER 23

Authorities quoted:

A great deal of the information in this chapter is taken from a private copy, at the School of Oriental Studies, Durham University, of Mrs. G. M. Culwick's *A Study of the Human Factor in the Gezira Scheme* which she gave to the author. This draft report of her social studies in the Scheme has many other interesting details, omitted here, and I hope it will some day be published. The position on any particular item would vary in the Gezira from village to village, but although this report is a sample from only three villages (there are now 900 in the Scheme), the broad outline emerging probably applied generally throughout the Scheme.

1. Page 312   The Gezira Scheme Ordinance, 1950, schedule IV, part II.

2. Page 316   See the Report of the Select Committee of the Legislative Assembly on the Future Administration of the Gezira (1950), where appendices 11 and 12 reveal these points of view of the management and tenants respectively on the tenants' costs of production.

3.   „   318   Sir Malcolm Darling, *The Punjab Peasant in Prosperity and Debt* (London, Oxford University Press, 1925).

CHAPTER 24

Authorities quoted:

The author was not present at the time of the transfer of power and the description given here is a condensation of papers in the files of the Sudan Gezira Board in Barakat. The author's reflections on the subject were stimulated by subsequent discussions with some of the present Sudanese leaders.

1. Page 324   Report of the Select Committee of the Legislative Assembly on the Future Administration of the Gezira Scheme (1950), para. 4 (*b*).

2.   „   325   Ibid., para. 9.

CHAPTER 25

Authorities quoted:

This chapter is entirely personal comment. The subject is extremely controversial but intimately concerns any work on international development.

1. Page 338   Montesquieu, 'Pensées Diverses', quoted in the journal *Western World*, July 1957.

INDEX

369